BEYOND THE NEW THEISM
A Philosophy of Religion

Beyond
the New Theism
A Philosophy of Religion

GERMAIN GRISEZ

UNIVERSITY OF NOTRE DAME PRESS
NOTRE DAME   LONDON

Quotations from Immanuel Kant's *Critique of Pure Reason* are
from the English translation by Norman Kemp Smith, published
by St. Martin's Press, Inc., Macmillan & Co., Ltd., and Macmillan,
London and Basingstoke, and are used by permission of the
publishers. Most scriptural excerpts are from the *New American
Bible*, copyright © 1970 by Confraternity of Christian Doctrine,
and are used by the generous permission of the copyright owner.
Other brief scriptural excerpts, including the selection from Psalm
104 on the dedication page, are from *The Jerusalem Bible*,
copyright © 1966 by Darton, Longman, and Todd, Ltd., and by
Doubleday and Co., Inc.

Library of Congress Cataloging in Publication Data

Grisez, Germain Gabriel, 1929-
  Beyond the new theism.

  1. Religion—Philosophy. 2. God—Proof.
3. Religion and language. 4. Apologetics—20th
century. I. Title.
BL51.G743   201'.1   74-27885
ISBN 0-268-00567-2
ISBN 0-268-00568-0 pbk.

This book is dedicated to my colleagues in
Campion College, University of Regina.
They have made the ideal of a community of scholars a reality for me
after I had almost given up believing it possible.

Glory for ever to Yahweh!
May Yahweh find joy in what he creates,
    at whose glance the earth trembles,
    at whose touch the mountains smoke!

I mean to sing to Yahweh all my life,
I mean to play for my God as long as I live.
May these reflections of mine give him pleasure,
    as much as Yahweh gives me!
                  Psalm 104:31-34

Contents

III. Criticism of Alternatives

IV. The Meaningfulness of God-Talk

V. Existential Objections to God

VI. The Meaningfulness of Christian Beliefs

Preface with Acknowledgments

The problems I investigate in this book are so many, so difficult, and so important that no one is likely to be completely satisfied with the results—no one, not even myself. The work is an essay rather than a finished treatise. I should be very pleased if any reader who writes—whether for publication or not—an analysis, discussion, or criticism of the work would send a copy of it to me. I also will appreciate receiving any specific suggestions for improving the work.

After two brief drafts I prepared a full-scale draft of the present work as notes for a course in Introduction to Philosophy which I taught at Campion College, University of Regina, in the Winter Semester, 1974. The material proved too difficult for an introductory course, yet the comments and questions of the members of this class were very helpful. In many cases class discussion led to clarifications incorporated in this final version. I am most grateful for the help of my students in this project and for their patience in struggling with an overly difficult first course in philosophy. I hope this experience does not kill their interest in the subject. Four members of the class—Sharon Hester, Nona Kent, Bart Leach, and John Pearce—kindly returned to me the critiques they wrote of each chapter during the course, and I have profited from many of the questions they raised.

On the basis of this experience I suggest that this book could be used as one of two texts in an advanced undergraduate or introductory graduate course in philosophy of religion or philosophical theology. Many works in the field, several of which I cite in notes, are written from a nontheistic point of view. A comparative study of one of these books and the present book could constitute an exciting course. Too often the only exposure students receive to

xi

theistic views is secondhand, or in the form of brief excerpts taken out of context in such a way as to render them wholly unintelligible.

I make extensive use of self-referential argumentation in this work. A self-referential argument shows that an attempt to assert a proposition either falsifies it or renders the assertion of it pointless. Dr. Joseph M. Boyle, Jr. has done pioneer work in clarifying the logic of this type of argumentation. His main work on the topic is his unpublished doctoral dissertation, *The Argument from Self-Referential Consistency: the Current Discussion*, which he completed under my direction at Georgetown University in 1969. Boyle and I have collaborated with Dr. Olaf Tollefsen—who also worked under my direction at Georgetown—on a full-scale application of self-referential argument to the problem of free choice: *Free Choice: A Self-Referential Argument.* Important aspects of the argumentation in chapters seven, eleven, eighteen, and twenty-three of the present book were first developed as part of the collaborative project on freedom. The present book, in fact, grew out of an overly ambitious attempt on my part to deal in a draft chapter of the book on free choice with the question of the compatibility between divine causality and human free choice. That draft chapter will not appear in the final version of the book on free choice in the form in which it was originally written; however, the criticisms Boyle and Tollefsen offered of it helped me greatly in developing several aspects of the present work. (*Free Choice* is scheduled for spring 1976 publication by the University of Notre Dame Press.)

In addition to those whose names I have already mentioned, the following persons read at least some part of some version of this work and made helpful suggestions: Owen Bennett, O.F.M.Conv., Richard J. Blackwell, Basil Cole, O.P., John Finnis, Dagfinn Føllesdal, John C. Ford, S.J., Anthony Kenny, Ronald Lawler, O.F.M.Cap., Ernest McCullough, Kenneth L. McGovern, George Marshall, Rev. Eric Mascall, William E. May, Hugo Meynell, Jerome Miller, E. Peter W. Nash, S.J., Rabbi David Novak, Thomas Rendall, Russell Shaw, and Ronald K. Tacelli, S.J. I should point out that while some of these critics were enthusiastic, others advised that the entire project should be scrapped. Since the present draft has been revised in the light of *all* the comments I received on previous ones, critics in *either* group might now take a different view, so I forbear indicating which were which. However, the fact that someone is kind enough to look at and criticize a work obviously does not constitute an endorsement of it. Thus none of those to whom I express my thanks should be considered guilty of anything I have done—perhaps against their good advice.

I also thank Campion College for a grant defraying research expenses and the Canada Council for a travel grant which enabled me to participate in the

Thomas Aquinas International Congress in Rome in the spring of 1974, and to stay on after the Congress to do research for this book.

The interlibrary loan department of the University of Regina library has been most helpful; special thanks are due to Mrs. Carol Olive.

My wife Jeannette encouraged and supported me at every stage of the work, patiently producing the typescript and helping with the mechanics of publication. Our closeness makes an expression of thanks to her seem inappropriate.

At the beginning of this study I was aware of the infinite disproportion between what we human persons can think and say about God and what he is in himself. At the end I remain aware of this disproportion. Indeed, I am far more acutely aware of it:

> One cannot lessen, nor increase, nor penetrate the wonders of the Lord.
> When a man ends he is only beginning,
> and when he stops he is still bewildered. (Si. 18:4-5)

Germain Grisez

Campion College
University of Regina
September 30, 1974

I: Faith and Reason

1: Introduction

What this work is about

Can any argument establish the truth of the proposition that God exists? Most contemporary philosophers think not, and many offer criticisms of the classical arguments for the existence of God. Are these criticisms cogent or can they be rebutted? If they can be rebutted, can one say anything more about God than that he exists? Language is used in peculiar ways in talk about God. How can these unusual uses of words be meaningful?

If God is an omnipotent and all-good creator of the universe, how can human persons be free and why is there evil in the world? If God is an infinite being, is not the created universe reduced to nothing? If God is unchangeable, how can there be creativity and novelty within the created universe? Are miracles and divine revelation possible? Are the paradoxical teachings of Christian faith logically coherent? Even if doctrines such as the Incarnation, the Trinity, and the Eucharist are not sheer nonsense, why should a reasonable person choose to believe them?

The present work is intended to clarify these questions and to propose answers to them. The questions I investigate here make up a subject matter which has been treated by some English-speaking philosophers in recent years under the heading "philosophical theology." However, I use this expression to designate a special *part* of philosophy of religion—the part indicated by the questions listed in the first paragraph above. "Philosophy of religion" I take to be a wider expression which designates all philosophical questions pertaining to religion, including those of philosophical theology and those listed in the second paragraph above, and also including many other questions often

2

treated by continental European thinkers but generally not discussed by English-speaking philosophers.

Philosophy of religion does not presuppose religious faith. It is concerned with matters religious, but it does not take for granted the truth of any religious belief. However, persons working in the field of philosophy of religion ordinarily have beliefs of their own. The rationality of a philosopher is not the neutral rationality of a computer.

Readers of the present work will be aware that its author is a believing Christian. Readers of any work in philosophy of religion written by a person who is an agnostic or an atheist usually are aware of the faith-position of the author. A philosopher, whether believer or nonbeliever, can deal philosophically with topics which also concern him precisely insofar as he is a religious believer, an agnostic, or an atheist. Everyone has beliefs before he begins philosophizing. A philosopher's antecedent beliefs suggest what ground he will try to defend and how he will try to defend it. The essential characteristic of a philosophical approach is that the defense be rational; a philosopher tries to avoid begging questions in favor of his own beliefs.

A major concern throughout this work is to develop a position which integrates what is sound in classical theism with important insights and concerns of what is called "the new theism." Classical theism, the set of positions and approaches common among Christians and Jews until the nineteenth century, stressed the separation between God and creation. The new theism is more interested in the relationship between them. Classical theism, stressing divine transcendence, also emphasized God's changelessness. The new theists argue that an immanent God, who cares about creation and who gives it real importance, must work and suffer along with his creatures. In short, classical theists held that God is an absolute being, perfect in himself, while new theists are more interested in God as a person to whom human persons can relate.

From the point of view of Christian faith perhaps the only final resolution of the tensions between classical theism and the new theism is a further refinement of the doctrine of the Incarnation. Philosophy of religion must leave the working out of such a final resolution to theologians who work in the light of Christian faith. But philosophy of religion can make a contribution of its own. Many classical theories of talk about God were best suited to clarifying the meaning of language used to talk about God in his transcendence; many contemporary theories, naturally enough, fit better with the new theism. Philosophy of religion can try to work out a more adequate logic of God-talk. A more adequate logic must distinguish nonrelational from relational predication about God.

I try to clarify this problem and to contribute to its solution, not by examining and criticizing various classical and contemporary theories of talk about God, but by articulating a view which I think is adequate both for metaphysics and for religion. I hold that the God of the philosophers and the God of faith are not two gods but one God, talked of in distinct but compatible ways. In talk about God, abstract metaphysical expressions and metaphorical, anthropomorphic expressions both have a role to play. I think that many philosophers who were classical theists tended to be overly ambitious and confident about the ability of man to talk about God as he is in himself, while many philosophers who might be called "new theists" too easily assume that relational predications concerning God must either tell what he is in himself or express only a special way of looking at the world of experience. My view is that the new theism contains much that is important and suggestive, but that it is ultimately irreconcilable with traditional Jewish and Christian faith. However, I do not think it possible to go back to the philosophy developed by classical theists in previous centuries; a Jewish or Christian philosopher who holds to the essential tradition of his faith must take the new theism into account and try to go beyond it.

The following brief outline might be helpful in grasping the structure of this work as a whole.

The first part, including this chapter and the next two chapters, is mainly concerned with the relationship between faith and reason. In the latter part of this chapter I try to clarify how faith and reason are related to each other in my own thinking. Chapter two provides an example of the interplay between reason and faith in a child's learning about God. Chapter three considers a number of positions which, if sound, would rule out any philosophical attempt to establish the truth of the proposition that God exists. I try to show that these positions are not sound.

In the second part, chapters four and five, I present an argument for the proposition that there is an uncaused entity. In several respects the argument is new, but it falls into a class of arguments usually called "cosmological" by philosophers. Arguments of this sort proceed from the existence of some aspect of the cosmos—the world of experience—to the conclusion that an uncaused cause exists. In my view an argument for the existence of an uncaused entity plays a double role in philosophical theology. An argument is essential to establish the conclusion that God exists; to establish this conclusion is useful, not so much to prove it to persons who do not accept it as to establish a real *referent* for the beliefs of those who do accept it. At the same time an argument showing that God exists provides a principle for making *sense* of talk about God; the ways in which language is used in the argument can be clarified and adapted for further talk about God.

The third part, chapters six to thirteen, considers objections philosophers are likely to make to the argument presented in the second part. If these objections are successful, then the argument fails to prove its point. Major modern philosophers, especially Hume, Kant, and Hegel, criticize classical examples of cosmological argumentation. I try to rebut such criticisms, both as they are found in the writings of the major philosophers, and also as they are reformulated today. During the twentieth century, moreover, several new philosophical methods sharing certain common features have emerged, and these methods sometimes are assigned the task of excluding as impossible the development of any philosophical theory, including one such as I am proposing. To exploit these methods to exclude theories obviously is to give them a theoretical task. I call such exploitation of these methods "post-hegelian relativism" and try to show that no form of this relativism presents an insurmountable obstacle to the sort of argument presented in part two.

In the fourth part, chapters fourteen to seventeen, I try to show how talk about God has sense. Here I reflect upon the argument presented in the second part. My view is that the *meaning*—not only the reference—of other God-talk *depends upon* some sort of reasoning to the existence of God. I do not mean that the argument must be articulated formally; I mean that God-talk logically originates in such a context, and always must be tied back to it. Once its sense is initiated, God-talk of course goes on to statements beyond the conclusion that God exists.

In the fifth part, chapters eighteen to twenty-one, I examine several problems in philosophy of religion which are probably more important to anyone who is not a philosopher than are the more technical problems of philosophical theology considered in previous chapters. The problems examined in part five are related to the humanistic concern to protect freedom and other human values against any possible threat from religious belief. Thus, these problems are about compatibility—for example: How can man be free if God causes everything? My way of dealing with such problems, in general, is to try to show that one who takes a consistent position should not be troubled by them. For instance, nothing we can learn about God by rational argumentation alone gives us any reason to expect that there should not be evil in the world; however, religious faith, if it is consistent, not only generates but also resolves the problem of evil.

The sixth part, chapters twenty-two to twenty-five, considers further problems related to the meaningfulness of religious faith. Some of these problems are quite general: How can talk about miracles and revelation, which underlies all specific Christian doctrines, be understood? There also are specific questions about the coherence of some major Christian doctrines. And, finally, there is the question of the existential meaningfulness of faith: What point might there be in believing Christian doctrines even if they are not nonsensical or necessarily false?

Readers who are not familiar with the history of modern philosophy and with the major trends in contemporary philosophy may find the third part especially difficult. Although this part is essential to the philosophical defense of the argument presented in the second part, the remainder of the work can be understood by someone who ignores the third part.

Some readers may feel that I pay too much attention to problems about the meaningfulness of religious language and too little attention to questions about its truth. However, language, including the language of faith, cannot express truth unless it has meaning. Moreover, the question of the truth of the teachings proper to Christian faith—or any other purportedly revealed faith—cannot be settled without consideration of questions belonging to the field of history. Thus, philosophical theology concentrates on problems of meaning. Even the argument of part two and the treatment of objections to it are mainly directed to a problem of meaning: Is there anything beyond human thought to which religious language refers?

Moreover, confusion of language used in speaking about God and in formulating tenets of religious faith causes many people to have serious problems in accepting what such language is intended to express. This content, if true, is of the highest importance; if it is not true, it is important that we not believe it. Therefore, any contribution to getting rid of misunderstandings which interfere with the use of religious language is important.

I think that religious language is multiform, not uniform. To adopt Wittgenstein's expression, religious language is not one language game but many distinct games. I do not think that all difficulties of faith are caused by linguistic confusions, but I do think that many of them are either caused or aggravated by such confusions. I hope the present work will help to show the butterfly of faith the way out of the chrysalis of linguistic confusion.

Faith, reason, and philosophy of religion

As suggested already, I do not think a philosopher's personal faith can be left behind when he moves onto the field where the combats of philosophy of religion are fought. For this very reason I believe that readers of works in this field are entitled to a clear statement of the author's understanding of the roles which faith and reason play in his own thinking.

In the first place, I do not think that philosophy of religion is irrelevant to religious faith. I have explained already why I think the philosophical clarification of the meaning of religious language and its many forms is important for theological progress and for removing obstacles to faith. I also think that any community of faith which is not a ghetto of obscurantism must have among its members some persons who can meet nonbelieving philosophers on their own ground. Otherwise, what assurance is there that the faith of the community can stand rational examination even by one who shares this faith?

In the second place, I do not think it is the philosopher's business, even in philosophy of religion, to be edifying. Someone has said that no treatise on God is sound unless it makes the reader get out of his chair and get down on his knees. I think this objective is too ambitious for philosophy; a philosophy which seeks to achieve it is likely to become ideological in its effort to be prophetic. It seems to me enough for a philosophical work on God to untie some of the bonds which keep the reader so firmly in his chair that he could not possibly get out of it.

I do think it is legitimate for the philosopher to argue for positions which he would hold on faith even apart from the argument. However, I do not think it legitimate for the philosopher to commend what he believes to readers *because* he believes it, or even precisely because he thinks it true. I try to avoid such commending in this work. I try to argue for what I think true to the extent, and only to the extent, that I think its truth can be established by arguments which deserve to be accepted by any reasonable person. If there is something wrong with my arguments, I am ready to be shown what is wrong with them. There is no point in trying to defend one's positions with unsound arguments.

Moreover, if my positions themselves are indefensible or false, I am ready to be shown this too. Frankly, I do not expect anyone to show that these positions are indefensible or false; if I expected that, I could not hold them and would not defend them. However, the thinking presented in this work has developed as I have wrestled with arguments which challenge what I believe.

I have always wished to test what I believe, to make sure that it can survive critical scrutiny in the full light of rational reflection. Long before I first heard of Socrates and his dictum that the unexamined life is not worth living, I troubled the teacher of my First Communion class and irritated the other children in it by insisting that I could not see how anyone could fit into the small dimensions of the Communion bread. Since I began studying philosophy twenty-five years ago, I have altered and refined my beliefs on many points. I do not expect this process to stop short of senility or death whichever comes first.

Since I do not ask readers to grant tenets of religious faith as grounds for the arguments in this book, when it is necessary to refer to religious beliefs I use the third person and the past tense. For example, "Christians believed that. . . ," not "I believe that. . . ," and still less "It is true that. . . ." Lest anyone be misled by the fact that I refer to propositions of Christian faith in the course of philosophical arguments without affirming them, I perhaps should make it clear here that I personally believe what the Roman Catholic Church believes and teaches. I make no reservations, but I do point out that most Catholics believe a great deal which the Church does not believe and teach, and I am not bound to agree with them in these extra beliefs.

If anyone thinks that an author's philosophical integrity is called into question by an affirmation of faith such as I make, I suggest that he ask himself whether the faith-positions of authors who wholly reject religious faith—whether the rejection is stated explicitly or not—put *their* integrity and objectivity in question. If anyone is really neutral on the matters treated in this book, is his thought likely to be worth considering seriously? If anyone claims to be strictly impartial, should a reader believe such a claim? And if no claim to neutrality should be accepted, is it fair to assume that only those who reject religious faith can be objective? Such an assumption would prejudice the whole discussion from the outset. I suspect some such assumption as this often is made by persons who feel it is necessary to protect reason against faith.

However, it seems to me that a philosopher who is also a religious believer should not feel it necessary to protect either faith or reason against the other, while a philosopher who is not a religious believer should have enough confidence in reason that he will not try to exclude from the philosophical arena those who openly avow their religious faith. Both the religious believer and the nonbeliever should be more firmly committed to truth than to their beliefs, because beliefs should be held only insofar as they are thought to be true.

An interesting exchange between two contemporary philosophers clarifies the point I am making. Antony Flew argues in an article, "The Presumption of Atheism," that in philosophical theology the presumption should be on the side of nonbelief. The burden of proof should be on the theist, Flew thinks, because the theist asserts propositions which are not evident. Flew points out that theists used to admit as much; Thomas Aquinas, for example, proposed five ways of proving the existence of God.[1]

Donald Evans, in response to Flew, points out that a theist should not be expected to give up his faith as a condition for engaging in arguments in philosophical theology. Evans makes an important distinction between a "procedural presumption" and a "personal presumption." The believer cannot take his faith-positions for granted in the argument without begging the questions he ought to treat philosophically. However, a believer need not deny the faith-positions which he forebears to assert and puts in question for the sake of argument.[2]

Flew comments on Evans's response, accepting Evans's distinction between procedural and personal presumptions. But Flew adds a further important clarification. If a person is to be reasonable, he must have reasons for believing what he does. If a believer enters into philosophical argument, he should not simply play a game, without any personal commitments. The game should be for keeps. A responsible person must be ready to accept the outcome required by reasons. He need not concede the role of judge to an adversary in argument, but he should play this role himself. One who argues philosophically commits himself to forego beliefs which he comes to realize cannot be sustained by reason.[3]

I think Flew and Evans both make some good points, and their exchange suggests several other related points which are worth making.

First, in the issue whether an uncaused entity exists or not, the procedural presumption is initially in favor of the person who doubts its existence. That there is such an entity is not obvious, either in the way that "This is a printed page" or in the way that "Two and two equals four" is obvious. Thus in this case there is a presumption in favor of atheism; it is unreasonable to posit entities arbitrarily.

However, it is worth noticing that once a plausible argument is proposed leading to the conclusion that there is an uncaused entity, the presumption shifts. It is unreasonable to reject the conclusion of a plausible argument unless one can show that the premises are false or the reasoning fallacious. Some critics of arguments for the existence of God write as though mere speculation that there might be a fallacy in the argument—even without a clear showing that there is one—suffices to maintain the presumption on the side of atheism.[4] This position seems to me dogmatic.

Second, if one can establish that there is a God, and the issue is about some other problem in philosophy of religion, the presumption is not necessarily in favor of the nonbeliever. For example, if a believer and a nonbeliever both admit that there are certain extraordinary phenomena, and if the believer wishes to explain these phenomena as miraculous, while the nonbeliever wishes to explain the same set of facts naturalistically, both parties to the dispute are offering hypotheses. Both hypotheses deserve to be judged by the rules of inductive logic; to establish a presumption in favor of either side, without grounding that presumption in a previously established principle, is simply dogmatic.[5]

Similarly, when we find language being used by many people in a way they think expresses important truths, there is a presumption in favor of the meaningfulness of such language. A nonbeliever can put forward reasons for thinking that various samples of religious discourse are nevertheless meaningless. His argument can shift the presumption. If the arguments pointing to meaninglessness are plausibly answered, however, the presumption once more is with the meaningfulness of the language in question. If anyone assumes that language which is actually used is meaningless until its coherence can be *demonstrated,* it is fair to ask him to demonstrate the coherence of *any* interesting philosophical or theological statement—for instance, his own statement of his position.

Where it is a question of the personal presumption, rather than the procedural assumption, Flew is correct, I think, in holding that one must take philosophical argument seriously. The believer and the nonbeliever must play for keeps. However, the personal presumptions of the believer and the nonbeliever differ. Flew seems not to notice this, perhaps because he thinks of philosophy too much on the model of an adversary procedure such as a legal trial rather than as a common effort of reasonable men to draw nearer to the truth.

It is reasonable for each person to continue to believe what he already does believe, unless he finds good reasons for altering his belief. The personal presumption of the believer does not allow him to ignore arguments against what he believes. However, it is not unreasonable for a believer to continue to believe what he cannot prove, so long as no weighty reasons are given for changing.

If anyone denies this, either he assumes *a priori* that religious faith as such is irrational or he condemns most human convictions. The *a priori* assumption against the rationality of religious faith would be in line with the personal presumption which is reasonable for a nonbeliever, but he cannot reasonably expect his personal presumption to be shared by a believer. (Perhaps Flew in responding to Evans overlooks the relativity of the reasonableness of personal presumptions.) A general position against the reasonableness of continuing to believe what one believes, even though one cannot support it with direct reasons, would condemn most human convictions as unreasonable, for most human convictions are based on authorities of one sort or another. A child believes his parents and teachers; an adult believes scientists, experts, historians, journalists, and so on. For only a few beliefs does anyone have good reasons which he can produce on demand, and no one can produce good reasons for all his beliefs.

If I know and trust a person and if he tells me something which he is in a better position than I to know, then I have a reason to believe him. In fact, it would be irrational to doubt what he says unless I have good reasons for thinking it false; still, I may not have any reasons other than my faith in the person for assenting to the truth of what he says.

Someone might ask what a person who shares my position would do if he encountered an apparently cogent argument against something he believed. This question is legitimate; moreover, it is important.

My answer is that in such cases—they do occur—I proceed with a threefold inquiry. First, is the argument really cogent? Second, is its conclusion really incompatible with what I believe? Third, is what I think I believe what I really believe? The third point requires explanation. No Christian holds his own current grasp of faith to be the sole norm of faith. Some Christians who encounter difficulties go back to the Bible and study it prayerfully. Roman

Catholics can do that too. But they also investigate what *the Church* believes and teaches. In this investigation one must interpret documents. In doing so one need not be simpleminded. The proper strategy is not to twist the language to fit one's wishes, but to recognize the considerable openness inherent in Catholic faith and to make the most of this openness in a creative way. If the argument which started the process of reflection going really does cogently demonstrate a truth incompatible with what one thought one believed, one must refine and develop one's faith to make room for this truth.

My method of dealing with an apparently cogent argument against something I hold on faith might seem evasive. It might be compared unfavorably with the rational procedure of natural science, in which one imagines the investigator giving up his theory the moment he encounters a fact which falsifies it. This model is much too simple even for the rationality of the experimental scientist, however, for a theory is much more frequently refined than given up when the facts seem to falsify it. Moreover, anomalies abound, and a scientist does not give up his theory in the face of them, so long as it holds together fairly well and there is no better alternative theory at hand.

Single bits of evidence against a complex theory, single arguments—or even many arguments—against a system of belief do not automatically render one's confidence in the theory or system of belief irrational. Religious faith is in many ways less vulnerable than any scientific theory. Doctrines which believers themselves do not claim to comprehend are not easily falsified; moral precepts which are coherent with a fundamental worldview and a basic commitment are not easily shown irrational. Certain historical facts are relevant to Christian faith, but historical-critical scholarship hardly seems to offer any plausible reasons for denying the essential facts, except to the extent that such scholarship proceeds upon assumptions—for example, the exclusion of miracles—which believers need not accept. It must be admitted that a religious faith can box itself in by too many overly specific commitments; some forms of fundamentalism make this mistake. However, traditional Jewish and Christian faith on the whole avoided unnecessary commitments, and adherents of these rather flexible systems have a great deal of room for maneuver when they encounter difficulties.

One final point. Readers will observe that I am more indebted to Thomas Aquinas than to any other previous thinker. This observation, together with the fact that I profess the Roman Catholic faith, might lead some readers to the mistaken conclusion that the philosophy I present is simply a variety of thomism. I have drawn much from Thomas's thought. However, I do not regard myself as a thomist. I do not assume anything true because Thomas holds it. I use him much as many empiricists use Hume—to the extent that his thought seems sound and that it can stand on its own philosophical feet.

It might be helpful to warn readers familiar with Thomas's thought of important points on which I do not agree with him. Thomas sometimes treats being (*esse*) as if it were an essential nature. "Ipsum esse subsistens" serves as a quasi-definition of God in attempts to demonstrate properties such as omnipotence.[6] I do not think this procedure correct. I also think that Thomas follows Aristotle too far. I do not think one can argue to an unmoved mover and legitimately call it "God." I do not think Aristotle's theory of substance is altogether sound, especially not in application to the human person. I do not think the human soul should be considered an aristotelian substantial form.[7] Moreover, I do not think the philosophical arguments Thomas uses to try to show that there is knowledge and freedom in God are sound.

I also pick up a number of hints from Thomas which I carry much further than he might have wished. Among these are the descriptive metaphysics of the four orders in chapter fourteen, the way of negation in chapter fifteen, the doctrine of relational predication in chapter seventeen, and the theory of divine inefficiency in chapter twenty-one. The position I take on a Christian's hope in chapter twenty-five goes well beyond anything Thomas says.

There are still some followers of Thomas Aquinas—as there are followers of Wittgenstein and of Marx—who think that their school has a corner on truth. But none of the scholasticisms seems to me to be so final as members of the various schools think. At the same time many who reflect upon the plurality of philosophies and the conflicts among them are quick to reduce every philosophic effort to a mere point of view, a personal option. Such pluralism really is a form of dogmatism—a relativistic dogmatism which makes an absolute of a sceptical rejection of absolute truth. I do not think the problems about which philosophers disagree can be swept away so easily. Some apparent disagreements can be dissolved, but real disagreements can be overcome only by a sincere effort to uncover the mistakes made by either or both sides.

As inquiry goes on, every person must take responsibility for his own beliefs. No philosophical authority can arbitrate the differences among all beliefs. Only a position identical with philosophy itself could play such a role. But philosophy is not a position, it is a quest; it is the persistence of reason. A man cannot escape the responsibility, imposed upon him by the fact that he has a rational mind, of deciding for himself what he ought to believe and of criticizing his own beliefs. This responsibility is to truth, not to any position, not to other men. The more perfectly this responsibility is fulfilled, the more probably will consensus be achieved.

2: A Child Learns to Talk about God

Preliminary remarks

In his "Lectures on Religious Belief" Wittgenstein remarks that "God" is one of the earliest words learned by children. He recalls learning it in connection with certain religious objects. Asked whether he then knew the meaning of the word, Wittgenstein answers that he would say:

> "Yes and no. I did learn what it didn't mean. I made myself understand. I could answer questions, understand questions when they were put in different ways—and in that sense could be said to understand."[1]

Reading this description, I ask myself whether it corresponds to my own memories of learning to talk about God and find that it does not.

Undoubtedly, everyone's experience differs. However, I recall my childhood rather clearly and find it easy to reconstruct conversations and thinking which occurred in a more diffuse form around the time I was five years old. I decided to include some of this reconstruction here, as an example of *a* way in which a child *can* learn to talk about God. I omit from the example many memories of the use of the word "God" in specifically religious contexts, because although the word picks up important aspects of its meaning in such contexts, I do not think these aspects of the meaning of "God" could stand alone, while those aspects of the meaning which I include in the example can stand alone.[2]

My learning to talk about God involved an interplay of faith and reason. I first began to understand "God," as I recall, when the word was used in answers to questions I asked about the movement of heavenly bodies. I

13

accepted the truth of the answers on faith; my mother answered my questions in light of her own religious faith. But reflection upon initial answers led to further questions, and these to further answers. At each stage reason suggested questions to which faith supplied answers.

This interplay, established early in childhood, perhaps explains the genesis of my view of the relationship between faith and reason, outlined in chapter one. The example of a child's learning to talk about God also will be put to use in chapter three.

One striking difference between Wittgenstein's childhood experience and mine is pointed up by his explanation of the remark quoted above:

> If the question arises as to the existence of a god or God, it plays an entirely different role to that of the existence of any person or object I ever heard of. One said, had to say, that one *believed* in the existence, and if one did not believe, this was regarded as something bad. Normally if I did not believe in the existence of something no one would think there was anything wrong in this.[3]

I never felt I had to say I "believed" in the existence of God; I always thought I *knew* that God exists, and I was unaware that this knowledge was a product of an interplay of faith and reason. I cannot recall any situation which could have suggested to me that not believing in God would be something bad until I learned in school about the existence of atheists and agnostics. I remember that when I first learned of such persons, I was puzzled by *their* existence, for it seemed strange to me that anyone could doubt or deny something so elementary as that God exists.

Because the following example involves reconstruction and is intended as illustration rather than as autobiography, I cast it in the form of a third-person narrative.

The example

It was summer and the ground was warm. The moon had not yet risen; the sky was clear and very black. A little boy lay on the grass in front of his home and gazed up at the stars. He was watching for shooting stars. Earlier in the summer the whole family had watched fireworks set off to celebrate July the Fourth by people from the city. Now there were only shooting stars, but they were not too bad. In between watching shooting stars he scanned the sky, making out the constellations he knew.

A few days later, after dinner, he was standing by the side door of the house, looking at the sunset. "Look, Mama, how pretty the sun is!"

"Yes, the sun is going down, and it is a beautiful sunset this evening." The little boy gazed at the horizon as the edge of the sun sank below it. He thought about the shooting stars.

"Mama, what makes the sun go down?"

"Why, God makes the sun go down."

"But the sun is very big. Why doesn't it fall fast like a shooting star?"

"God doesn't let it fall fast. The shooting stars fall fast but they get all burned up, like the cinders in the fireplace. God wants to keep the sun, so it can come up tomorrow. So he doesn't let it fall fast."

"God must be very big and strong."

"Oh, he is. He is much bigger and stronger than you can imagine."

"Is he bigger and stronger than Daddy?"

"Yes," she laughed, "much bigger and stronger than Daddy."

"Some God!"

Daddy brought home a dozen doughnuts. Each member of the family was entitled to two of them. The little boy took two doughnuts and put them on the table at his place. Finally it was time to eat them. "If we are very careful when we eat the doughnuts to save the holes in the middle," one of the older children teased, "Daddy can take them back and get free doughnuts."

The little boy knew what "free" meant. He began to eat his first doughnut very carefully. Soon there was only a thin ring of crust left. He was quite pleased with himself. "Here is a hole!"

"Oh, no. You have to eat *all* of the doughnut and save the hole. You haven't eaten it all yet."

The little boy ate carefully, but as he finished the last of the doughnut, the hole was all gone too. He took his second doughnut and tried again.

"You have to be more careful. You weren't careful enough last time, and you lost the hole."

He ate very, very carefully. But as he finished the doughnut the hole vanished with it. He was frustrated. "When you eat *all* of the doughnut, the hole goes away too," he said with some irritation, realizing he had been kidded. Everyone laughed.

After dinner, the little boy watched the sun go down again. He was thinking about what Mama said about God. "Mama, if God gets tired out, won't the sun fall down fast like a shooting star, and get burned up like a cinder?"

"God never gets tired out. He doesn't have to work to make the sun go down the way he wants it to. He just thinks how it should be, and it does what he wants."

The little boy thought about this for a while. When *he* thought how he wanted something to be, it didn't get to be that way. And Daddy would talk about how something should be, as when the grass needed to be cut, but then one of the bigger boys had to cut it. If God made things be the way he wanted just by thinking about them, would they stay that way if he went to sleep? "Mama, you remember the hole in the doughnut?"

"Yes," she laughed, "it went away when you ate the doughnut all up, because there really isn't anything there."

"You said God makes things be the way he wants just by thinking about them. When he goes to sleep, why don't things go away like the hole in the doughnut?"

"Because God doesn't go to sleep. He doesn't have a body like we do. We get sleepy because our bodies get tired out. But God doesn't have a body. He just thinks, so he never gets sleepy."

"God doesn't have a body?"

"No, and that is why we can't see him. But he is right here with us all the time."

The little boy thought about this for many days. God must be like the wind. You can't see the wind, but it is there. Even inside the house, if you run fast, you can feel the wind. And if you blow hard on your hand, you can feel the wind you make. God must be like the wind. He is here with us, but he doesn't have a body, and so we cannot see him.

The little boy went with Mama to stay with Auntie Min. Auntie Min was dying, and Mama had to care for her. Auntie Min did not seem to know the little boy; she used to give him cookies when he came to visit. But now she was in bed and she didn't seem to know him. She kept talking and singing; sometimes she would cry and scream, and try to get out of bed and fall down. Mama said Auntie Min was dreaming even when she was awake. Finally, one afternoon, Auntie Min was quiet. The little boy was there with Mama when Auntie Min became very still.

Mama went to the dresser and took a mirror. She rubbed it on her dress, and then held it very close to Auntie Min's face over her nose and mouth. Mama looked at the mirror. "Auntie Min is dead," Mama said. "She isn't breathing."

The priest had been there that morning, but he came back. The doctor came too. Then some men came and they brought some strange things and worked on Auntie Min in her room far into the night. The little boy was supposed to be asleep, but he stayed awake and listened as long as he could. Finally he went to sleep. In the morning he was awake before anyone else and went downstairs to the living room. The furniture had been moved around. In front of the windows was a long thing with a little step in front of it. The little boy stood on the step and looked inside. Auntie Min was there and she seemed to be sleeping peacefully. The little boy touched her. If he could wake her up, perhaps she would be all right now, and she would give him some cookies.

Auntie Min felt cold. She didn't move at all. She didn't wake up. The little boy remembered that Mama had said Auntie Min is dead. He knew what "dead" meant; he had seen plenty of dead flies and dead trees and he once had a pet rabbit which died. Auntie Min was not breathing, Mama had said. God was not there any more. She was cold, like a cinder from the fire which burned in the fireplace yesterday but had been allowed to go out in the evening. God must have stopped thinking about Auntie Min, and she had fallen dead, like a shooting star.

The little boy got out some of his toys and began to play quietly. In a little while one of his other aunts came down and found him playing there. She scolded him and made him go to another room, at the back of the house. Soon Mama came down and began to make some breakfast.

"He was right there in the living room, playing in front of the coffin. I made him go play back here."

"All right. I'll tell him not to go in the living room again. He doesn't understand. Anyway, he didn't disturb anyone."

Mama was not angry with the little boy at all. She snuggled him and told him to come and eat some breakfast in the kitchen. The other aunt had left.

"I wasn't bad, was I Mama? I tried to wake Auntie Min up, but she won't wake up. Then I remembered you said she was dead."

"No, you weren't bad. Never mind."

"Auntie Min isn't breathing. She's cold."

"That's what happens when someone dies."

"God isn't there. He must have stopped thinking about her and let her fall."

"Oh, no. God is there. He hasn't stopped thinking about Auntie Min. She was very sick and she hurt a great deal. So God has taken her to live with him."

"She lost all her breath."

"Yes, her body is dead. But she is still alive, with God. We can't see her, just as we can't see God. But she is alive with him."

"She lost all her breath, and it went out into the wind, with God. She is in the wind now?"

"No, she isn't in the wind."

"But I thought God is like the wind. You can't see the wind, but it is there."

"No, God isn't like the wind. We can *feel* the wind. We can't feel God, we can't see him."

"Then he isn't there!"

"He is, but we only know him by thinking, because he doesn't have a body, and he is not like the wind."

The little boy thought about this for some time. God is not *there*. He is like the hole in the doughnut. It isn't there either. If everyone and all the animals and insects and trees and flowers were dead, God would not be there anymore, just like the hole in the doughnut, which goes away when you eat up the doughnut. "Mama, if everyone and all the animals and insects and trees and flowers were dead, God wouldn't be there anymore, would he?"

"Yes, he would. You know he makes them all be, just by thinking. He makes the sun set and lets the shooting stars fall, just by thinking. A long time ago, there were no people or any living things, but God thought and wanted them, and they came to be. A long, long time ago, long before God made living things, there were no stars, there was no sun. The ground and the sky were not here. But God always was, and he thought of all he wanted to be, and everything started and came to be as he wanted it to be."

"Then God is not like the hole in the doughnut."

"No," she laughed. "The hole in the doughnut isn't really something there. We only think about the hole because the doughnut is there. But the hole doesn't make the doughnut be there. We think of God because we see the stars and sun, and people and living things, and the wind and everything there is. God makes everything be there by thinking of it and wanting it. He is real, and he always was, before anything else came to be, and he will always be."

"Will everything go away, like the hole in the doughnut? Is that what happened to Auntie Min?"

"No," she said gently, seeing how worried the little boy was. "God didn't make things to let them go away. He loves us, and when we die we go to live with him. That is what has happened to Auntie Min."

"Then *where* is she? Where does God live?"

"God doesn't live here or there. He isn't something here or there. He is everywhere, and he is right here with us. But he lives in a different way, a way we don't understand. We can only think of God."

"Auntie Min is living with God?"

"Yes, but in a way we don't understand."

"Is she right here with us too?"

"I think so," she said slowly and thoughtfully. "I don't think Auntie Min is far away from us. But we can be sure she is living with God. She is not sick any more and she is happy now."

3: The Necessity
for Reasoning toward God

Introduction

In part two I will try to show how a sound argument can proceed from something in the world of experience and ordinary, nonreligious talk to the conclusion that there is an uncaused entity. But is such an argument necessary? Many thoughtful persons who believe in God think not. There are various versions of the position that argument from the world to God is superfluous and perhaps even dangerous, and there is a vast literature articulating, attacking, and defending this position.

Even if there were cogent reasons for thinking that it is not necessary to reason toward God, the argument developed in part two could be sound and interesting, but it would not be very important. I think that it is necessary to reason from the world toward God. Still, it seems to me that those who hold the opposite view make some points worth considering, and that a brief examination of some of the reasons proposed for this view will throw further light on the relationship between faith and reason. Therefore, although I cannot hope to do full justice to them, I wish to take a quick look at some attempts to articulate and defend the position that reasoning from the world toward God is unnecessary.

This position takes at least four forms: first, that the reality of God is somehow evident, and so there is no need to prove that God exists; second, that the reality of God can only be accepted by a commitment, and that reasoning merely gives this commitment a pseudorational appearance; third, that the reality of God can only be encountered in his free self-revelation, and that any attempt to reason about God is a product of sinful presumption; and

19

fourth, that the reality of God is obvious to anyone who reflects clear-headedly on what he means by "God," and that reasoning from the world toward God, even if possible, is unnecessarily indirect.

Is the existence of God evident?

To some people it seems evident that God exists. What is puzzling to such persons, as it was to me when I was a child, is that there are people who doubt or deny the existence of God. Thomas Aquinas considers the view that the proposition that God exists is so obvious that its contradictory is simply unthinkable. He begins his criticism of this opinion:

> In part, the above opinion arises from the custom by which from their earliest days people are brought up to hear and to call upon the name of God. Custom, and especially custom in a child, comes to have the force of nature. As a result, what the mind is steeped in from childhood it clings to very firmly, as something known naturally and self-evidently.[1]

The point Thomas is making can be restated in contemporary terms by saying that the seeming obviousness of the reality of God arises from the fact that belief in God is a product of conditioning; the conviction caused by this conditioning is strong because the conditioning began in early childhood and continued for a long time. The example of the child in chapter two could be used to support this point. The child learns how to use the word "God" by hearing the word used in answer to certain questions which he asks. The meaning of the word is built up from the context in which these questions are asked and answered.

Someone who thinks that the reality of God is obvious might object that although the child learns from others how to use the word "God," he himself must form the idea which the word expresses. The little boy anticipated the answer to the extent that he asked a question; perhaps he only needed help to express his insights. When children ask about various objects—"What is this?"—they often seem only to seek the name; when they are told the word for the object, they seem to be satisfied, although this sort of answer clearly adds nothing to what they already knew about the object itself.

This argument does point to a fact worth noticing. The child is not passive in the learning process. But the manner in which a child learns about God is quite different from the manner in which he learns about objects perceptible to the senses. The existence of the latter is evident. The question a child asks which elicits an answer using the word "God" is not the question "What is this?" asked about an experienced object. The question "Why does such-and-such occur?" is asked with respect to a state of affairs which arouses wonder. (This is not to say that children only learn to use the word "God" in this way, but they can do so; the child whose experience is described in chapter two did so.)

A "why" question begins from something obvious, but it asks for what is not obvious. Answers to "why" questions need not be—and perhaps never are—self-evident. "Why" questions seek reasons; they are requests for explanations of some sort.[2] When a child begins asking questions of this kind, we know that the child has begun to reason. Reasoning goes beyond the obvious, points to something not obvious, and asks: "What is the nonobvious factor which explains the given state of affairs?"

A child who learns about God in the way exemplified in chapter two is engaged in a reasoning process. The child's questions reveal that he is "putting two and two together." At the same time the child is being conditioned. The answers he receives to his questions are not the only possible answers. Mother might have said that the sun sets because the earth rotates on its axis; she might have illustrated this answer with a globe and a light bulb. This answer would have led to quite different further questions. Of course, the child might have asked some other question which would have elicited an answer involving the word "God."

In any case the question is likely to be one which presupposes reasoning, not one of the form "What is this?" about something directly experienced. In English the word "God" is not the name of a particular object given in experience, because "God" names an object of worship, and English-speaking people do not usually worship material objects. We may doubt that members of other civilizations who regard particular objects—for example, idols, the sun, and so on—as divine altogether identify the perceptible object with the reality of what they call "God."

Someone who holds that the existence of God is obvious might argue that he "sees" God present in the beauty and goodness of experienced things. The child described in chapter two, it might be argued, really has an experience of God as part of his experience of the beauty of the sunset. One's attention must be called even to what is obvious; thus the fact that children learn from the suggestions of parents and teachers does not eliminate the possibility that the reality of God is evident to all. Parents and teachers themselves learned how to use the word "God," and the language of religion is not a technical language, like that of nuclear physics, but is part of ordinary langauge. One finds talk about some sort of divinity in every human culture. God is part of the common-sense world. Thus, the argument concludes, the reality of God must be obvious to anyone willing to pay attention to it.

This position has been developed systematically by a number of philosophers who maintain that one can have immediate experience of God, not as part of the world, but as a distinct reality given along with the world of objects. Norman Kemp Smith, for example, holds: "We never experience the

Divine sheerly in and by itself; we experience the Divine solely through and in connection with what is other than the Divine."[3] Smith suggests that we experience God immediately with our experience of the material world much as we experience other minds immediately with our experience of other person's bodies. Dom Illtyd Trethowan speaks of a *contuition* of God; he maintains that God is immediately experienced along with experiences of moral and existential reality, including in particular one's sense of one's own contingency and finitude.[4]

Perhaps John Hick's development of this approach is the fullest and most plausible. Hick maintains that the natural world is not a set of brute facts, but a world of facts shot through with meanings. The moral order is mediated by the natural world, but the former is not reducible to the latter. One can enter neither the natural world nor the human, moral world without a personal act of interpretation of the given meanings. This interpretative act is not super-added to experience, according to Hick; rather, it is constitutive of experience. In a similar way, there is an encompassing situation of being in the presence of God and belonging within an ongoing divine purpose. This situation is related to the human world as the human world itself is related to the natural world. Thus we experience God by interpreting meanings given with and mediated by other dimensions of significant data, but we do not reason to the existence of God. Hick concludes:

> Thus the primary religious perception, or basic act of religious interpre-
> tation, is not to be described as either a reasoned conclusion or an
> unreasoned hunch that there is a God. It is, putatively, an apprehension of
> the divine presence within the believer's human experience. It is not an
> inference to a general truth, but a "divine-human encounter," a mediated
> meeting with the living God.[5]

Hick's conception of access to God by experience, it must be noted, does not rest upon specifically "religious experiences," such as mystics and some other people claim to have.

However, religious experience also sometimes is alleged to provide imme-
diate evidence of the existence of God. The experiences cited range all the way from the awareness of the presence of God experienced during prayer or a liturgical celebration, through the experience of divine grace some people have when they are converted to Christian faith, to the peculiar experience of mystics such as St. John of the Cross.[6]

But there are serious difficulties involved in any appeal to specifically religious experiences. If one admits the testimony of all who claim to have had mystical experiences, excluding none in advance as false witnesses, mystics disagree about *what* it is that they experience; moreover, many mystics do not claim to experience anything Jews or Christians would call

"God."[7] More run-of-the-mill religious experiences which purportedly involve an "encounter with God" also seem questionable if they are offered as instances of immediate evidence of divine reality, for if the analogy with human interpersonal relationships is preserved, then God is reduced to the human level, while if the analogy is not preserved, the meaning of "encounter" becomes obscure.[8] So far as other religious experiences are concerned, it seems fair to ask whether persons who are not deeply religious, or not religious at all, might not have similar *experiences,* which would be articulated in other ways—for example, by saying that one "has a strange feeling of confronting a great power," "is aware of having an unusual sense of security and encouragement," or something of the sort.

In other words, some experiences are called "religious" by those who believe in God and who therefore refer the origin or some aspect of the content of such experience to God. The experiences themselves do not reach the whole reality which these believers themselves would call "God"; the reality adumbrated by such experiences might be merely subjective or it might be an undiscovered natural factor.

A believer who claims to know God directly in religious experiences will be challenged by nonbelievers to show that the content of these so-called religious experiences is not susceptible to psychological or other naturalistic account. Unless it is possible to establish an independent ground for referring such experiences to a reality distinct from the self and the world, the nonbeliever is likely to regard these religious experiences much as healthy persons regard the hallucinations of the mentally ill.[9]

It seems to me that where it is a case of claiming specifically religious experiences as instances of the immediate awareness of God, the objections of nonbelievers against using these experiences *as evidence* are decisive. Nonbelievers can admit the phenomena, yet consistently challenge the believer's interpretation of the phenomena, for the religious believer brings to his interpretation of the facts a framework of beliefs and expectations. If the believer does not discount this framework, his use of the experience as evidence is question-begging; if he does discount it, the residual experience will not be sufficient to prove that God transcends experience. For example, I sometimes experience the presence of Christ while participating in the Sacrifice of the Mass; however, I can imagine that if I did not believe in Christ's presence in the Eucharist I might have a very similar experience, but take it to be of *someone else.*

John Hick's position does not rely upon specifically religious experiences, but I do not think it fares better against sceptical criticism. If awareness of the divine depends upon a voluntary act of interpretation, as Hick maintains, it is hard to understand in what sense this awareness is by acquaintance, or noninferential knowledge. Hick's problem is to establish that there is a distinct *referent* for his talk about God; he seems to assume that there is a genuine viewpoint from which the world and human life can be *seen as* in the presence of God and under his providence. This assumption is natural enough for a believer, but an unbeliever who does not "see" the religious realities which are taken for granted by a believer is in no position to "see" everything else in their light.[10]

If the claim that God can be immediately experienced is not accepted, how can one explain its plausibility to many thoughtful persons? I think the answer is that nonformalized, spontaneous inferences easily lead to the conclusion that there is a possible referent for the word "God," and nonformalized inferences also enter into experience and shape the way one habitually "sees" the world. A brief explanation of these points is necessary.

Informal inference which is not articulate about its own logic often, if not always, precedes logically articulated argument. I imagine that every scientist and philosopher has had the experience of thinking about a problem and reaching a conclusion, only to find it difficult to articulate his reasoning. Students beginning in logic can find a correct solution to many problems, but they often are at a loss to explain how they reached it. Similarly, when beginning logic students sense that an argument is fallacious, they often cannot tell what is wrong with it. Perhaps no one who thinks philosophically about the question of the existence of God initially reaches the conclusion that God exists by a formal argument. Thus, like the child in chapter two, many people who think they *know* that God exists as a matter of immediate evidence perhaps only conclude by a nonformal inference that there is a principle on which the world of experience depends, and learn by faith to identify this principle with the object of worship called "God."[11]

Informal inference also enters into experience and shapes the way in which one habitually perceives the world. It is notorious that witnesses called to testify in legal cases often state what they *infer* when asked to tell what they *observed.* For example, a witness who observed a defendant receive a telephone call, apparently become angry, hang up the telephone, take a gun from a drawer, and leave the room hastily, might testify (until interrupted by defense counsel): "The defendant became enraged by something which the deceased said to him on the telephone, slammed the phone down, grabbed a gun, and rushed out of the house to kill him." Less dramatically, a policeman observes a person displaying many signs of alcoholic intoxication, perceives a drunk, but might nevertheless be dealing with a diabetic having an insulin reaction. One use of the expression "see x as F" is in cases in which x is interpreted in accord with expectations by nonformal inferences: if x has properties $G, H, \ldots$, then x is F; x has properties $G, H, \ldots$; therefore, x is

F. This is the pattern of reasoning a physician uses in diagnosing cases of disease which he does not immediately recognize.

It follows that religious believers çan have—and should be expected to have—an awareness of God which seems to them direct. Yet this awareness does not show that God's reality is immediately experienced. If, as I am suggesting, the awareness is based upon nonformal inference, it ought to be possible to articulate the inferential pattern and its steps, just as a physician can articulate his diagnosis to a colleague.

Must the existence of God be accepted on faith?

William James holds that the reality of God must be accepted on faith if it is to be accepted at all. James, considering Kant's criticism of classical arguments for the existence of God decisive, regards any attempt to prove that God exists as an unnecessary and futile attempt to endow a nonrational commitment with an aura of rationality. James says:

> An intellect perplexed and baffled, yet a trustful sense of presence—such is the situation of the man who is sincere with himself and with the facts, but who remains religious still.[12]

James also maintains that refusal to believe is a self-fulfilling pessimistic expectation, while the will to believe, although not rationally justified in any direct way, is grounded in the hope which it makes possible. If one accepts James's position that one can never be certain that he knows the truth about *anything,* then his theory about the need for faith as a way to God will be more plausible than if one rejects this supposition.[13]

Wittgenstein seems to take a position somewhat similar to James's. Wittgenstein admits that religious beliefs are somehow meaningful, and he does not assert that they are false. But he rejects as ludicrous any attempt to make religious beliefs appear *reasonable:* "If this is religious belief, then it's all superstition."[14]

Some followers of Wittgenstein claim to find in his thought the position that religion is a form of life which is self-enclosed. Within the language-game appropriate to a religious form of life the question whether God exists does not come up. As a self-enclosed system, each form of life has its own criteria of rationality and intelligibility. Thus belief—a continuing acceptance of the religious form of life—is necessary and sufficient to settle the question of God's reality.[15]

There is a difference of opinion as to whether this position—which has been called "Wittgensteinian fideism"—is a correct interpretation of Wittgenstein's own thought.[16] In any case, the position has been attacked for its relativistic implications. If each religion is a self-enclosed form of life, then every religious system is equally valid, equally immune from criticism, and equally without reference to anything beyond itself.[17] This lack of transcendent reference is explicit in D. Z. Phillips, a leading Wittgensteinian fideist. He argues that Christians learn in context to forgive, to thank, and to love. In this way "the believer is participating in the reality of God; *this is what we mean by God's reality*" (italics his).[18] Phillips also maintains that such participation in God's reality constitutes human immortality, but he holds that neither one who believes in eternal life nor one who disbelieves in it will survive his own death.[19]

One might attempt to develop a view more plausible than Phillips's along lines suggested by Wittgenstein's remarks. Instead of regarding a religion as a self-enclosed form of life it might be more plausible to think of religion as a universal phenomenon which plays a part in all forms of life. Every culture has some sort of religion; every ordinary language has a word corresponding to "God." This being so, perhaps Wittgenstein only means to point out that religious language is irreducible to other language-games. Everything talked about in ordinary language has some sort of reality. Thus, God undoubtedly is real. The important point is not to confuse God's reality, which is unique, with the reality of physical objects, human persons, and so on.[20]

One answer to this sort of argument for God's reality is that although religious language is part of ordinary language, God is not part of the common-sense world. Many people today do not regard the reality of God as evident; they either doubt it or deny it. Many people would answer the child's initial question narrated in chapter two with elements of a scientific worldview instead of with a religious answer. Many critics of religious belief assert that most children believe what their parents believe and that most individuals would believe differently if they had been exposed to a different early training. Moreover, various psychological and sociological explanations of religious belief have been proposed. These suggest that religion might be a widespread illusion, based on such factors as human fear of the power of nature, wonder about unknown forces, projection of human ideals into a "supernatural" being, or projection of an idealization of one's father.

These attempts to explain religious beliefs and practices have prima facie plausibility. The example of a child's learning to talk about God in chapter two probably is not typical, but I think that most religious believers would admit it as possible. The child began with an anthropomorphic conception of the explanatory factor called "God" because his mother's initial answer led to such a conception. Even when the child was led beyond anthropomorphism, he still conceived God as a natural cause or force. In identifying God with breath or wind he reached a conception common in many primitive religions. Important psychological factors, relating to fear of death and other emotions, were involved in the developments by which the child finally came to think of God as a reality unlike human persons yet somehow personal, hidden but powerful, mysterious but loving.

Of course, it is too facile to say that children grow up believing what their parents believe. The fact is that today many persons whose parents were very religious and who were given an extensive religious formation are non-believers. Also, some persons brought up without any religious formation eventually become firm believers. Changes from one mode of religious belief to another also occur. But despite these facts religious belief might be explained psychologically.

Moreover, a psychological explanation of the fact of religious belief does not preclude its being true. A person who has paranoid delusions might also be a victim of genuine persecution. Psychological explanations of religion are devastating only to those who base everything on unsupported belief and incommunicable experience. The religious believer also can point out that there might well be psychological factors to account for unbelief and the efforts of unbelievers to explain away God. For instance, a believer might suggest that those who reject religious faith are trying to reconstruct reality in such a way that an amoral way of life can be rationalized and their responsibility to anyone or anything beyond their own desires negated.

The religious believer can argue that if a mother answers her child's questions about natural phenomena in purely naturalistic terms, she also is conveying belief, not evident truth. People are likely to suppose that the rotation of the earth is evident because they have been taught this explanation of the phenomena from childhood, but the currently accepted explanation of the apparent movements of heavenly bodies is really a conclusion drawn from arguments which few people understand.

The preceding argument tends to show that naturalistic theories which reduce God to some immanent factor are not as plausible—let alone cogent—as they are often thought to be. But a more serious problem remains. How can a person who claims that God is knowable neither by immediate experience nor by argument establish any *possible* referent for "God" as it is used in "I believe that God exists"? Only if the possible reference of the word is somehow established is the believer in a position to tell what he believes in—something or other, not nothing at all—when he says he believes in God.

If "God" did not function as a proper name, the problem would not be acute. But, clearly, in traditional Jewish and Christian belief "God"—or "God the Father Almighty"—does function as a proper name. If the believer did not hold that God is transcendent and unique, he might offer a definite description, much as a child who believes in Santa Claus can give a description to indicate a possible referent for his belief. But, sceptics argue, if the believer proceeds in this way, the result either will be some combination of the properties of nondivine entities—some of these properties perhaps qualified in logically paradoxical ways—or it will be some entity intelligible but religiously inadequate, because merely immanent.[21]

It seems to me that the problem of the referent of "God" can be solved, but not by one who denies the possibility of arguing to the existence of a principle which can be identified by the believer as identical with that in which he believes. Given an argument that there is an uncaused entity, and given a clarification of "uncaused entity" such that the expression is neither incoherent nor its referent reducible to a merely immanent entity, one is in a position to believe that the uncaused entity is God, and *thus* that God ("God the Father Almighty") exists.

Those who argue that God can only be approached by faith sometimes point out that philosophic arguments seem worthless in real life. No one was ever converted by a syllogism, so the argument goes. If it is possible to establish the conclusion that God exists by argument, why are arguments so ineffective?

In considering this question it must be noticed that no reasoning process is effective in establishing conviction unless certain conditions are met. First, one who encounters the reasoning process must be willing to ask the necessary questions and to follow the steps in the argument. Children wonder naturally, but such wonder is only one possibility among others for an adult; there are many reasons why an adult might choose *not* to ask questions which would lead to knowledge of the existence of God. Second, effort is needed to understand a reasoning process. Interpretation of the language used can be hard work. A logically tight argument for the existence of God requires language which few people can understand without careful study. The linguistic expressions can be made into material for endless quibbles by anyone who is clever and who does not wish to follow the reasoning to its conclusion. Third, it is not easy to construct a sound argument, plausible to one not already a believer, concluding that God exists. Many attempts to reason toward God fail for the simple reason that they are logically fallacious. Even a person who is willing to follow the argument and who makes the necessary effort to interpret the language in which it is articulated cannot reach the conclusion if the "proof" is fallacious.

One who feels that he has good reasons for disbelieving in God's reality is unlikely to be easily moved to change his mind by any abstract argument concluding that there is an uncaused entity which could serve as the referent of "God." Such good reasons are suggested by the following existential questions, some of which I will consider in chapters eighteen to twenty-one. If God exists and is good, why is there so much evil in the world? If God causes everything, how can man be free? If God is unchanging, how can there be room for real development and change in the world? If God destines man to a supernatural end, does he not expect man to abandon his natural life, with its meaning and values? Isn't belief in God a distraction from one's responsibilities in the human community? Do religious experiences show more than that human persons have certain peculiar characteristics, characteristics which perhaps can be changed, but which in the past have made them posit as a reality the bundle of ideals which define what they themselves would like to be? Perhaps honesty requires men and women to work for such ideals in this world, not to seek them in some other world.

No argument for the *existence* of God can answer these questions. However, it seems to me that a sound argument for the existence of God, while not sufficient, is necessary for a rational response to these questions. The word "God" itself, as well as words such as "good" and "causes" predicated of God, must be clarified if one is to think clearly about the existential questions. I do not think that these words can be clarified except in the context of an argument and reflection upon it along the lines I will undertake in parts two and four.

Is every attempt to reason toward God irreligious?

The third view to be considered is that any reasoning toward God is a form of presumption arising from human arrogance. Many theologians during the past one hundred and fifty years have maintained that the reality of God can be encountered only in God's free revelation of himself. This position considers faith and reason to be contrary to one another.

Søren Kierkegaard, for example, states:

> Without risk there is no faith. Faith is precisely the contradiction between the infinte passion of the individual's inwardness and the objective uncertainty. If I am capable of grasping God objectively, I do not believe, but precisely because I cannot do this I must believe. If I wish to preserve myself in faith I must constantly be intent upon holding fast the objective uncertainty, so as to remain out upon the deep, over seventy thousand fathoms of water, still preserving my faith.[22]

In a similar vein Karl Barth argues that the word "God" in the Creed should not be assumed to have some meaning derived from experience and reflection to which the articles of faith add further information. Of ourselves, Barth claims, we do not know what we mean when we say "God"; our expressions do not reach God who reveals himself, but only some self-made idol.[23]

One point to be noticed about Barth's position is that it is not immune from the difficulties of other positions which reject reasoning toward God. If "revelation" is some sort of religious experience which is supposed to make the existence of God evident, then Barth's view is susceptible to the criticisms proposed above against the position that the existence of God is evident. If "faith" involves reference to God apart from experience, argument, or intelligible description, Barth shares the common lot of fideists.

Barth might say that "God" refers to the one who speaks and is spoken of in the Bible. A sceptic would apply to the God-talk of the Bible itself the same analysis and criticism applied to other instances of such talk. But one need not be a sceptic to challenge positions such as Kierkegaard's and Barth's, for their opinions seem to conflict with the teaching of the Bible itself. St. Paul says:

> Since the creation of the world, invisible realities, God's eternal power and divinity, have become visible, recognized through the things he has made. (Rom. 1:20)

Barth points out that this statement occurs in a context in which Paul is showing that the truth about God was rendered ineffective, since the pagans fell into idolatry.[24] This observation is correct to the extent that Paul is insisting upon the need for faith; Paul's point in the epistle is that no one can be rightly related to God except by God's own saving gifts. But Barth seems to be confused in his reading of the passage in question. Paul wishes to show the shortcomings of the pagans in view of the evidence in creation of the power and deity of the *true* God. It would be absurd to say that pagan idolatry was blameworthy because the pagans grasped *idols* and responded inappropriately to them. Moreover, Paul's formula seems to have been inspired by another passage in the Bible:

> The heavens declare the glory of God, and the firmament proclaims his handiwork. Day pours out the word to day, and night to night imparts knowledge. Not a word nor a discourse whose voice is not heard. Through all the earth their voice resounds and to the ends of the world, their message. (Ps. 19:2-5)

If man cannot learn anything about the true God from the created world, the statements of the Psalm would be pointless.

Much of the point which Kierkegaard, Barth, and others wished to make could be preserved without excluding the possibility of establishing the existence of God by a sound argument. One can hold a Christian position according to which some knowledge about God is possible to human persons through reason, although such knowledge is inadequate for salvation. Without faith, it may be argued, sinful man inevitably falls into many errors about God, similar to the mistakes made by the child whose learning was described in chapter two.

A Christian also can maintain that without divine grace an individual presented with a sound argument concluding to the existence of God will evade the force of the argument. As Terence Penelhum points out in a discussion of self-deception, the existence of God might be *proved* from a purely cognitive point of view, yet "only people not hindered by their own wilfulness from knowing that God exists" might assent to the conclusion. [25] A Christian also can hold that even if a person had all the knowledge reason can give about God and even if he made no mistakes and indulged in no self-deception, still divine revelation and faith would be necessary for salvation, since God's plan for mankind transcends human understanding.[26]

A further point, much stressed in contemporary Christian thought, is that commitment to Christ demands much more than merely rational reflection. Thus rational reflection can be admitted as a preliminary to commitment without removing the need for faith. Kierkegaard was in reaction to Hegel. One might suppose that if Kierkegaard with his Socratic temperament were alive today, confronted with widespread misology and with sceptical attacks on the possible *meaningfulness* of religious language, he would admit a legitimate although limited role for reasoning toward God.

All of these points suggest that the exaltation of God's grace intended by Barth might be achieved without his rejection of reasoning toward God. Indeed, Barth's objectives might have been better served had he allowed a modest place for reason. Rudolf Bultmann agreed with Barth in rejecting natural theology, but Bultmann proceeded to demythologize Christian doctrine by using existentialist categories to interpret the Gospel in a way acceptable to contemporary man.[27] Langdon Gilkey recounts how Bultmann's development of Barth's neoorthodoxy had results Barth surely would not have wanted.[28] Many of Bultmann's recent followers reduce the Bible to nothing more than some insights into the complexities and incomprehensibilities of human existence; theology thus becomes a subdivision of anthropology, and the religious ministry becomes a form of psychological guidance and therapy.

Despite the sincerity of the religious concern of Kierkegaard, Barth, and their followers, it seems to me they make a mistake in rejecting all possibility of reasoning from the world toward God. The problem with their position which I have pointed out has been stated more graphically:

> Without natural theology the divine message not only remains a foreign body; it remains unintelligible and ceases to be a message. A message which cannot be received, a communication which can never be understood, makes no sense. Likewise a message of and about God makes no sense, if the word 'God' can have no meaning for man *as man*. It turns into an enigmatic sign on the wall, which nobody can interpret.[29]

Is the reality of God evident to reflection?

About nine centuries ago St. Anselm developed an argument—some say two arguments—which seems to show that the reality of God is implied by the very meaning of the word "God." If Anselm's approach is correct, the existence of God is evident, not as a matter of experience, but as a matter of insight based upon intellectual reflection. It would follow that reasoning from the world toward God, if possible, is unnecessarily indirect.

Anselm's argument has fascinated philosophers down through the ages, and has been attacked and defended by some of the greatest of them. Among its critics are St. Thomas Aquinas and Immanuel Kant. The latter dubbed this form of argumentation "ontological." A vast body of literature has developed around old and new forms of ontological argument in recent years. I do not consider it necessary to discuss this argument fully here; there are good, up-to-date introductions for interested readers.[30]

However, because it will be necessary to refer to this argument at several points later on and because my critique of it will be useful as a point of departure for part two, I offer the following, nontechnical version of the type of argument invented by Anselm. My version does not pretend to reconstruct Anselm's original argument(s).

We think of God, the argument begins, as the Supreme Being. "Supreme Being" means not merely the highest being which happens to exist, but the highest possible being—the Supreme Being is the one to which there cannot possibly be anything superior. (If we imagine a Godless universe, we might suppose that in it among all the finite beings there would happen to be one—perhaps some great man—to whom nothing in the universe happened to be superior. But we still could *think of* a superior being; the great man would only *happen to be* superior to all others, and so he would not be the Supreme Being.)

Now, the argument goes on, if we think of God as the Supreme Being, we also must think of him as really existing. For if we thought of an infinite being, absolutely perfect in every possible way, yet not existing, we could think of a still higher one—namely, one just like it but *also* really existing. An infinite, absolutely perfect, but non-existent being—if, indeed, that makes sense at all—is just not what we think of when we think of God, the *Supreme* Being.

Thus, the argument concludes, since we are not thinking of God at all unless we think of him as the Supreme Being, if we do think of God, then we must think of him as actually existing. If some people—atheists and agnostics—say that they do not think God really exists or are not sure whether he exists, then one of two things must be the case. Either they do not mean

"Supreme Being" when they say "God"; they are denying or doubting the existence of something other than what Jews and Christians believe in when they believe in God. Or atheists and agnostics are confused, for they suppose one can think of a Supreme Being as a merely possible being, or as an idea of something in one's mind which might or might not really exist.

What is wrong with this argument? A common criticism, which I think is valid so far as it goes, is based upon a distinction between two meanings of "thinking of something as." In one sense, to think of something as such-and-such (to think of x as F) is to think that *if* x really exists, *then* x must be F. For example, to think of a phoenix as immortal is to think that if a phoenix really exists (were to exist), it is (would be) immortal. In another sense, to think of x as F is to think of something already known to exist, and to believe that this x is F. For example, to think of light as that which moves fastest is to think of the light which we know exists in the physical universe, and to believe that nothing in the universe moves faster than this light does.

Using this distinction, one can see that "thinking of God as the Supreme Being" has two meanings. In one sense, one thinks of God as the Supreme Being when he considers what it would be like for God to exist. Such a being, if there is one, would be Supreme, necessarily so, and thus really existent. But the question remains, Is there a God? In another sense, one thinks of God as a Supreme Being when he takes it for granted that God actually exists, and believes that God, being who he is, *naturally* is the Supreme Being and *of course* cannot help but exist.

In the first sense, it is true, one cannot say "Supreme Being" without including *really existing* in the very meaning of what one is saying. Yet the problem of the referent remains. To what if anything do the honorific titles belong? A sceptic might admit that he understands perfectly well what Anselm *means*, yet still deny that Anselm's words refer to anything. Anselm and others who regard this sort of argument as sound obviously assume that God really exists. For one who assumes that God really exists, it is not easy to make or to keep clearly in mind the difference between including *really existing* in the meaning of "Supreme Being" and asserting *that there is* a Supreme Being.

W. Donald Hudson sums up this point neatly:

> The very meaning of the question 'Is God an ontological reality?', or 'Does God exist objectively?', implies that it cannot be answered by any analysis of the meaning of the word 'God'. For *within the meaning of that question* a distinction is drawn between what is being *said* and what, if anything, it is being said *about*.[31]

Being the *Supreme Being, necessarily existing,* and so forth might be included in what is being said when one asks whether God exists. But even after one has spelled out everything one means in asking the question, one is no nearer to answering it.

This distinction between knowing what it would be like for a question to be answered in the affirmative and knowing that the question must be answered in the affirmative will play an important role in the argument set out in part two.

II: There Is
an Uncaused Entity

4: Provisional Statement of the Argument

Introduction

The argument that there is an uncaused entity which I propose at the end of this chapter is provisional in the sense that it must be completed by points considered in chapters five to seventeen. In the first two sections of chapter five I try to establish two necessary and especially difficult steps in the argument. In part three—chapters six to thirteen—I offer an exposition and criticism of leading modern and contemporary philosophic alternatives to the position, which I defend, that there is a sound argument for the existence of an uncaused entity. Part four—chapters fourteen to seventeen—includes a reflection upon and a clarification of the meanings of the words used in saying that there is an uncaused entity which causes other states of affairs to obtain.

The word "God" has many meanings. The argument I propose here concludes that there is an *uncaused entity*. In the argument itself I do not use the word "God" at all. In the final section of chapter five I distinguish various meanings of the words "God," "god," and "gods." Whether one who accepts the soundness of the argument that there is an uncaused entity will regard it as establishing that God exists will depend upon what he means by "God."

I do not claim that the argument I propose here was developed by autonomous reason. I think that in my own childhood experience, reconstructed in chapter two, some nonformal reasoning was prior to faith. But I doubt that I would have arrived at the present formulation, even though I think it articulates my earliest reasoning, except in the light of faith. More-

36

over, readers familiar with Thomas Aquinas's treatise *On Being and Essence* might notice similarities between the present argument and one which he proposes.[1]

Religious authority and the opinions of previous thinkers do not settle anything in philosophy, since philosophy seeks to test beliefs, not to proceed from them. But the argument I propose does not appeal to authority. The subjective genesis of an argument and its logical force should not be confused. As Peter Achinstein notes, many philosophers of science distinguish between the contexts of discovery and of explanation:

> Questions pertaining to the discovery of a hypothesis are empirical matters best left to the psychologist. Questions pertaining to the justification of a hypothesis once it is discovered are matters for philosophical scrutiny; it is in this context that the scientist reasons and that his reasoning can be appraised.[2]

While Achinstein insists that similar reasoning can appear in both contexts, he does not reject this useful distinction. It surely applies to philosophical inquiry and argument as well as to science. If one keeps this distinction in mind, one will avoid the fallacy, often committed in philosophical debate, of impugning arguments and positions because of their suspect origins.[3]

Cosmological argumentation originates in wonder at the reality of the world around us. This wonder is expressed by questions, and one important difference among cosmological arguments is the diverse questions from which they begin. To forestall confusion, it will help to consider some questions which are similar to, but distinct from, the question from which the argument I propose begins.

J. J. C. Smart examines some versions of cosmological argumentation and comes to the conclusion that all of them involve irremediable logical faults. Yet, while he sees no difficulty in supposing that particular entities might exist without an ultimate explanation of their existence, toward the general question "Why should anything exist at all?" Smart expresses a different attitude:

> Logic seems to tell us that the only answer which is not absurd is to say, 'Why shouldn't it?' Nevertheless, though I know how any answer on the lines of the cosmological argument can be pulled to pieces by a correct logic, I still feel I want to go on asking the question. Indeed, though logic has taught me to look at such a question with the gravest suspicion, my mind often seems to reel under the immense significance it seems to have for me. That anything should exist at all does seem to me a matter for the deepest awe. But whether other people feel this sort of awe, and whether they or I ought to is another question. I think we ought to.[4]

Smart adds that this raises a further problem, "What sort of question is this question, 'Why should anything exist at all?'" Absolutely excluding as illogical an interpretation after the manner of a cosmological argument, Smart concludes: "All I can say is, that I do not yet know."[5]

Smart's remarks may have been inspired by some similar thoughts of Wittgenstein, who rejects "I wonder at the existence of the world" as a misuse of language, but who nevertheless regards such a sentence as a futile attempt to express something both inexpressible and important.[6] Martin Heidegger also regards as important the question "Why are there existing entities, why is there anything at all, rather than nothing?" Like Smart, but for other reasons, Heidegger rejects treating this question as a point of departure for an argument that God exists.[7]

The wonder at being which is thus expressed by contemporary philosophers already found expression in Leibniz's version of the cosmological argument for the existence of God. Leibniz maintains that the present state of the world raises two questions: *how* the world came to be as it is, and *why* there is a world rather than no world. The first question, Leibniz thinks, can be answered by a description of the previous states of the world and of how the world as it is developed from those earlier states. But the second question must be answered by reference to a being beyond the world and all its successive states. If one asks why the earth exists and is told that it was spun off from the sun, one can go on to ask why the sun itself exists. Wonder at being is finally put to rest only if the question "Why is there a world rather than no world?" is answered by saying that there is a cause of the world, God, who exists of himself. Since he exists of himself, God needs no cause; thus the question "Why does God exist?" can be answered: "Because God is God." This answer prevents further questions.[8]

The questions raised by Smart and Heidegger on the one hand and by Leibniz—and perhaps Wittgenstein—on the other are not exactly the same. Smart and Heidegger ask why *anything* exists, while Leibniz asks why the *world* exists. To ask why anything exists rather than nothing presupposes that it could have been true that nothing at all exists; to ask why the world exists assumes at most that the world might not have existed. The first question is peculiar in ways in which the second is not.

For example, it has been plausibly argued that the supposition that nothing exists is logically coherent. But if nothing exists, it seems to follow both that the proposition that nothing exists is true, and that there is no such proposition. The latter would follow because, no matter what one thinks is necessary for there to be a true negative proposition, clearly something must exist if there is to be any proposition at all.[9] Again, Heidegger entertains the supposition that nothing at all might exist, but at the same time he takes for granted principles of existing entities—namely, Being (which for Heidegger is not God and is not any existing entity) and Man. Man, Heidegger holds, constitutes the ontological space in which existing entities gain and have their actuality.[10]

Thus even if the question "Why is there anything rather than nothing at all?" is not meaningless, still it seems to involve a presupposition from which one cannot think consistently except, perhaps, by positing ontological principles which are neither existing entities nor reducible to existing entities.

If one assumes only that the world, including one's own thinking, might not have existed, one can suppose that if such were the case the truth about the situation would be known to God. This supposition, of course, is compatible with an attempt like Leibniz's to explain the existence of the world by reference to God.

Thus the argument I propose here does not begin from the question "Why is there anything?" In fact, I do not even set out from the question "Why does the world exist?" If one assumes that the world is all there could be, then the latter question becomes equivalent to the former and shares its peculiarities. However, if one assumes with Leibniz that there could be something other than the world, then an argument like his from the world to God is question-begging, because "world" in Leibniz's question includes everything but God, and God according to Leibniz is necessarily existent if he is possible.

Instead of the existence of something rather than nothing or of the world rather than no world, I take as point of departure a particular state of affairs, for example, someone reading some sentence printed in a book entitled *Beyond the New Theism: A Philosophy of Religion.* I call this state of affairs "*SRS*" (that is, "someone's reading a sentence in this book"). Sometimes, as now, *SRS* is an existing state of affairs, sometimes not. The question is, Why is *SRS* an *existing* state of affairs?

Smart points out that questions of this sort about particular objects are perfectly legitimate, but he thinks they also are easily answered. He suggests, for instance, that one can ask why a certain table exists, and answer the question by saying that a certain carpenter built it.[11] It seems to me that if this sort of answer would do, then all questions of the form "Why does x exist?" could be answered by specifying the relationship of x to other things in the world, and the question "Why does the world exist?" would be nonsensical in the same way that the question "Where is the world located?" is nonsensical.

But Smart's answer will not do. The existence and work of the carpenter who made the table only partially explains why the table *began* to exist. Once the man did his job, perhaps he died of a heart attack brought on by the exertion, yet the table still exists. Smart himself holds that questions of the form "Why does x exist?" are legitimate because statements of the form "x

exists" are not logically necessary. Clearly, a contingent entity does not acquire logical necessity by some sort of metaphysical inertia once such an entity is launched in existence.

Preliminary clarifications

Several expressions and distinctions which are required for the argument must be clarified. The first of these is "proposition."[12] I do not attempt to give a complete theory of propositions, but only propose some points to forestall possible misunderstandings.

Let us imagine a conversation among four individuals who are making camp. What they do first depends upon the weather.

> A. (At 7:00 p.m.): "It's going to be raining one hour from now."
> B. (Immediately afterwards): "That is true."
> C. (A few seconds later): "It won't rain."
> D. (At 8:00 p.m.): "A was right. What he said is true. It's raining."

I call what A's sentence expresses a "proposition." The proposition it expresses is what B refers to by saying "that." Thus A expresses a proposition and B refers to the same proposition. A and B also express a common attitude and take a common stand with respect to the proposition. The attitude they express is belief in the proposition, and the stand they take is the asserting of the proposition. C expresses disbelief; C denies the same proposition which A and B assert. Since the distinctions between belief and assertion and between disbelief and denial are not important for my present purpose, from now on I generally ignore belief and disbelief.

When D says "what he said," he refers to the proposition which A and B asserted and C denied. When D says "It's raining," D also asserts this same proposition. That D asserts the *same* proposition previously asserted by A and B is perhaps not obvious, because of the difference in tenses. However, the proposition could be expressed in a pidgin-English which dispenses with tenses and uses adverbial modifiers to express times—for example, "It rain 8:00 p.m. today." Assertion could be expressed by nodding one's head while uttering the sentence expressing the proposition; denial, by shaking one's head. Even if A, B, C, and D used the single pidgin-English sentence to express the proposition, their *statements* of the proposition would differ in that A, B, and C still would be predicting whereas D would not be predicting.

Thus propositions can be true or false; they can be asserted or denied. They also can be believed, doubted, disagreed about, and so forth. A proposition stated as a prediction can be proved true by the eventuality.

A proposition, p, is distinct from someone's asserting p, since p also can be denied. To assert or to deny *p,* one must *do something* which counts as asserting or denying *p. A, B,* and *D* do somewhat different things—that is, utter different words—all of which count as asserting the same proposition. By nodding his head in agreement *B* could have made the same assertion which he made by saying "That is true."

Since the same proposition can be expressed in different ways and since the same assertion or denial can be made in different ways, it is clear that one proposition cannot be identified with the many different ways of expressing it, nor can one assertion be identified with the many different ways of making it. Moreover, since there is no special reason to identify a proposition with any one of its expressions rather than with another, a proposition must be distinguished from all of its expressions. An analogous point can be made with respect to assertions of propositions.

Thus if *A, B, C,* and *D* spoke German rather than English, they would use different sentences to express the same proposition. An accurate translation exchanges expressions of one language for expressions of another, while expressing the same propositions. Thus propositions are distinct from sentences; languages can express propositions, but propositions themselves are not linguistic entities. An analogous point holds for assertions.

The sense of a sentence is determined by the meanings of the words which make it up and by its grammar. A proposition must be distinguished from the sense of any sentence which expresses it. When *A* says at 7:00 p.m., "It's going to be raining one hour from now," and *D* says at 8:00 p.m., "It's raining," and someone using pidgin-English says at any time the same day, "It rain 8:00 p.m. today," all three sentences express the same proposition. However, the three sentences have different senses. If *A* repeats at 8:00 p.m. the sentence he uttered at 7:00 p.m., the sense of the sentence is no different, but the proposition it expresses is different.

The reason why sentences having different senses can express the same proposition and different utterances of the same sentence can express different propositions is that the context in which a sentence is uttered helps to determine what proposition the sentence expresses.

To nod one's head in agreement always has the same sense, but it is not always the same assertion, either in the sense of being the same act of asserting or in the sense of expressing the same asserted proposition. In different contexts the same gesture refers to different propositions. Similarly, "I see rain falling" has the same sense regardless of who says it or when it is said, but the utterance of the sentence by different speakers and/or at different times expresses different propositions. Said by different persons "I see rain falling" refers to different persons and their different acts of seeing; said at different times, the same sentence refers to different rain.

However, the reference of a sentence is not solely determined by the context in which it is uttered. When *A* says at 7:00 p.m., "It's going to be raining one hour from now," and *D* says at 8:00 p.m., "It's raining," the difference of the sense of the two sentences precisely compensates for the difference in contexts, so that both sentences refer to the same rain falling. The two different sentences can express the same proposition because if one discounts those differences in sense required to establish sameness of reference in the different contexts, then the residual sense would be the same—for example, the sense of the pidgin-English expression of the proposition.

The sense of sentences also depends upon the context. "He has water on the brain" has a different sense when it is uttered by a physician as a medical diagnosis than it does when it is uttered by a student as an evaluation of a professor.

Propositions are composed of parts having distinct functions. I call the parts of a proposition which determine its sense and reference "concepts." Some concepts primarily determine the reference of a proposition; others primarily determine its sense. For example, if I assert that John is sitting down, *John* primarily determines the reference of the proposition while *sitting down* primarily determines its sense.[13] I call a concept which primarily determines reference a "name" and a concept which primarily determines sense a "predicable." Since propositions are not linguistic entities, it is not necessary that concepts correspond one-to-one with words or groups of words. "Name" and "predicable" are not synonymous with "noun" and "verb."

Names determine reference by standing for some entities rather than others, and thus names limit what a proposition is *about*. For example, *John* stands for one individual human person rather than for any other entity in the universe, and thus limits the proposition that John is sitting down to being about John and no one else. Not all names are proper names. In the proposition that water is a compound of hydrogen and oxygen, *water* stands for a certain substance.

Predicables determine sense by signifying something definite—that is, by including one understandable aspect rather than any other—and thus predicables demarcate that which one knows of that for which the name or names in the proposition stand. (Of course, one *knows* only if the proposition is true and one accepts it as true.) For example, *sitting down* signifies a certain arrangement of the parts of a human or animal body; the predicable includes this understandable aspect, which is marked off from *standing, kneeling,* and so on. If the proposition that John is sitting down is true and if one accepts it as true, then one knows John's bodily arrangement.[14]

Playing their roles within the unified proposition, the name and the predicable contribute to the whole their distinct ways of determining. The result is that the proposition as a whole has a delimited content. I call this delimited content of a proposition a "state of affairs." I call a proposition's delimiting of its content "picking out a state of affairs." Thus "picks out" does not mean the same thing as "determines" in the expressions "a name determines" or "a predicable determines." It follows that states of affairs are not entities such as John nor understandable aspects such as being seated.

The proposition that John is sitting down picks out the state of affairs of John's being seated. If one entertains and accepts this proposition, however, one can be mistaken. John's being seated might not be an existing state of affairs—for example, if John happens to be standing at a level sixteen inches lower than one supposes he is, so that he looks as if he is sitting down although he is actually standing. In this case I say that the state of affairs picked out by the proposition that John is sitting down "does not obtain." However, if John's being seated obtains, then one who entertains and accepts the proposition that John is sitting down is not mistaken.

"Obtains" used in this intransitive sense in sentences about states of affairs means the same as what I have meant by "existing" in the expression "existing state of affairs," except that "obtains" is tenseless, inasmuch as temporal determinations are consigned to the content of propositions. Thus I now dispense with this use of "existing." In other uses, "exists" cannot be replaced by "obtains." For example, "Do unicorns really exist?" cannot be translated into "Do unicorns really obtain?" A possible translation might be: "Is there a nonextinct species of horned animal characterized by having one and only one horn?" Moreover, "John's being seated exists" will not do as a substitute for "John's being seated obtains," not merely because the former is poor English, but because it has the misleading implication that the state of affairs which is John's being seated is an entity something like John or his chair.

"Obtains" could replace "happens" or "occurs" in some expressions. For example, two automobiles colliding with each other is a state of affairs; this state of affairs is called a "two-car collision" or, more generally, an "accident." Accidents are said to "happen" or "occur."

"It is raining" and "It is not raining" express the same proposition—that is, pick out the same state of affairs. The two sentences differ in that they are used in taking different stands in respect to the proposition.

One who asserts that it is raining asserts a true proposition if the state of affairs picked out by the proposition obtains; he asserts a false proposition if the state of affairs picked out by the proposition does not obtain. One who denies the proposition that it is raining wrongly denies a true proposition if the state of affairs picked out by the proposition obtains; his denial is wrong because that in respect to which he takes this stand is a true proposition. One who denies the proposition that it is raining rightly denies a false proposition if the state of affairs picked out by the proposition does not obtain; his denial is right because that in respect to which he takes this stand is a false proposition.

Putting things in this way, it is unnecessary to suppose that there are negative states of affairs corresponding to rightly denied propositions and positive states of affairs corresponding to rightly asserted propositions. Problems are raised, however, by the fact that the meaning of some words must be explicated in terms of rightly denied propositions. "There is cheese in the icebox" and "There is no cheese in the icebox" express the same proposition, just as "It is raining" and "It is not raining" express the same proposition. Cheese being in the icebox is a state of affairs which obtains or not. But "There are holes in the cheese in the icebox" does not mean that there is not only cheese but also holes in the icebox. "Save the hole in the doughnut" is misleading because it suggests that when one finishes eating the doughnut there will be a hole to be saved.

These difficulties can be cleared up by noticing that "hole" expresses neither a name nor a predicable. "Hole" expresses the denial of a certain false proposition—for example, that there is solid cheese within the outer surface of a piece of cheese. One can describe the shape of a doughnut without introducing and denying any propositions, but in that case one would not talk about a hole; one is not likely to say that there is a hole in a tire unless there is an abnormal hole in it.

The meaning of some words can be explained as expressing predicables in some contexts but requires analysis in terms of denied propositions in other contexts. For example, "fresh" said of cheese might express a cluster of concepts which includes *recently purchased, moist,* and so on. But "fresh" sometimes, perhaps usually, expresses the denial of propositions such as that the cheese is abnormally dry, that it is moldy, and so on.

It would be interesting, but I do not think it is necessary, to consider the meaning of "whole cheese" and "piece of cheese." In what follows I use as examples sentences made up of words which clearly do not require analysis in the way that "hole" clearly does and that "fresh" sometimes does.

From what I have said, it should be clear that one need not posit negations within states of affairs. The negations which one might suppose to be within a state of affairs can be reduced to propositional attitudes such as disbelief and to stands such as denial. Disbelief itself is a positive attitude contrary to belief, and one who denies takes a positive stand against one who asserts. To shake one's head is not simply not to nod it; to shake one's head is to make a gesture which expresses the positive stand of denial.

But what about the nonobtaining of a state of affairs which does not obtain? Nonobtaining seems to be something negative in addition to disbelief and denial. As a matter of fact there is an additional factor, namely, mistaken belief. Above, I introduced the expression "does not obtain" by use of the example of one entertaining and mistakenly believing the proposition that John is sitting down. It is tempting but confused to think of *obtaining* and *nonobtaining* as if they were predicables signifying contrary, understandable aspects, as *black* and *white, here* and *elsewhere,* and many other pairs of opposites do. But contrary predicables are conceptual constituents of propositions. "Obtains" does not express any conceptual *constituent* of a proposition. The meaning of the proposition—both sense and reference—is precisely the same whether or not the state of affairs picked out by the proposition obtains.

But, it might be urged, finding that one has a mistaken belief means observing or otherwise discovering that the state of affairs picked out by the proposition in which one believed does *not obtain.* Thus *nonobtaining* must be something one can observe or discover. This objection is important; I do not think it is insurmountable.

If one believes that John is sitting down and then observes John standing upright, the situation might be put as follows. One adds to the proposition that John is sitting down the predicable *standing upright,* and disbelieves the newly formed proposition. One then forms the propositions that John is standing upright and that John is sitting down, believes the former and disbelieves the latter. The statement of the latter proposition in such a case is as rejecting or setting aside, and this is what is meant by "finding that one was mistaken." To observe that it is not raining when one expected rain is not to observe the nonobtaining of the state of affairs of rain falling. What does one observe? One's view is steady and sharp in a way which is different from the blurred and shifting view one has when it is raining. In other words, one sees things as they look when it is not raining, and how they look then is different in positive ways from how they look when it is raining.

I think a similar analysis could be carried out of other cases in which one might be tempted to say that the nonobtaining of a state of affairs is itself a predicable. Still, one feels that it is plausible to suppose that one sees a hole in a doughnut, not merely a doughnut and something behind it which one would not see if one were looking at a fried cake. I think the feeling that one sees holes can be explained as an effect of nonformal inference and belief upon experience; as I suggested in chapter three, such factors enter into experience and shape the way in which we perceive the world.

The criticism of the ontological argument which was formulated at the end of chapter three (pages 33-34) now can be reformulated as follows. If the sentence "The Supreme Being necessarily exists" expresses a proposition, the meaning of the proposition both as to its sense and as to its reference could be complete, yet the state of affairs picked out by the proposition not obtain. In other words, one could know what it would be like for the state of affairs picked out by the proposition to obtain without knowing whether it obtains, unless the reference of the proposition can be established only *if one knows* that the state of affairs picked out by the proposition does obtain. In the latter case, however, one is not proceeding, as Anselm tried to proceed, from one's understanding of the meaning of "God" to the conclusion that he exists in reality. One rather is proceeding from one's knowledge that a certain state of affairs obtains to an understanding of the meaning of "God." The argument I propose proceeds in this direction, opposite to Anselm's.

Many philosophers have criticized the ontological argument by saying that "existence" is not a "predicate," does not signify a "real property," and so on. This criticism is imprecise, because of the ambiguity of "exists," which sometimes expresses one or more predicables. However, the sense of the criticism can be more precisely expressed by saying that *obtains* is not a predicable.

Because *obtains* is not a predicable, it is possible to understand the meaning of many propositions—if not of all—without knowing whether they are true. In general, one can know what it would be like for a certain state of affairs to obtain without knowing whether it obtains. This is evident inasmuch as one who does not know whether a certain state of affairs which might or might not obtain does obtain, can wonder and ask a question of the form, "Is such and such the case?"

It might be argued that if "John" is a proper name, then one cannot understand the meaning of the proposition, whatever it is, expressed by "John exists" without also knowing that the state of affairs picked out by this proposition obtains. Whether this position is defensible depends, it seems to me, on what one means by "proper name" and "exists." But assuming these expressions can have meanings such that the position is defensible, one might be tempted to infer that the meaning of a proposition and the obtaining of a state of affairs picked out by it are distinct only in the case of general propositions. This inference might in turn lead one to suppose that *obtains,* after all, is a predicable concept.

But there are several reasons for rejecting this conclusion. One, already considered, is that obtaining and nonobtaining are not contraries, but they would be contraries if *obtains* were a predicable.

Again, one can understand not only a general proposition but also a proposition picking out a unique state of affairs without knowing whether the state of affairs picked out by the proposition obtains. For example, the reader can entertain the proposition that there is a crisp, new, Canadian $100.00 banknote, series 1954, serial number A/J 7289748, bound between pages 100 and 101 of this copy of this book. Still, one does not know whether this state of affairs obtains until one looks.

If it is true that "John exists" expresses a proposition and that one cannot understand the meaning of this proposition without knowing that the state of affairs picked out by it obtains, this can be explained without supposing that *obtains* is a predicable. One need only suppose that the reference of the proposition can only be determined if one knows that John exists.

The sentences of logic, arithmetic, and so on, including certain sentences of ordinary language, such as "Bachelors are unmarried men," often are thought to express propositions of a peculiar sort, namely, propositions which are necessarily true and are such that to understand them is to know their truth. One might suppose that such sentences, at least, express propositions in which *obtains* is a predicable.

There are various ways of dealing with such sentences, at least three of which can be accepted within the framework I am articulating.

First, one can say that such sentences do not express propositions. This solution is drastic, but it would suit my purposes if it were correct.

Second, one can say that such sentences express propositions which are about linguistic expressions. This position also suits my purposes. I would prefer to say that these propositions pick out states of affairs involving concepts and other constituents of propositions but no extrapropositional entities. Thus "Bachelors are unmarried men" can be taken to express a proposition which picks out a state of affairs in which either of two distinct predicables can fulfill a certain set of roles in propositions without affecting those propositions, or, at least, without affecting them in certain specified ways. On this theory, one can easily explain why one often (surely not always; there are proofs in mathematics) knows the truth of such a proposition in understanding its meaning, namely, because the meaning of the proposition or the meanings which one must understand to understand it, being what they are and being related as they must be, precisely is the state of affairs which the proposition picks out. One also can explain the necessity of such truths or falsities on this theory by saying that concepts are nothing but relational entities, and therefore the predicables which signify understandable aspects of concepts, by defining what the concepts are, establish them in a certain state of affairs or in a certain set of states of affairs.

This second approach seems to me more plausible. The sentences in question can be considered to be expressions of propositions without assuming that they pick out extrapropositional states of affairs.

A third solution is to suppose that the sentences of logic and so on express ordinary propositions, but that the states of affairs they pick out are different from those picked out by other propositions. On this approach one knows the truth of the proposition in understanding its meaning, because the reference of the proposition is established only by knowing that the state of affairs picked out by the proposition obtains. The state of affairs picked out by the proposition obtains necessarily, on this theory, because it is an aspect of the structure of the world.

This last view seems to me mistaken *as an account of the truths and falsities of logic and mathematics.* It might be a sound account of certain other propositions—for example, that one cannot return to an earlier time.

However the sentences of logic and other sentences which are not informative about extrapropositional states of affairs are to be explained, I call them "formal truths and falsities." From now on unless the context demands otherwise, "proposition" should not be taken as referring to formal truths and falsities.

As already explained, one can know what it would be like for certain states of affairs to obtain without knowing whether they obtain. This is true of any state of affairs which might or might not obtain, provided that one can know the meaning of the proposition which picks it out without having prior knowledge that it obtains. I call such states of affairs "contingent" and the propositions which pick them out "contingent propositions."

Therefore, for a contingent state of affairs to be the state of affairs it is, and for the same contingent state of affairs to obtain, are not identical. "Obtains" does not express a predicable. Nevertheless, to say that a certain state of affairs obtains is to say something about it—something which makes a difference not by making the state of affairs different, but by making it be extrapropositional. Consider the proposition that there is a crisp, new Canadian $100.00 banknote bound between pages 100 and 101 of this copy of this book. If the state of affairs which the proposition picks out obtains, the banknote does not become a new denomination—for example, $100.01. Rather, the owner of the book gains exactly $100.00.

The nonidentity between a state of affairs which obtains being the state of affairs it is and the same state of affairs obtaining can be expressed by saying, "There is a real distinction between a state of affairs which does obtain and its obtaining." But to say this is neither to say that the obtaining of a state of affairs is itself a larger state of affairs—which would imply that *obtains* is a predicable—nor to say that a state of affairs and its obtaining are two realities for which names might stand in a proposition.

One further question must be considered. What is the principle of individuation for states of affairs?

Understanding "individuation" in one sense, this question cannot be answered, for it is based on a false assumption. Often if one asks about an individuating principle, the question concerns entities of a sort for which names can stand in propositions. Since states of affairs *as such* are not entities for which names can stand, but rather are what are picked out by names and

predicables working together in propositions, there is no individuating principle for states of affairs in the sense in which there might be individuating
principles for sorts of entities for which names can stand.

Taking "individuation" in another sense, some states of affairs are not
individuated and others are, because some propositions pick out states of
affairs which can have many instances while other propositions pick out
states of affairs which can have only one instance. The proposition that men
are mortal is of the former type, inasmuch as the state of affairs which it
picks out has as many instances as there are mortal men. The proposition
about the $100.00 banknote is an example of the latter type; there can be
only one instance of this state of affairs. Precisely why and how propositions
of these two types differ seems to me to be a very difficult question which
cannot be answered—if it can be answered at all—without going deep not only
into logical theory but also into ontology. Fortunately, so far as I can see, I
do not need to explain this distinction. Also, even if no one can explain it,
everyone admits it.

Taking "individuation" in a third sense, one can say that states of affairs
are individuated by the propositions which pick them out. Since states of
affairs are picked out by propositions, there is a one-to-one relationship
between states of affairs and nonmolecular propositions.

I call a proposition "molecular" if it is formed by linking other propositions by logical connectives—such as some uses of "and," "or," or "if . . .
then"—*in a manner which does not affect the inner structure* of the propositions linked. Thus the truth of a molecular proposition is a function of the
truth of the propositions of which it is compounded. A nonmolecular
proposition is one which cannot be divided into propositional components,
because all of the names and predicables in it are interrelated in such a way
that removing any of them would affect the functioning of the others.

The proposition that Jack and Jill went up the hill to fetch a pail of water
seems to me to be nonmolecular. If one attempts to divide this into the
propositions that Jack went up the hill and that Jill went up the hill, their
going together is omitted. If one attempts to divide it into the propositions
that Jack and Jill went up the hill together and that they went to fetch water,
the means-end relationship between hill climbing and fetching water is
omitted. And so on.

However, if one entertains the proposition about Jack and Jill going to
fetch water and also entertains the proposition that Jack and Jill went down
the hill to fish in the brook, the two propositions are related truth-function-
ally. They cannot both be true. Expressing the two propositions—as the
children's father might do, noticing that both they and the pail were missing,
as he set out to find them—"Either the children went up the hill to fetch

water from the spring or they went down the hill to fish in the brook"—
makes the incompatibility of the two propositions clear. But this way of
considering the two propositions does not alter their inner structure.

If, as I think, the proposition about Jack and Jill is nonmolecular, still this
rather complex proposition does entail several less complex ones: that Jack
went up the hill, that Jill went up the hill, that Jack and Jill went somewhere
together, that each went to fetch water, that they shared a common purpose,
and so on. Each of these propositions is nonmolecular and each picks out a
different state of affairs. Thus one state of affairs includes many states of
affairs. However, the many states of affairs do not constitute as a compound
the one state of affairs in which they are included. If they did, the original
proposition would be molecular. It is also worth noticing that some—if not
all—of the included states of affairs have many instances. They are included
only as to one or some instances.

This clarification of the one-to-one relationship which holds between
nonmolecular propositions and states of affairs should suffice for my present
purpose as an answer to the problem of the individuation of states of affairs.
It should be noted that one need not—and I think definitely ought not—to
suppose that the world is made up of states of affairs, as if they were
building-blocks of reality. Thus one need not assume that all the distinctions
and relations among states of affairs as such mirror ontological distinctions
and relations.

If one knew the truth about the ontological structure of the universe, that
knowledge itself would be *contained* in propositions; in other words, the
structure of the universe is itself a certain state of affairs. Whatever the truth
about the ontological structure of the universe, the preceding explanation
only requires that the world be such that if one accepts a true proposition,
the content of that proposition *so far as it goes* is extrapropositionally as one
believes it to be. I say "so far as it goes" because the limitations of the
content need not be regarded as a reflection of limits in the extrapropositional. The limits of our knowledge only indicate that there is *something*
about the extrapropositional which makes possible knowledge of it which,
while true, nevertheless is limited as ours is.

If what I have proposed as a reply to the question about individuation of
states of affairs avoids unnecessary metaphysical commitments, still it might
seem that the previous clarifications presuppose many questionable logical,
epistemological, and ontological commitments.

It might be true that in trying to lay the foundation for the argument I
have made more commitments than necessary; the foundation required for
the argument actually does not amount to much. However, I do need
"proposition," "picks out," "state of affairs," and "obtains," and I wished to
give these expressions fairly clear senses. Also necessary are the distinction

between the meaning of a proposition and its truth and the corresponding distinction between a state of affairs which does obtain and its obtaining. I hope that if the reader finds certain aspects of the preceding clarifications objectionable but unnecessary for the argument, he will dispense with what is unnecessary, and, if possible, substitute for what is objectionable something adequate for the argument and acceptable to himself.

However, it is worth noting several respects in which I might seem to be making commitments but am not making them.

In the first place, I am not committed to the subject-predicate form as the sole or even primary form of proposition. I think that what I say about propositions and their structure is in some ways more easily reconciled with modern logic than it is with aristotelian logic, which kept too close to ordinary language. I have not dealt at all with the many logical problems in respect to quantification, modal operators, and so on, but I do not think anything I have said about propositions creates any special obstacles to dealing with such problems.

In the second place, nothing I have said commits me to an epistemology according to which one intuits essences, forms, or anything of the sort. I make no greater claim in saying that predicables signify understandable aspects than anyone makes who supposes that various people and/or the same person on various occasions can sit down, and that one can tell in clear-cut cases whether someone is sitting down or not. Again, some of my examples might suggest that I am committed to an epistemology which would reduce all knowledge to basic propositions, but nothing I have said demands that such a reduction be undertaken or even that it be possible.

In the third place, I am committed to very little about the ontological status of propositions other than that they are not linguistic entities. This commitment will be objectionable to physicalists who hope to account for entities like propositions in terms of linguistic behavior. However, I think I have a good case for denying that propositions are linguistic entities, and additional reasons will be given in chapters fourteen and twenty-three for thinking physicalism mistaken. I do not maintain that propositions are some sort of ghostly entities. For a proposition to be, is for it to be entertained, believed, asserted, debated, and so on. If some states of affairs obtain without being known to anyone, one can say that there are unknown truths to be discovered, but in this context "truths" does not refer to actual propositions. It refers to possible propositions: that is, to the knowability of extrapropositional reality and to the ability of propositional knowers to learn what they do not already know.

In the fourth place, the ontological status of states of affairs also can be dealt with simply and without getting into metaphysical quicksand. States of affairs, considered simply as such, do not exist at all, because to consider a state of affairs simply as such is just to exclude from consideration any question of existence. States of affairs insofar as they are contents of propositions exist by virtue of being picked out by propositions. A state of affairs insofar as it obtains has the extrapropositional status appropriate to the sort of state of affairs it is. Physical states of affairs obtain in the processes of the physical world; fictional states of affairs obtain in the thinking up of a story, in the writing or telling or enacting of it, in the reading or hearing or seeing of it, and so on.

Finally, in the fifth place, it is not required by anything I have said that one assume that the world is made up of substances and accidents. All that is required is that the world be such that names in propositions can stand for something or other and that words in sentences expressing propositions can be used according to some criteria so that they can express predicables. If these conditions are not met, it is hard for me to see how one could say anything about anything, whatever the makeup of reality.

Thus the commitments presupposed by the preceding clarifications are more modest than might at first appear.

The argument

A nontechnical summary of the argument, although not completely true to it, might be helpful for orientation.

As everyone knows, things don't just happen. There has to be something which makes them happen. Everything we're familiar with which makes things happen also happens, and would not have happened if something hadn't made *it* happen. There are only three possibilities.

The first comes in two versions. One version is that the whole universe is a big, perpetual happening machine, in which the happening of some things makes other things happen, and the happening of the latter things makes the former things happen, and all things making each other happen makes the whole universe happen. Another version of this first possibility is that the whole universe is a train which happens to be without a locomotive. We see the caboose coming up hill toward us, as if the train were backing up, and there are cars as far as we can see. We suppose that the train happens to go on and on forever, because that is the only way the caboose could keep coming toward us without a locomotive.

A second possibility is that the universe is just one big happening, which could as well not have happened, but just happens to happen, for no particular reason at all.

In chapter five I'll try to show that the first "possibility" is impossible and the second possibility is possible but ridiculous.

This leaves only the third possibility, and since this is the only reasonable possibility, this is the way it has to be. Possibly there is something—call it "God" for short—which has what it takes to make everything which happens happen. God doesn't just happen to make things happen, but he does make things happen, and nothing makes him make anything happen. God himself doesn't happen to be, he has to be; other things don't have to be, they happen to be. God makes other things happen to be, and nothing makes him have to be, except that he's the sort of being who can't help being, even if he happened to want to, which he can't.

* * *

Tomorrow someone will read some sentence printed in a book (B) entitled *Beyond the New Theism: A Philosophy of Religion.* The preceding sentence (S) uttered at the time the reader reads it expresses a proposition (P), namely, that the day after the reader reads S someone will read some sentence printed in B. P picks out a state of affairs (SRS)—someone reading on the day after the reader reads S some sentence printed in B.

SRS might obtain and then again it might not. One can know what it would be like for SRS to obtain without knowing whether it obtains. P is stated as a prediction, and it will be proved true or false by the eventuality.

If P is to be proved true, certain conditions prerequisite to SRS and not included in SRS will have to be fulfilled. By "conditions" here I mean extrapropositional conditions, not logical conditions.[15] For example, there will have to be sufficient light for someone to read a sentence in B, he will have to be alive and conscious, and he will have to know how to read English.

The need for sufficient light to read could be satisfied in various ways—for example, by daylight, by electrical light, or by candlelight. Thus SRS does not include any of these in particular, since SRS might obtain without all but one of them and any one would do. The requirement that someone be alive and conscious cannot be fulfilled unless many complicated neurophysiological processes go on. These in turn depend upon the environment. It is clear that SRS does not include these processes and the whole complex environment, since P, which picks out SRS, could be known to be true by someone who knows little or no biology or physics. But one could not know P to be true without knowing that SRS obtains, and one could not know that SRS obtains without knowing what is involved in SRS. As for knowing how to read English, this requirement could not be fulfilled if there were not a culture which has English as its language. Someone need only spend a few seconds in reading for SRS to obtain; the culture which makes reading possible is a complex system with a history. Thus SRS does not include this condition, since the duration of SRS and of the presupposed culture are not equal.

From these remarks it is clear that *SRS* cannot obtain simply by itself. *SRS* might or might not obtain because the prerequisites which must be satisfied for *SRS* to obtain might or might not be satisfied. Each of the conditions of *SRS* has its own prerequisite conditions, which might not be satisfied. This is true even though for all practical purposes we can take it for granted that some of these conditions will be satisfied. For example, we assume that tomorrow there will be someone who can read English, but this optimistic assumption might be falsified—for example, if everyone who speaks English is wiped out in a sudden nuclear war.

Some of the requirements which must be satisfied for *SRS* to obtain are included in it—no one can read a sentence unless he sees words. Other prerequisites, as the examples already given show, are not included in *SRS*.

Thus there are extrapropositional prerequisites which (1) must be satisfied for *SRS* to obtain, (2) are states of affairs which might or might not obtain, and (3) themselves obtain only if further prerequisites not included in themselves are satisfied. I call the entire set of such prerequisite conditions "*C*." It does not matter to the argument whether *C* is part of the universe or the entire universe. It does not matter if some of the entities involved in the constituents of *C* existed only in the past or will exist only in the future. *C* includes whatever *SRS* requires to obtain unless *SRS* requires something which does not meet the second or the third of the three criteria for membership in *C*.

C is not merely the collection of the distinct states of affairs included in it. In other words, *C* is not an arbitrarily constructed class. The preceding discussion described conditions of *SRS* which meet the criteria for membership in *C*. *C* is the set of these conditions and any others like them in specified respects. It follows that the states of affairs included in *C* have in common an extrapropositional relationship to *SRS;* each of them, in its own way, is a prerequisite extrapropositional condition which must be satisfied *for* SRS *to obtain*. That all these conditions be so disposed as to provide what is required for *SRS* to obtain is itself a state of affairs. Thus *C* is itself a state of affairs. The proposition which picks out *C* I call "*Q*."

Given any two states of affairs, SA^1 and SA^2, such that SA^2 includes extrapropositional prerequisite conditions which are not included in SA^1 but which must be satisfied for SA^1 to obtain, I call SA^2 a "cause of" SA^1, and say that "SA^2 causes SA^1."

Thus *C* causes *SRS*. But why does *C* itself obtain?

One could say that *C* obtains because it is self-sufficient otherwise than in the way in which the content of a formal truth is self-sufficient. *C*, after all, includes *every* condition of *SRS* which might or might not obtain and which obtains only if extrapropositional requirements not included in it are satisfied. Perhaps the elements of *C* are mutually complementary in such a way that they satisfy one another's requirements. Moreover, if a finite set of states of affairs reciprocally related to one another cannot obtain by itself, perhaps the elements of C are an infinite set, and perhaps an infinite set of contingent states of affairs can obtain by itself. In other words, although C only includes states of affairs none of which obtains without the satisfaction of some requirement extrinsic to it, perhaps C itself obtains by itself, without the fulfillment of any *extrinsic* condition. I postpone consideration of this supposition to the first section of chapter five. There I will argue that it is impossible to explain in this way why C obtains. I assume, for the present, that this argument will be successful.

Assuming the argument is successful, C is a contingent state of affairs; Q is a contingent proposition. It must be remembered that "contingent" said of a state of affairs simply means that it might or might not obtain. Thus even if some entities involved in constituents of C always existed—for example, if C includes the whole universe and if the universe has some permanent constituents or unalterable structural features—still C and the states of affairs included in it are contingent. Moreover, according to the third criterion, constituents themselves of C obtain only if further prerequisites not included in themselves are satisfied.

From these considerations it follows that C does not obtain simply because its constituents are *what* they are. If a proposition picks out a state of affairs which does not obtain necessarily and extrapropositionally, yet the proposition is true simply by virtue of its own content, such a proposition is a formal truth. But since Q is a contingent proposition, it cannot be a formal truth.

Thus, assuming the argument in chapter five will be successful, there is no answer to the question "Why does C obtain?" in C itself and in its constituents. Furthermore, since all of the extrapropositional prerequisites of *SRS* which meet the three stipulated criteria already are included in C, there is nothing which might be called upon to explain why C obtains which is not included in C but meets the same criteria. In other words, what explains C must not be subject to the set of criteria for inclusion in C.

But *must* there be an answer to the question "Why does C obtain?" Perhaps the entire universe—that is, all states of affairs which obtain only if prerequisites extrinsic to themselves are satisfied—is included in C. Every state of affairs within the universe which might or might not obtain, but which actually does obtain, can be explained to the extent that other states of affairs provide what is required for it to obtain. But perhaps the universe as a whole simply obtains. It must be noticed that the supposition here is *not* that Q is about the universe as a whole, and th t the universe as a whole necessarily obtains—although no part of it obtains both extrapropositionally and necessarily—because it is *the state of affairs* it is. This supposition, previously considered and excluded, would make Q a formal truth. Nor is the supposition here that the universe might have no prerequisite conditions except its own contingent constituents; this is the supposition discussed and postponed for consideration in the first section of chapter five.

The present supposition is that the universe, while it might or might not obtain, simply obtains because it obtains. In other words, the universe is merely because it happens to be. This supposition is the one which J. J. C. Smart suggests when he says that a proper answer to the question "Why should anything [the universe] exist at all?" might be "Why shouldn't it?"

Many people are inclined to dismiss this supposition as absurd. If "absurd" means logically impossible, I think such a dismissal is a mistake. I do think this supposition utterly unreasonable, but postpone stating the reasons why I think so to the second section of chapter five.

In sum. C does not obtain merely because—although no part of it obtains both extrapropositionally and necessarily—it is the state of affairs which it is; C is not such that Q is a formal truth. The supposition that its own constituents might explain why C obtains—especially if these constituents are an infinite set—will be considered in the first section of chapter five. The supposition that the universe *is* because it *is* will be considered in the second section of chapter five.

Thus, for C to obtain—which is required for SRS to obtain—there must be a further extrapropositional prerequisite for C to obtain rather than not. This additional factor I call "Dc." Since Dc's relationship to C satisfies the previously stipulated definition of "cause," I call Dc the "cause of C." Being the cause of C, Dc also is required for SRS to obtain, since Dc, as a prerequisite for C to obtain, also is required for anything to obtain which C causes to obtain.

C and what is included in it do not explain why C obtains. Hence if Dc does explain why C obtains, Dc must be distinct from the set of factors already included in C. Since Dc is like the states of affairs included in C in being an extrapropositional requirement which must be satisfied for SRS to obtain, Dc must not be subject to one or both of the other criteria which define factors included in C.

The second of these criteria is to be a state of affairs which might or might not obtain. Dc *must meet this criterion.*[16] Dc causes the causing of SRS. SRS might or might not obtain. If Dc obtained noncontingently, SRS would obtain noncontingently.

Only the third criterion remains. Dc is not subject to the third criterion; Dc obtains without requiring anything not included in itself. In other words, Dc is the cause of C, but Dc itself does not require that some further prerequisite not included in itself be satisfied. Dc is not related to anything as

SRS is related to *C* and as *C* is related to *Dc* itself. There is no cause of *Dc*. I therefore call *Dc* "an uncaused cause."

Corresponding to *Dc*, there is a proposition (*Xc*) that an uncaused cause causes *C*, which, in turn, is the proper cause of *SRS*.

Dc might or might not obtain, but it requires nothing which is not included in itself to obtain. The arguments I present in chapter five against the possibility of *C* being explained by contingent states of affairs included in it and against the rationality of assuming that *C* is simply inexplicable also apply to *Dc*. Thus *Dc* must include in itself a peculiar state of affairs. This state of affairs must be noncontingent. Being the state of affairs which it is must be the sole requirement for it to obtain. This state of affairs, included in *Dc*, I call "*D*."

D is included in *Dc*. The whole characterization of *Dc* is that it is an uncaused cause. Insofar as *Dc causes C* and *SRS* to obtain, *Dc* is contingent since *Dc* does not cause *SRS* if *SRS* does not obtain, and *SRS* is contingent. *D* is distinct from *Dc* precisely because *D* is the prerequisite required by *Dc* to obtain. Therefore, *D* is simply an uncaused entity.

D does not obtain because any condition apart from *Dc* is fulfilled; nor does *D* obtain simply because it obtains. *D* obtains because it is *what* it is. It must be noticed that to say that *D* obtains because it is what it is, is not to say that even in this case *obtains* is a predicable. *D*'s obtaining is not what *D* is. Rather, what *D* is, is the sole condition for *D* to obtain, and since *D* does obtain, this condition obviously is fulfilled.[17] The proposition *X*, which corresponds to *D*, is that there is something which is not caused—an uncaused entity.

Assuming as we are that *SRS* obtains, if one also understands what the proposition *X* means, then one knows that it is true. But it does not follow that *X* is a formal truth. *D* obtains extrapropositionally; *SRS* cannot obtain unless *D* obtains.[18] The truth of *X* follows from its meaning together with the assumption that *SRS* obtains because *X* is derived from a relational proposition, *Xc*, and *X* has no meaning apart from this derivation. *Xc* is reached from *Q*; *Dc* is necessary for *C* to obtain. Both the sense and the reference of *X* emerge from the argument itself; *D* must obtain for *SRS* to obtain.

Throughout the argument I have been assuming that *SRS* obtains. But tomorrow might never come. To assure that this factual assumption of the argument is fulfilled, therefore, I substitute for the first sentence in this section the following: Someone has written a book entitled: *Beyond the New Theism: A Philosophy of Religion*. The preceding sentence is uttered at the time the reader reads it, and appropriate adjustments are made throughout the section.

D is not a contingent state of affairs, and yet it obtains although it is uncaused. I call such a noncontingent, extrapropositional state of affairs a "necessary being." Since X picks out a necessary being, X is necessary truth.

The preceding argument remains provisional in the sense that two important steps in it are reserved for treatment in the first two sections of chapter five. After these two steps are supplied, I will restate the argument more concisely in the third section of chapter five. In the final section of chapter five I consider the question whether D should be called "God."

No doubt objections have occurred to the reader. Many potential objections will be considered in part three. How the sense and reference of Xc, and thus of X, emerge from the argument itself will be explained in part four.

5: Development of the Argument

A self-sufficient set of contingent states of affairs?

In the argument provisionally stated in the previous chapter certain conditions required for *SRS* to obtain are grouped together in a class defined by three criteria: (1) these requirements must be satisfied for *SRS* to obtain; (2) they are states of affairs which are contingent—that is, they might or might not obtain; and (3) they themselves obtain only if prerequisites not included in themselves are satisfied. States of affairs meeting these criteria are included in a state of affairs, *C*, which causes *SRS*.

The first question raised in the previous chapter and postponed for consideration in this chapter is whether *C* might not be self-sufficient, otherwise than as a formal truth is self-sufficient. Although *C* includes states of affairs which might or might not obtain and which obtain only if further conditions are fulfilled, could not *C* itself obtain without requiring anything not included in itself? It might be supposed that *C* could be self-sufficient either because its elements mutually satisfy one another's requirements or because they are caused causes ordered in an infinite series.

I think the supposition that *C* obtains without requiring satisfaction of any condition not included in itself can be shown to be impossible by a single, general argument, but the force of this argument is unlikely to be appreciated unless various cases are also considered one by one. I present the general argument first.

The question "Why does *SRS* obtain?" arises because *SRS* is contingent. One can suggest that at some point the question "Why does *x* obtain?" must be set aside as unanswerable; this suggestion will be considered in the next section.

Nothing is explained by itself, nor is anything's being F explained by something else which is precisely like it in being F. Therefore, if a certain state of affairs is contingent and if explanation of its obtaining as contingent is not impossible in principle, either something in that state of affairs is not contingent or something not included in that state of affairs itself is required. The second alternative is incompatible with the supposition under consideration. In other words, if it is shown that to obtain C needs something not included in itself, then this step of the argument is completed. Thus if the supposition that C is self-sufficient is to be sustained, either C must be noncontingent or C must include something noncontingent in itself.

Whether the elements of C are few, many, or infinite, they are prerequisites of *SRS*, as is C itself; thus all *as such* are contingent, inasmuch as *SRS* is contingent. A noncontingent factor which would explain C's obtaining as self-sufficient would have to be some state of affairs within C which obtains simply by being the state of affairs it is. Thus, within C there would be an uncaused entity. Either this uncaused entity itself is within a state of affairs which is an uncaused cause, or not. The former alternative is impossible; an uncaused cause is excluded from C by definition. The latter alternative—that is, that there is an uncaused entity in C but that this uncaused entity is not within a state of affairs which is an uncaused cause—would make the assumed uncaused entity inaccessible to human inquiry beginning from contingent states of affairs.

The last point might seem obvious. However, it has been denied.

If C includes everything normally regarded as a contingent state of affairs, at least one major philosopher holds that there is an uncaused entity somehow identical with C and unlike D precisely in not being the nucleus of an uncaused cause. The philosopher in question is Hegel, and the uncaused *entity* which is not an uncaused *cause* is Hegel's Absolute Spirit. For Hegel, inquiry begins from what seem to be contingent states of affairs, but ends by discovering that the universe as a whole and all its parts as such obtain necessarily. In the end the rational is the real. Hegel intends his system as a whole to express a single rationally necessary proposition. This proposition, although necessary, like a formal truth, also picks out all states of affairs ordinarily thought of as obtaining contingently.

Hegel considers what is normally regarded as the contingent, extrapropositional world as the content of the thought of Absolute Spirit. This content in the past was like an incomplete formal truth gradually unfolding itself. At the culmination of this development, which Hegel claims occurs in his own philosophy, Absolute Spirit, fully self-conscious, completes the proposition. Its rationality as a quasi-formal truth appears; Absolute Spirit recognizes as its own the content which previously seemed contingent. Thus meaning is united with actuality. According to Hegel everything is explained by Absolute Spirit, which is an uncaused and necessary entity, although not an uncaused *cause*. Absolute Spirit does not cause anything; it is everything.

In chapters ten and eleven I expound and criticize Hegel's thought. I try to show that an uncaused entity, such as Hegel's Absolute Spirit, which is not an uncaused *cause*, cannot consistently be posited as the outcome of a human inquiry beginning from contingent states of affairs.

Since Hegel, many philosophers—in other ways quite diverse from one another—have proposed self-contained, uncaused entities on a more human scale than Hegel's Absolute Spirit. According to these philosophies human thought and action are inseparable; together they constitute certain states of affairs, which are limited, unlike Absolute Spirit, but which are similar to Absolute Spirit in that understanding these states of affairs is inseparable from knowing that they obtain extraproposi.ionally.

John Dewey, for example, holds that knowledge is achieved only in the actual resolution of real problems; the satisfaction of the requirements for understanding a problematic situation and for the obtaining of the state of affairs projected as a solution to it coincide in problem-solving action. Wittgenstein, in his later work, holds that philosophy is an activity which aims at clarification. Clarification is achieved by bringing together understanding and extrapropositional states of affairs involving linguistic activity. Many existentialists and dialectical materialists also seek explanatory principles in man himself, where meaning and existence meet.

Philosophies such as these center upon action. If they do not consider human action somehow *constitutive* of reality in general, they do not conflict with the thesis that *C* and states of affairs like it, which are made up entirely of contingent factors, are not self-explanatory. Sometimes interpretation of a philosopher's writings is difficult and hotly disputed, as in Wittgenstein's case. Only on some interpretations or in the work of some disciples, perhaps, does a method become a metaphysics. When such a method does become a metaphysics, essences are denied; amorphous obtaining is shaped into a world by the meaning which human action confers. All meaning *originates* in use; existence is *prior* to essence; things are seen truly *only when* they are seen in the perspective of revolutionary action. What I am concerned with here is not a particular philosophy, so much as it is the exploitation, sometimes contrary to their originators' intentions, of a variety of contemporary philosophical methods. I call this metaphysical exploitation of such methods "post-hegelian relativism."

The plausibility of such metaphysical theories arises from a certain noncontingency within human action, namely, from the reflexivity present in it. Suppose I had begun the argument in chapter four: "Someone is now reading some sentence." Anyone who understands the meaning of this sentence also knows that the state of affairs picked out by it obtains extrapropositionally. However, such a state of affairs does not obtain simply by being *what* it is; rather, the state of affairs picked out by such a proposition obtains because a certain human action, which is necessary for understanding the meaning of the proposition, is picked out by the proposition.

In chapter twelve I expound the positions shared by various forms of post-hegelian relativism and in chapter thirteen criticize these positions. The noncontingency of certain states of affairs because of the reflexivity present in human action is conditioned upon prior states of affairs which are contingent; thus states of affairs which are relatively noncontingent still require an uncaused cause.

Assuming that hegelianism and post-hegelian relativism cannot satisfactorily explain why contingent states of affairs obtain, the general argument already proposed shows that C and what is included in C cannot explain why C obtains. However, the general argument can be specified to various cases.

The simplest case is that of two mutually interdependent contingent states of affairs. These must be included in one state of affairs, for if they were not, there could not be a proposition picking them out as mutually interdependent. The larger state of affairs itself is contingent or not. If it is contingent, it must be explained; moreover, since the states of affairs included in it obtain only if it obtains, why they obtain also still must be explained. If the larger state of affairs is not contingent, the project of showing the self-sufficiency of a set of contingent states of affairs fails. The logical situation is represented by the relationship of four conditional propositions: If p, then q, if q, then p; if r, then p and q; if p or q, then r. If either of the two mutually interdependent states of affairs obtains, then both obtain; if both obtain, then each obtains. But this says nothing about whether either or both do obtain. No set entirely composed of conditional propositions can yield any unconditional conclusion.

The next case is the circle: for example, four states of affairs such that SA^1 depends upon SA^2, SA^2 depends upon SA^3, SA^3 depends upon SA^4, SA^4 depends upon SA^1. This system also forms a larger state of affairs. If this larger state of affairs obtains yet is contingent, why it obtains must be explained. The included states of affairs can only explain why the larger state of affairs obtains if something explains why each of them obtains, for each of them is contingent. The logical situation is: if p, then q; if q, then r; if r, then s; if s, then p; if t, then p, q, r, and s; if p, q, r, or s, then t. The circle closes upon itself; if any of the interlocking states of affairs obtains, they all do; if they all do, each one does. But this relationship still provides no premise for an unconditional assertion.

Unless either the system itself or some included state of affairs is noncontingent, an additional principle still is required. The question why each state of affairs in the system obtains is partially answered by reference to the others only if the others obtain. I call such a partial answer a "conditional explanation." A conditional explanation does not forestall further questions. The question why each state of affairs obtains only becomes more acute as the potentiality within the system for conditional explanation approaches its limit.

This case is the one I referred to in chapter four as a "perpetual happening-machine." The reference could be misleading. If one imagines a frictionless mechanism which does no work, then one could suppose that the mechanism might run forever without being started by anything. I do not think this is logically impossible; *moving* is a predicable. But if such a machine exists, a proposition picking out the state of affairs still would be contingent; one knows what it would be like for this proposition to be true without knowing whether it is true. Thus, one could still ask "Why?" —not why the parts of the machine move, but why the state of affairs obtains which is picked out by the proposition that there is a perpetual motion machine.

Sometimes opponents of cosmological argumentation suggest that to ask for a cause of a state of affairs in addition to the mutual causality of its members is like asking for an explanation of the grouping of a crowd of people on a street corner in addition to the reasons why each member of the group happens to be there. But as an objection to the argument proposed in chapter four, this analogy fails. The argument begins from the fact that *SRS,* which might or might not obtain, does obtain. *C* includes conditions *required* for *SRS* to obtain. *C* explains *SRS* to some extent, but as a state of affairs made up of contingent states of affairs, *C*'s obtaining itself raises a further question. If *SRS* requires *C,* and if *C* is no less contingent than *SRS,* then both *SRS* and *C* require something else.

An apt analogy would be a circle of four persons, all with arms tightly linked, standing together a few feet off the ground in thin air. Each is asked in turn: "What is holding you up?" Each gives the same answer: "My friends to my right and left." At this point, although the answers are partial explanations, it is clear that even taken together they are not satisfying. What is holding them all up? The question becomes acute precisely when the conditional explanations come full circle.

If this is true, why do people think that such circles, if large enough, might be self-contained? I think there are two reasons.

First, there is the logical necessity of an interlocking set of conditional propositions. This necessity mirrors causal relations among the states of affairs involved, and these causal relations, whatever philosophers might think of them, are felt to have some sort of necessity. Thus it is easy to slip from "Things have to be so" to "Things have to be," not noticing that nothing must be so unless it is. This mistake is the basis of the ontological argument, criticized at the end of chapter three and further analyzed in chapter four. Even when one is not trying to demonstrate God's existence it is easy to suppose that necessity within a state of affairs unconditionally explains its obtaining.

Second, the multiple members in a circle of interdependent states of affairs do, to some extent, explain one another's obtaining. The sharp dichotomy sometimes made between explaining how and explaining why is mistaken. The satisfaction of the requirements included in C is required for SRS to obtain. Science begins when one asks why some state of affairs obtains. Science, unlike logic and mathematics, does not merely trace ideal relations among possible states of affairs. Thus, as long as one takes for granted that the world exists, an explanation of why a contingent state of affairs obtains by reference to other contingent states of affairs is appropriate and satisfying. Again, the situation recalls the ontological argument, which seems convincing if one takes for granted that God exists.

But an explanation of a contingent by reference to contingents is incomplete and unsatisfactory just to the extent that the states of affairs which provide the explanation do so only if they themselves obtain. To assume that the latter states of affairs obtain without knowing why they do and to stop at this point, would be to stop with something as much in need of explanation as that from which one started.

The most common case in which it is supposed that some set of contingent states of affairs might be self-sufficient is that in which an infinite series of contingent states of affairs is posited. Why could SRS not be explained by a particular cause, and this cause by another cause, and so on *ad infinitum?*

It might be objected that this supposition lacks plausibility, because contemporary scientific cosmology strongly suggests that the universe is not infinite. A proponent of the infinite series might answer that the scientific evidence is not complete and that future theories might make an infinite series more plausible than present theories do. This argument seems to me rather weak as an answer to the objection, because it involves speculation against the best available information on the subject. If someone arguing for the existence of God had scientific cosmology against him, his opponents would make the most of it. However, nothing in the argument I propose depends on the physical universe being finite. Therefore, I grant for the sake of argument that the physical universe is infinite and that a particular state of affairs might have infinite antecedent causal conditions—whether antecedent in time or not—each of them itself a contingent state of affairs.

The infinite series can be considered in two ways. In one way, it is a set of discrete states of affairs. Each is contingent; why any one obtains is explained only if one assumes that the one before it obtains. No one of them explains what it causes except to the extent that it itself obtains, and all of the members of the series obtain because infinite prerequisites are satisfied. In another way, the members of the series are a single state of affairs, unified by their common disposition in respect to the particular state of affairs, *SRS*, which they all help to explain.

It makes no difference whether one considers the states of affairs which make up the series one by one or considers the single state of affairs in which they are included. The proposition picking out each particular state of affairs is contingent. Therefore, no conjunction of such propositions, even though they be infinite, can provide a premise for any unconditional assertion.

The state of affairs as a whole—assuming such a state of affairs possible—is equally contingent. One can know what the infinite series of contingent causes would be like without knowing whether such a state of affairs obtains. This is evident from the occurrence of the argument mentioned previously between a proponent of the infinite series and a defender of scientific cosmology. If an infinite series of causes does happen to obtain, it still makes sense to ask why it does.

Frederick Copleston, S.J., used an argument somewhat like the preceding in a debate with Bertrand Russell. Russell replied that Copleston's argument involves a fallacy of composition. Russell illustrated his point: "Every man who exists has a mother, and it seems to me that your argument is that therefore the human race must have a mother, but obviously the human race hasn't a mother—that's a different logical sphere."[1] The short answer to Russell is that the argument does not involve composition, and so cannot be guilty of a fallacy of composition.

If someone denies that an infinite series of contingent causes would be a single contingent state of affairs, it is hard to see what he is denying; he must refer to something which is a unity to deny its unity. If it is a single state of affairs, it is either contingent or not. If someone wishes to hold that the whole state of affairs is noncontingent, then a noncontingent proposition must correspond to it, and this noncontingent proposition will entail the propositions picking out the states of affairs included in the whole. Only something like Hegel's philosophy of Absolute Spirit could begin to make plausible a noncontingent whole which includes and explains its contingent parts. If the infinite series as a whole is contingent, then the question remains: "Why does this state of affairs obtain?"

If Russell, when he said "human race," meant the species rather than the totality of human persons, his analogy was unsound. For, on any account, the supposed infinite series is not merely a class; it is an infinite number of actual individual states of affairs. With this distinction in mind, one can construct a more apt analogy than Russell's to illustrate the preceding argument. One can imagine that an insane mendicant becomes world ruler and decrees that no one can eat anything he has obtained otherwise than by begging. Each member of the human race might live on begged food. The food supply of each individual would be accounted for by reference to those from whom he begged. Still, there would be a question how the human race obtained its food. One cannot imagine a system, even with infinite members, in which no one ever gathered, hunted, or raised any food, yet everyone ate quite well on the rations he managed to beg. To suppose that since all individuals could live on begged provisions, the whole race could live on begged provisions, would be to commit a fallacy of composition.

The following parable also might be helpful. A certain Tweetlebottom needed money and asked a friend for $100. to tide him over. The friend said he did not have the cash, but would be glad to try to raise it, if he could have a little time. Much later, the friend returned, dragging a long strip of paper which reached over the horizon. Putting the end of the paper on Tweetlebottom's table, the friend wrote, "Pay to the order of Tweetlebottom," and signed his own name. "Here, Tweetlebottom," the friend said, "is your money. Just endorse this and I'll hand over the cash." Tweetlebottom did as he was told and received the crisp $100 bill mentioned in the previous chapter (which is one reason the reader did not find it between pages 100 and 101 of this copy of this book). Feeling a slight curiosity, Tweetlebottom looked at the reverse side of the end of the strip of paper. There he saw all the usual information found on a check, except that it lacked the signature of the maker. "I expect the name of the person on whose account it is drawn is somewhere along the strip," Tweetlebottom said. But his friend answered, "No, this isn't your usual check. It's not drawn on anyone's account at all. I couldn't find anyone with $100. to write a check, so I asked my fairy godmother to get an *infinite* group of people to *endorse* this check. Now that you've endorsed it, you can keep the $100, and I'll take the check, and pass it back along the line. No one needs to worry about the check ever getting to the bank." Tweetlebottom was pleased to receive the $100, and he promised to pay it back, but he still did not quite understand how a check could be without a maker.

The logical situation with respect to the infinite series is that the links correspond to an infinitely long chain of conditionals. *SRS* if *p*, *p* if *q*, *q* if *r*, and so on. This set of logical relations reveals that *SRS* does not obtain unless all its infinite antecedents obtain. Thus, if *SRS* does obtain, we know that all the propositions in the series are true. But all of them, taken as nonmolecular propositions, are contingent. Thus neither the fact that all of these states of affairs obtain nor the causal chain linking them explains unconditionally why any one of them obtains.[2]

It is also worth considering why infinite regresses are generally regarded as unacceptable in philosophy. If one asks a question and receives an answer, and if this answer raises a further question the answer to which reveals that the line of questioning is *inevitably* interminable, then the first answer is rejected, because it is no answer at all. The point of questioning a position is to see if it can stand; a position which retreats every time one approaches it is no position at all. Each step in the regress is an instance of a common model; as soon as the common features of the question-answer complex make clear that continuing the line of questions will not alter the questionableness of the initial state of affairs, there is no point in continuing. The purpose of asking questions is to get answers, and any satisfactory answer will explain all states of affairs similar in relevant respects to that from which one started. If the same question must be asked over and over, it was not answered the first time.

Thus, if one is seeking an explanation of why a contingent state of affairs obtains and if one is not satisfied with conditional explanations, there is no point in positing an infinite regress of contingent causes. What, then, is the point of positing such an infinite regress?

As explained previously, the awareness of the incompleteness of conditional explanations grows as the conditional character of the explanation of one contingent state of affairs by reference to other contingent states of affairs becomes clear. To posit an infinite regress is to suggest that conditional explanations might be endless, as well they might be. This move in the argument seems to me to be a symbolic way of suggesting that science might be an inexhaustible quest—as well it might be—and that one ought to settle for the conditional explanations of science, instead of asking why *all* the contingent causes of anything obtain.

It is the last position which must be challenged. This position is not that the contingent as a whole is self-sufficient, as if it were somehow non-contingent. Thus the question to be considered next emerges: Must there be an answer to the question "Why does C obtain?" C is a state of affairs which includes all of the causal conditions of SRS which themselves, if they obtain, require the satisfaction of conditions distinct from themselves. One who answers this question in the negative is not saying that the whole system of contingent causes constitutes a state of affairs somehow noncontingent. Rather, he is saying that the demand for explanation somehow becomes inappropriate when one reaches this point.

Must there be an explanation of the contingent?

The argument provisionally stated in the previous chapter does not begin from the existence of the world as a whole. The argument begins from a particular state of affairs, someone's reading a sentence or writing a book.

From this starting point the argument proceeds to conditions which must be satisfied for the initial state of affairs to obtain. All the prerequisites which themselves obtain only if further prerequisites are satisfied are grouped together in a class, C, which is not only a collection but also a single state of affairs—namely, all the prerequisites for a certain state of affairs to obtain being so disposed that it does. It has now been shown that C itself and the states of affairs included in it, whether finite or infinite, cannot unconditionally explain why C obtains. An unconditional explanation would answer the question why C obtains by reference to a state of affairs which is noncontingent, the necessary entity D, which obtains because it is what it is.

Some critics of cosmological arguments insist that proceeding to this question is inherently fallacious, either because one need not explain a whole if its parts can be explained scientifically, or because any question about the entire universe is meaningless. For example, Paul Edwards, in an influential article, argues that just as the explanation of a group of five Eskimos standing on a street corner in Manhattan might be nothing more than the statement of the different reasons why each happens to be there, so the explanation of the whole of contingent things need be nothing more than the explanation of each contingent thing. Edwards also says: "I may hold that there is no 'universe' over and above individual things of various sorts. . . ."[3]

Now, the first of these objections is the point with which the previous section dealt. What is at stake in the argument to an uncaused cause is not the explaining of a group after its members have been explained, but the attempt to more fully explain a particular state of affairs, which is only explained by the whole set of its contingent prerequisites to the extent that one takes for granted that they obtain. The second objection is closely related to the first. But it is worth noting that C, in the argument I propose, is not defined by reference to the universe or to any other totality selected arbitrarily, but by reference to SRS.

I am willing to grant that C might include every contingent state of affairs which obtains; if it does, as the preceding discussion reveals, one can pursue conditional explanations in the largest possible domain. For this very reason, those who do not care to seek an unconditional explanation are usually the ones who suggest that the universe as a whole is adequate to explain each particular state of affairs in it. I accept this formulation of the problem as a concession to the opposition, not as something my own argument requires.

The present issue, to repeat, is whether there *must* be an answer to the question "Why does C obtain?" The supposition which I wish to show unacceptable here is that C—which might be the universe as a whole—simply obtains because it obtains. This is the supposition which J. J. C. Smart suggests when he says that a proper answer to the question "Why should anything [the universe] exist at all?" might be "Why shouldn't it?"

Another way of expressing this supposition would be to say that perhaps *C*—or the universe as a whole—is an extrapropositional prerequisite for *SRS* to obtain, and that *C* itself meets the three criteria which are listed at the beginning of this chapter, but that *C* meets the third criterion in a peculiar way. The third criterion for counting a state of affairs among the prerequisite conditions which are included in *C* is that it be a state of affairs which does not obtain without conditions not included in itself being satisfied. On the supposition being considered, *C*—or the universe as a whole—would meet this third criterion merely by being nonidentical with its own obtaining, just as is any lesser state of affairs. But unlike any lesser state of affairs, the obtaining of *C*—or of the universe—would be the *sole* extrinsic determinant of its obtaining rather than not obtaining. *C*—or the universe—on this supposition is because it is, and that is all there is to it. *C*—or the universe—need not be and nothing causes it to be. Yet it is.

Smart himself and other philosophers cited in the introduction to chapter four, although they do not admit that the existence of things is to be explained by positing an uncaused cause, do admit that it arouses deep awe. Smart also says that he thinks other people and himself ought to feel this awe. Why do we feel this awe? Why does even someone like Smart say that we ought to feel it?

Often proponents of the cosmological argument have answered this question much too quickly by saying that if one does not posit an uncaused cause, then nothing is explained at all. But this answer would be seriously misleading. If one does not posit an uncaused cause, contingent states of affairs do partially explain each other's obtaining, but these partial explanations remain conditional. The argument of the previous section, if it is correct, has made clear that the conditional explanations which science provides are not only incomplete insofar as they raise further questions which can be answered by further conditional explanations but also are inevitably incomplete. To the question "Why does *x* obtain?" only an answer which posits a noncontingent state of affairs, such as *D*, precludes asking *the same question* of that to which one refers in answering the initial question.

But it must be admitted that even if one posits *D* as an unconditional explanation of why *C* and *SRS* obtain, this answer does not preclude asking additional questions about why *SRS* obtains. Only a few of the conditions included in *C* are known. Until one knows not only that there is an uncaused cause but also precisely what are the contingent causes of the states of affairs being investigated, one does not have a complete explanation. In other words, if one responds to the awe one feels in the face of the contingent by positing an uncaused cause, one does not render scientific inquiry any less necessary.

Leibniz and other rationalists make quick work of the step in the cosmological argument from contingent beings to a necessary being. Contingent states of affairs might be or not be. If there is no necessary being, yet contingent states of affairs do obtain, they simply happen to obtain. But this is incompatible with what Leibniz calls the "principle of sufficient reason." He formulates it as follows: "No fact can be real or existent, no statement true, unless there be a sufficient reason why it is so and not otherwise, although most often these reasons cannot be known to us."[4]

If this principle were true, the question "Why does C obtain?" must have an answer, and since, as has been shown, the answer cannot be found in the contingent itself, there must be a necessary entity. If D is not, then C simply obtains because it obtains, and this is not a sufficient reason, in Leibniz's sense, because C is contingent—that is, it might be otherwise, it might not obtain. But is the principle of sufficient reason true? I think not.

It has often been pointed out that the principle of sufficient reason can hardly be regarded as a mere generalization from facts. As Leibniz and other rationalists state it, the principle pretends to be absolutely universal and necessary. However, it is not a formal truth. Formal truths cannot be denied without contradicting oneself, because the reason why the formal truth is true is intrinsic to it. The principle of sufficient reason is designed precisely to deal with cases in which something is so but could be otherwise; if the reason why it is so were intrinsic to what is to be explained, then it could not be so *or* otherwise, it would simply be so.

Another way of putting this important point is as follows. When the question "why" is asked, there is always some gap between what is given and what is understood. If someone says that a certain logical or mathematical conclusion follows, and one does not understand the formal necessity, one asks to be shown why the conclusion follows. If one is faced with a fact, such as an eclipse, and does not know how this fact fits into a regular system, one asks why the fact occurs. If one's friend behaves in a peculiar way and one cannot comprehend his intentions, one asks the friend why he is behaving so oddly. Similarly, faced with contingent states of affairs and their obtaining, and with the gap between meaning and obtaining, one asks why. If in all these cases the reason were identical with that which is to be explained, the gap would not exist; there would be no occasion for asking "why." Thus, whenever there is an occasion for asking "why," the reason which is sought cannot be found in the intelligibility of the state of affairs which raises the question. Thus one can suppose, without *self-contradiction,* that there is no reason at all.

Richard Taylor proposes a brief and clear version of the cosmological argument. To set the stage for the introduction of the principle of sufficient reason, he describes an imaginary situation in which one, while walking in a forest, comes across a large ball, about one's own height, perfectly smooth and translucent. One certainly would wonder how it got there. If one does not come across a ball in the forest, one does not wonder why there is no ball in the forest. The existence of the world, Taylor argues, is apt to be taken for granted. But, in fact, it is strange indeed. Taylor thus formulates the principle of sufficient reason "by saying that, in the case of any positive truth, there is some sufficient reason for it, something which, in this sense, makes it true. . . ." Noting that the principle is neither a factual generalization nor a logically necessary truth, Taylor suggests an alternative: that it is a presupposition of reason. One could not prove it without assuming it. If one tries to deny it, he is likely to find that he is not denying what the principle asserts. The principle, Taylor thinks, is "something which all men, whether they ever reflect upon it or not, seem more or less to presuppose."[5]

Now, although I think the principle of sufficient reason is false, I think that what Taylor says about it is close to being correct. The first thing which must be done is to show that the principle is false.

The question "What makes this individual teacup different from that individual teacup?" is a perfectly intelligible question. One can point out slight differences in shape and so forth. But suppose the two were exactly alike in these respects? One could say that they are made of different clay, but this only pushes back, not answers, the question. One might say that they are in different places, but their places can easily be exchanged. Finally one might say that they are not in the same place at the same time. But this seems to say no more than that they are different individuals.

Medieval philosophers devoted much attention to this problem, and as far as I know never solved it. Leibniz, following out his principle of sufficient reason, said that any two individuals must differ by at least one predicable. If not, they would be the same. This is Leibniz's "identity of indiscernibles"— everything must be *intelligibly* distinct from everything else. This might seem harmless enough, but it implies that ideally names can be dispensed with in favor of predicables. Such a scheme might be suited to logic and mathematics, but it is unsuited to empirical knowledge. Propositions which are not formal truths must have reference, and the something to which they refer cannot in principle be reducible to predicables. Following Leibniz's principle of sufficient reason to the end would eliminate empirical knowledge. Leibniz more or less saw and accepted this implication of his position, and he drew a number of peculiar conclusions from it.[6]

There are other areas in which the principle of sufficient reason leads to strange conclusions. In a discussion of scientific cosmology an author of a recent article remarks:

> There are some interesting problems at a more fundamental level that seem not so much to invite an answer from within the framework of the model as to demand an explanation in order that the model itself seem less arbitrary. Choosing to work backward from the present state of the

universe to gain some knowledge of the initial conditions is not at all arbitrary, but it does not suffice to *explain* the initial conditions. Probably the most we can expect from this approach is that we shall be able at least to *describe* those conditions.[7]

Someone who believes in God might easily be led from this sort of observation to meditate upon divine causality. And, it is true, the work of physics, as it reaches the ultimate boundaries and tries to understand a system with no boundary conditions, does point up the conditionality of all scientific explanations. However, it would be a mistake to suppose that the initial conditions of the physical universe can be explained if this means showing why these conditions, rather than some other imaginable conditions, obtain.

But is this not to admit that there is no need to posit an uncaused cause? No, an uncaused cause is posited, not to explain why states of affairs which obtain contingently are *contingent,* but to explain why they *obtain* despite their being contingent. To put the point in another way. Scientific questions ask both why a state of affairs obtains and why this state of affairs, rather than some other state of affairs, obtains. Both questions are answered by science with conditional explanations, which leave gaps to be filled. What I am saying is that the gap between states of affairs being what they are and the same states of affairs obtaining can be closed if there is an uncaused cause which is a necessary entity. But the gap between some states of affairs rather than others obtaining cannot be completely closed, just as differences among individuals cannot be completely explained.

"But," the believer might object, "one can explain why the initial conditions of the universe are what they are. God chose that they be so." This answer leads to a further question: "Why does God choose just this set of conditions rather than any other?" "God chooses freely," is the answer. "Precisely. He chooses *freely.* Therefore, there is no sufficient reason for his choice." If a choice really is free, then while there might be many reasons for this choice, there must be the same total set of reasons for this choice and for its alternative. When all the reasons and conditions common to the alternatives are given, there is no sufficient reason for this choice being made rather than for an alternative choice being made. Thus, if one supposes that God creates freely, this supposition explains why contingent states of affairs *obtain,* but it does not explain why God chooses to create certain contingent states of affairs rather than others.[8]

The principle of sufficient reason, then, does not underwrite reasoning to the existence of God from contingent things. Instead, it eliminates contingency from things, and thus removes the starting point of cosmological argumentation. Indeed, since the possibility of explanation depends upon a gap in intelligibility and since the point of explanation is to close the gap, if everything could be explained, then everything would be one, and so nothing could be explained.

One of the most persuasive arguments of determinists against human free choice appeals to the principle of sufficient reason. If a choice is free, the only reason why this choice *rather than its alternative* is made is the choice itself. Determinists generally protest that this is unintelligible, absurd, and so forth. In protesting thus, determinists sound very much like leibnizian rationalists. It is clearly not self-contradictory that there be free choices, and I think it has been convincingly argued that someone can make a free choice.[9] The odd fact is that many of the same philosophers who invoke the principle of sufficient reason—without calling it that—in arguing for determinism reject it when they are criticizing arguments for the existence of God.

Thus I think the principle of sufficient reason is false. If it is true, there simply is no contingency.

However, this conclusion does not mean that explanations are not to be sought or that one can determine *a priori* what is allowable as explanation. Many who attack the cosmological method of arguing to an uncaused cause say that such argumentation "involves an obscure and arbitrary redefinition of 'explanation,' 'intelligible,' and related terms."[10] Often they offer some very simple model of scientific explanation, and triumphantly conclude that since the question why contingent states of affairs obtain—if an unconditional answer is demanded—cannot be answered according to the model proposed, the question must be illegitimate.

Apart from the fact that this approach tends to reduce all explanation to the paradigm of scientific explanation, although there are many other forms of explanation,[11] it is not at all clear that "explanation" in science is as uniform as is often suggested. One need only look at contemporary writings in philosophy of science to see that it is by no means clear that scientific explanation is reducible to a single model.[12] What is more important, the question is not, in the first instance, to find something which everyone will say is an "explanation." The question is why *C*, the cause of *SRS*, obtains, although it might not. If one admits the legitimacy of the question, it makes no difference whether its answer would be called an "explanation." Someone might say that this question is not legitimate. If he explains why it is not, his explanation is unlikely to look much like a scientific explanation.[13]

Another mistake sometimes made when the principle of sufficient reason is rejected is to conclude that there is no sufficient reason for anything. Since not everything can be explained and since every explanation we actually give leaves room for further questions, it is easily assumed to be an error in principle to seek explanations which answer a question with more than practical finality. Any satisfactory answer to a "why" question renders the original fact intelligible by reference to something which does not admit of being questioned in the same way, and which the person asking the question thinks reasonable to take for granted. In many cases what is reasonably taken for granted does depend upon one's practical purposes. "Why is my favorite brand of tea not on the shelf?" "The boy will get it from the basement." It is reasonable to take for granted the tea's being in the basement and the boy's working in the store and a great many other things, so long as the tea is forthcoming.

Children's questions seem endless partly because they do not have very limited purposes in asking them, and so do not see that it is reasonable to take much for granted. But in a purely theoretical inquiry, whether in science or in philosophy, some things are taken for granted for reasons which are more than merely practical purposes. One can see why one should not ask why. In a biological theory of evolution one finds it reasonable to take reproduction for granted; the data to be explained, not a practical purpose, determines this limit of inquiry.[14] Plato's treatise on unity and multiplicity in his dialogue *Parmenides* provides excellent reasons why both unity and multiplicity must be taken for granted by philosophers.

Thus, I reject the principle of sufficient reason as false, and I also reject *a priori* restrictions which would rule out the question "Why does *C* obtain?" But must there be an answer to this question? If one answers affirmatively, is one not supposing a more restricted version of the principle of sufficient reason?

A more restricted version suited to the case can easily be designed along the following lines: If a cause of a contingent state of affairs obtains, and if this cause is itself contingent and such that every causal factor included in it itself requires a cause, then there must be an uncaused cause. This restricted version of the principle of sufficient reason would be adequate, but to posit it as a justification of the step in the argument in question against someone who denies the need to take the step would be question-begging. Thus, it seems to me that this step in the argument cannot be underwritten by a theoretical principle.

Still, it seems to me that the obstacle to carrying through the argument can be surmounted. Contingent states of affairs do obtain. There is a gap between what they are and their obtaining. Therefore, it is legitimate to ask why they obtain. It might not be prudent or practical to ask this theoretical question at a given moment, but many people have asked and do ask the question. To ask the question with regard to particular states of affairs leads to some success in theoretical science, which provides conditional explanations. The question "Why does *C* obtain?" is formed in such a way that a conditional explanation will not be acceptable as an answer. But any radically new and interesting theoretical question in some respects precludes a standard reply or a reply worked out according to a standard method. If there were not something very *odd* about the questions which great scientists ask, there would never be any revolutions in scientific theory.[15]

It is not clear that there is anything wrong with the question "Why does C obtain?" which would prohibit us from asking it, as there is something wrong with "Why do individuals differ?" and "Why are certain choices—assuming them to be free—made rather than others?" In the case of C's obtaining it is reasonable to ask the question and to expect some sort of answer to it. The positing of an uncaused cause, which is a necessary being, does provide a partial answer to the question why C and other contingent states of affairs obtain. It provides a partial answer because given Dc, the question why it obtains is answered by saying that it includes D, and D obtains because it is *what* it is.

It is clear that answering the question "Why does C obtain?" by positing D is not very satisfactory. One knows nothing about what D is in itself; it is a theoretical entity introduced because it is required to satisfy the conditions of the problem. But positing D is at least some sort of answer, and it puts one in a position to raise the further question: "What is D in itself, and precisely how does Dc cause C to obtain?" Since the positing of the uncaused cause and of the uncaused entity which is its nucleus moves the inquiry forward, one *must* answer the question "Why does C obtain?" by saying, "Because an uncaused cause causes it to obtain."

It will not do, in this situation, to say that while contingent states of affairs need not obtain but do, they simply obtain by their obtaining. It is unsatisfactory to say that things just happen to be when one can posit something which would explain them; it is unreasonable to stop the inquiry at C when one can move on to D. Making this move does not explain everything, but it does open the way to a question "What is D in itself?" which, if answered, would be a reasonable place to stop. "Why is D what it is?" is meaningless, because it demands an explanation of the self-identity of the entity. Explanation closes a gap; there is no gap to be closed where there is self-identity.

Many philosophers will object to this argument that there is something radically wrong with the question "Why does C obtain?" or with the answer "Because an uncaused cause, which is a necessary being, caused it." Hume and philosophers who follow his lead object along these lines. Hume's position will be expounded in chapter six, and the objections he and others raise will be answered in chapter seven.

Other philosophers will argue that the implicit analogy in the preceding argument to the procedure in theoretical science is fallacious. Human understanding, they will maintain, is limited to the world of experience. One can think beyond this world, but if one does so, and imagines that he is gaining theoretical knowledge of nonexperienced things, such thinking will end in absurdities. Kant raises this sort of objection. Kant's position will be expounded in chapter eight and criticized in chapter nine.

Assuming that objections such as those of Hume and Kant can be met, I think the preceding line of argument shows that one must make the step from things which happen to be to something which has to be. The reasoning depends upon certain suppositions, which I call "rationality norms." They include the following.

If a question arises and if one sees no good reason not to ask it, one should ask it. If a question of a certain form has been asked and answered, one can expect another question of the same general form to be answerable if it is asked. ("Why does x obtain?" is not unanswerable in principle, so why should it be unanswerable when one arrives at C?) If one asks a question, one ought to suppose that things are as they must be if the question is to be answered. If one can provide a partial answer to a theoretical question by positing a theoretical entity, and if doing so opens the way to further questions which, if answered, promise a satisfying answer to the initial question, then one ought to posit such a theoretical entity.

The rationality norms to which I am appealing are, in a certain sense, presuppositions of reasoning, as Richard Taylor suggested the principle of sufficient reason might be. But they are not, directly and in themselves, statements about the way things are. They lack the metaphysical ring of Leibniz's principle of sufficient reason. However, many perennial puzzles can be clarified by noticing that a rationality norm, rather than a theoretical principle, is what is presupposed.

For example, one can justify the use of various forms of deductive inference. But how can one justify the simplest forms, such as *modus ponens?* (*Modus ponens* is reasoning of the form: if one proposition, *p*, is true, then another proposition, *q*, also is true; but *p* is true; therefore *q* is true.) Max Black has argued very plausibly that it is unreasonable to expect a theoretical justification of *modus ponens;* a person who uses it without reasons is not behaving irrationally, and one who refused to accept it would be unreasonable. But at the same time there is nothing conventional about *modus ponens.*[16] Black's position, it seems to me, amounts to saying—although he does not put it this way—that there is a rationality norm which might be formulated: If one is presented with a deductive argument which seems valid, and if no justification of it is possible, then one ought to accept the argument as valid.

Similarly, Black makes a strong case against a variety of efforts to justify or to vindicate inductive reasoning. "Why should we accept the conclusions of inductions which, after all, are not necessarily true?" Black's conclusion is that human beings belong to what he calls "the inductive institution"; we are all necessarily subject to "norms of belief and conduct imposed by the institution."[17]

I think the puzzle about the uniformity of nature can be reduced to a rationality norm: If certain uniformities have been observed and one has no special reason not to expect them to obtain in the future, then one ought to expect them to obtain. Simplicity rules, used in evaluating hypotheses, although notoriously difficult to formulate—for reasons which the subsequent discussion will partially clarify—also express rationality norms for theory construction.

Probability is based on rationality norms. When one knows that the proportion of women who live to age seventy is greater than the proportion of men who live to age seventy, and when one knows that a certain husband is older by ten years than his wife, then one ought to expect the wife to outlive her husband, assuming one knows nothing special about the couple which would indicate life expectancies different from the average, with a probability which can be calculated from past experience registered in mortality tables.[18]

Michael Slote, in arguing against scepticism with respect to the existence of the external world, explicitly formulates a number of rationality norms, although he calls them "principles." An example is his *Principle of Illusion and Evidence:*

> . . . one who is (even in the slightest degree) rationally justified in believing any (fairly specific) causal claim must have evidence which he is rationally justified in trusting or using in order to support that claim, and must, therefore, not be rationally justified in believing that all his sense and memory experiences are illusory (non-veridical).[19]

The heart of the matter might be put more briefly: If one cannot possibly have any good reason for rejecting experience as illusory, one ought to accept it as genuine. Obviously, this is a very strong norm.

A person who believes what he is told is acting on a rationality norm: One ought to believe others unless there is some reason to doubt their word or their competence. A person who asks questions acts on rationality norms, some of which I have set out in the preceding argument. A person who reasons relies on rationality norms such as the general dependability of deduction and the justifiability of taking the measured risks of induction. Even a person whose motto is "Seeing is believing" follows a rationality norm similar to that stated by Slote.

There are many other rationality norms. They are not often articulated explicitly, and they have not, so far as I know, been recognized as a class having many common characteristics. All asking of questions, all reasoning, and all judging are governed by such norms.

What are these rationality norms? Children follow them spontaneously, although children oversimplify them. Children ask questions, accept and use various forms of argument, and make judgments, all of which can be questioned by a sceptical adult. But children are not sceptical. They do not realize that one need not ask and cannot answer every question which comes to mind, that sometimes there is something wrong with a question. They do not realize that one need not accept the conclusion of an intuitively valid deductive argument even if one has granted the premises, for they are not aware that even the simplest forms of argument can be fallaciously used. Children do not imagine that life as a whole might be merely a dream; they are not sensitive to the extent to which illusion infects what seems evident. In these matters children are innocent, naive, and trusting, just as they are in their relationships with other people. They believe what they are told; they take for granted that they are loved; they do not wonder whether mother might be putting poison in the porridge.

Experience shows the fallibility of knowledge, just as it shows that mothers sometimes murder their babies. One learns that the steps of questioning, of reasoning, and of judging which one can take, can fail. One sees that one need not take them. One acquires the ability to make a choice. One finds it possible to be critical and cautious, if not sceptical. And the more sophisticated the adult, the more he is able to decide whether he will ask a question, follow an argument, or make a judgment. Thus, the policies which children follow spontaneously must grow up into adult rationality norms. Adults do not simply enshrine their childhood ways of thinking—at least one hopes they do not. They refine them, qualify them, and orchestrate them so that they can use them in concert.

Yet this whole process is for the most part inarticulate. Rationality norms only become explicit in one or another area of inquiry, not as a unified system. As long as these norms are not violated, no one calls attention to them. When violations occur, the norms are articulated. Often the first articulation is too simple, as is Leibniz's formulation of the principle of sufficient reason.

And often, as in this case, rationality norms are expressed as if they were universal, necessary, descriptive statements about reality. The reasonableness of rationality norms, their obviously objective normativity, leads people to express them in a form appropriate to what is not normatively but factually objective. However, rationality norms are not descriptive. Yet they are objective; they are nonconventional, not relative to individual purposes, and cognitive. Their cognitivity is not descriptive; they do not tell what reasonableness is. But rationality norms do provide a guide to straight thinking—to asking legitimate questions, developing sound arguments, and making critical judgments.[20]

There are some pragmatic rules of thought which are relative to particular purposes and even conventional. These are not rationality norms. One must have such pragmatic rules only to the extent that one wants something from thinking besides knowledge—for example, success in some specific task. Rhetoric, in Aristotle's sense, provides pragmatic rules of thought and expression for the purpose of persuasion. The working out, the use, and the justification of such pragmatic rules of thought always *presuppose* rationality norms.

Because they are not pragmatic norms, rationality norms are not conditioned by particular purposes. But they are not simple, unconditional principles or laws of thought. They have built-in qualifiers, provisions for exceptions, other-things-being-equal clauses. The various rationality norms limit and complement each other.

Since rationality norms are not laws of thought, one can choose to violate them. To do so is to indulge in rationalization, self-deception, obscurantism, bias, or the like. In the face of the categorical demands of the rationality norms that one face the facts, quit evading the issues, get one's head out of the sand, take an opponent's objection seriously, and so on, one can be unreasonable. This possibility arises from the fact that one can be concerned about values other than knowledge of the truth, and that one can prostitute one's thinking, not merely make it an honorable handmaiden, to these other values.

"Be reasonable!" is very like a moral demand, if it is not precisely a moral demand. Rationality norms are very like a code of ethics for asking questions, arguing, judging. Someone who violates them cannot be convicted of self-contradiction for violating them, because rationality norms direct all and only the moves which admit of choice, and one who is face to face with an inconsistency no longer has a choice. I have explained elsewhere how moral norms can be cognitive though nonnaturalistic, and how one can apply moral norms with sensitivity while avoiding moral relativism.[21]

Most people recognize that knowledge of truth is a basic human good. This does not mean that one must never pursue other goods, and it does not mean that one may not seek knowledge as a means, not merely as an end in itself. It does mean that one ought not, where truth is at stake, act contrary to it, by concealing it from oneself, by cherishing opinions one would not wish to submit to critical examination, by refusing to accept the essential risks of making mistakes which are inseparable from a fallible knower's pursuit of knowledge and wisdom. Rationality norms are the law of the love of truth, but dedicated scientists and true lovers of wisdom do not feel this law as a constraint, because it is second nature to them.

Sophists of every age realize that rationality norms are usages which need not be followed. If challenged, sophists point out that their procedure is not self-contradictory and claim that they are therefore not irrational. The sophist follows rationality norms for the most part, but he does not admit them to be categorical. He insists upon his freedom to invoke the principle of sufficient reason—or some more accurate expression of the norm which that principle imprecisely expresses—when it suits him, and to point out that it is no law of thought when this suits him. No doubt one is free to be immoral. The sophist asks for a demonstration from extramoral principles that one ought to be moral, and not receiving such a demonstration, he declares that his immorality is rationally vindicated.

Rationality norms initially are shaped by experience. For example, one accepts inductive arguments because one has learned by experience that while they are not an infallible means for coming to know, they are a necessary means for coming to know many things. Is this a circular justification of induction? No, it is not a justification at all. Children have no choice about whether to expect the future to resemble the past, to expect data to be veridical, to believe what they are told, and so on. Experience teaches how well these natural dispositions work in thinking toward truth. The most basic rationality norms, once learned, are subject to little modification.

But experience also teaches the need for sophistication. The child gradually learns that there are ways in which questioning, reasoning, and judging can go wrong unexpectedly. Thus by the time one is aware of his ability to make choices, one also has a considerable body of experience. One who loves the truth follows policies which, so far as he knows, are more likely than alternative policies to lead to the truth.

Sophists adopt other policies, policies which are conducive to the goods they love more than truth. Yet they are adept at articulating a rationality norm when it suits their convenience, often without its necessary built-in qualifiers, provisions for exceptions, and other-things-being-equal clauses. Each sophist seems to develop a special skill in using one or a few rationality norms as irresistible weapons for coercing honest persons who are seeking truth.

Someone might object that if the principle of sufficient reason is replaced in the version of the cosmological argument I propose by a mere rationality norm, then the argument attains only a certain degree of probability, not certitude. If this objection means that the argument does not achieve the sort of absolute cogency which Leibniz hoped for, I concede. However, rationality norms underwrite all human thinking, even deductive argument in logic and mathematics, and thus it is too simple to suppose that if a rationality norm is explicitly adverted to in an argument, the argument is thereby admitted to be weak.

In some cases, such as the norms governing probability judgments, judging in accord with the norms is reasonable, but one is aware of specific reasons why, in the nature of the *sort of case* one is concerned with, one's judgments will sometimes turn out mistaken. In some cases, such as the choice of one's own career, one knows that there are incalculable risks, but one cannot estimate how great they are, since one's judgment as to what career would be best for him cannot be considered as a mere instance of a class of cases.

In other cases one has no specific reason whatever for supposing that the question is illegitimate, the reasoning unsound, or the judgment mistaken. Some strong rationality norms, such as the principle of illusion and evidence which Slote formulates, apply in such cases. One only has a choice in these cases if he considers the general fallibility of human thinking and averts to the lack of logical necessity which accompanies the acts of thinking at every step of the way.

All *acts* of thinking do lack logical necessity. For necessity is in the content of propositions, not in the acts of questioning, reasoning, and judging. Acts of thinking are just as distinct from the content of propositions as contingent states of affairs are from their own obtaining.

Methodical doubt or heuristic scepticism can be justified as reasonable procedures for testing how far one can proceed in doubting before coming to rock bottom. However, to insist at every step of a philosophical argument that the contradictory judgment is logically possible, that the reasoning could be unsound, and that the question might be meaningless is to speculate against the value of rational discourse. Speculation against the value of rational discourse, like monetary speculation, causes inflation. Elaborate arguments are constructed to show that rationally necessary acts of thinking are not logically necessary, and then a great deal of time and effort is wasted in futile attempts to show that rationally necessary acts are logically necessary.

To say "Still, this might be mistaken" can be salutary as a reminder of general human fallibility. But "might" which expresses mere logical possibility is strictly equivalent to "might not." A great deal of confusion is engendered by using "might" in this logical sense as if one had some basis for assertion—that is, as if "might" meant "more *likely*," when, in fact, what might be is altogether unlikely. A question might be meaningless, but if one has no good reason to think that it is, it is irresponsible to suggest that it might be in a way which is likely to lead someone to undertake the task of showing that the question *is not* meaningless.

I think that the rationality norms which replace the principle of sufficient reason in the version of the cosmological argument I am proposing are very strong. They are open to sceptical challenge. But unless specific objections, such as those proposed by Hume and Kant, are sustained, it seems to me that it is rationally—although not logically—necessary to ask why contingent states of affairs obtain, to assume that the question is answerable, to posit an uncaused cause which is a necessary being, and to be ready to pursue the inquiry into what this necessary being is. If specific objections, such as those of Hume and Kant, are not sustained, it would be unreasonable to block inquiry with an obscurantist refusal to proceed in this case as one would proceed in other investigations.

The argument is not, as the saying goes, knockdown. But the conclusion, assuming specific objections are met, should not be qualified as "probable." When one thinks as straight as one can and sees no special reason to suppose that the outcome might—"might" in a more than logical sense—be mistaken, one is entitled to say that one knows. To ask for more is to demand something which perhaps the angels have, but which is not available to human persons.

Summary restatement of the argument

Having developed the argument, I now restate it in summary form. This summary is not intended to replace the statement of the argument in the previous chapter, but only to help the reader to see the relationship among that statement of the argument, the treatment of the two important steps in the argument in the previous sections of the present chapter, and the matters still to be considered in parts three and four. It is especially important to notice that several concepts essential to the argument, including "cause" and "necessary entity," are defined only in the context of the statement of the argument in chapter four.

1. *Some contingent state of affairs obtains.* Nothing in the argument depends upon the particular content of the state of affairs from which it begins. Thus the argument can be generalized; it proceeds from any contingent state of affairs *which obtains.* "Contingent" here does not mean dependent or transitory. A contingent state of affairs is one which might or might not obtain; its obtaining does not follow from its being the state of affairs which it is. The primary evidence that there are contingent states of affairs is that we can know what it would be like for many states of affairs to obtain without knowing whether they obtain.

2. *It is reasonable to ask why any particular contingent state of affairs obtains and to expect an answer which would begin to provide an unconditional explanation.* An unconditional explanation would explain why a contingent state of affairs obtains otherwise than by reference to other contingent states of affairs themselves assumed to obtain. Although it is not reasonable, according to the preceding argument, to expect an explanation of why contingent states of affairs are *contingent,* it is reasonable to expect an explanation of why they *obtain,* unless there are good reasons for not

proceeding with the inquiry. Hume, Kant, and philosophers who more or less closely follow them argue that human knowledge is necessarily limited in certain ways which would rule out the question, the answer, or both. I argue in part three, chapters six to nine, that such attempts to delimit knowledge fail.

3. *The question why a contingent state of affairs obtains is not satisfactorily answered by positing a necessity which is identical with some or all contingent states of affairs.* Hegel attempts to overcome the distinction between what contingent states of affairs are and their obtaining by his theory of Absolute Spirit. Post-hegelian relativism limits philosophic explanation to cases in which meaning originates in human action and thus coincides with a state of affairs which obtains. I argue in part three, chapters ten to thirteen, that such attempts to comprehend obtaining—that is, to explain it without an uncaused cause—fail.

4. *The question why a contingent state of affairs obtains is not satisfactorily answered by saying that it obtains because it is the state of affairs which it is.* A noncontingent state of affairs can be explained in this way. Thus, if formal truths pick out states of affairs, it is reasonable to say that such states of affairs obtain—in the sense in which they do obtain—because they are what they are. It also is reasonable to say that an uncaused entity obtains simply because it is what it is. But since a contingent state of affairs is the state of affairs which it is whether it obtains or not, what a contingent state of affairs is cannot explain its obtaining.

5. *The question why a contingent state of affairs obtains can and must be answered by saying that there is an uncaused entity, which necessarily obtains, and which causes contingent states of affairs to obtain.* It must be admitted that in saying this one uses language in irregular ways. But an irregular use of language need not be arbitrary. If the way in which the irregular use is derived from ordinary uses can be clarified, extension and stretching of ordinary language and the bending of linguistic rules can be reasonable. In part four I try to clarify the ways in which language is used in the conclusion of the argument and argue that the irregularity of these uses is reasonable.

6. *To say that a contingent state of affairs is caused by an uncaused cause is only a partial answer to the question why it obtains.* This answer is only partial for two reasons. No particular contingent state of affairs obtains in isolation. The relationship of contingent states of affairs to one another is part of the explanation of why they obtain. Philosophical and scientific explanations complement one another and in a sense bear upon the same subject matter, but they cannot substitute for one another. Moreover, the uncaused cause, Dc, and the uncaused entity which is its nucleus, D, emerge

from the argument only as theoretical entities which are posited to satisfy the conditions of the problem. What is D in itself? How does Dc bring about contingent states of affairs? Such questions naturally arise, and it is false to suggest that one has a complete unconditional explanation of why contingent states of affairs obtain unless these questions are answered.

God, god, and gods

If the preceding argument were not somehow relevant to religion and to the great human concerns centered in the religious aspect of life, it would be of little interest. But the histories of philosophy and theology make clear that there is some relationship between an argument of this sort and him with whom—or that with which—religion is concerned. The main point of the present section is to clarify the relationship between the theoretical entity posited through the argument and the divine entity or entities worshipped in religious rites. A secondary point is to relate the argument I propose to other ways of reasoning toward God—I use "God" here as equivalent to the cumbersome phrase "God, god, or the gods."

Thomas Aquinas ends each of the Five Ways with a phrase identifying the entity to which that way of reasoning points as God: "and this everyone understands to be God," "to which everyone gives the name 'God,'" and so on. Perhaps Thomas—who, after all, was writing theology—used "everyone" to refer to a well-defined group, namely, philosophically sophisticated Christians of his own time. But still one feels that he made a crucial, final step of the argument too easily.

If one is to identify a theoretical entity, such as the uncaused entity toward which the preceding argument points, with an entity called "God," some clarification is needed of the relationship between reasoning of the sort involved in the argument and religious concerns. I do not mean that a further clarification is needed of the relationship between philosophy and theology, reason and faith. The question rather is how acts of reasoning and religious acts are related to one another.

This subject is important, vast, and difficult. However, the main lines of a sketch which I hope will be adequate for the present purpose can be marked out quite briefly.

Part of the difficulty of the question is the logic of the concept of *God*. Is *God* a proper name, a predicable, or some other sort of concept? A recent book-length study is devoted to this question. To try to fit *God* into any one of these categories—while attending to the use of "God" in a variety of religious contexts—leads to logical difficulties.[22]

The author of the study to which I refer refrains from drawing a conclusion which, I am afraid, incautious readers of his book are likely to draw, namely, that since *God* does not easily fit into the logical categories which are used in thinking about what is not God, "God" is a meaningless word and God does not exist. Unfortunately, fallacious inferences of this sort are not uncommon. Thus it is worth giving the fallacy a name. I call it the "procrustean-bed fallacy."

To dissolve the puzzles engendered by arguments involving a procrustean-bed fallacy, one must show how to put God to bed elsewhere or how to stretch the bed to fit him. In other words, one must show that there are other categories than those admitted in the argument or that the categories admitted in the argument need not be applied in so restrictive a way. Thus, the present section must also suggest a solution to the problem of the logical status of the concepts expressed by "God," "god," and "the gods."

The first and most obvious point is that these words need not be taken as having a single meaning in all their many occurrences, nor need the concepts they express be assumed to have a single logical role. Still, the words are not used with altogether different meanings, and this suggests that there is some consistent logic of the various roles played by the concepts which these words express.

The meanings of "God" are partly the same and partly different. Thus, when pagans said "the gods" and when Christians said "God" ("God, the Father of Our Lord, Jesus Christ"), they obviously did not mean the same thing. Still, when pagans said "the gods" and Christians said "God," their expressions had related meanings. St. Paul in Athens was able to pick one of the many gods worshipped there as a suitable referent for his preaching about Christ crucified; the god he picked was one worshipped at a shrine dedicated "To an Unknown God." Paul said that the God he proclaimed was the one the Athenians already worshipped without knowing it (Acts 17:23).

Many who believe in God and whose main interest in philosophical arguments such as the one I propose is a religious interest undoubtedly feel considerable disappointment when they read of an "uncaused cause," an "uncaused entity," and so on. As I explained at the beginning of chapter four, the argument I propose does not presuppose a meaning and reference for the word "God," and then set out to prove that God exists. Each reader can decide for himself whether *D* is what he calls "God" or not. How might one make this decision?

The initial reflections of some believers might be along the following lines. "When I think of God, I do not think of some peculiar state of affairs called 'an uncaused entity.' What I think of is someone much more personal and relevant to my own life. The world is in a complete mess. We are all likely to be wiped out in an eventual nuclear war. Corruption abounds. We've tried everything to solve our problems. First education became progressive and then it became permissive. What is worse, my own life is a mess too. I know I am a bum. My wife went to a psychiatrist who talked her into the idea that she needed broader experience of interpersonal relationships—with him. I just can't believe that life as we know it is all there is. There must be something better, or nothing makes sense. Personally, I just cannot accept the idea that nothing makes sense. So I believe in God. As far as I am concerned, God is someone up there who *cares* and who will make things come out right in the end."

This way of thinking about God seems utterly different from the argument of the preceding section. But there is a relationship between the two.

The rabbis, in commenting upon Genesis, noticed that when Abraham makes his first appearance (Gen. 12:1), he is being addressed by God, who orders him to leave his home and native land, and to move to a distant country. Why did Abraham pay any attention to the order? How did he know that there is a God who is Lord of the world? To answer this question a parable was constructed. Abraham was like a traveler who came to a place where he saw a building ablaze ("doleket," which means either *brightly lighted* or *burning down*). The traveler did not see anyone around and he wondered, "Is it possible that this building has no owner who cares for it?" The owner looked out and said, "I am the owner of the building." Similarly, because Abraham wondered, "Is it possible that the world has no Lord?" the Holy One looked out and said to him, "I am the Lord; I care for the world."[23]

The parable, being ambiguous, was interpreted in two ways. One interpretation was that Abraham reasoned to the existence of a Lord of the universe from the evidence of divine causality one finds in it. This interpretation most naturally fits the pattern of an argument from design, but it might be stretched to fit a cosmological argument. Finding the world ablaze with the metaphysical brightness of *obtaining,* which brings it out of the night of *nonobtaining,* Abraham reasons that there must be an uncaused entity. Another interpretation was that Abraham was ready to receive God's orders because he was looking for a redeemer. The world is destroying itself with evil; is it possible that there is no one who cares enough to put things right? This interpretation, obviously, is nearer to the thinking of the believer, sketched above, who considers God to be someone "much more personal and relevant to my own life."

In fact, the ways of thinking have a great deal in common. In each case one encounters a set of facts which raise a question to which one finds no satisfactory answer in the world of experience. At this point one might give up wondering and accept the absurdity of it all. But acceptance of absurdity is not easy for the human mind. There is an alternative, namely, to suppose that there is an answer to the question, but that this answer points outside the world of experience to an unseen reality, to a being or beings unlike anything in the world of experience.

This general pattern of reasoning can be carried out in many diverse ways. These differ not only in their starting points but also in the mistakes to which they are liable. Thus the entities at which various examples of such reasoning arrive are described quite differently.

No matter how reasoning of this sort is carried out, the conclusion is of more than theoretical interest. Such reasoning begins in wonder, and reasoning which begins in wonder normally ends with an attempt to adjust oneself more adequately to reality. Thus, those who follow this pattern of reasoning to its conclusion make an effort to take into account in their dealings with the world and with other persons the reality of the unseen to which that conclusion points. But since the details of the ways in which such reasoning is carried out vary considerably, the efforts to take into account the that-to-which instances of it point also vary considerably.

In most cultures of the past and in many of the present, reasoning of this sort is not an individual project, although individuals obviously contribute to the common inquiry. A tribe, a society, or a whole cultural group carries on such reasoning, draws the conclusions, and experiments with ways of adjusting life to the reality of the unseen as it comes to be conceived.

For example, if a couple happen to have sexual intercourse in a field and if that field produces an unusually good crop the following season, then since there clearly is a relation between the two events, and since it is not clear how the first caused the second, it is only natural to assume that the invisible reality makes the connection. Having intercourse in the fields at an appropriate time thus becomes part of the right way to take the reality of the unseen into account when dealing with the world.

Thus a basic reasoning pattern establishes a referent which, once available, readily becomes a dumping ground for anything which cannot be easily disposed of in one of the other categories built up by experience and available for use in a given culture. A system of behavior grows up around the unseen reality in an attempt to deal with it suitably. Obviously, what happens to be dumped in each culture's dumping ground will lead to even greater diversities among the complexes of behavior adopted for dealing with the unseen. This diversity multiplies the diversity which arises from the variety of ways in which people reason to the unseen.

Furthermore, there is a dynamic relationship between a conception of the unseen and the pattern of behavior intended to adapt life to it. People seek what they expect and expect what they get. Man experiments with the unseen just as he experiments with the visible world and with society itself.

The word "god" is used in one sense, at least, to refer to anything which is arrived at by the general pattern of reasoning to something unseen. Not every *invisible* reality is regarded as a god. The whole pattern of reasoning defines the meaning of "god." In other words, any entity can be called "god" in this sense only if it is posited to answer questions for which one otherwise has no answer and for which having no answer at all seems rationally unacceptable.

Corresponding to "god" in this sense is religion in general. In other words, any way of adjusting to the reality of an entity which is a god is religious. An integrated system of such ways of adjusting is a religion. Whatever is necessary to integrate the system is added to the concept of god; there is considerable freedom to make such additions, since the concept to begin with is quite broad. Thus the characteristics of gods differ greatly from place to place and vary from time to time.

The functional relationship between a god and a religion obviously entails that there are at least as many gods as there are religions. If two religions are partly alike, their gods will be partly the same and partly different. This consideration clarifies many puzzles—for example, whether Moslems and Christians worship the same God, whether Lutherans and Roman Catholics worship the same God, and so on. The answer in each case is "more or less"; in the latter case rather more than less, and more than in the former. But both cases can be contrasted with the much greater difference between St. Paul's God and the Unknown God of his Athenian audience.

The multiplying of gods and of religions not only occurs among different cultural groups. Within one culture the unseen can be found to have incompatible properties or can be assigned incompatible roles. Since a single entity cannot have incompatible properties or fulfill incompatible roles, as many gods as necessary are posited. There is a corresponding multiplication of religions, or of subsystems within a religion. Religious systems also are affected by various social stresses and strains. If one group of worshippers cannot get along with another group—perhaps for reasons which initially have nothing to do with their god—their religions will diverge and their gods consequently begin to differ.

When a group of people pays attention to the facts that other religions are different from their own and that the unseen entities to which others are devoted are not identical with the unseen entity to which they are devoted, they naturally give their own god a proper name. At the same time, recognizing the similarities among unseen entities, they need a common name or a descriptive phrase for gods and they need predicables to signify the characteristics of divine beings. The proper name can be used interchangeably with a suitably definite description—for example, "Yahweh" with "the God of our Fathers." Moreover, there is nothing inconsistent in saying both that Yahweh is the only God and that he is the God of gods. "God" is not used in the same sense in all three cases, although the senses are closely related.

In his *Metaphysics* Aristotle offers an argument to the existence of an unseen entity, a primary, self-thinking thought. He wishes to call this entity "God," although obviously it is very different from the gods with which most of his readers were familiar. (It also is quite different from *D*.) Reflecting upon the discrepancy, Aristotle remarks that the ancestors had handed down a myth that the divine encloses the whole of nature and that the primary reality is God. But the myth picked up accretions in the course of its tradition, and Aristotle suggests that if the accretions are stripped away, the residual myth—which is compatible with his own view—must be regarded as an inspired utterance.[24]

Aristotle obviously is engaging in persuasive definition. He is rejecting the establishment gods and proposing what he considers a better idea—a god built to satisfy a philosopher's mind and heart. That there is heart as well as mind in Aristotle's reflection is evident from the following beautiful passage:

> If, then, God is always in that good state [contemplative thought] in which we sometimes are, this compels our wonder; and if in a better this compels it yet more. And God *is* in a better state. And life also belongs to God; for the actuality of thought is life, and God is that actuality; and God's self-dependent actuality is life most good and eternal. We say therefore that God is a living being, eternal, most good, so that life and duration continuous and eternal belong to God; for this *is* God.[25]

Aristotle builds his ethics on a religious principle proportionate to this god. His religion is simple and austere: to imitate God as much as possible by devoting oneself to the philosophic life of contemplation. "We must not follow those who advise us, being men, to think of human things, and, being mortal, of mortal things," Aristotle urges, "but must, so far as we can, make ourselves immortal, and strain every nerve to live in accordance with the best thing in us," namely, the intellect, "for even if it be small in bulk, much more does it in power and worth surpass everything."[26]

Such reasoning exemplifies a philosophical reduction of the divine to rational categories. The reader might wonder whether the argument to the uncaused entity, which I propose, is intended to accomplish a similar reduction.

I will argue in chapters fifteen through seventeen that there cannot be many uncaused causes and that there is a sense in which there is just one. However, I am not proposing the uncaused entity as such as an object of religion. In other words, my intention is not to suggest, without adding anything further, that *D* is God. The concept of *D* is considerably less rich than that of Aristotle's god, and Aristotle's god is not a very adequate object of worship. What I am ready to call "God" without qualification is the Trinity in whose name and names I bless myself whenever I make the sign of the cross. The logical relationship between *D* and the Trinity is that *D* is a definite description of that for which "the Father and the Son and the Holy Spirit" is a proper name and of them for whom "Father," "Son," and "Holy Spirit" are proper names. How these names are introduced into discourse and how a single definite description can correspond to four proper names are matters considered to some extent in chapter twenty-four.

Arguments quite different from the one I propose also yield definite descriptions of something which I would call "God" without qualification. For example, many philosophers and theologians reject a straightforward cosmological argument in favor of a moral argument for the existence of God. Some moral arguments so clearly beg the question that they can hardly be taken as articulations of the manner in which anyone actually reasons to God. However, many such arguments proceed along lines which are illustrated by Plato's thought, at least according to some interpretations of it. Plato seems to argue that there must be a transcendent Good which backs up fundamental human values even when men ignore and violate them—backs them up not by enforcement but by giving them an objectivity which stands up against human weakness, ignorance, and malice. I think most Jews and Christians tend to identify this Good as God, even though Plato does not call it "god."[27]

Perhaps every morally good person reasons along the lines Plato marks out. If so, every morally good person accepts the reality of something which most Christians and Jews would identify with God. Everyone, of course, is an atheist relative to the gods in which he does not believe. However, if moral reasoning along Plato's lines is correct, then any morally upright person who received a revelation—if revelation is possible—would be able to refer the revelation to the reality toward which he directs his moral aspiration, respect, and submission.

If this conclusion is correct, then those who maintain that there can be no reasoning to God apart from faith also might be correct; on their view a person's first morally right act cannot occur before the grace of faith, by which sinful man is justified.[28] Of course, the view that God is known implicitly in all moral knowledge also implies that if the religious act of faith is itself a morally good act, then there is some rational knowledge about God antecedent—not necessarily temporally, but logically—to the act of faith. For on this position the knowledge which a person requires to do any morally good act would imply some rational knowledge of the Good which backs up fundamental human values. Of course, this knowledge would not need to be explicitly articulated; it could be a matter of nonformal inferences.

If there are different sound arguments for the existence of something transcendent which a believer would call "God," the difference among such arguments which is philosophically interesting is what they yield for reflection. Arguments which are closer to moral and emotional needs always will have more existential force and will be preferred by those whose main orientation in talking about God is ethical. The argument I propose, if it is sound, has the advantage of being defensible against the philosophical objections to be examined in part three and of serving as a good point of departure for the further linguistic clarifications proposed in part four.

III: Criticism of Alternatives

6: The Empiricist Alternative

Introduction to part three

The other sections of the present chapter provide a brief exposition of Hume's criticism of the cosmological argument and of the philosophic perspective, alternative to the one I am developing, from which he made that criticism. But before beginning this exposition, I think it very important to clarify the purpose of this part of the book and to enlist the reader's cooperation in achieving this purpose.

Like the present chapter, the even-numbered chapters of part three are expository; the odd-numbered chapters are critical. The exposition is not offered as history of philosophy in any strict sense; more important, the criticism is not intended as polemic.

I offer an exposition of only those aspects of the thought of Hume, Kant, and Hegel with which I am directly concerned. Similarly, in chapter twelve I try to describe more clearly and fully the metaphysical exploitation of contemporary philosophical methods which I call "post-hegelian relativism." These expositions are hardly more than rough résumés, which must be supplemented—and perhaps corrected—by more complete and accurate historical knowledge already in the reader's possession or available to him in scholarly histories of philosophy.

In many cases diverse interpretations of a position are defensible. If on some interpretation a philosophy does not present the obstacle to the philosophical theology which I am trying to develop that I think it does, then I simply am not concerned with the philosophy interpreted in that way. I have no desire to make straw men of great philosophers; I am aiming at real

94

obstacles confronting my own argument, which I *think* were articulated in the work of these philosophers and which I *think* can be surmounted by means of the criticisms I propose. But it is the reality of the obstacle and the effectiveness of the criticism, not the accuracy of the résumé, which is most essential for my purposes.

The philosophies with which I am concerned in this part are not important to what I am attempting to do in the book as a whole merely because they happen to include particular objections which can be made and answered within very limited perspectives. They do include some objections of this sort, and I have already tried to deal with some of these as the argument proceeded in part two. However, these philosophies also raise diverse fundamental challenges to my whole approach. Many of the most important objections, in each case, go back to a single, fundamental issue of principle.

The various issues can be summarized as follows. The philosophical theology which I am developing embodies the position that the distinction we find in experienced things between *what* and *that*—between what a contingent state of affairs is and its contingent obtaining—points to an extraempirical entity which explains why contingent states of affairs obtain. In this extraempirical entity, *D, what* and *that* are unified, although not identified, since the only requirement for it to obtain is that it be what it is.

One radical alternative to this philosophical theology is presented by philosophies in which *what* and *that* cannot be unified by any extraempirical principle or by anything within experience. I take Hume to be the most important representative of this alternative.

A second alternative is presented by philosophies in which *what* and *that* cannot be unified by anything within experience, and also cannot point human inquiry beyond experience to any possible extraempirical principle of explanation. I take Kant to be the most important representative of this alternative. Kant does not deny the reality of the extraempirical, but he closes the path of *theoretical* inquiry to it.

A third alternative is presented by philosophies in which *what* and *that* are theoretically unified, not by any extraempirical principle, but by a principle which man can understand as pervading experience as a whole, once experience becomes fully articulate to itself. I take Hegel to be the most important representative of this alternative.

A fourth alternative is presented by a set of contemporary ways of thinking which agree with Hume to the extent that Hume excludes theoretical explanation which would unify *what* and *that*, which agree with Kant to the extent that Kant excludes any principle for unifying *what* and *that* which could be articulated in the language appropriate for making descriptive statements about the empirical world, and which agree with Hegel in positing a principle of unification within experience itself. Here, as I have explained, I am concerned not so much with any single philosophy as with a certain manner of exploiting a variety of philosophical methods for metaphysical purposes.

In some cases the originators of these methods probably would object strenuously to the metaphysical exploitation of their methods, which they intended for more modest purposes. In such cases I only attack the exploitation of the method; I by no means attack the method and its legitimate uses. No obstacle arises for me unless these methods are exploited in such a way as to *confine* philosophical explanation within islands of intelligibility formed within experience by human action, when such action generates certain *relatively* noncontingent unities of *what* and *that*. I call this fourth alternative "post-hegelian relativism"; a brief introduction to it already was given in chapter five (pages 61-62).

In view of my stated purpose of dealing with radical philosophical alternatives to the philosophical theology I am developing, the reader might wonder why I do not simply sketch out the positions, without referring at all to actual philosophers. The answer is that I think the historical references will provide a kind of bridge—perhaps shaky, yet helpful—between my arguments and the philosophical world in which any working philosopher already has his own bearings. Using this bridge, I hope, a reader will be better able to understand the obstacles which I am struggling to surmount. Moreover, many contemporary philosophers assume that classical modern philosophy permanently destroyed any possibility of developing a philosophical theology along the lines proposed in part two. I think that the arguments proposed in the critical chapters of the present part render this assumption implausible. But these arguments could not alter an assumption about history if it were not possible for the reader to see a relationship between the criticisms I propose and the works of Hume, Kant, and Hegel which one might suppose definitively block my project.

I realize how maddening it is to encounter an exposition of the thought of some philosopher whom one greatly respects, and to find the exposition not as perfect as it should be. I also realize how maddening it is to find oneself seemingly consigned to the box of some "ism," weighted with the cast iron of opinions one does not recognize as one's own, and unceremoniously cast into the sea of rejected counterpositions. I realize these things because I myself have read numerous résumés of Thomas Aquinas's thought which I would hardly have recognized if his name had not been mentioned, and I have found myself being dismissed by the attachment of the label of the "ism" which is derived from his name.

There is a depth of wisdom in the work of every great philosopher, and there is a uniqueness in the vision of every genuine philosopher; the individuality of the thought of even a beginning student must be respected. Thus, it always is possible to see how the description of a position which is criticized is not exactly one's own—nor precisely that of any philosopher whom one respects. But when one meets criticism, even if it seems not quite on target, there is something to be gained in working with the critic, rather than in dismissing him as an inept opponent.

Much of what is *different* in the preceding part of this book—whether it is ultimately defensible or not—I reached in trying to see what is effective in criticisms of views I used to hold, criticisms which in many cases could have been dismissed without dishonesty. "I don't hold that God is a logically necessary being"; "I don't consider the principle of sufficient reason to be true"; "I don't make the specific logical mistakes in using the word 'God' pointed out in this article." Rejoinders such as these are fair enough. But I also began to realize that in many cases I was holding some indefensible view somewhat similar to the one being objected to, somewhere in the neighborhood of the target of the criticism.

Thus if the reader finds himself dissatisfied with specific points in the argument of the preceding part, I ask him to attempt to correct and improve the argument so that it is more adequate and more satisfying. If it is not possible to improve the argument by touching it up, however, I ask the reader to try to find something in the present part which can be applied to his own thinking as a legitimate criticism of it. Once this criticism is taken into account and necessary adjustments made, perhaps such a reader's revised position will permit the argument I propose to go through, after some necessary revisions.

If a reader has objections which would exclude as *impossible* the approach I am trying to develop, although nothing in the present part of the book touches his position, then perhaps it will be found that I have wholly missed one or more fundamental philosophical alternatives. The uncovering of such alternatives will show that the line of thinking I am attempting to develop has further obstacles to overcome, or else that it is altogether futile.

I am not so self-confident as to rule out the last possibility. However, I am confident that no one can *exclude* one metaphysical attempt unless he endorses and supports some alternative attempt. The sceptic who simply doubts and doubts excludes nothing; the sceptic who tries to show the impossibility of some sort of knowledge has taken philosophical ground which he must rationally defend, just as any other position must be defended. No philosophically interesting position can be rationally defended, so far as I can see, unless one at least implicitly takes a definite stand on the question of the relationship between *what* and *that.*

Hume's criticisms of a cosmological argument

One classical set of objections to a cosmological argument, somewhat similar to that proposed in part two, was first developed by David Hume. Many recent philosophers adapt and develop Hume's arguments. For the sake of having a convenient label I call those who do so "empiricists" and call the underlying position "empiricism," although some philosophers sharing the views with which I am concerned might not regard themselves as empiricists and some who consider themselves empiricists might not share these views.

What follows is a summary of the main points Hume makes against the version of the cosmological argument he criticizes; some of his fundamental philosophical positions which are essential for understanding these objections also are briefly explained. The historical background and the arguments Hume offers in favor of his positions will not be developed here; interested readers might consult standard works.[1] Nor will I consider here Hume's positions on topics—for example, miracles—which I will discuss in later parts of this book, and adaptations and developments of Hume's positions by other empiricists which I will consider in chapter seven.

The place in Hume's works most relevant to the argument which I proposed in part two is Part IX of his *Dialogues Concerning Natural Religion.* Although the criticism of the cosmological argument outlined there is put in the mouth of one of the characters in the dialogue, this criticism expresses Hume's own view; it squares with the rest of his philosophical work.

The argument proposed for criticism is said to be "a priori." Hume uses this expression here in a special sense. The argument from design is called "a posteriori," because it begins from a description of special features of observed facts—namely, the orderliness of the world—while the cosmological argument requires only the fact that something exists, together with general principles.

The argument which Hume outlines and subjects to criticism proceeds as follows.

"Whatever exists must have a cause or reason of its existence, it being absolutely impossible for anything to produce itself or be the cause of its own existence." But infinite regress is excluded; therefore, there must be an "ultimate cause that is *necessarily* existent." The argument against infinite regress grants a regress in time, and seems to admit that the chain of causes and effects could be eternal. But "the question is still reasonable why this particular succession of causes existed from eternity, and not any other succession or no succession at all." If there is no necessarily existent being, then why should something else not have existed, rather than what does, or nothing at all? The determination among possibilities requires an explanation.

External causes are ruled out by hypothesis; chance is assumed to be meaningless; nothingness does not explain. "We must, therefore, have recourse to a necessarily existent Being who carries the *reason* of his existence in himself, and who cannot be supposed not to exist, without an express contradiction." This entity is identified as God.

The first criticism Hume proposes, and the one on which he asserts his willingness to rest the whole argument, is that it is absurd to try to demonstrate a matter of fact or to prove it by argument *a priori*. Only something the opposite of which implies a contradiction is demonstrable. Nothing distinctly conceivable implies a contradiction. One can imagine the nonexistence as easily as one can imagine the existence of any being. Thus, no entity can be demonstrated to exist.

Hume develops this point by saying that the argument under attack supposes that just as one who understands "two plus two" perceives it to be impossible for the sum not to be equal to four, so if one knew God's whole essence, one would perceive it to be impossible for him not to exist. Hume replies that "it is evident that this can never happen, while our faculties remain the same as at present." One always can conceive the nonexistence of whatever one has conceived to exist, and thus the expression "necessary existence" is meaningless.

Hume drives the point home by suggesting that perhaps the necessarily existent being, if there were one, could be identified with the material universe itself. Hume wishes to point out that one supposes the material universe not necessarily existent precisely by application of the following criterion: One can conceive the nonexistence of any particle of matter or any natural form. Hume suggests that it is equally possible to conceive God nonexistent or his attributes altered.

Hume next argues that there cannot be a general cause of an eternal chain of causes and effects, because the first cause would have to be prior to its effect and thus before eternity. Moreover, any effect must begin at some time; something both eternal and an effect is absurd. Moreover, Hume suggests that an infinite chain of causes and effects would need nothing outside itself, since every element would be adequately accounted for, and the whole is nothing but an observer's summation of the parts.

Hume next suggests that perhaps the universe as a whole is necessary in all its parts and arrangement. This suggestion is put forth speculatively. The possibility being proposed is that perhaps the entities from which the argument was intended to begin contain within themselves the sufficient reason of their existence. The implication would be that there is a necessarily existent being, but this being would be the universe itself, not God the creator. The necessary being would be a pantheistic god, not the God of Christians.

Hume ends the attack by urging that arguments of the sort being criticized are not very convincing even to believers. He supposes that this fact indicates that there is a source of religion other than in such reasoning. This comment is a bridge to other arguments in the following parts of the *Dialogues*.

Hume's argument with respect to infinite regress adds nothing to the arguments considered in the first section of chapter five. It is worth noticing that the version of the cosmological argument Hume criticizes uses the principle of sufficient reason in a way that would eliminate contingency. The argument also assumes a regress of causes and effects in time, and then moves to the necessary being as a principle outside time. Hume's criticism of the argument also assumes that a cause must precede its effect. This assumption is essential to Hume's general theory of causality, as I shall explain.

Hume's suggestion that the universe might itself be its own cause or sufficient reason is an important possibility later developed fully by Hegel. Hume is not in a position to provide arguments which would make this possible approach plausible, since the position in its developed form is inconsistent with Hume's general philosophical outlook.

Thus there remain to be considered the contentions that a matter of fact cannot be demonstrated and that the expression "necessary existence" is meaningless, as well as Hume's general theory of causality.

One not familiar with Hume's philosophy is likely to wonder why he supposes that matters of fact are not demonstrable. Surely the sciences demonstrate laws—for example, did not Darwin demonstrate the evolution of species, which is a matter of fact? The opposite obviously is not inconceivable, yet the evolution theory seems to be established as an account of the biological facts. And must not the ultimate stuff of the universe, particles of matter or quanta of energy or whatever, exist necessarily? Any change presupposes this stuff as substratum; thus it seems absurd that the ultimate stuff itself should ever cease to exist.

Such objections, which might seem plausible in themselves, do not touch the point Hume is making. He is not denying the demonstrability of matters of fact, if "demonstration" is taken to mean *scientific proof.* Thus objections of this sort are simply irrelevant. To see why, one must go back to the foundations of Hume's attack upon the cosmological argument.

The basis of Hume's attack

The fundamental principles of Hume's philosophy, on which the points about demonstrability, necessity, and factuality are based, are stated concisely and adequately for present purposes in Sections II through VII of Hume's *An Enquiry Concerning Human Understanding.*

Hume grounds his position, in Section II, on a distinction between impressions and ideas. These together he calls "perceptions of the mind." The two differ by their force or liveliness. An impression is a lively perception, as when one sees, hears, feels, desires, loves, hates, or wills. Ideas are less lively perceptions, formed when one reflects. Ideas can be combined, altered, and so on. One can form with ideas, and thus conceive, anything which does not imply an absolute contradiction.

Given this distinction, Hume sets up an extremely important methodological principle. Ideas are faint; one is likely to become confused in working with them; one can use words supposing them to have a meaning when their meaning has been lost. Impressions are vivid; their distinctions are clear; one cannot easily make mistakes with them. Thus, if one suspects

> ... that a philosophical term is employed without any meaning or idea (as is but too frequent), we need but enquire, *from what impression is that supposed idea derived?* And if it be impossible to assign any, this will serve to confirm our suspicion.

Hume's point is that thinking must be reduced to immediate experience. Hume puts this point in psychological terms, but the methodological implications can be translated in line with Hume's purposes into a theory of meaning.[2]

In Section III Hume goes on to assert that ideas in memory and imagination are connected together. There are laws of their association. The three relations which he considers adequate to account for the connections of ideas are resemblance, contiguity, and cause-and-effect. The working of these laws of association indicates how one can have more in his thinking than he does in his experience; the fact that the organization of ideas is a matter of psychological laws *of association* suggests at once that the "more" one thus gets in his thinking is not necessarily more knowledge of the real world.

In Section IV Hume lays down a distinction which has come to be called Hume's "fork." Objects of human inquiry are of two kinds: relations of ideas and matters of fact. Inquiries of the former sort do not depend upon the existence of anything. One can get answers which are absolutely certain by mere thinking, for the questions only concern the way in which different ideas are related to each other. Inquiries of the second sort are concerned with existence. The contrary of any matter of fact is still possible: one cannot tell what is the case merely by thinking; one must look and see. If one cannot immediately settle questions of fact by looking and seeing, one must fall back on reasoning by cause and effect.

This distinction is called Hume's "fork" because it is a strict either/or. Either a statement is about relations of ideas or it is about matters of fact. If the former, it can be necessarily true, but it is not informative about anything in the world; if the latter, it is informative, but it cannot be necessarily true.

The distinction Hume is making can be exemplified, first, with respect to reasoning about relations of ideas. The examples he mentions are mathematical studies. A simple, nonmathematical example would be: "All bachelors are unmarried men, and no unmarried men have wives, therefore, no bachelors have wives." The reasoning is sound, but it merely relates the various expressions to each other. The premises would remain true and the argument valid even if every man on earth were to get married. The opposite of such a proposition is not simply false, but self-contradictory. One cannot imagine a bachelor who is not an unmarried man. Of course, bachelors do get married, but then they cease being bachelors.

The point also can be exemplified with respect to reasoning about matters of fact. If one wishes to know whether a certain old friend, who used to be a bachelor, has married or not, one cannot find out by mere thinking. One might look into the records of marriages. This is not the same as seeing the marriage itself, but one reasons: "All whose marriages are certified in the records are married; this man's marriage is certified; therefore, he is married." One's reasoning might or might not be sound, but that is not the point. The point is that one is relying upon certain cause-effect connections: marriages are certified in the public records only after a couple has married. Hume's example is more striking. That the sun will not rise tomorrow is no less intelligible than that it will rise. Neither of these propositions is self-contradictory. In this sense one cannot *demonstrate* that the sun will rise tomorrow. One must wait and see. Meanwhile, one expects sunrise at a certain time tomorrow on the basis of causal laws.

But how does one learn about causes and their effects? Not by mere reasoning, Hume says, but by experience. Effects and causes are distinct from one another. No matter how long one considered something which is an effect or something which is a cause, one would never suspect the relation except one finds it by experience. There is never anything inconceivable in either the cause or the effect existing just as it now exists without the other, nor is there anything self-contradictory in the relationship being other than one experiences it. The only reason such suppositions might seem absurd is that one is so used to some connection between causes and effects that one finds it hard to imagine things going otherwise than one has learned by experience that they do go.

Hume goes on in the second part of Section IV to argue that the basis in experience of cause-effect reasoning cannot itself be reduced to reasoning.

The point is that the causal connections can be very strong, but they cannot have logical necessity. Reasoning on the basis of cause and effect proceeds from cases previously experienced to further cases not yet experienced. One supposes that experience points to hidden properties, and that these hidden properties remain constant if outward appearances remain constant. But this expectation has no absolute necessity about it. Logically, one is going from "All the x's I have experienced have been followed by y's" to "All x's whatsoever always will be followed by y's." The generalization step which is at the basis of every cause-effect argument is natural enough, but it has no logical necessity. Hume is here pointing very strongly to the difference between induction and deduction; his point is that the induction which is required for empirical reasoning is itself grounded not in logical necessity but in the mere fact that one expects the future to resemble the past. This itself is a fact one has grounds for in experience, but not logically compelling grounds; the only grounds are in induction.

In Section V Hume further develops this point. A grown man, suddenly waking up in the world, would not be able to reason about matters of fact until he had gained some experience. The connections which are observed have no obvious necessity. A subjective principle—custom or habit—leads one to expect previously experienced sequences to recur. Even animals learn by experience. Imagining something fictional and believing something factual differ in this: the factual belief is "more vivid, lively, forcible, firm, steady." The peculiarity of conceptions involved in belief "arises from a customary conjunction of the object with something present to the memory or the senses." One expects a piece of wood, thrown onto the embers, to make the fire burn more rapidly, because one has experienced this sort of thing before. One can conceive that the wood might instead put the fire out.

It is easy to find a more plausible illustration of Hume's point. The gas in a bottle of compressed oxygen appears very similar to that in a bottle of compressed carbondioxide. If one had no experience of what happens when each is released near a fire, one never could predict the effects simply by examining the two gases. Yet one knows by experience that the oxygen makes the fire flame up while the carbondioxide is a good extinguisher. The point is more difficult to see when one thinks about logs, because their effect on fire is more familiar. But if one had no prior experience, how would one know what might happen when one puts a log in a fire?

Hume also is aware, of course, that one can draw some factual conclusions from established scientific laws. But the fact that one can do this does not undermine his point. These laws themselves must ultimately be reduced to experience; they only express very strong expectations based upon connections which, ultimately, are given. Scientific laws are not based on relations of ideas to which one can reason; one must first look and see what the world is like. Only then can one use logic and mathematics to help *organize* what one learns by experience.

In Section VI Hume offers an explanation of probability, which fits it into his general position.

In Section VII Hume rounds out his argument. Assuming the principle that ideas must be derived from impressions, he looks for the impression from which the idea of necessary connection, which is involved in relations of cause and effect, is derived. One assumes that there is a power in the cause which necessarily brings about the effect. Hume considers various possible ways of locating the required impression and concludes that there is none. All the cases of the operations of bodies or minds that he can think of do not yield any impression of a power or necessary connection, so long as one only considers a single instance in which one event is observed to follow another.

But when one often experiences similar events connected together, one feels there is a connection between events in such pairs. This feeling of connection, which is altogether a matter of human psychology, is the impression from which one gets the idea of necessity which is built into the idea of cause. The objectification of this necessity is a mistake, but a mistake quite naturally made. The first instance of one billiard ball hitting another is just like later ones, but only after many experiences does one learn what to expect. The only difference between later instances and the first one is that the later instances are later; instances accumulate to make many like instances. The difference is not in the instances, but in the observer, who eventually expects what he did not at first expect. Thus, the idea of necessity in the causal relation really is nothing but the pull one feels toward what one expects because of the habit which is built up by repeated past experiences.

With this theory of causality Hume excludes any ground for arguing by causality from experience to anything which one has never experienced at all. One can argue from what one now experiences to something one does not now experience, working by connections learned from past experience. This process might be very complex, since one can proceed by way of the whole of natural science. But ultimately all arguments about matters of fact must begin with given facts and must proceed by way of connections, based upon experience, from one fact to another.

Hume does not maintain that anything begins to exist without a cause; in fact, he characterizes the supposition that something might arise without a cause as absurd.[3] But he believes that this general principle is like particular causal laws in that it also must be learned by experience. Thus, the causal principle as Hume understands it cannot be used as a basis for arguing to an extraempirical entity. The cause which is always to be looked for—and which one can expect will be found—will be a prior state of affairs within experience itself. And it too, if it began, also has a cause, and so on *ad infinitum.* This throws light on Hume's understanding of the infinite regress aspect of the argument regarding the existence of God.

This summary of the foundations of Hume's philosophy should be adequate to clarify the four main points which are usually made in attacks by empiricists against arguments such as the one Hume criticizes for the existence of God.

First, facts as such do not of themselves require or demand anything outside themselves. One only feels that a certain sort of fact requires something beyond itself because one has often experienced the two phenomena in conjunction. Therefore, one should not demand or expect that anything be unconditionally explained.

Second, no factual argument can lead to anything which has never been experienced directly. Therefore, if God is not an object of direct experience, one cannot argue to his existence by causal argument; if he is an object of direct experience, no such argument is necessary.

Third, it is never possible to demonstrate the existence of anything, in the sense that reasoning by connecting ideas does not tell one anything about the real world, and reasoning on the basis of experience is always open to falsification by further experience, so that the contradictory of any factual conclusion always remains possible. Thus, no reasoning process can conclude to the existence of anything, including God, in such a way that the conclusion is absolutely established.

Fourth, necessity itself is attributed to the relations of ideas or reduced to a subjective feeling of impulsion to expect sequences similar to those previously experienced. Hence, necessity is wholly separated from existence; thus it is clear why Hume regards "necessary existence" as a nonsensical expression.

Hume's position as a metaphysical alternative

In the second section of chapter five I criticized the principle of sufficient reason proposed by Leibniz. Hume's attack is directed against the same sort of rationalism; against this outlook his attack is devastating. Hume undoubtedly is right in asserting that one cannot have logical necessity in *acts* of thinking as Leibniz and other rationalists supposed one might have.

But the obstacle which Hume's philosophy poses to the argument which I have proposed also is clear. Hume has grasped the distinction between *what* and *that* in respect to contingent states of affairs. The only necessity he admits is logical necessity, which cannot take one beyond the *content* of states of affairs. If this position is sustained, clearly one cannot reason that any uncaused entity, such as *D,* obtains necessarily. The question is, Can Hume's position be sustained as a metaphysical alternative to the philosophical theology which I am developing?

The very suggestion that Hume's position might be regarded as a *metaphysical* alternative might seem to be an odd distortion of Hume's intentions. Probably no major philosopher has been less a metaphysician than Hume. But I do not think that it is unreasonable to interpret Hume as a metaphysician, considering my present purpose, nor do I think such an interpretation wholly betrays his intentions.

It must be admitted that Hume can be read as a psychologist, who merely describes in general terms some peculiarities of human understanding as he finds it. In many observed instances, he would be saying, ideas are reducible to impressions, knowledge of matters of fact differs from knowledge of relations of ideas, the nonexistence of something can be as easily conceived as its existence, and awareness of cause-effect relationships arises from the observation of the regular pairing of two events in sequence.

But if Hume really only means his theory of human understanding in this way—that is, as a psychology based on empirical evidence—nothing he says constitutes an obstacle to the argument I have proposed in part two. I can grant that human understanding, in general, works as Hume describes it. Unlike arguments of rationalists such as Leibniz, the argument I propose does not require that knowledge on the whole be very different from Hume's description of it. All that the argument I propose does require is that human knowledge not be *in every instance* as Hume describes it. The idea of an uncaused entity, the relationship between fact and idea in reasoning toward and thinking about this entity, the necessary existence of this entity, and the way in which the cause-effect relationship is known in this case—all of these are unique. In fact, as the whole of part two makes clear, the argument could not possibly work except in virtue of its unique features and the peculiarity of the uncaused entity which it reaches.

Thus Hume's theory of human understanding poses no obstacle to the philosophical theology I am developing if his theory is regarded merely as psychology. Like any psychological theory of human knowing, it would be open to falsification by counterexamples; it would not exclude the argument I propose and its outcome as impossible. To anyone who thinks Hume ought to be read as a psychologist, I suggest that part two provides the falsifying counterexample. In other words, Hume's theory, like any scientific theory, is fine as far as it goes, but since there is a fact it does not cover, it must be modified and extended to cover this fact.

Obviously, to answer Hume in this way would be outrageous. One cannot respond to a philosophical challenge to one's position by saying that one's

position itself is a fact which falsifies the *philosophical* view of one's opponent. It must be noticed, however, that the outrage is only committed if
Hume's theory is taken to be a philosophical position, not merely a psychological account of human understanding.

If Hume's theory is taken to be a philosophical one, it does pose an
obstacle to the philosophical theology I am developing. For understood as a
philosophical position, Hume's theory of human understanding involves
theses which I cannot accept: that an idea irreducible to an impression is
impossible, that a factual proposition which is necessarily true is *impossible,*
that a necessarily existent entity is *impossible,* that reasoning toward God by
cause and effect is *impossible.*

If Hume is maintaining theses such as these, then his position is a
metaphysical alternative to the view I am developing. He is not merely saying
how the world happens to be, but making claims about how it has to be—or,
rather, about how it *cannot* be. Making claims such as these is precisely the
business of metaphysics, as distinct from a science such as psychology.

Therefore, in the criticism to which I proceed in chapter seven I take for
granted that Hume is making metaphysical claims, that he thinks his statements about human knowledge and its objects are somehow necessarily true,
and that this necessity is more than that of the generalizations established in
an empirical science such as psychology. *If Hume is not to be read in this
way, I have no quarrel with him.*

However, I do not think this reading of Hume betrays his own intentions.
Hume is not talking like a psychologist when he says in Part IX of the
Dialogues:

> . . . there is an evident absurdity in pretending to demonstrate a matter of
> fact, or to prove it by any arguments *a priori.* Nothing is demonstrable
> unless the contrary implies a contradiction. Nothing that is distinctly
> conceivable implies a contradiction. Whatever we conceive as existent, we
> can also conceive as non-existent.

Nor is he speaking as a psychologist in Section IV, Part I, of the *Enquiry*
when he says of the cause-effect relationship: "I shall venture to affirm, as a
general proposition, which admits of no exception, that the knowledge of this
relation is not, in any instance, attained by reasonings *a priori.* . . ."

At the very end of the *Enquiry* (Section XII, Part III) Hume makes clear
what force he intends his theory to have:

> When we run over libraries, persuaded of these principles, what havoc
> must we make? If we take in our hand any volume; of divinity or school
> metaphysics, for instance; let us ask: *Does it contain any abstract reason-
> ing concerning quantity or number?* No. *Does it contain any experimental*

reasoning concerning matter of fact and existence? No. Commit it then to
the flames: For it can contain nothing but sophistry and illusion [italics
his].

The humor of this passage might easily distract one from its serious point,
which is expressed clearly in the final phrase: "For it can contain nothing but
sophistry and illusion." The words "can . . . nothing but" stake out Hume's
metaphysical claim.

7: Criticism of Empiricism

Empiricism and meaning

Hume bases his empiricism upon the distinction between impressions and ideas. Ideas ultimately must be reducible to impressions. As I explained in chapter six, this position is the foundation for Hume's "fork"—that is, his absolute distinction between knowledge of relations of ideas and knowledge of matters of fact—as well as for his theory of causality, and these positions, in turn, are the basis for Hume's critique of a rationalistic version of a cosmological argument for the existence of God. Hume's argument for the reducibility of ideas to impressions is twofold: the experience of those lacking certain senses and the challenge that anyone produce an idea which is not derived from an impression.

That a person born blind does not have the idea of *red* because he has never had a perception of red can be admitted. That a person born deaf does not have an idea of *loud* because he never has perceived a loud sound also is obvious. But Hume does not merely say that some ideas are reducible to impressions. He challenges anyone to produce any idea which is not reducible to impressions.

Fortunately, it is easy to meet this challenge. Hume's statement of the distinction between impressions and ideas makes use of the expressions "perception of the mind," "impression," and "idea." Hume is in no position to say that these words do not express ideas. But it seems clear that there can be no impression from which any of these ideas is derived.

Let us consider, for example, the idea of *idea*. If there is any impression from which the idea of *idea* is derived, that impression must be quite odd, since one neither sees it, nor hears it, nor experiences it in any analogous way.

109

Moreover, that impression must be an impression by hypothesis, but it also must be nothing but idea, for if it were anything but idea, the idea derived from it would not be the idea of *idea*, but the idea of *idea* together with whatever else was included in that perception.

The situation with respect to *perception of the mind* is no better. One can reduce the idea of *red-and-white-striped* to a single impression or to simple ideas which can be reduced to impressions. "Perception of the mind," however, signifies an idea which is at once and equally an idea of *impressions* and of *ideas*. Thus, any impression to which this expression could be reduced would have to be both an impression of *impression* and of *idea*.

Recent empiricists prefer to set aside the psychological theory in which Hume's initial distinction is embedded. Antony Flew, for example, proposes the logical translation: "No term can be understood by anyone unless its meaning can be given in terms of his experience, and no term can have any public meaning in a public language except what can be given by reference to the public world."[1] This formula avoids the difficulties of Hume's psychological theory, but its advantage is bought at a considerable price in vagueness.

Undoubtedly, if the words which make up this formula are given sufficiently broad meanings, then words such as "terms," "understood," "meaning," "public," "language," "reference," and "world" can meet the test suggested by the formula. For in some fashion or other one does learn the meanings of words by using them in suitable contexts, and one alters and develops the meanings of words under pressure of what one can call "experience," provided that one includes the experience of thinking or theorizing. But if the formula is understood loosely enough so that all its own words are meaningful, it is not easy to see how it can be used either to support Hume's "fork" or to underwrite even an updated version of his theory of causality. At the same time, understood broadly enough, the formula proposed by Flew is no obstacle to the philosophical theology I am developing. Chapter two illustrates how a child can learn to use the word "God" through experiences which include observing some facts about the world, reasoning, being told certain things and accepting them on faith in his parents, and the like. Studying the present book, if the argument is successful, is an experience which, together with other experiences, and even without faith, can provide a way of understanding the word "God."

Verificationism falsifies itself

In any case, some recent empiricists have used a criterion of meaningfulness, as Hume did, to establish requirements for true or false statements such that talk about a necessary being turns out to be neither true nor false but meaningless. Hume, as I explained in chapter six, formulated his "fork" by distinguishing between inquiries concerned with relations of ideas, which can conclude with such necessity that the opposite would be self-contradictory, and inquiries concerning matters of fact, which can only achieve the strong probability of a scientific generalization. Statements expressing truths based on relations between ideas cannot tell anything about contingent facts; statements which tell something about the world never tell what is necessary. The nonreality of any contingent state of affairs always is possible.

A. J. Ayer, in his book *Language, Truth, and Logic,* first published in 1936, provided an influential modern formulation of Hume's "fork." According to Ayer's version no sentence is cognitively meaningful—that is, expresses a proposition—unless it is either analytic or synthetic. An analytic statement merely draws out the implications of definitions; it states necessary connections between expressions themselves, as in logic and mathematics. Synthetic expressions say something about the real world; they must be verifiable by reference to some possible sense experience.

If one considers a sentence such as "God exists," one sees that it is not intended to be analytic; the sentence claims that something *exists,* not merely that various meanings are related in a certain way. However, no possible sense experience could show that this sentence is true. It is supposed to be about a reality which transcends the world of experience, not about any particular fact in the world. Thus, no fact can either support it or count against it. "God exists" is neither true nor false; it simply lacks any cognitive meaning. It perhaps expresses emotion or something of that sort.[2]

Ayer's original formulation was several times modified by others because of technical objections. Nevertheless, many empiricists still accept the view which underlies the "verifiability criterion," as Ayer's formulation of Hume's "fork" was called. They still do not admit as either true or false sentences such as "God exists."[3]

This form of empiricism must be met decisively if the argument proposed in part two is to stand. I am maintaining that X—that there is an uncaused entity—is a true proposition, that it is necessarily true, but that it is not a formal truth. The verifiability criterion rules out the possibility of a proposition such as X.

However, in ruling out the possibility of such a proposition the proponent of the verifiability criterion falls into self-referential inconsistency. In metaphorical language one might say that the proponent of the verifiability criterion takes a position which undercuts itself. The self-referential inconsistency of the position of those who hold the verifiability criterion provides grounds for a much more damaging argument against it than do any technical objections to various statements of it, since technical objections might be resolved by technical reconstruction, but the self-referential inconsistency of the position is irremediable.

To clarify what self-referential inconsistency is, it will be helpful first to look at a simple example which does not have the complexity of a philosophical thesis. Suppose someone should say, "No one can put words together to form a sentence." Obviously there is something queer about this sentence. One might be inclined to think it expresses something self-contradictory or paradoxical. Strictly speaking, it does neither. What the sentence expresses is coherent, and its reference is definite, not shifting as is the case with semantically paradoxical sentences. The trouble with the proposition that no one can put words together to form a sentence is that it is false.

Of course, nobody is going to assert that no one can put words together to form a sentence. But suppose someone did try to defend this peculiar position. It would not be necessary to go into the arguments he offered in support of it. No matter how ingenious and plausible they might be, they would not help him a bit. In fact, every time he offered some argument, he would put together more words into additional sentences. This would not make his position any worse—it cannot be more false than false—but it would make it more ludicrous.

How would one show that the thesis is false? It would not be a matter of producing a *reductio ad absurdum* argument. Such arguments show that a position implies something *logically* inconsistent. No, one would simply say: "Friend, if someone does put words together to make sentences, then someone can. And every time you say that it cannot be done, you are doing precisely what you say cannot be done." The position that no one can put words together to form a sentence is falsified not by relations of ideas—to use Hume's phrase—but by a matter of fact.

It must also be noticed that the position under consideration is not like that of someone who says, "This sentence is false." In this case one asks, "Which sentence?" If some other sentence is referred to, then one can consider it on its own merits. But if this very sentence itself is referred to, then one takes it to mean, "This sentence 'This sentence is false' is false." The reference of the original sentence cannot be established, and neither can the reference of any sentence used in a subsequent attempt to establish the reference of the original sentence. This is a semantic paradox. But there is no problem of reference of this sort in case someone says that no one can put words together to form a sentence. In fact, this proposition, unlike a semantically paradoxical sentence, has a true contradictory, namely, that someone can put words together to form a sentence.

Noting the dangers of semantic paradox, some philosophers have tried to exclude self-reference from language completely. But such an attempt cannot succeed. Either one uses *some* language to talk about *other* language when one sets down the rule excluding self-reference, or one uses the very language for which one also sets down the rule. If the former, one does not exclude self-reference from all language, but only from the *other* language—the language to which one refers without referring to the language one uses. If the latter, one provides an example of that which one attempts to exclude.

It must be noticed that the *sentence* "No one can put words together to form a sentence" is not necessarily self-referentially inconsistent. Someone might say this to a child, meaning that it is wrong to write: "Noonecanputwordstogethertoformasentence." In other words, one merely means that one must leave spaces between words. However, it is self-referentially inconsistent to express by means of a sentence made up of words the proposition that no one can do what one does when one expresses in this way this proposition *and other propositions.*

It also must be admitted that someone who tries to defend a self-referentially inconsistent position can modify his position to avoid the inconsistency. For example, someone might maintain that no one except himself can put words together to form a sentence. This position would still be false, but it would not be self-referentially inconsistent. However, if the proponent of this peculiar thesis had been trying to defend it in the first place in order to forbid others to form sentences, it obviously would be arbitrary for him to maintain that he could do what no one else could do, unless he could give some very good reasons for the difference between his ability and that of others.

In sum. A self-referentially inconsistent position is not logically incoherent nor is it semantically paradoxical. It is false; it does not square with facts. What is peculiar about a self-referentially inconsistent position is that it carries in itself or in its expression the fact which falsifies it. Thus, whenever one takes a self-referentially inconsistent position, in that very act he provides all that is necessary to refute his position.[4]

It follows that self-referentially inconsistent positions do not simply happen to be false; they are inevitably false. I call this inevitability "self-referential noncontingency." Since a self-referentially inconsistent position is noncontingently false in the sense defined, it can be called "impossible," provided that one does not confuse this impossibility with logical impossibility on the one hand or with physical impossibility on the other. The true proposition which is contradictory to a self-referentially false one also is self-referentially noncontingent. The noncontingency of such a true proposition can be called "necessity," provided that one keeps in mind the distinctions already indicated.

The impossibility of self-referentially false positions and the necessity of their contradictory opposites can be philosophically interesting. As I explained in the final section of chapter six, a theory of knowledge such as

Hume's poses no obstacle to my attempt to develop a philosophical theology unless that theory is taken to show that what I am trying to do is *impossible*. But, obviously, as soon as someone begins taking positions about what is impossible, he could exclude too much—that is, he could cut the ground from under his own feet. Whether he does cut the ground from under his own feet depends upon *what* he holds to be impossible. If the position he holds to be impossible includes his own position among others then he has cut the ground from under his own feet.

If a philosopher is involved in self-referential inconsistency, a strong rationality norm comes into play. The norm in question can be expressed: One ought never to defend a self-referentially false position and one ought never to make merely ad hoc modifications to save such a position. In other words, it is rationally necessary to give up any position which is self-referentially impossible. It also is rationally necessary that one then move to a position which is significantly different from the one which one has had to give up. It is not enough to say, "Except in my own case, no one can. . . ."

The necessity of the rationality norms must not be confused either with logical necessity, self-referential necessity, or physical necessity. Rational necessity is more closely allied to—if not identical with—the moral necessity which renders immoral behavior irrational. For example, if a head of a constitutional government claims that no one can prosecute him for his crimes, since their doing so would put them above the law of the republic, and no man is above the law, then his behavior is irrational in this sense. Similarly, if a philosopher were to attempt to rule out the prosecution of a line of inquiry leading to an uncaused entity, since pursuing this line of inquiry would lead one to say things which only those who wish to block this line of inquiry are permitted to say, then his behavior clearly is irrational.

Ayer's verifiability criterion, which like Hume's "fork" draws a strict, either/or division between necessary logical truths and contingent empirical truths, and which excludes truths of other kinds, is a self-referentially false position. This is shown by the following argument.[5]

1) The verifiability criterion (*VC*) is the proposition: Any sentence (*S*) which expresses a proposition has a certain property (*LTF*-or-*ETF*)—that is, the property of expressing either a logical truth or falsity, or an empirical hypothesis which would be factually true or false.

2) Any expression of *VC* is an instance of *S*, and the sentence which expresses *VC* can express a proposition only if it has the property *LTF*-or-*ETF*.

3) If a statement of *VC* expresses an empirical hypothesis, the making of the statement is pointless, and it will not forbid anyone to hold the truth of the proposition, *X* (that there is an uncaused entity, which is the conclusion reached by the argument proposed in part two). Such an empirical hypothesis

could claim no more than that one *has not found* any propositions which do not fit into one or the other of these two types. The final section of chapter six developed this point with reference to Hume.

4) If a statement of *VC* expresses a logical truth, the making of the statement also is pointless, and it will not forbid anyone to hold the truth of the proposition, *X*, for the logical truth of *VC* will follow only if the required definition of "proposition" is stipulated, and one who does not accept *VC* need not accept the definition stipulated. In other words, a proponent of *VC* must claim more than that *X* is not a proposition by his own special and technical definition of "proposition"; he can define as he wishes for himself, but his objection only succeeds if he can maintain that *X* is not a proposition in the sense in which the argument in part two says that it is.

5) Any statement of *VC* lacks the property *LTF*-or-*ETF* (from steps [3] and [4]).

6) Any statement of *VC* does not express a proposition (from steps [2] and [5]).

7) *VC* is a proposition (shown below).

8) Any statement of *VC* does express a proposition.

9) *VC* is a proposition any statement of which is falsified by its own performance (since [8] falsifies [6]).

A proponent of *VC* might argue—in fact, some have argued—that *VC* is not a proposition. For example, some say that *VC* is a rule of meaning or something of the sort. Now, it is possible that someone might utter sentences which seem to express *VC* without in fact stating any proposition. One might utter such sentences in his sleep or in a drama. However, if the proponent of *VC* wishes to exclude rationally the possibility of a proposition such as *X*, then he must take some sort of stand in favor of what he is saying, and as soon as he does take a stand, he *is* asserting a proposition, whether he intends to do so or not. Of course, this proposition will not be a proposition according to *VC*, but the proponent of *VC* nevertheless is making a claim that his position is one which it is rationally necessary to hold. In making such a claim he expresses a proposition. If he refuses to make any claim, then he poses no obstacle to the philosophical theology I am attempting to develop. He cannot deny the meaningfulness of *X* for the simple reason that without asserting something he cannot deny anything.

In short, if a proponent of *VC* is to deny the possibility of a proposition such as *X*, then his position is a proposition, but this proposition itself is one for which his position leaves no room.

Antony Flew proposed a variation on *VC*, which has been called the "falsifiability criterion," in a brief article entitled, "Theology and Falsification." His position is that since the assertion of any proposition is equivalent to the denial of its contradictory, the meaning of both members of a pair of purportedly contradictory propositions must be established in the same way. If a supposed assertion does not rule out anything, then it does not assert anything either. Thus, if no facts are permitted to count against theological assertions, they do not exclude anything at all, and so they do not affirm anything at all. To believers Flew would address the question: "What would have to occur or to have occurred to constitute for you a disproof of the love of, or of the existence of, God?"[6]

Flew's argument gains plausibility because he deals with God's love along with—and more extensively than—God's existence. It does not seem implausible to suppose that the believer does mean to rule out some conceivable states of affairs when he says that God loves man. As I explained in the final section of chapter five, there is a sense in which those who engage in religious acts experiment with the divine. But to admit that some religious propositions might be confirmed or falsified by facts and to admit the relevance of the falsifiability criterion in the matter of the existence of God are two quite different things.

The argument that there is an uncaused entity does rule out something—that there is no uncaused entity. Moreover, since the premise of the argument is the fact that some contingent states of affairs do obtain, the conclusion that there is an uncaused cause—from which the meaning of "There is an uncaused entity" is derived—would be falsified if there were no contingent states of affairs at all.[7]

Undoubtedly Flew would not be satisfied with this answer. He probably would demand that some particular contingent state of affairs be picked out, so that the proposition that there is an uncaused entity might be definitively falsified while other contingent states of affairs would continue to obtain. But such a demand clearly would amount to a restatement of *VC;* it merely says in another way that it *is* a necessary truth about the extrapropositional that everything be contingent—that is, that there *be no* necessary truths about the extrapropositional.

It also is interesting to notice that some statements which are certainly empirical, meaningful, and true could not possibly be falsified by any experience. An example is that one learns the truth of many propositions by experience. Obviously, any *experience* which could possibly throw further light on the psychology of the genesis of propositional knowledge could never falsify this proposition about learning by experience.

Empiricism falsifies itself

Ayer's verifiability criterion is accepted by hardly anyone today. Ayer himself realized the difficulties in trying to hold it, modified it, and finally admitted that it is merely a persuasive definition.[8] Nevertheless, many philosophers today are still empiricists. They still defend a certain kernel of the position Hume and Ayer held.

In reaching this kernel they strip away a great deal. The psychology Hume relied upon can be dispensed with. In fact, psychology and epistemology are not the heart of the matter. Perhaps there is no way to set down hard and fast limits of meaning in terms of the possibility of empirical verification. The sharp distinction between formal, logical, or analytical truths (falsities), on the one hand, and empirical hypotheses or contingent propositions about extrapropositional states of affairs, on the other, perhaps is untenable. The line is not necessarily sharp. The same sentence can be regarded either as analytic or as synthetic, depending upon the way in which it functions within a whole theory or other larger linguistic context. Furthermore, some defend the position that even the propositions of logic and mathematics are not strictly necessary.

After all this stripping away, what kernel of truth remains, so far as contemporary empiricists are concerned? Part of it, at least, is the position that no proposition picking out an extrapropositional state of affairs can be necessarily true.[9] This empiricist position is closely related to two of the theses of Hume which I discussed in the final section of chapter six: a factual proposition which is necessarily true is impossible, and a necessarily existent entity is impossible. The empiricist position, whether expressed in a single statement or in two statements, obviously is incompatible with the argument I propose in part two. Hume was ready to rest his whole case against the cosmological argument on this position: matters of fact cannot be "demonstrated"—that is, shown to obtain necessarily—since every existent can as easily be conceived to be nonexistent.

The empiricist position, stripped down to the kernel, certainly has a great deal of plausibility, in view of the fact that the extrapropositional states of affairs with which one is most familiar are contingent—they might or might not obtain. The *what* and the *that* of such states of affairs are really distinct, in a sense I explained in the second section of chapter four. Empiricists who maintain that no proposition picking out an extrapropositional state of affairs can be necessarily true might seem to be saying little more than I say myself when I insist upon this distinction.

But the appearance is deceptive. In fact, either empiricists are saying a great deal more or they are not saying anything with which I disagree.

If empiricists are simply saying that propositions picking out extrapropositional states of affairs are not formal truths, I agree. I do not hold that the proposition that there is an uncaused entity is a formal truth. If they are simply saying that they cannot think of any necessarily true proposition which picks out an extrapropositional state of affairs, I refer them to the previous section for examples of such propositions. If they are simply saying that nothing they would *call* a "proposition" can pick out a noncontingent, extrapropositional state of affairs, I do not disagree; how they use words is their own affair.

However, if empiricists mean that extrapropositional states of affairs are such that one can rationally dismiss proposition X as impossible—that is, the conclusion of the argument in part two, namely, that a necessary entity exists—then I of course must disagree. But if this is what empiricists are saying, their position, although considerably stripped down from the verifiability criterion, remains self-referentially inconsistent.

For they are claiming that *there is one thing necessarily true* about extrapropositional states of affairs, namely, that *nothing can be necessarily true* about extrapropositional states of affairs. The self-referential falsity of the empiricist position, even in this very stripped down version, is inevitable. The position does not merely happen to be false; it is self-referentially impossible. Therefore, its contradictory is self-referentially necessary. This self-referentially necessary proposition is that there can be some necessary truth about extrapropositional states of affairs.

This self-referentially necessary proposition also is rationally necessary. One ought to assert it and to deny its contradictory; one may not make an ad hoc exception to this position in its own favor.

The preceding use of self-referential argumentation perhaps will leave some readers feeling that a trick has been played on them. "Perhaps," someone could argue, "one cannot assert empiricism, yet it might still be true. Maybe the difficulty is only that the position's very truth prevents one from consistently asserting it." This reaction might be expressed by saying that even if empiricism is not true, even if it is perhaps in some sense meaningless, still it is important or useful nonsense. As such it must be preferred to the insignificant nonsense of metaphysical argumentation such as I propose in part two.

The objection that even though empiricism is self-referentially falsified, still it might be true, can be taken in two ways. The first turns out to be a reassertion of the position. The second points to a position somewhat different from empiricism which ought not to be confused with it.

The first way to take the objection is to understand it as claiming that empiricism might be true and that one could somehow know or think it to be so, and make use of it in other thinking.

Now, in one sense empiricism *might* be true; it is not self-contradictory. Logically, empiricism is a contingent proposition, which simply happens to be false. But the self-reference which falsifies empiricism is not merely logical; the self-reference involves both a proposition and an extrapropositional state of affairs. Self-referentially, empiricism cannot be true; it is an impossible position. An empiricist, quite naturally, assumes that whatever is logically possible is possible without qualification, since the only sort of strict necessity he admits is the necessity of formal truths. Hence, he slips from the purely logical "might"—empiricism is not self-contradictory—into a weakly assertive stand in its favor: "Perhaps, after all, it *is* true." But as soon as this weak assertion is made, whether it is made out loud or not, the one who makes it again asserts empiricism and, as usual, falsifies it.

Someone might object to this argument that inasmuch as the empiricist does not admit self-referential noncontingency, I am begging the question against him by appealing to it to defend my own project against empiricism. This objection fails. Self-reference is not a peculiar position I hold; it is a trap into which anyone can fall. The empiricist, without any help from me, falls into it.

This point can be made clearer by recalling the example "No one can put words together to form a sentence." If someone were to maintain this position by uttering a sentence, then one who pointed out that person's predicament to him would not be begging any questions; the self-referential impossibility is a fact, even if no one notices it. It is worth noting in passing that since the proposition in this example is *about* words and sentences, one could consistently think it true if it is possible to think without words and sentences. Empiricism is about extrapropositional states of affairs. Thus, the empiricist does not have the option to think extralinguistically that his position might be true. If an empiricist prefers to talk about the ability to use language rather than about human knowledge, this preference makes no difference, because either the capacity to use language is itself extralinguistic or there is no extralinguistic haven into which one can retire to think empiricist thoughts.

Thus to point out that empiricism falsifies itself is not to *say* that it is inadequate because it does not admit self-referential necessity. Rather, to point out that empiricism falsifies itself is to *show* its self-referential impossibility. This impossibility is a fact which would be as it is whether anyone pointed it out or not. The argument that empiricism falsifies itself is not based on assumptions I hold and the empiricist denies. The argument only formulates an observation which I make and which anyone, including the empiricist himself, can verify, merely by following out a simple reasoning process.

A very strong rationality norm, already mentioned, requires that one not assert—not even weakly assert—a self-referentially impossible position, and that one significantly modify one's position when it is found to be self-referentially impossible. One who is imbued with empiricism cannot submit to this norm without a struggle. The feeling that although empiricism is self-referentially inconsistent, nevertheless it *might* somehow be true, and so one can permit oneself a very weak assertion of it without too seriously violating one's rationality, could be a symptom of this struggle with temptation.

There are many other symptoms of it. One is the protean character of verificationism. As I said earlier, today hardly anyone, if anyone at all, would defend the verifiability criterion. But one constantly reads arguments in which it is assumed and used. For example, many philosophers appeal to the principle that if one has no criterion for using an expression, then the expression is meaningless. This principle is unobjectionable if it only means that nothing is a linguistic expression unless someone knows how to use it, which implies that some uses of any expression are acceptable, others are not, and others are borderline cases. But if it means that some expressions which are part of a living language—"God," "soul," "heaven," "sin," "Incarnation"—are meaningless because one cannot produce criteria for using them meeting some empiricist criteria of what is a criterion, then the criterion criterion is simply a reincarnation of the verifiability criterion.

Despite all this the objection that even though empiricism is self-referentially falsified, still it might be true, can be taken in another way. In his early work *Tractatus Logico-Philosophicus* Wittgenstein is attempting to clarify the relationship between extrapropositional states of affairs and the language used to talk about them. He proposes very strict criteria for propositions having sense, with the result that the propositions of his own work turn out not to have sense. Wittgenstein says at the end of the book:

> My propositions serve as elucidations in the following way: anyone who understands me eventually recognizes them as nonsensical, when he has used them—as steps—to climb up beyond them. (He must, so to speak, throw away the ladder after he has climbed up it.)
> He must transcend these propositions, and then he will see the world aright.
> What we cannot speak about we must pass over in silence.[10]

The *Tractatus* often has been read as an empiricist work. If it is read in this way, the passage quoted is a version of the objection to which I have been replying. In this case the self-referential inconsistency is hidden in the metaphor of the ladder. As Max Black remarks: "It is one thing to say we must throw away the ladder after we have used it; it is another to maintain that there never was a ladder there at all."[11] Or, to put the point another way, if in the *Tractatus* Wittgenstein is defending empiricism, then all through the work he is pretending to his reader that there is a ladder, although there really is none, and asking the reader to climb it: "Come on, don't be afraid! It's just a few more steps to the top"; then at the end of the book, after the reader has climbed up, Wittgenstein tells his reader to look back and notice that there is no ladder to climb.

Fortunately, a nonempiricist interpretation of the *Tractatus* is possible. The nonempiricist interpretation is that there is more to reality than empiricists admit, but that the more cannot be expressed in empirical language. There are truths which in a certain sense cannot be known, cannot be expressed discursively in descriptive language. This interpretation, which does more credit to the author, is supported by Wittgenstein's talk of the "mystical."[12] If Wittgenstein was thinking along these lines, his metaphysics when he wrote the *Tractatus* was close to that of Kant, and would pose the same obstacle which Kant's critical philosophy does to the philosophical theology I am attempting to develop. The metaphysical alternative Kant proposes is expounded and criticized in chapters eight and nine.

Causes and explanations

The concepts of *cause* and of *explain* are closely related. If one asks, "Why?" the answer often begins, "Because...." What follows "because" does not always refer to what one would call a "cause," but sometimes it does.

Hume proposes a conception of causality according to which a cause and its effect must be events experienced in temporal succession, and this succession must be an instance of a set of similar cases. Clearly, on this theory reasoning to an uncaused cause is impossible. An uncaused cause is not experienced; it is not antecedent in time to its effects, since time itself is an intrinsic determinant of contingent states of affairs; moreover, the cause-effect relationship between an uncaused cause and its effects is not an instance of a set of similar cases previously experienced.

I already discussed explanation to some extent in the second section of chapter five; however, since this topic is related to causality, and since recent empiricists frequently attack arguments similar to the one I propose in part two by claiming that such arguments rest upon misconceptions about explanation, some additional comments about it are appropriate here.

Many contemporary empiricists believe with Hume that causality involves temporal sequence, and that this precludes causal reasoning toward an uncaused cause.[13] Actually, examples readily come to mind in which states of affairs which anyone would say are related as cause and effect are not in temporal sequence. The spring in my watch, at this moment, is causing the hands to move; the wind is causing an annoying noise; my finger slips off the key and causes a typographical error. It makes perfectly good sense to say that a safecracker died immediately when he jolted a bottle of nitroglycerine and blew himself to pieces. The blast, the destruction of the man's body, and his death were all empirically simultaneous—that is, a surviving accomplice could not have noted any temporal sequence. Still, he could very easily recognize and report the facts as a cause-effect sequence: the jolt caused the blast, which caused the man's body to be blown to pieces, which caused his death instantaneously.

Since Hume's theory of cause and effect has no principle for telling which is which except the supposed temporal priority of cause to effect, such counterexamples conclusively show that the theory is mistaken.

What about Hume's view that the supposed necessary connection between cause and effect is only a psychological disposition induced in an observer by a succession of similar experiences? Obviously, if this view is correct, one cannot reason to any reality beyond one's experience.

However, there is some psychological evidence that children learn certain causal connections from a single instance—for example, that fire burns or that an animal scratches.[14] It also has been argued that adults often grasp a cause-effect relationship in a single instance; for example, one sees a machine and understands that a piston moves because a connecting rod pushes and pulls it.[15]

An empiricist who holds that causal explanation must always be in terms of some general law could say that in the example last mentioned one understands the particular case only because it is similar to many others one has experienced. It is similar, but it also is different. In relevant respects, the empiricist could say, it is precisely similar; the same mechanical laws apply. But how does one recognize the *relevant* respects? They are the ones that are picked out by the law. Does the law indicate some necessary connection between cause and effect? No, the empiricist must say, it only tabulates a regular correlation. But on this view any correlation which happens to hold is a law. One can easily construct imaginary examples of correlations which it would be odd to call "laws." For example, it might be the case that everyone who has a full-time daylight job and who lives in a city, the name of which begins with the letter X, leaves for work between 7:00 a.m. and 8:00 a.m. (local time) each morning.

What is more important, regular correlation does not include all that is usually meant by cause-effect relationship. There is a regular correlation among the temperature, the pressure, and the volume of a gas. But one says that assuming the volume remains constant, changes in the temperature cause changes in the pressure, but not vice versa; and assuming the temperature remains constant, changes in the volume cause changes in the pressure, but not vice versa.[16] Similarly, there is regular correlation among symptoms of diseases, but one does not say that the symptoms cause one another; in fact, one reason medicine has progressed in recent centuries is that causes of diseases have been distinguished from symptoms, and attention has been directed to trying to remove the causes rather than merely treat symptoms.

Such considerations show that Hume's theory is mistaken in supposing that regular correlation and psychological conditioning are sufficient to explain what one usually calls a "cause-effect" relationship.

It is interesting to notice that in positing a psychological disposition to explain the necessity built into the idea of causality Hume actually is stating what he takes to be the *cause* of the supposed necessity which one naturally but mistakenly regards as objective. Hume does not call the custom or habit a "cause," but his account of causality is only plausible if the relationship of the custom or habit to the belief is that of a cause to its effect. It also is a causal relation without temporal succession, and it is between something experienced—the sense of necessary connection—and its nonexperienced cause. For, obviously, custom or habit is not an empirical object.

I am not concerned here with the supposed circularity of Hume's account of causality; it could be circular and true. I am concerned with the inconsistency between the account and Hume's giving of it in a philosophical context. Hume is saying that the necessity one supposes to hold between causes and effects is not in the objects, because it can only be a matter of conditioning. One cannot help but expect the second of a pair of regularly correlated events after one has experienced the first of the pair; one cannot help but feel that there is more of a connection between the events than there is.

Why did Hume try to explain the idea of cause in terms of regular temporal sequence and psychological conditioning alone, to the exclusion of any real connection between causes and their effects? I think there are several important reasons.

In the first place Hume is attacking a rationalist conception of the cause-effect relationship. As Hume perceives, if the rationalist conception were correct, the connection between a cause and its effect would be logically necessary. Hume rightly insists that logical necessity is not involved in the relationship. If it were, contingency would be eliminated from the world. Thus Hume certainly was correct in what he wished to exclude. But why did he propose such an inadequate alternative?

I think the answer to this question is to be found in Hume's conception of experience. Throughout his works Hume supposes that experience has three properties. First, it is altogether distinct from reason. Reason has an active role, but it only deals with materials already given, ultimately with the impressions to which Hume turns when he looks to experience. Second, these impressions are atomic units, one following another with no intelligible connection. Hume was influenced to take this view by the successes of mechanistic and atomistic theories in the natural sciences of his time; Hume aspired to explain the human person as scientifically as Newton had explained the physical world. Third, Hume considers the impressions to be self-contained givens. These perceptions of the mind are passively received; they *refer* to nothing; they simply stand before the mind's eye, as it were, for inspection.

Thus, if for Hume the causal connection is to be objective, it must be found in some impression. This is why Hume searches for and does not find an impression of power or necessity, and this is why, not finding such an impression, he concludes that the necessity must be reduced to a psychological disposition.

I think that Hume might have reached a quite different result if he had paid more attention to examples in which a person himself is involved in a cause-effect relationship, actively or passively playing a role *in* nature, with other persons or nonpersonal entities playing the complementary role. Only once in the *Enquiry* does Hume consider the experience of a knower involved in nature as a possible source of the idea of causality. This single consideration of an involved knower is in a footnote, where the possibility is brought up and swiftly dismissed.[17]

Hume says that someone could suggest that the idea of causal power or necessity might arise from the impression one has when one exerts his power against the resistance he meets with in bodies. But Hume rejects this suggestion for two reasons. First, this feeling of exertion cannot be identified with causal necessity, since God, the mind, and inert matter are regarded as causes, yet none of them can have this feeling. Second, there is no known connection—Hume means no logically necessary relation—between this feeling and any event; one must find out by experience what is associated with it. At the end of the note Hume makes a significant admission: although this feeling of effort cannot serve as a principle for defining causal necessity, it enters very much into the common, inaccurate idea people have of such necessity.

In other words, Hume reduces the experience of an involved knower, for the purpose of his analysis, to a single feeling. Looking at this feeling, although he knows it is somehow related to the common-sense conception of causality, he cannot find how it might serve as a defining characteristic of causal necessity. In any case, the assumptions Hume is making about the atomic character of experience on the one hand and about the logical character of necessity on the other guarantee that no impression can possibly connect cause and effect. Atoms cannot connect atoms with atoms.

It becomes clear at this point that Hume's theory of causality is related to Leibniz's as a photographic print is related to the negative; one is the inverse of the other. Leibniz's theory taken to its limit imposes logical necessity on everything and thereby eliminates contingency and multiplicity; Hume's theory taken to its limit imposes absolute contingency on everything and thereby eliminates necessity and unity. Thus, the difficulties in Hume's theory of causality are not incidental to his empiricism.

Any philosopher who holds that there can be no necessarily true propositions about extrapropositional states of affairs is bound, if he is consistent, to reject the possibility that reasoning in unifying multiplicities might gain some otherwise inaccessible knowledge. The difficulty with this position is that by some reasoning one clearly does acquire knowledge about extrapropositional states of affairs. An instance of such reasoning is the self-referential argument by which one can learn the truth of the proposition that there can be something necessarily true about extrapropositional states of affairs.

Thus the self-referential falsification of empiricism not only shows that its basic position is impossible; it also shows that any theory of causality compatible with empiricism, and any theory of explanation which would correspond to such a theory of causality, is certain to set excessively narrow limits to what one can know by cause-effect reasoning.

In recent works by empiricists criticizing arguments similar to the one I proposed in part two, certain objections involving the concept of *explanation* are commonly made. In many cases these objections assume that one who proposes a cosmological argument must be assuming a rationalistic theory of causal explanation; the difficulties in this theory are attacked. In other cases the objections assume an empiricist theory of causality or explanation—the two tend to merge under some such rubric as "laws of nature."

Objections of the first kind and short replies to them include the following. If everything must be explained, then what explains God? The answer is that nothing does; I deny the rationalistic assumption. What would it be like to have a complete explanation of everything, anyway? I do not know, but the argument I propose does not involve any such ideal. Even if there is an uncaused cause, how could that explain anything—there is still the question why it causes and why it causes this world rather than any other? I deny that contingency can be explained. What I claim is that an uncaused cause explains why contingent states of affairs which do obtain *do obtain*.

Objections of the second kind and short replies include the following. If there is an uncaused entity which explains why contingent states of affairs obtain how can they be contingent? Its causality need not be a matter of turning the logically contingent into something logically necessary; in other words, the model does not yield explanation by deduction. Since one cannot explain everything anyhow, why not admit that the world is inexplicable? Some places are better than others to end a line of explanation, and the best place to stop the explanation of why states of affairs obtain is with one which obtains simply by being what it is. How can one explain the whole world? One cannot, if explanation is limited to showing how states of affairs fit into the regularities of a system, but explanation is not necessarily limited to stating laws of nature. The argument I propose does not explain at all in that sense.

The preceding criticism of an empiricist approach to causality and explanation is likely to remain dissatisfying unless I at least suggest an alternative. The topic is too large and complicated to allow more than a brief sketch.

In the first place, physical necessity is experienced, if one sets aside Hume's narrow conceptions of experience. "Daddy, I *can't* hold it any longer!" said by a child whose father unwisely failed to make a rest stop on the highway—this is physical necessity. "I'll hold the dog on a tight leash so that he *can't* jump on the guests." "Peek-a-boo, you *can't* see me." "If you bash that lump of coal hard enough with the poker, it *has to* break; it's only soft coal." "There's too much noise here; I *can't* hear a word you're saying." "I *couldn't help* getting angry; he kept stepping on my foot." "You *have to* eat something or you'll die of starvation."

In the second place, the experience of physical necessity involves both an understanding of distinct states of affairs at least one of which could obtain separately and an understanding of a larger state of affairs including them. I pull the two ends of a piece of paper in opposite directions and the paper's two halves part. One might be tempted to suppose that this is one state of affairs expressed in two ways. But no. A machine cuts through the middle of a piece of paper and the paper's two halves part. If I try to pull the two ends of a piece of paper in opposite directions, perhaps the paper is too tough to tear, and then the paper's two halves do not part. Where, then, is the causal necessity? Only if the cause causes. Then, my pulling the two ends of the paper in opposite directions is the separating of these parts; the separating of these parts is the paper's being divided in two; therefore, my pulling the two ends of the paper in opposite directions is the paper's being divided in two. But not necessarily vice versa. The machine's cutting through the middle of the paper also is the paper's being divided in two. The necessity is from cause to effect, not from effect to cause. My tearing the paper in half and the machine cutting the paper in half are states of affairs each of which include a state of affairs which can obtain without the other. The unity in this case is that of an action-passion state of affairs; I think that when one says "cause" in current English, one most often is talking about an action-passion state of affairs with agent and patient states of affairs included in it.

In the third place, the experience of causality includes reasoning. One can only think of one thing at a time. The question, then, is how to think of three states of affairs at once. If one cannot somehow do it, one cannot know causes. The answer is that one knows the cause in knowing the action-passion state of affairs in a particular way. One does not simply observe it as a state of affairs which obtains. One knows the truth of the proposition which picks out the action-passion state of affairs *insofar* as the truth of this proposition is conditioned by the truth of the propositions which pick out the agent state of affairs and the patient state of affairs, both of which are required for the truth of the proposition picking out the action-passion state of affairs. To know a proposition to be true in the light of other propositions being true is to know the first as a conclusion of reasoning from premises which include the others. Someone might object that one hardly proves anything with reasoning on the model of the example proposed. This may be true, but proof of a conclusion is only one goal of reasoning. Knowing causes is another point, and it is not necessarily coincident with proof.

In the fourth place, a state of affairs once known either as an agent or as a patient state of affairs is not fully understood if it is found obtaining without its counterpart. I have torn paper in two and know about this physical connection. Now I see paper being divided and I am not tearing it. The separating of its two halves is the paper's being divided; the separating of its two halves *is not* my pulling the two ends in opposite directions; therefore, why? There is a gap between the data and understanding. An explanation is called for. The shiny part of the machine's moving down to the paper and then back up again is the separating of its two halves. I *see.* The shiny part of the machine makes the paper divide; the paper can't help dividing when the shiny part of the machine does that to it.

What I have said so far, if it is correct at all, makes clear why Hume could not find any *impression* from which the idea of causal necessity might be derived. Regarding the content of experience as a set of atomic givens to which reason takes a purely detached approach assures that the experience of causality will be missed.

Causal necessity in making an effort also is less obvious than that involved in being overcome. Being a patient is more clear-cut phenomenologically than being an agent, perhaps because one's attention as a patient is directed upon the causality itself, whereas one's attention as an agent is directed on what one is causing. "I *make* the kiddie-car go" is accompanied by attention to the effect as a state of affairs in itself; "I *can't* hold it any longer" is accompanied by attention to the passion-action state of affairs in which the child loses control.

Perhaps it will be admitted that the preceding account of how one knows a physical cause-effect relationship has some plausibility. Nevertheless, it could be objected, such reasoning takes one no further than agent and patient states of affairs which can be unified in an action-passion state of affairs. The uncaused cause, if there is one, which causes contingent states of affairs to obtain, cannot be an agent for which a contingent state of affairs which obtains is a patient, since in that case both would be within the physical world.

In the argument which I propose in part two I introduce "cause" and "uncaused cause" by stipulation. I do so to avoid many irrelevant connotations which these expressions have. However, the argument uses without defining such expressions as "extrapropositional conditions," "requirements which must be fulfilled," and "prerequisites for something to obtain." Each of these expressions could be interchanged in some contexts, but not in all, with "cause." It would be odd to say that the light being on or one's being conscious caused one to read a sentence. That there is an English-speaking culture does not cause one to read a sentence written in English. But it is not odd to refer to such factors as these with the looser expressions I use. Using such expressions, I develop in the context of the argument the schema "SA^1 is an extrapropositional requirement which must be fulfilled for SA^2 to obtain." This schema is then used to define "cause" and "uncaused cause."

The result of this procedure is that "cause," as I define it in the argument, is a much wider conception than is "cause" in the immediately preceding discussion, which I limited to action-passion situations since these are near to what Hume was talking about and near to what "cause" usually means in English today. If one treats all extrapropositional requirements for something's obtaining as elements of its cause, as I do in the argument, one has a concept of *cause* at least as broad as Aristotle's, who distinguished four modes of causality, only one of which involves action and passion. In all of these modes there is a unifying state of affairs in which a condition of something's obtaining and the state of affairs it conditions are included. Other unifying states of affairs are only analogous to the action-passion situation.

Departing from empiricism, many recent philosophers have admitted *necessity* into the concept of cause. The result is a conception close to mine. I adapt the following definition from Richard Taylor,[18] substituting my language of states of affairs for his of events:

> An expression of the form "One state of affairs (SA^1) is the cause of another (SA^2)" means that both SA^1 and SA^2 obtain and that SA^1 is that set of extrapropositional conditions, among all those which obtain, which is such that each condition included in it is necessary for, but logically independent of, the obtaining of SA^2, given only the other conditions which obtain. More loosely, this means that the causal condition of any state of affairs is any condition which is such that did it not obtain, the state of affairs in question would not obtain, given only those other conditions which obtain, and that the totality of these conditions is the cause of the state of affairs.

Using this understanding of "cause," the causal necessity one comes to know by reasoning is of various modes. If the unifying state of affairs is an action-passion situation, then the causal necessity one comes to know is physical necessity. If the unifying situation is of some other sort, then the causal necessity one comes to know is not physical necessity, but a causal necessity of some other sort, perhaps one of the other three distinguished by Aristotle.

The causal necessity which is known in reasoning is the noncontingency of the effect obtaining if the cause obtains; the necessity is conditional and the explanation also is conditional. The argument proposed in part two defines "uncaused cause" by analogy. The basis of the analogy is the common schema of causal reasoning. As I explained in the second section of chapter five, it seems reasonable to ask and answer the question why all the contingent causal conditions of a state of affairs which require something not included in themselves to obtain, do obtain.

The immediately preceding argument makes possible a restatement of the point of the second section of chapter five. There I am arguing for the reasonableness of extending the schema of causal reasoning to accommodate the question why contingent states of affairs obtain, apart from the fact that they are caused by other equally contingent states of affairs. The alternative to extending the schema is to say that at least one contingent state of affairs simply obtains because it obtains. To say this is unintelligible, not in the sense that it is self-contradictory, but in the sense that "because" is being used vacuously. The given is given, but it would be unreduced to intelligibility by reasoning. To posit unintelligibilities unnecessarily is to go against the thrust of a truth-loving reason. There are enough such unintelligibilities which must be accepted: for example, the uniqueness of individuals, contingency as such, and freedom of choice.

How an uncaused entity is a necessary being

"Necessity" has been used in several senses in this chapter. There is causal necessity, logical necessity, self-referential necessity, rational necessity, and the necessity of D, the uncaused entity. Is the last-mentioned necessity an instance of one of the other types? If not, what is it? Here I try to answer this question; while doing so, I recapitulate what I have said about each of the modes of necessity and make a few additional remarks about them, without undertaking a synthetic treatment of all the modes of necessity.

Causal necessity is the inseparability of the obtaining of two states of affairs which are related in such a way that if one obtains, the other also obtains. Two states of affairs which are connected by causal necessity are united in a state of affairs which includes them both.

One knows causal necessity *in reasoning.* "In reasoning" does not mean "as a result of reasoning." One knows the causal necessity which relates two states of affairs only if one knows the truth of the proposition which picks out the state of affairs in which they are united in the light of the known truth of the propositions which pick out the two states of affairs linked by causal necessity.

If one knows that a cause obtains, one also knows that its effect obtains. For example, if one knows that one is pulling the two ends of a piece of paper away from one another, one knows that the two halves of the paper are being divided. However, as the preceding discussion of this example shows, the causal necessity of this connection is not logical necessity. The causal connection unites two states of affairs insofar as they obtain, not merely insofar as they are picked out by propositions entailed by the proposition picking out the larger state of affairs in which they are included.

In many cases one refers to an entity which is sometimes involved in a causal state of affairs as a "cause" when the entity is merely observed, not known to be a cause. What is a cause in this sense is not necessarily followed by its effect. Hume was correct in maintaining that one must learn by experience whether, or with what probability, a physical cause in this sense might be about to become involved in an action-passion state of affairs.

Even if certain physical entities—such as ultimate particles or energy or space and time—never came to be and never will pass away, such entities remain contingent in the sense that propositions picking out states of affairs in which such entities are involved might or might not obtain. However, if there are entities of this sort, they can be said to be "physically necessary" in the following sense: no proposition picking out a state of affairs in which such entities come to be or pass away is true, because every agent state of affairs and every patient state of affairs involves these entities. In other words, nothing can physically cause such entities to come to be or pass away; thus their coming to be and passing away is physically impossible, and their existence is physically necessary.

Some authors suggest that "God is a necessary being" means that he always was and always will be, that nothing can make him come to be or pass away. This suggestion is mistaken. If it were correct, God would be physically necessary. To speak in this way can be useful as a metaphor—for example, in religious discourse—if nonsymbolic expression would be unintelligible.

Not all causal necessity is physical necessity. Aristotle distinguished other modes of causal necessity, and there are modes of causal necessity which Aristotle did not distinguish. Nonphysical modes of causal necessity differ from it by including the causally connected states of affairs in something other than an action-passion state of affairs.

One mode of nonphysical, causal necessity is formal necessity. Formal necessity becomes known in reasoning such as the following. A square has four sides; what has four sides has more sides than what has three sides; a triangle has three sides; therefore, a square has more sides than a triangle. A square's having more sides than a triangle is formally necessary because a square and a triangle are what they are.

It might be objected that one need not reason to know this; the necessity is not causal, but logical. If the objection means that once one has come to know formal necessity, one cannot deny the proposition that a square has more sides than a triangle, I concede. But if the objection means that one cannot know what a square is and what a triangle is without knowing that a square has more sides than a triangle, I deny. A child knows squares and traingles as shapes; then he learns to count. The difference between the shapes is learned by experience.

For example, a child who plays with a toy having holes each of approximately the same area, but of different shapes, through which he pounds pegs of corresponding shapes, discovers by experience that the square peg will not go into the triangular or the round hole. When the child later learns to count, he makes the interesting discovery that one of his pegs has one side which goes all the way round, none of his pegs has two sides, one has three sides, and one has four sides. By reasoning he then learns that the shapes he already has known as square and traingle are such that a square has more sides than a triangle. Thus, experience is as essential to knowledge of formal necessity as reasoning is to knowledge of physical necessity, although reason and experience do not operate in exactly the same way in the two cases.

The causal necessity of the relationship between an uncaused cause and the obtaining of contingent states of affairs which require such a cause to obtain is neither physical nor formal necessity. Such causal necessity is distinct from any of the modes of causality mentioned by Aristotle, for he does not clearly distinguish between states of affairs and their obtaining.[19]

Since causal necessity is the inseparability of two states of affairs which are included in some state of affairs uniting them (in one of several ways), the uncaused entity, D, must not be called a "necessary being" if "necessary" is used to express causal necessity (of any mode). There is no state of affairs including and uniting what D is and that D obtains, because D's obtaining is not a state of affairs distinct from D, although D's obtaining is not what D is. In other words, the only state of affairs involved in D's obtaining is D; the sole requirement for D to obtain is for D to be the state of affairs which it is; and for anything to be what it is, one state of affairs suffices.

If I were undertaking a synthetic treatment of necessity, I would ask at this point whether logical necessity is reducible to formal necessity together with the necessity of asserting some propositions and denying their contradictories, provided that one entertains these propositions in or after coming to know them to be formally necessary. "Necessity of asserting" refers here to a psychological instance of the physical mode of causal necessity, or to rational necessity.

To investigate this question is unnecessary for my present purposes. However, it is interesting to notice that if logical necessity is reducible in the way suggested, then *D* cannot be a logically necessary being. For if logical necessity is reducible to causal necessity, and *D*'s necessity cannot be causal necessity, then *D*'s necessity cannot be logical necessity.

Hume rightly insisted that the expression "necessary existence" has no meaning, for he meant by "necessary"—as his argument makes clear—formal or logical necessity, and he meant by "existence" the obtaining of an extrapropositional state of affairs. In arguing that it is possible to conceive the nonexistence of any entity, Hume asserted the real distinction between *what* and *that*. This point is correct, and it is an effective criticism of the ontological argument, as I explained above (pages 33-34 and 45-46). This point is not an effective criticism of the argument I propose in part two. The argument I propose is based on this precise point.

In the provisional statement of the argument in the final section of chapter four, I carefully proceed from a future state of affairs—someone's reading a sentence the next day—in order to make clear that the meaning of *D*, which emerges from the argument, does not include its obtaining. The unconditional assertion that there is an uncaused entity can only be made at the end of the argument when the factual assumption is replaced by a true proposition about a past state of affairs. One cannot know what *D* is without also knowing that it obtains only in the sense that one cannot know that *D* refers to anything unless one knows that all of the following obtain: some contingent state of affairs, its caused cause, the uncaused cause, and *D* itself.

Thus, if *D* is God, God's existence is not logically necessary. Does it follow that God might not exist? Yes, provided that "might" refers to logical possibility. It is clearer to say that "God exists" does not express a formal or logical truth, or that the proposition that God exists does not pick out a state of affairs which is logically necessary. At least on some conceptions of *logical necessity* only propositions can be logically necessary; if one conceives logical necessity in this way, it ought not to seem odd to say that God's existence is not logically necessary.

I think that there is a rather strong tendency, which results from the heritage of rationalism, to regard logical necessity as somehow fundamental, and to think of it as having an ontological as well as a logical status. Many logicians and mathematicians have thought of their work as a description of the structure of the world.. If it is possible to think of logical and mathematical entities as intrapropositional, I do not see any reason to consider them extrapropositional. If someone maintains that formal or logical necessity is a property of the extrapropositional world as a whole, then I think that if he is consistent, he holds a metaphysical alternative similar to that proposed by Hegel. This alternative will be expounded and criticized in chapters ten and eleven.

Hume's statement that nothing is demonstrable unless its contrary implies a contradiction is true in one sense and false in another. It is true in the sense that nothing can be shown to be logically or formally necessary unless its opposite implies self-contradiction. It is false in the sense that the argument proposed in part two—which rejects the principle of sufficient reason as firmly as Hume does himself—shows that it is reasonable to assert and unreasonable to deny that there is an uncaused entity.

Hume's argument would be effective against the philosophical theology I am developing only if he were correct in thinking that there cannot be any necessary truth about extrapropositional states of affairs. However, this assumption of Hume's argument is self-referentially impossible. Hume surely is not expressing a formal or logical truth when he says about extrapropositional states of affairs: "Whatever we conceive as existent, we can also conceive as non-existent. There is no being, therefore, whose non-existence implies a contradiction."[20] Nor can this be taken as a merely empirical statement, for if it is, the "evident absurdity" which Hume is trying to demonstrate—and which he does demonstrate against the ontological argument—is not *necessarily* absurd.

The self-referential impossibility of Hume's position does not depend upon any peculiarities of his form of empiricism. It depends upon the attempt, characteristic of empiricism, to say that there can be no intelligible unity, but only experienced concomitance, of *what* and *that*.

It must be noticed that self-referentially necessary and impossible propositions such as the empiricist position and its contradictory are peculiar in that in such propositions *obtains* and *state of affairs* function as concepts. For example, when Hume argues that no extrapropositional state of affairs can obtain necessarily, his position cannot be understood unless "state of affairs" expresses something like a name and "obtain necessarily" something like a predicable. Similarly, one cannot point out what is wrong with the ontological argument without saying that *obtains* is not a predicable, and to say this is to use "obtains" to express something like a name. Similarly, the argument proposed in part two cannot proceed unless the obtaining of contingent states of affairs can itself be regarded as if it were a state of affairs picked out by a proposition in which *obtains* functions rather like a predicable.

The points mentioned in the preceding paragraph, all of which I think are correct, are closely related to what is involved in self-reference. A further explanation of self-referential necessity and impossibility will help to clarify these points. I will try to provide the required explanation in the final section of chapter nine. Pending that explanation, it might be helpful to say that at least some self-referential propositions can be regarded as metapropositions, in which *state of affairs* is a metaname and *obtains* is a metapredicable. By taking this position I do not fall into self-referential inconsistency, since the clarifications I propose in the second section of chapter four are not framed in an exclusivistic way. Nor is the potential infinite regress embarrassing, because higher levels of propositions are not invoked as principles to establish lower-level ones. That there is an uncaused entity is a metaproposition of the same order as the metaproposition which points out what is wrong with the ontological argument.

The necessity of an uncaused cause cannot be self-referential necessity. Self-referential necessity is opposed to self-referential impossibility. Self-referential impossibility characterizes positions which are impossible because they attempt to delimit what is possible so narrowly that they leave no room for themselves; thus the single counterinstance found in the self-referentially impossible position itself decisively falsifies the proposed position. Self-referentially impossible positions, in other words, are expressed in a form such as "No x can be y." Therefore, self-referential necessity is the necessity expressed in a form such as "Some x can be y." Thus the necessity picked out by a self-referentially necessary proposition is the irreducibility of the *possibility* of some state (or metastate) of affairs. The necessity of an uncaused entity is something more than an irreducible possibility.

It follows that the self-referential necessity of the proposition contradictory to the empiricist thesis does not establish the existence of an uncaused entity, but it does establish that there *can be*—self-referential possibility—an intelligible unity between *what* and *that*. If there is an uncaused entity, this possibility is fulfilled; if there is no uncaused entity, its existence cannot be excluded by an *a priori* argument such as empiricism proposes. The *a priori* character of the empiricist argument *against* the existence of a necessary being is another respect in which empiricism inverts rationalism, which tends to argue *a priori for* the existence of such a being.

Rational necessity is the inseparability from love of truth of certain modes of asking questions, reasoning, and judging. Rational necessity is closely related to—if not identical with—the categorical demand of moral norms. Rational necessity characterizes acts of thinking, not propositions or extrapropositional states of affairs generally.

The rationality norms which are relevant to acts of knowing certain sorts of cause-effect relationships perhaps are part of what Hume had in mind when he spoke of "custom" or "habit." The necessity of the rationality norms, of course, is distinct from causal necessity. Thus, if Hume had in mind rational necessity when he spoke of "custom" or "habit"—he perhaps also had in mind the psychological necessity of causal reasoning in children—he was correct in refusing to posit such necessity as the connection between cause and effect.

Rational necessity also must be distinguished from formal or logical necessity. One can choose not to be rational; one cannot choose not to understand a formal or logical necessity which one knows, except by not thinking about it.

Rational necessity belongs to the act of reasoning toward an uncaused entity. However, the necessity of such an entity cannot be rational necessity, for the latter belongs to human acts of thinking. Some recent philosophers have suggested that "God is a necessary being" means that if God exists, then it is necessarily senseless to ask further questions of the form "Why does x exist?" where x is a contingent entity.[21] This view confuses rational necessity with the necessity of an uncaused entity.

Many contemporary philosophers argue that there is no plausible explanation of the nonanalytical necessity of the proposition that God exists. Terence Penelhum, for example, argues that "God is a necessary being" might be thought to mean "that the explanation for God's existence lies within him and not outside him" if this statement can be interpreted as expressing neither physical nor logical necessity. To avoid making "God exists" analytic, Penelhum thinks, "We would have to claim that God's nature or essence is somehow causally related to his existence, but this claim is surely nonsense." Penelhum gives two arguments for rejecting causal necessity. The first is that causality implies temporal precedence; here Penelhum shows how closely he follows Hume and Kant. The second is that causality implies a distinction between cause and effect which cannot be maintained in this case.

Penelhum thinks that the only remaining alternative is to say that "a necessary being is one about whom it makes no sense to ask why he exists, a being at which demands for explanation come to a stop." But, Penelhum asks, why should demands for explanation stop here? He suggests two possible answers to this question, both of which he rejects. The first is that God is self-explanatory; Penelhum takes this to mean that the necessity would be either logical or causal, and therefore rightly rejects it. The second is that as uncaused cause God needs no explanation. Penelhum rejects this possibility because he thinks that if it were accepted, the necessity of the necessary being would have to be established independently of the argument, because the argument "is based upon the principle of sufficient reason, which would compel us indefinitely to seek its cause if it were not self-explanatory and would be violated by such an uncaused and un-self-caused being."[22]

Thus Penelhum correctly rules out as candidates for the necessity of an uncaused entity logical necessity, causal necessity, and rational necessity. He is not altogether accurate in his reasons for ruling them out, however, especially insofar as he supposes that the argument is based on the principle of sufficient reason. Since I reject the principle of sufficient reason, I can and do say that an uncaused entity needs no explanation.

In the argument I propose at the end of chapter four I introduce the expression "necessary being" by stipulative definition. I call D, the uncaused entity, a necessary being because it is not a contingent state of affairs, it obtains, and it is uncaused. All three of these factors are indispensable. Dc, the uncaused cause, also obtains and is uncaused, but it is not a necessary being because it is contingent. A square-circle is noncontingent and uncaused, but it is not a necessary being because it does not obtain. What is either logically, causally, or self-referentially necessary is noncontingent—in various senses—and perhaps obtains, but it is not a necessary being, because it is caused. D is a noncontingent, extrapropositional state of affairs, which obtains but requires nothing other to obtain than to be the state of affairs which it is.

Although *what* and *that* are distinct in D, D's necessity is not causal, because D and its obtaining are not united in any state of affairs distinct from D itself. This necessity is not logical, because "obtains" does not signify what D is. D requires only to be what it is to obtain; however, the ontological argument does not follow from this conclusion. Rather, it follows that if D obtains, then D cannot fail to obtain, because it cannot fail to be what it is. Since D obtains, it necessarily obtains. The necessity of the uncaused entity is as unique as the uncaused entity itself is, for this necessity simply is the inseparability of D and its own obtaining. To insist that such inseparability is unintelligible is to commit the procrustean-bed fallacy.

To maintain that D's necessity is intelligible, however, is not to claim to understand it. D is a theoretical entity, posited to satisfy the requirements of the problem. What D is, apart from what is specified by the argument, remains to be investigated.

The necessity of the proposition, X, that there is an uncaused entity is strictly derivative from the necessity of D. One can understand this proposition through an argument based on a factual assumption. However, if one understands the proposition X through the argument and if one also knows the truth of this proposition because one knows that the contingent state of affairs from which the argument begins does obtain, then one knows that X is a necessary, categorical truth about an extrapropositional state of affairs. If X were not true, no other proposition could be true, not because X is a premise from which one can deduce other truths as conclusions, but because X picks out a state of affairs such that if it does not obtain, no state of affairs obtains.

8: The Alternative
of a Critique of Knowledge

Kant's problem and strategy for solving it

It is a curious fact that while almost no philosopher today regards the philosophy of Immanuel Kant as a defensible system, practically everyone assumes that proofs for the existence of God are definitively shown to be impossible in Kant's great work, the *Critique of Pure Reason*.

Kant is confronted with Leibniz's rationalistic metaphysics, which maintains that in principle all judgments could be reduced to identity, and which thus points to an ultimate intelligible synthesis of all extrapropositional states of affairs, a synthesis unifying everything into a solid block of intelligible necessity. But Kant also is confronted with Hume's empiricist alternative, which holds that no proposition picking out an extrapropositional state of affairs can be necessarily true. Hume rejects any intelligible unity in extrapropositional states of affairs, even the intelligible connection between cause and effect, and thus divides experience into atomic units which are concomitant only by unintelligible contingency. For Hume the idea of a necessary being is nonsense; for a completely intrepid rationalist, such as Hegel, who takes Leibniz's principles to their ultimate conclusions, reality as a whole, all being, is necessary.

Thus Kant is the man in the middle. He attempts to solve the problem by admitting against Hume and with Leibniz that there are necessary truths about extrapropositional states of affairs, and by admitting at the same time against Leibniz and with Hume that one cannot demonstrate the reality of a necessary being. Kant maintains that the world of experience includes intelligible unity, such as that of causes and their effects, but he also maintains that it is a mistake to attempt to project such intelligible unity upon an uncaused entity in which *what* and *that* come together in the obtaining of a necessary being.

Thus, unlike Hume, Kant does not fall into the self-referential impossibility of holding that there can be no necessary truth in respect to extrapropositional reality, but Kant holds that human knowledge of such necessary truth is limited to objects within human experience. This limitation of human knowledge to the world of experience Kant opposes to rationalistic metaphysics, which he calls "dogmatism" or "transcendent metaphysics"; Kant opposes his vindication of the claims of human knowledge to achieve necessary truth about the world of experience to Hume's empiricism, which he calls "scepticism." Kant refers to his own position as "critique of knowledge" or "criticism."

The task of criticism is to make a discriminating appraisal. Critique of knowledge discriminates legitimate claims to knowledge of necessary truth from illegitimate claims to such knowledge. This discrimination between claims in the field of knowledge, like a surveyor's discrimination between conflicting claims to land, establishes a boundary. But the boundary, Kant insists, is only a boundary for *human knowledge.*

To project this boundary upon extrapropositional states of affairs as they are in themselves is as bad as to transgress this boundary by making illegitimate claims to knowledge of realities beyond experience. To do either is to become "transcendent"—that is, metaphysical in a bad sense. The reification of the boundary of knowledge, scepticism, and the transgressing of this boundary, rationalist dogmatism, both create difficulties for theism, according to Kant. These difficulties are removed

> ... by combining with Hume's principle, "not to carry the use of reason dogmatically beyond the field of all possible experience," this other principle, which he quite overlooked, "not to consider the field of experience as one which bounds itself in the eyes of our reason." The *Critique of Pure Reason* here points out the true mean between dogmatism, which Hume combats, and skepticism, which he would substitute for it. . . .[1]

Thus Kant's critique avoids self-referential falsity, at least the self-referential falsity into which empiricism falls. Yet his critique, if successful, rules out the possibility of reasoning toward an uncaused entity.

Hence, Kant proposes a metaphysical alternative to the philosophical theology which I am attempting to develop, which poses an obstacle distinct from the one empiricism poses. Yet Kant agrees with Hume to a considerable extent.

Kant is much impressed by Hume's critical work, especially by Hume's treatment of causal necessity. Kant tends to take for granted Hume's basic notion that knowledge begins by a passive reception in sensation of many impressions, diverse and isolated in their initial givenness. Kant also accepts Hume's view that experience as such does not contain any necessity. He admits Hume's position that analyzing concepts only clarifies the meaning they contain and tells nothing about the real world.

However, Kant disagrees with Hume on several very important points. Kant insists that sensations and concepts—Hume's impressions and ideas—are distinct not in degree but in kind. Sensation is marked by singularity; understanding involves patterns which are applicable universally. Kant is convinced that Euclid's geometry and Newton's physics are permanent knowledge. In these sciences, Kant believes, man has achieved knowledge about extrapropositional states of affairs, knowledge which has necessity.

Kant also passionately believes that persons are morally responsible, that this responsibility is based on their freedom of choice, that every person has an obligation to strive toward moral perfection, that this effort cannot be completed in this life, that there must therefore be a life after death in which endless growth toward perfection will be possible, and that there is a God who will harmonize virtue with happiness in the next world as they are not harmonized in this world.

With such beliefs Kant obviously has serious difficulties when he accepts Hume's critical conclusions. How could he uphold the absolute necessity and universality of scientific knowledge if Hume's theory of knowledge were correct? How could Kant solve the problem Hume poses? How can the causal concept be anchored in the world of experience, where everything seems to be contingent? Moreover, how could Kant uphold the existence of God against Hume's criticisms, and how could he uphold human freedom in a world which was assumed to be completely mechanistic?

Kant's first step is to notice that geometry and physics involve and presuppose a kind of truth for which Hume's theory leaves no room.

Kant, like Hume, holds that there are truths based on relations of ideas or pure analysis of concepts; Kant calls such truths "analytic." There also are truths concerning the real world which lack necessity; these are the truths Hume calls "matters of fact"; Kant calls them "synthetic *a posteriori*," because they put concepts together on the basis of (and so posterior to) experience of the way the world happens to be. Like Hume, Kant holds that analytic truths are necessary but tell us nothing about how things are; synthetic *a posteriori* truths do report how things are, but since they tell us nothing more than what is contained in experience, they have no necessity.

But, Kant argues, what about the very principles of mathematics and natural science? A simple equation in arithmetic, such as, seven plus five equals twelve, involves something more than an analysis of meanings. To know it requires an operation, counting, at least in imagination; moreover, arithmetic holds true in an informative way about the real world. In fact, one applies arithmetic all the time in handling the real world and it always works, but one's certitude of the truth of arithmetic goes beyond this experience. The same, Kant thinks, is true of a principle of geometry, such as, the shortest distance between two points is a straight line, or for a presupposition of natural science, such as, every alteration which begins in anything is preceded by the action of something else upon it. Propositions of this sort are informative, but they also are necessarily true.

Propositions of this sort, which are both informative about the world and necessarily true, Kant calls "synthetic *a priori.*" They are synthetic because sentences used to state them do more than merely express equivalent concepts in different ways; they express a unity of different concepts. These propositions are *a priori* because their necessity and universality is not derived from experience; they are somehow known to be true for all future experience.

Hume had denied that there can be any truths which will necessarily hold for all future experiences. How, according to Kant, are they possible? Kant's solution is that propositions of this sort express the basic structure of human knowledge of the world of experience; they are based upon conditions which make it *possible* for man to know the world. Like Hume, Kant is locating the necessity in the knower rather than in the stuff of sensation. Unlike Hume, Kant is making the necessity more than psychological. Kant is saying that the knower supplies organizing principles which build his knowledge of the world and are built into such knowledge. The materials come from perception, but the plan already is in the knower beforehand; it is *a priori.* Thus, what one knows is structured by one's built-in ways of knowing, because otherwise one simply could not know anything.

Long before Kant it was suggested that the content of immediate sensation is, not a precise replica of the world, but a product of the action of the world on man's peculiar sensibility. One hears sounds, for example, but in the world there are only waves in the air—at least, this is the assumption of the mechanistic theory of nature widely taken for granted in Kant's time. It seems to follow that one does not hear anything as it is in itself; one only becomes aware of certain effects which things outside have upon oneself. The world one perceives is the world of human perception; one cannot perceive anything apart from his perception of it. It is really meaningless—according to this view—to ask what things are like *in themselves* or apart from human perception of them.

Kant takes this basic idea and extends it very far. Is there any impression of space as such or of time as such? No, all one's outward impressions are in space and all of one's impressions are experienced in a temporal succession, but space and time themselves are not givens. Still, one can imagine empty space and time, while one cannot imagine anything without also imagining the space-time framework into which it fits.

Kant uses an example of two gloves. One can see that they are not alike; the right glove and the left one are counterparts. But although the gloves cannot replace each other, no amount of conceptual analysis would tell that. Nevertheless, the relationship one finds is necessary. From this Kant concludes that space is a kind of framework which neither is given in experience nor is a mere idea. Space and time are concrete, like particular things given in experience, but they have their own necessary structure. Space and time make human experience possible and organize the stuff which is fed in by sensibility; man can experience the world only under spatiotemporal conditions.

The fact that space and time are *not* given in experience, Kant thinks, furnishes a basis for explaining necessity in mathematics. The shortest distance between two points is a straight line because the structure of space requires it; the structure of space cannot change, because it is not merely something which is experienced; rather it is a condition for the very possibility of experience. In other words, space and time are located in man who experiences the world; they shape the world man experiences; thus the truths which express how space and time are will always be true of the world, for they go into its very construction.

If one accepts this view of Kant's and adds it to the older notion that the direct objects of the senses such as color and sound are produced in the perceiver, then all human concrete experience turns out to be of a world which is, and only can be, a world for experience. Somehow what is beyond experience acts upon sensibility and gets the whole process going, but what one reaches in one's immediate experience is an organized world-out-there, which in its qualities, in its organization, and in its being "out there" spatially, wholly depends on the human manner of sensing and perceiving.

If this strategy works for space and time, and thus explains how mathematics can achieve necessary and universal truth about the world, Kant reasons that the same strategy should work for concepts such as substance and cause, with a like benefit to natural science.[2] In this case it is not only a matter of putting sensations together into a unified perceptual field at the concrete level but also a question of shaping experience into a world of "real" objects intelligibly connected by cause-effect relations. The underlying principles of natural science, in other words, express requirements which are set by the built-in way in which man *must understand* the world.

Thus, the physical world ultimately is a construct, which is built out of the raw material of what happens to a man when things apart from him act upon him, organized by his own ways of experiencing and understanding and explaining. Things in themselves, which start the process of knowledge going, never can be known as they are in themselves, because one can never know anything without knowing it, and one can only know with the equipment one has.

It might be admitted that man cannot peek around, as it were, his own cognitional apparatus in order to steal a glance at the world without "knowing" it. But how does this incapacity on man's part guarantee the certitude—the universality and necessity—of natural science? The impossibility for a human knower to get around his built-in way of knowing the world guarantees the laws of nature just because man cannot possibly think of things otherwise than as he does.

The things one thus thinks of, according to Kant, are real things in the real world (in the ordinary person's sense of "real"), but they are not things in themselves. Kant does not hold that the world man experiences and knows is an illusion. He is saying that the world of experience is *objective* precisely because it is the correlate of man's way of knowing. Man's way of knowing is subjective, not in positing a psychological necessity, as Hume thought, nor in depending upon changeable interests, as pragmatists think. Man's way of knowing is subjective because it is a merely human—although the only human—way of understanding extrapropositional states of affairs.

This solution to Hume's problem answers the question about the necessity of knowledge of things experienced—necessity in the physical world as an object of natural science. But what about metaphysics? Man still wishes to ask questions about himself, as a knowing subject; about the whole world, as the total system of what he can know; and about God, as the ultimate cause of all things.

How Kant attempts to dissolve metaphysics

Kant grants that man has ideas of the self, of the world, and of God. He also grants, even insists, that man does want to ask questions about these ideas, that one cannot help asking questions. These ideas are necessarily formed by man at the boundaries of knowledge. The self as ultimate knower would be the final subject, the "I" *doing* the thinking which, as such, is never thought about. The universe would be the whole of what could ever be known, the whole which man projects because knowledge grows and he knows there is still more to investigate. God would be the final explanation of it all, the last answer which would provide a "because" for every "why." Such ideas, Kant says, are necessary and useful at the boundaries of knowledge, because one needs these ideas of unity and completeness to keep knowledge moving. But the fact that man has ideals does not mean he will ever reach them, or even that there really is anything to reach.[3]

It is important to notice that Kant does not *deny* that the ideas of reason might correspond to something in things in themselves. In fact, he thinks that a practical approach, based on moral considerations, can lead one to the view that one must *act* on the belief that God and the self are somehow realities. But Kant is anxious to keep God and the self outside the field of theoretical argument; in this way he can protect these entities against theoretical attacks. Kant is limiting the possibility of knowledge in order to make room for a practical orientation toward extraempirical reality; Kant regards this practical orientation as a kind of "faith," although it is not necessarily religious in character.[4]

In this way Kant deals with the problem of finding a middle position between rationalist metaphysics and empiricism. Leibniz engaged in transcendent judgments, that is, in bad metaphysics; Hume forbade such judgments. Hume limited the extrapropositional to the contingent; it seemed to Kant to be in harmony with reason and with the requirements of morality to forbid this restriction:

> If we connect with the command to avoid all transcendent judgments of pure reason the command (which apparently conflicts with it) to proceed to concepts that lie beyond the field of its immanent (empirical) use, we discover that both can subsist together, but only at the boundary of all permitted use of reason. For this boundary belongs to the field of experience as well as to that of the beings of thought, and we are thereby taught how these so remarkable Ideas serve merely for marking the bounds of human reason. On the one hand, they give warning not boundlessly to extend knowledge of experience, as if nothing but world remained for us to know, and yet, on the other hand, not to transgress the bounds of experience and to think of judging about things beyond them as things in themselves.[5]

In other words, Kant takes a middle way in which it is permissible to think of an uncaused cause as a possibility, but impermissible to claim to know that there really is an uncaused cause.

In this respect Kant's critique is obviously a metaphysical alternative to the philosophical theology I am developing. If Kant really succeeds in establishing the boundary he proposes, then the path of theoretical inquiry about the extraempirical is closed.

But how could Kant establish the boundary without himself offering some description of the extraempirical which would make clear why no one could know it? Obviously, if he did this, his position would be self-referentially impossible. But such is not Kant's approach. Instead, he argues that if one is to think of nonempirical entities as if they were real, one must think of them by using the same apparatus one uses to understand the world of experience—

object, cause-effect, and so on. But if one does proceed in this way, reason unintentionally reveals that the procedure is illegitimate in the only way in which this fact could come to human attention, namely, by leading to inevitable nonsense. If one assumes the reality of extraempirical entities as objects theoretically known, one can perform a *reductio ad absurdum,* Kant thinks, which will show the falsity of the assumption.[6]

Kant offers four *reductio* arguments, which are called "antinomies." The first two are not directly relevant to the present project and can be disposed of fairly easily.

Kant argues that if one treats the universe as if it were one big object, one is going to ask questions about it, such as, "Are space and time finite or boundless?" and "Are there elementary particles or is matter divisible ad infinitum?" Kant claims that apparently valid arguments can be built from true premises for answering these two questions either "yes" or "no." Thus, the supposition behind them—that the world as a whole is one big object—leads to antinomies.

Kant tries to solve these first two antinomies by arguing that in trying to think about the whole universe as if it were an object which could be studied scientifically, one is making a mistake. The statements "The world is finite" and "The world is infinite" appear to be contradictory opposites, but Kant suggests that they are contraries. Both can be false together because they share a common assumption. Kant calls such a pair of contrary positions "dialectical opposites." The assumption in this case is that one can talk meaningfully about the totality of the world. This presupposes, Kant thinks, that one can experience the totality, and Kant regards this as impossible.

Once one realizes that the totality of possible objects of experience is not one big object which could be given in actual experience, then one should see that it simply does not make sense to ask the questions which generate the first two antinomies. To solve such questions is to dissolve them—that is, to make clear that they do not make sense. When one sees this, he will not keep asking such questions as if they were legitimate topics for theoretical inquiry.[7]

There are several reasons why these first two antinomies need not concern me. First, when I discussed in the first section of chapter five the question whether a self-sufficient set of contingent states of affairs is possible, I avoided assuming for my own argument that the universe can be considered as one big object; I allowed the assumption, for the sake of argument, only to the extent that it is introduced by those who deny the need to posit an uncaused cause. Second, so far as I am concerned, it does not make any difference whether the supposed issues involved in these antinomies are pseudoquestions; my conception of reason is sufficiently removed from rationalism that if these arguments show that some things about the world are inexplicable, I can accept these inexplicables as additional items on a list which already includes more important items than these.

Third, competent critics of Kant do not find his arguments cogent.[8] If a *reductio* is not cogently argued on both sides, it remains possible that the conflict has been generated by the critic himself. Finally, one can argue that these issues are empirically meaningful and that they are being dealt with by modern physics, which does not hesitate to consider the whole universe as one big object.[9] If one cannot talk about the universe as a whole, what could it mean to say, for example, that hydrogen is the most abundant element in the universe?

The third antinomy Kant proposes is the conflict between the assertion of free choice and of determinism. Does the world include any causes which act freely? Or is everything in the world, including all human acts, determined by causes which operate according to natural laws. In this antinomy, Kant argues, both positions can be correct from different points of view. If one is concerned only with the world studied by the sciences, including sociology and psychology, it must be the case that everything in the world, including all human action, is a product of natural laws which form an absolutely tight network. However, it is not impossible that the human person as a moral agent escapes scientific observation and that in reality the moral self responds to the demands of moral law with a spontaneous, free causality which is of an altogether different order; thus, for the moral point of view man's actions also can be the result of freedom.[10]

Clearly, the third antinomy poses no obstacle to the philosophical theology I am developing. It does not show more, at most, than that the causality of free choice must not be reduced to the causal necessity of action-passion states of affairs. Since I agree with Kant that these ought not to be confused— although I do not think he is correct in supposing that each obtains in a different metaphysical domain—I have no quarrel with him here.

The fourth antinomy seems to come to the heart of the matter. The thesis is that there belongs to the world, either as part of it or as its cause, an absolutely necessary being. The antithesis denies this.[11] What arguments can Kant propose for each side? The arguments for both must be completely cogent if his case that reason, by falling into self-contradiction, reveals its incompetence to press theoretical inquiry beyond the boundary of the empirical world.

The proof Kant proposes for the thesis begins from change in the world of experience, argues that such change is conditioned, invokes the principle of sufficient reason, and concludes to an unconditioned condition. Kant then assumes that this unconditioned condition, if it is a principle of change, must cause by action and must be temporally antecedent to what it causes. Thus, he concludes, there is a necessary being which, on the given assumptions, must be part of the world.

Since Kant uses the principle of sufficient reason in this argument, and I already have argued in the second section of chapter five that this principle is false, I can ignore this supposed proof. Thus the whole burden of proving Kant's claim that the dialectic of reason demonstrates that reason cannot press theoretical inquiry beyond the bounds of experience rests upon his proof of the antithesis. In other words, Kant only poses an obstacle for me—in terms of his own strong claims—if he here demonstrates that there is no uncaused cause. How does he proceed?

First he argues that the world itself cannot be a necessary being. Either there is a beginning of the series of conditions, which is both contingent as a physical cause of effects, and yet a necessary being, or the total series of conditioned conditions constitutes a necessary being. The former is absurd and so is the latter, for it implies that a whole made up of contingent parts nevertheless can be necessary. In some ways Kant's argument here is similar to mine in the first section of chapter five. However, he is concerned with *change,* which is a predicable, not with *obtaining.* Moreover, since he does not propose an adequate analysis of contingency and necessity, it is not clear that his argument does not involve a fallacy of composition.

But, Kant goes on to argue, there can be no necessary cause of the world existing outside it, for if there were

> ... then this cause, as the highest member in the series of the causes of changes in the world, must begin the existence of the latter and their series.[a] Now this cause must itself begin to act, and its causality would therefore be in time, and so would belong to the sum of appearances, that is, to the world. It follows that it itself, the cause, would not be outside the world—which contradicts our hypothesis.

In note "a" Kant explains that he is taking "begin" in both an active and passive sense, reasoning from one to the other.[12]

What Kant is arguing here is that an agent in an action-passion state of affairs cannot be extratemporal. I agree. This argument has nothing to do with the uncaused entity to the existence of which I reasoned in part two. However, I will comment on it in chapter nine.

At this point I could declare that Kant's attempted dissolution of metaphysics fails. He only succeeds in showing that one cannot reason to extrapropositional states of affairs beyond experience if he shows that any attempt to do so leads to self-contradiction. The antinomies were supposed to show this. They do not do so. But how could they possibly have done so? Unless one has some sort of principle which establishes that all attempts must fail, one can only show that no one has succeeded thus far. But, as I mentioned previously, if Kant offers some description of the extraempirical which would make clear why it cannot be known, he would fall into self-referential inconsistency.

Arguments for the existence of God

Still, there is more to Kant. One cannot assume that simply because he stakes everything on the antinomies, his critique might not have other resources which could pose a serious obstacle to the position I am developing. In fact, he offers specific criticisms of the cosmological argument, and these must be examined. But before proceeding to them, it is worth noticing Kant's own solution to the fourth antinomy.

The issue was whether or not there is a necessary being, either in the world or apart from it. Kant's resolution, surprisingly, does not reject both alternatives as dialectical contraries, both based on a false supposition. Instead, Kant suggests that a possible solution to this conflict would be to suppose that the whole series of causes and effects which makes up the world is contingent; each entity has a conditioned existence and only exists in virtue of the fact that a prior cause brings it about. At the same time there *could be* an intelligible principle of the whole series of conditions. It would not enter into the temporal sequence. It would not make any of the empirical entities unconditioned. The world of experience would be left unaffected. This entity would have to be completely beyond the world of experience.[13]

Kant does not think that the movement of reason from the conditioned entities of the world of experience to an unconditioned entity is unnatural or easily avoidable. The unconditioned being is not given as real in experience, nor is it an entity which follows from concepts by definition. Here, Hume was correct. But an unconditioned entity is

> . . .what alone can complete the series of conditions when we proceed to trace these conditions to their grounds. This is the course which our human reason, by its very nature, leads all of us, even the least reflective, to adopt, though not everyone continues to pursue it. It begins not with concepts, but with common experience, and thus bases itself on something actually existing. But if this ground does not rest upon the immovable rock of the absolutely necessary, it yields beneath our feet. And this latter support is itself in turn without support, if there be any empty space beyond and under it, and if it does not itself so fill all things as to leave no room for any further question—unless, that is to say, it be infinite in its reality.
>
> If we admit something as existing, no matter what this something may

be, we must also admit that there is something which exists *necessarily.* For the contingent exists only under the condition of some other contingent existence as its cause, and from this again we must infer yet another cause, until we are brought to a cause which is not contingent, and which is therefore unconditionally necessary. This is the argument upon which reason bases its advance to the primordial being.[14]

Clearly, Kant, unlike Hume, understands fairly accurately how the argument should proceed.

But Kant now takes one more step. Reason seeks a concept by which to characterize the necessary being. The best concept it can find is that of the *most real entity,* a being capable of accounting for everything because it is endowed with the sum total of all perfection, a being therefore supreme among realities. Kant maintains that if one had *to decide* what sort of thing a necessary being would be, this characterization would be plausible. But Kant claims that while the argument "If there is an unconditioned being, it is the most perfect being" might be plausible, this argument does not exclude the possibility that any other entity in the world might not also be a necessary being. One cannot show by any concepts that entities in experience are unconditionally necessary, says Kant, but this does not mean that they are not. Thus, the argument is defective.

Still, if practical considerations demand that one suppose that there is a supreme being, then perhaps one should accept the result of this sort of argument, although it is inconclusive in itself. In any case, it is not to be brushed aside lightly, for it has influenced people of all cultures to form some idea of God. In this matter, Kant thinks, people are led "not by reflection and profound speculation, but simply by the natural bent of the common understanding."[15]

At first glance the preceding argument, far from posing any obstacle to what I argue in part two, seems to agree with it, provided that a couple of modifications are made. In the first place Kant here introduces expressions I do not use, such as "infinite in its reality," "most real entity," and "most perfect being." I have no use for these expressions. They tend to suggest that *reality* or *being* is a predicable. In the second place Kant supposes that there is no proof that entities in the world of experience are not necessary beings. He supposes this because he understands "necessity" as the opposite of the physical contingency of what comes to be or passes away. The necessary being to which the argument points, as Kant understands it, is a physically necessary being—one which cannot come to be and pass away. Hence, Kant is correct in thinking that the argument he outlines is defective. The situation is altogether different if one begins from states of affairs which obtain although they might not obtain.

Kant now proceeds to criticize arguments for the existence of God. First he considers the ontological argument, as formulated by Descartes and Leibniz.[16] The argument is that an absolutely necessary being must be; a most perfect being must actually exist. An absolutely necessary being, as Kant understands it, would be logically necessary. Thus, the conclusion seems to follow that a nonexistent absolutely necessary being would be a contradiction in terms; a nonexistent most perfect being would be somewhat less than perfect.

Kant begins his criticism of the ontological argument by making the sound point that the idea of an absolutely—that is, logically—necessary real being is nonsense. Kant rightly insists that such necessity and existence must be separated; necessity of this sort properly characterizes certain propositions, not existing things. Kant also points out that existence is not part of a concept of what anything is. One can understand what it would be like for anything to exist; if it does exist, this does not change what it is in the least, but simply makes it be:

> By whatever and by however many predicates we may think a thing— even if we completely determine it—we do not make the least addition to the thing when we further declare that this thing *is*. Otherwise, it would not be exactly the same thing that exists, but something more than we had thought in the concept; and we could not, therefore, say that the exact object of my concept exists. If we think in a thing every feature of reality except one, the missing reality is not added by my saying that this defective thing exists. On the contrary, it exists with the same defect with which I have thought it, since otherwise what exists would be something different from what I thought. When, therefore, I think a being as the supreme reality, without any defect, the question still remains whether it exists or not.[17]

Here, Kant continues, is the heart of the matter. If one is thinking about empirical objects, whether they are given in experience makes a difference, though not a conceptual difference, to one's whole state of knowledge.

But when it comes to an extraempirical entity, one *cannot* have this sort of evidence of existence. In fact, Kant maintains, nothing at all can distinguish the existence of an extraempirical entity from bare possibility. Thus, although there might be some extraempirical entities, a human knower cannot be in a position to know about them. Human consciousness of existence

> ... (whether immediately through perception, or mediately through inferences which connect something with perception) belongs exclusively to the unity of experience; any existence outside this field, while not indeed such as we can declare to be absolutely impossible, is of the nature of an assumption which we can never be in a position to justify.[18]

This argument of Kant's will be carefully considered in chapter nine, for it directly challenges the argument I propose in part two.

After completing his demolition of the ontological argument, Kant proceeds to deal with the cosmological argument once more. This time he proposes a more metaphysical version of it, based upon existence. If anything exists, then a necessary being exists. I exist. Therefore, a necessary being exists. Kant points out that this argument proceeds from a basis in experience. But, he asks, what can "necessary being" mean here?

If it is to be necessary, he argues, it must be determined by one of every pair of contradictory predicates. The assumption which Kant is making is that if it were not in itself wholly definite, it would not be necessary. Now, he says, only the concept of *ens realissimum*—the most real entity, which possesses the sum total of all perfection—can be totally determinate. Thus, the necessary being must be thought of as the most real being. But to fit the concept of *most real being* to something which is supposed to be a necessarily existent being, Kant continues, one must assume precisely the sort of coincidence between the two which is involved in the ontological argument. Thus, this cosmological argument presupposes and involves the ontological argument, and falls with it.[19]

Moreover, Kant argues, the cosmological argument depends upon four fallacious assumptions. First, the argument assumes the principle of causality in proceeding from the contingent to its necessary cause. But this principle, Kant says, is valid only in the sensible world; it has no meaning and no criterion of application apart from the sensible world. Second, the argument infers a first cause from the impossibility of an infinite series. But such a series cannot be excluded even in the sensible world. Third, the argument excludes all conditions without which one can have no concept of necessity, and thus renders it impossible that the necessary being be necessitated, yet pretends that this absurd outcome is an explanation, because one can conceive nothing further. Fourth, the argument confuses the logical concept of a being uniting in itself all the perfections of reality and the real possibility of such a being. Real possibility, Kant maintains, can be established only within the field of empirical knowledge.[20]

One might suppose that Kant is being inconsistent. On the one hand he maintains that it is natural and almost inevitable to argue to the existence of God as a necessary being, as the unconditioned condition. On the other hand he rejects the cosmological argument as invalid. His position is that the argument is theoretically invalid; one cannot press theoretical investigation beyond experience, since the human mind is built only for knowing things in the world of experience. But at the same time the ideal of reason is useful, for it tells us to pursue the investigation of the world as if it depended upon a necessary and all-sufficient cause. This ideal is perfectly legitimate and it provides a way of looking at things which is fruitful in guiding inquiry; yet the tendency to make this ideal into an object, then into a substance, and finally into a personal God is simply a confusion, understandable but altogether deplorable.[21]

Kant's conception of regulative principles is somewhat similar to the conception of rationality norms I developed above (pages 74-81). The precise character of Kant's regulative principles and how they differ from rationality norms will be considered in chapter nine.

In sum, Kant's position with regard to the possibility of an uncaused entity is more open than Hume's. Kant understands more accurately the way that an adequate argument would work. But he is convinced that there is no way to *know* that something exists of which man has no experience. The existence of something means that the object is posited in itself, beyond the mere thought of it. For Kant what is beyond thought is contained in the data of experience. Only there does one have any contact with anything as it is in itself—at least this is his official position. By concepts alone can one never come to a new existent, and "it is useless to appeal to experience, which in all cases yields only appearances."[22] Thus, on the matter of arguing to the existence of an uncaused entity Kant's position is quite similar to Hume's. In addition, Kant claims he has shown why men try to argue that God exists, and why that attempt is bound to be fallacious.

It must be noticed that Kant does presuppose the existence of God in the practical domain. There he feels a case can be made for supposing that God is a reality, even though this position cannot be established theoretically. Does it then turn out that God, even as believed in, is only a sort of pious fiction? No, this is not Kant's position. A fiction is an imaginary object, which we suppose as if it were out in the world, while knowing it is not there. God is neither a thing in the world nor a fiction. To believe in God is not to regard him as falling into the category either of real object or of fiction. Rather, it is to act with a certain confidence and expectation, to orient oneself by a moral principle, confident that reality is not at odds with this attitude.

A position very similar to this has been suggested by many philosophers in recent years. Like Kant, they wish to avoid claiming theoretical knowledge about God; they think that descriptive language applicable to the world of experience cannot possibly be suited to talking about God if he is to play a moral and religious role in life. Nevertheless, they think that from a practical point of view one sees the world differently if it is seen as related to God. This way of thinking is at the root of many of the positions which I criticized in chapter two.

9: Criticism of Critique as Metaphysics

The inconsistency of Kant's critique

Kant's critical metaphysics rests heavily upon Hume's empiricist metaphysics. For Kant, Hume's results are data of the problem to be solved. Although Kant does not accept everything Hume says, Kant accepts too much of it. Thus, to the extent that Hume's position is impossible, Kant's position is groundless.

The problem from which Kant sets out is how to account for the necessity of truths about the extrapropositional, in view of Hume's sceptical attack upon such necessity. I argued in chapter seven (pages 126-129) that necessary truths about extrapropositional states of affairs can be learned by experience and reason working together. It is unnecessary to posit built-in structures on the side of the knower, as Kant does, to account for human knowledge of causal necessity. Of course, these truths are not necessary in the way Kant thought they were; he imagined that Newton's physics and Euclid's geometry were as final as man's ability to know, but this ability has relativized these systems and qualified the necessity of their truths.

Of course, Kant does not follow Hume in everything. Kant rejects Hume's restriction of true propositions to synthetic propositions about contingent matters of fact and analytic propositions about necessary relations of ideas. Kant inserts between these two categories a third kind of propositions—synthetic *a priori* truths. But Kant claims that such truths are possible only with respect to the empirical world, for their necessity derives from the conditions on the part of the human knower which make possible his knowledge of the empirical world. Hence, Kant completely agrees with Hume

152

in rejecting the possibility that man can know any necessary, extrapropositional truth other than the conditional truth of causal relationships and the absolute truth of logical necessity. Kant states explicitly that the only nonconditional truth is that of logic: reason "recognizes that only as absolutely necessary which follows of necessity from its concept."[1] Self-referential necessity, which is neither logical nor conditional, shows that Kant is mistaken in accepting this position from Hume.

Kant follows Hume too closely on other points. One of the more important is the assumption that a causal relationship must involve time-sequence. Hume needs this assumption to distinguish cause and effect from one another; he cannot distinguish them by the direction in which, as it were, the necessity flows, since the necessity, on Hume's theory, is projected by the knower.

Kant adopts this assumption and makes it central to his own theory of knowledge. Kant's theory requires that the application of the *a priori* concept of causality be determined by an empirical ordering principle, and, following Hume, Kant takes time-sequence to be the principle which distinguishes cause from effect. Yet Kant himself is aware that the assumption that causality is partly defined by time-sequence is vulnerable.

Kant proposes the objection that causes and effects often are simultaneous and grants the objection. Most causes and effects, Kant says, are simultaneous; the time-sequence in the relationship is due to the fact that the cause does not have its full effect at once. But the beginning of the effect as effect is always simultaneous with the acting of the cause as such. "If the cause should have ceased to exist a moment before, the effect would never have come to be." How, in view of this admission, can Kant continue to maintain the position that the cause-effect relationship depends upon time-sequence? His explanation is the following:

> Now we must not fail to note that it is the *order* of time, not the *lapse* of time, with which we have to reckon; the relation remains even if no time has elapsed. The time between the causality of the cause and its immediate effect may be *vanishing,* and they may thus be simultaneous; but the relation of the one to the other will always still remain determinable in time. If I view as a cause a ball which impresses a hollow as it lies on a stuffed cushion, the cause is simultaneous with the effect. But I still distinguish the two through the time-relation of their dynamical connection. For if I lay the ball on the cushion, a hollow follows upon the previous flat smooth shape; but if (for any reason) there previously exists a hollow in the cushion, a leaden ball does not follow upon it.[2]

This is a remarkable argument, and since it is so vital to Kant's whole theory of knowledge, it is worthy of close examination.

Whatever is in time can have an order which is not temporal—for example, the order of more-and-less in some respect. But temporal order is not simply order of something *in* time; it is order *according to* time—according to before-and-after. Kant's use in his example of "follows" and "previously" in a temporal sense reveals that he admits the need to find something ordered according to time. He suggests that the interval may be *vanishing.* Yet if "vanishing" means "approximating zero," then this suggestion does not help, because an interval which approximates zero still is not zero, while if "vanishing" means "zero," then simultaneity is saved but time-sequence is lost.

The example of the leaden ball denting the cushion does not help; this example merely shows that cushions can be dented by causes other than leaden balls. If, instead, one considers a flat cushion with springs and makes the observation that the surface becomes concave only when someone is sitting (or something is setting) on the cushion, then it is the case that if (for any reason) the cushion begins to become concave, someone sitting (or something setting) upon the cushion does follow.

What is more, one never sees light go on or day break before light goes on or day breaks, yet one supposes that light causes sight, not sight light.[3] To some extent one can act upon both sight and light, but one acts on each in different ways, for example, by opening and closing one's eyes one at a time and both at once, and by turning lights on and off. By such experiences one learns in reasoning what depends on what.

I think that the probable reason for the confused character of this very important argument of Kant's is that he tends to take for granted a common-sense view of cause-effect relationship at the same time he is trying to explain that relationship in a manner very far from the common-sense supposition that it involves an objective necessity *found* in the real world. Another important example of this mixing of common-sense views and Kant's own critical views is his blending of a physical-physiological-psychological account of sensation with a critical account of it.

The former account is that external objects act physically upon the human organism and bring about sensations in the conscious awareness of the subject. All this, for Kant, is correct; it is part of the world of experience. But this world is constituted by human knowledge. Thus, Kant gives a second account, which begins with the unknown thing in itself which acts upon the knower. Kant does not say how the thing in itself *can* act upon the knower. There is a difficulty in his saying that it does, for he is regarding it as a cause, yet it is extraempirical. In other words, Kant is making an object of what cannot on his own theory be an object, since it never can be present to any subject. In any case, Kant thinks that the thing in itself does act upon the knower and produces in him the raw material of experience, a raw material which becomes a world of experience only by the automatic organizing work of *a priori* principles which are built into the knower. Yet the knower himself, also, is an empirical object; he, too, must be constituted *by his own knowing process.*

Thus, corresponding to the thing in itself which generates the stuff of experience Kant also posits an "I" which is not one's familiar self, but is a principle of the unity of all cognition. This principle accompanies all cognition and is the real ultimate subject of the whole knowing-process. If this distinction were correct, there could be no personal self-reference. For while the familiar, empirical self is such that reference can be made *to it*—it is, for Kant, one object of knowledge among others—this empirical self cannot make reference to anything, because *it* does not know anything. And while the ultimate principle of cognition can make reference, one cannot refer to it, because it is not an object.

Kant ought, on his own principles, to use no personal self-referential expressions. Since personal pronouns cannot be distinguished from one another without self-reference, they also should drop out of his vocabulary. However, Kant does not hesitate to say:

> In lifeless, or merely animal, nature we find no ground for thinking that any faculty is conditioned otherwise than in a merely sensible manner. Man, however, who knows all the rest of nature solely through the senses, knows himself also through pure apperception; and this, indeed, in acts and inner determinations which he cannot regard as impressions of the senses. He is thus to himself, on the one hand phenomenon, and on the other hand, in respect of certain faculties the action of which cannot be ascribed to the receptivity of sensibility, a purely intelligible object.[4]

In this passage Kant has man, the ordinary, common-sense entity who refers to himself without any critical difficulty all the time, knowing both of the entities with which critical philosophy is trying to replace him. One need only attempt to read this passage within the rules of Kant's system to see that he himself does not play by them.

Kant seems to assume that the general principles of his system admit of dispensation to the extent necessary to permit *him* to know things in themselves which cannot be known, and to permit *him* to think the self which is never given for thought. What is absolutely impossible according to the system is occasionally possible despite the system, because this occasional possibility is absolutely necessary to construct the system in such a way that it will be absolutely impossible for anything extraempirical outside the system to be known in a way Kant considers illegitimate.

Kant is claiming to know that one cannot know things in themselves, and he purports to prove that what one really knows instead—that is, instead of the unknown things themselves which one knows initiate knowledge—are things as they appear to one knowing (not, ultimately, to you and to me, but to an unknown knower which one nevertheless does know is the only real knower there is).[5]

In other words, Kant has fallen into self-referential inconsistency, just as empiricists fall into it. Empiricism claims that it is necessarily true of extrapropositional states of affairs that there is nothing necessarily true about them. Kant claims to know that it is necessarily true of things in themselves that no one can know them. His claim easily slips by because it is ambiguous. In one sense it can be taken to mean that one cannot know some entities—for example, an uncaused entity and oneself as ultimate subject of knowledge—in the same way one knows others. In another sense it must be taken to mean that one cannot know such entities at all.

The claim that one cannot know things in themselves at all is self-referentially impossible. But what about the more modest claim?

A defender of Kant would point out that unlike Hume, Kant permits *thought* to range beyond experience, but limits *knowledge* to empirical objects. This is true, but Kant's assumption that unknown things in themselves affect sensibility involves positing an objective causal relationship outside experience, not merely thinking a rational connection of ground with consequent. What is more, Kant's identification of the ultimate subject of knowledge with the bodily person—an identification which is inevitable for a human knower—opens the way to some knowledge of oneself as a cause. Kant, it is clear, is assuming that there is at least one other kind of necessary propositions in addition to the analytic ones and the synthetic *a priori* ones his doctrine admits. Of these other necessary propositions Kant offers no critique.

In other words, while Kant seeks the grounds of the possibility of other real and purported knowledge, he does not reflect upon the grounds of the possibility of his own critical thought. Lacking a critique of critique, Kant wavers between dogmatism and scepticism, allowing himself whatever knowledge of extraempirical entities he requires for his purposes—which vary from passage to passage—and forbidding to human knowers generally whatever knowledge of extraempirical entities he considers would be excessive.

The indefensibility of Kant's claim that one cannot know things in themselves comes into even sharper focus if one notices Kant's assumption that he knows other persons and that their cognitional apparatus is identical with his own. How can he know this?

If the description of the *a priori* principles of knowledge is in any sense derivative from the experience of knowing, then it has a psychological character, and there is no necessity to ground the assumption of uniformity. In other words, there is no more reason to assume necessary order in human cognitional processes than in any other part of the natural world.

If the description of the *a priori* principles of knowledge is in no sense derivative from the experience of knowing, then it must depend altogether on what Kant calls "transcendental deduction"—an explanation of the presuppositions which must be accepted to account for the very possibility of knowledge such as man has. But this procedure cannot work unless it is assumed that facts which reveal possibilities also reveal thereby a certain necessity. If this necessity is merely logical, it contributes nothing to the solution of the problem from which Kant set out—namely, the explanation of how empirical knowledge can attain some necessary truth. If the necessity which is uncovered is not merely logical necessity, then Kant must admit that at least in the knower's constitution there is a real necessity which is accessible to human inquiry.

Once any ground is given for admitting necessity, it is difficult to see why one should not reverse Kant's "Copernican revolution" and posit this necessity in what is known in general, rather than appropriating it for the constitution of the knower. In other words, once one begins to become critical of critique itself, one sees the possibility of looking to the known for the principles which make it knowable: What are the necessary conditions which must hold of possible objects of knowledge in themselves such that they can become known to human knowers, as in fact they are known? This realistic question admits of some consistent answers; Kant's inquiry into conditions of knowledge on the side of the knower which would somehow constitute objects of empirical knowledge admits of no consistent answer, unless one also grants that man does know things in themselves.

Such a realistic inquiry could begin by noticing that human knowing is not only a synthetic unity governed by formal principles; it also is a dynamic process filled with variety. All of the changes and all of the variety in human knowledge must arise from somewhere; *a priori* forms of intuition and understanding—if one grants these to Kant for the sake of argument—only give the unifying features of knowledge. Thus, even if things in themselves were not known fully and directly, they would be known to the extent that only their effects upon the knower would account for the variety in knowledge. These consequences would reveal something about their proper causes.

If one need not posit necessity on the side of the knower, what gives Kant's attempt plausibility? Two factors, I think. One is the underlying assumption—which is not Kant's own assumption—that knowledge is a set of replicas or pictures of objects. The other is an ambiguity in the phrase "know things in themselves."

If one begins from the assumption that knowledge is a replica, then one is likely to be impressed with the difference between the content of sensation and its physical conditions—for example, the difference between color and light waves. Since color is not a replica of anything, least of all of light waves, the realism of sensation is easily denied. One might still continue to think of propositions as pictures of the world. But Hume's researches—if one assumes the outcome correct—indicate that propositional knowledge also falls short of being a replica of anything.

Whatever its merits or limitations, the thesis that sense-perception is not realistic is intelligible. But this thesis depends upon the assumption that one knows in another way that sense-perception is not realistic, and that one has a plausible theory why it is not. If knowledge in general is assumed not to be realistic, the ground for calling the realism of any part of it into question is removed. If one does not know things in themselves by propositional knowledge, one simply does not know them, and one cannot know that one does not know them.

Someone might suggest that there is a still higher type of knowledge, a type which cannot be expressed in propositions, and that from this higher standpoint one could call into question the realism of propositional knowledge. This, in fact, is what Kant implicitly assumes. He thinks of the critical standpoint as if it were outside propositional knowledge altogether, and thus exempt from the rules he lays down.

I do not deny that there could be propositions which cannot be expressed in a given language. Nor do I deny the possibility of knowledge other than propositional knowledge. However, if one having other knowledge knows by it anything about the truth of propositions, whether to assert them or to deny them, then he has what can be known to be true, and what can be asserted or denied—propositions. And if anyone can introduce by philosophic discussion any thought which can question, limit, or otherwise bear upon propositional knowledge-claims, then he has sentences which express propositions—not, perhaps, in some special and technical sense of "propositions," but in the sense in which he thinks his own sentences expressing questions, setting limits, or otherwise bearing on propositional knowledge-claims are *saying* something significant which others might agree or disagree with.

Kant himself recognized that there is an important difference between sensation and propositional knowledge. Sensation does not involve truth-claims. It does not provide replicas of objects, but it is not false on that account. Indeed, because sensation does not involve any truth-claims, it cannot possibly be false in the sense in which propositions can be false. If sensation did provide replicas of objects, one would not have a better point of departure for knowledge. One would still have the problem of *knowing* the thing—whether the thing were an object outside or a replica inside the knower. The replica, precisely in virtue of its character as a precise duplicate, would not be any nearer to knowledge.

Apart from the implications of the assumption that knowledge is a replica, I think the other factor which lends plausibility to Kant's critical project is the ambiguity of "know things in themselves." In one sense, "to know something as it is in itself" would be to know it without knowing it, to slip around the modes of knowing which one has and to engage in some sort of immediate encounter or direct intercourse with reality, so that one could lose oneself in and literally become what one knows. This ideal is not bad, but it is the ideal of love, not of knowledge. In some respects love is better than knowledge, but each has its merits; one loses something by trying to make knowledge into love.

In another sense, "to know something as it is in itself" represents the legitimate ideal of propositional knowledge itself. Often one knows, but one's knowledge is mixed with many defects. Some of these defects originate in sensation and in experience generally—for example, in defects of memory and the like. Others perhaps originate in other ways apart from propositional knowledge itself.

But some of the defects of propositional knowledge arise from within itself. Propositions are limited to the states of affairs they pick out; the extrapropositional world need not be limited in the same way. This is evident because some propositions pick out states of affairs which include the states of affairs picked out by others; one often in learning discovers the limits of previous knowledge. Moreover, one discovers in a similar way that the ordering of propositions—both the sequence in which one comes to know them and the logical relationships among them—does not necessarily correspond to anything in the extrapropositional world. Finally, one discovers that distinctions marked by propositions—for example, between doughnuts and holes—do not correspond directly and simply with distinctions in the extrapropositional world.

In asking questions, in reasoning, and in making judgments one must try to take into account the respects in which properties of propositions cannot be taken as indicative of corresponding properties of the extrapropositional world. To take into account and to *discount* at its proper rate what the knowledge process itself puts into propositional knowing is the task—or, at least, one task—of logical thinking. Logic as a reflective discipline seeks to cultivate this necessary critique. But this critique is a self-criticism of propositional knowledge. It does not establish boundaries around what can be known, but only makes clear mistakes which must be avoided if the extrapropositional world is not to be dressed in the misplaced properties of propositional knowing. Stripped of such misplaced properties, extrapropositional states of affairs can be known as they are in themselves. They are known as they are in themselves to the extent that the propositions to which one assents are true. Still, even true propositions fall short of exhausting a subject matter. One can always ask additional questions. In doing so one points toward the ultimate legitimate sense of "knowing the thing in itself"—that is, knowing all the true propositions which can be known about it.

Perhaps this ideal is unattainable in practice, but it is not inherently nonsensical, and it does not entail that one does not now know things in themselves.

Thus "know things as they are in themselves" has two senses. In one sense it is absurd to think such knowledge possible; Kant, I think, unconsciously trades upon this sense. In another sense one can know things as they are in themselves, and the attainment of such knowledge is in part aided by a critical discipline. But the critical discipline is ordinary logic, which helps make clear what are properties of propositions as such, and what belongs to the content picked out by propositions. Also, the proper methods of various inquiries help in the progress of knowledge toward the ideal limit of answering all the questions which can be asked. But no legitimate critique of propositional knowledge can establish the self-referentially impossible position that one cannot know things in themselves.

Specific arguments concerning God

In the fourth antinomy, as I explained above (pages 145-147), Kant argues that a necessary being, either in the world or outside it, which could serve as unconditioned principle of alteration is impossible. Such a being, he holds, would have to initiate change as an agent in an action-passion state of affairs. Thus it would be included in time; yet, as the origin of all change, it must also be antecedent to time. I pointed out that this argument, since it is concerned with change, has nothing to do with the uncaused entity to the existence of which I reason in part two.

However, this argument of Kant's suggests the following problem relevant to my reasoning from contingent states of affairs (SA) to an uncaused entity (D). I name the propositions corresponding to SA and D, "P" and "X" respectively.

How can two entities as disparate as SA and D and two propositions as disparate as P and X be connected by a rational process? If SA obtains at certain times, for example, then its condition, D, must obtain only at those times; if D is a condition which obtains in virtue of itself, then D is necessarily given, and its consequences also must be necessarily given.

This objection is plausible, but it rests on false assumptions. First, it assumes that "obtains" can be modified temporally, but "obtains" is tenseless. Temporal determination belongs to the content of propositions. This point makes clearer the difference between arguing to a principle of change and arguing to a principle of being.

The objection also assumes that a principle (D) and what follows from and depends upon the principle (SA) must be homogeneous. However, it is clear that the condition required for SA to obtain *cannot* share all the properties of

SA. If the more immediate cause (*C*) of *SA* shared all *SA*'s properties, *C* could not be a condition for *SA*; the two would be identical in what they require to obtain. We often notice the similarities between physical causes and effects. These are important, but the differences also are essential, for a cause must be somehow different from its effect if the cause is to satisfy any requirement which the effect does not satisfy for itself by itself.

If *SA* obtains, the entities it involves must somehow exist; if they are physical entities, they must exist at a certain time. If *SA* obtains, then an uncaused cause (*Dc*) and an uncaused entity (*D*) also must obtain. But the temporal determinants of the entities involved in *SA* need not characterize *Dc* and *D*. One is likely to suppose that they must only because one thinks of *Dc* in its *relationship* with *SA*. Physical, causal relationships are transitive in respect to time; causes of changes are prior to or simultaneous with their effects, and effects are simultaneous with or subsequent to their causes. However, the relationship of *SA* to *Dc* is not that of patient to an agent. The obtaining of states of affairs is not a predicable determination of their content, and thus the relationship of states of affairs to what they require to obtain need not be transitive in respect to time, even if all the content of *SA* is temporally determined.

Similarly, the relationship of *Dc* to *SA* need not be transitive with respect to the necessary being of *D. D,* the uncaused entity, is included in *Dc,* the uncaused cause. *D* obtains necessarily, but *Dc* is contingent, since *Dc* does not obtain unless *SA* also obtains. There is no uncaused cause without effects.

SA obtains contingently; it might or might not obtain, but does. The relation of *SA,* which obtains contingently, to *Dc* is not a matter of logical necessity; if it were, I would have been able to use something like the principle of sufficient reason in the second section of chapter five rather than argue on the basis of rationality norms. Thus, it is possible to apply the causal schema, although the relationship of *D, Dc,* and *SA* is unique; it is not one of physical, formal, or any other sort of causality having other instances. The causal schema here is of the contingent states of affairs, *SA,* and the necessary state of affairs, *D,* united in a larger state of affairs, which can be looked at either from the side of the cause or from the side of the effect. From the side of the cause, *Dc* satisfies what *SA* requires, over and above other causal conditions, to obtain; from the side of the effect, *SA* obtains rather than not obtaining, its need for an unconditional principle satisfied by *Dc.*

This cause-effect relationship is contingent *because* it includes *SA. Dc* is contingent, but *D* is not; the relationship between *Dc* and *D* is not the same in both directions. I discuss this further in chapter seventeen. It is worth recalling at present, however, that *D* is included in *Dc* abstracting from the latter's causing of *SA*—in other words, the uncaused entity is that which is an uncaused cause apart from the latter's contingent relationship to its effects. If

D is God and *Dc* is God creating, that God freely creates the contingent does not entail that God himself is contingent.

In treating the arguments for the existence of God Kant begins by calling into question the very meaning of "necessary being." I first consider his argument on this point, and then consider the specific points he makes in reference to the ontological and cosmological arguments.

People always talk about a "necessary being," Kant observes, assuming that this expression is meaningful. One can easily define the expression: "something the nonexistence of which is impossible." But it is not so easy to state "the conditions which make it necessary to regard the nonexistence of a thing as absolutely unthinkable." Normally a thing is necessary in virtue of the fact that the conditions for it are given.

> The expedient of removing all those conditions which the understanding indispensably requires in order to regard something as necessary, simply through the introduction of the word *unconditioned,* is very far from sufficing to show whether I am still thinking anything in the concept of the unconditionally necessary, or perhaps rather nothing at all.[6]

Kant obviously learned his Hume, and this argument proceeds on the same assumptions which I criticized in chapter seven. Kant thinks that if one says that there is something unconditioned, one removes all the conditions for *regarding* the entity as necessary, because Kant assumes that necessity properly belongs to the logical relationship of condition to consequent. He confuses the exclusion of conditions for obtaining with the exclusion of conditions for *regarding*—that is, for knowing. Also, after Hume's fashion, Kant takes for granted that if the existence of a necessary being were possible, its nonexistence would be unthinkable—that is, self-contradictory. As I explained in chapter seven (pages 129-133), the uncaused entity to which the argument in part two leads might—it is a logical possibility—not exist.

As I explained in chapter eight (pages 149-150), Kant's criticisms of the ontological argument are not relevant to the argument I propose in part two except in respect to one point. Kant maintains that knowledge of existence amounts to knowing how an entity fits into the framework of experience. Consequently, so far as human knowing is concerned, nothing can distinguish the existence of an extraempirical entity from its mere possibility. Human consciousness of existence, according to Kant,

> ... (whether immediately through perception, or mediately through inferences which connect something with perception) belongs exclusively to the unity of experience; any existence outside this field, while not indeed such as we can declare to be absolutely impossible, is of the nature of an assumption which we can never be in a position to justify.[7]

In my language this amounts to saying that since one knows some state of affairs obtains if one is given experience of it, one cannot know that any extraempirical state of affairs obtains.

There are three points to be made in answer to this argument.

First, the argument I propose in part two does proceed mediately through inferences which connect the uncaused cause with something experienced as obtaining. Someone's reading a sentence or writing a book is an empirical fact. But the argument I propose does not terminate in an empirical fact. Apart from empiricist assumptions, I do not see why it should.

Second, Kant himself argues from experience to what is extraempirical—things in themselves, the *a priori* conditions of knowledge, the self as ultimate subject of knowledge, and so on. He treats these extraempirical entities as real conditions which make possible empirical knowledge. Once one sets aside Kant's untenable claim that one cannot know things in themselves, there is nothing to stop one from arguing beyond experience in a manner analogous to that by which Kant himself argues to extraempirical entities. The conditions which make knowledge possible can be traced back; these conditions include what is required on the part of things known. Among these conditions on the part of states of affairs directly known to us is the uncaused cause which explains why states of affairs which might not obtain nevertheless do obtain.

Third, Kant's argument that knowledge of existence is fitting entities into the empirical framework either does not succeed or proves too much. It does not succeed if it is even possible to know that something could exist which would not fit into the empirical framework; it proves too much if it shows that existence can be nothing but being-there in space and time. Extraempirical entities, by hypothesis, cannot be given in experience; thus, if to be is to be given in experience, Kant must declare that such entities are absolutely impossible.

It could be objected that this argument merely shows that Kant ought not to have admitted the possibility of extraempirical entities. This objection amounts to rejecting Kant's metaphysical alternative, perhaps in favor of a hardheaded empiricism. An empiricist cannot rule out extraempirical entities without claiming to know that extrapropositional states of affairs are necessarily limited to empirical ones. However, the necessity of such limitation, like extrapropositional necessity generally, is not something which one knows by experience. The self-reference into which the empiricist cannot help falling also shows that there is something extraempirical.

Kant criticizes a rationalistic version of the cosmological argument. In this version "necessary being" is defined as "the most real being." Such an entity is determined by one of every pair of contradictory opposites; it includes in itself the greatest possible sum of perfections. It is only as a consequence of this conception of "necessary being" that the cosmological argument which Kant criticizes either does invoke or at least seems to invoke the ontological argument.

At the end of chapter seven (pages 135-136) I explained what I mean by "necessary being." The concepts used in the rationalistic argument play no part in mine. As a matter of fact, however, I of course grant that the uncaused entity must be characterized by one or the other of each pair of contradictory predicables. However, as I will explain in chapter fifteen, this characterization does not result in a concept of a sum-total of perfections—that is, of intelligibilities predicable of entities which might or might not obtain. Rather, all propositions predicating such intelligibilities of the uncaused entity must be *denied*. Understanding "perfection" as Kant understands it here—that is, in a rationalistic way—one must say that the uncaused entity, far from being the greatest possible sum of perfections, is an absolute zero.

The first of Kant's four specific objections to the cosmological argument is that it assumes the principle of causality, which is valid only in the empirical world, and applies it beyond experience. The argument I propose in part two does not assume any *a priori* principle of sufficient reason or of causality, but argues—in the second section of chapter five—for the use of the schema of causal reasoning to render intelligible the obtaining of contingent states of affairs. Kant himself uses causality extraempirically. Moreover, Kant's justification for restricting the use of the principle is altogether dependent upon his general theory of knowledge, which I criticized above.

Second, the cosmological argument Kant considers infers a first cause from an infinite series. I discussed infinite series in chapter five (pages 64-67), but my argument does not depend upon regarding the uncaused cause as the limit of such a series. Rather, whether contingent states of affairs are finite or infinite in number, they are not self-sufficient.

Kant's third objection to the cosmological argument he is considering is simply a restatement of the point, already criticized, that "necessary" presupposes conditions which make something necessary. What Kant claims, however, is not true of every sort of necessity. Kant's fourth objection to the rationalistic version of the cosmological argument is that it confuses logical with real possibility by supposing that the logically possible "most perfect being" is really possible. This objection merely restates what Kant has said about existence in reference to the ontological argument.

Thus Kant's specific criticisms of arguments for the existence of God do not touch the argument proposed in part two. The reason they do not is that I took Kant's points seriously and was careful to avoid coming into conflict with the truths he points out. Kant also grasped further truths with reference to human knowledge of extraempirical entities. In the technical sense of "know" he claims officially that one cannot know them. But one can think them, and Kant proceeds to indicate how to do so.

> If, in connection with a transcendental theology, we ask, *first,* whether there is anything distinct from the world, which contains the ground of the order of the world and of its connection in accordance with universal laws, the answer is that there *undoubtedly* is. For the world is a sum of appearances; and there must therefore be some transcendental ground of the appearances, that is, a ground which is thinkable only by the pure understanding. If, *secondly*, the question be, whether this being is substance, of the greatest reality, necessary, etc., we reply that *this question is entirely without meaning.* For all categories through which we can attempt to form a concept of such an object allow only of empirical employment. . . .[8]

Thus Kant holds that one can and must think that there is something extraempirical, which is the ground of the world of appearances. He rejects the application to this entity of concepts which have positive meaning in the world of experience. It is neither substance nor not a substance, neither the greatest reality nor something less than the greatest, neither necessary—in the sense in which empirical entities are not necessary—nor merely contingent.

This position of Kant's, setting aside his distinction between appearances and things in themselves, is consonant with the argument I propose in part two and with the view, already mentioned, which will be developed in chapter fifteen, that the uncaused entity cannot be positively characterized by any of the predicables which are used in propositions picking out contingent states of affairs.

Kant goes on to suggest that it also is legitimate to think of this extraempirical entity by analogy with objects of experience, but this analogy, which might even include certain anthropomorphisms, is valid only for the idea, not for the thing in itself. One not only may but must think this principle of being to be a wise and omnipotent author of the world.

In his *Prolegomena to Any Future Metaphysics* Kant explains what he means by "analogy" in this context. If one limits one's knowledge claims to the relationship which the world has to its extraempirical ground, then one safely stops at the boundary of knowledge. Why?

> For we then do not attribute to the Supreme Being any of the properties in themselves by which we represent objects of experience, and thereby avoid *dogmatic* anthropomorphism; but we attribute them to the relation of this Being to the world and allow ourselves a *symbolical* anthropomorphism, which in fact concerns language only and not the object itself.[9]

By such analogy one considers the world as if it were the work of a supreme understanding and will. One thinks of the world in relation to its unknown ground on the model of the relation of human effects to intelligent causes in the world of sense. But one does not thereby *know* the unknown principle "as it is in itself but as it is for me, that is, in relation to the world of which I am a part." This analogy does not tell what the unknown is like. Still, by means of it

> . . .there remains a concept of the Supreme Being sufficiently determined *for us*, though we have left out everything that could determine it absolutely or *in itself;* for we determine it as regards the world and hence as regards ourselves, and more do we not require.[10]

Kant goes on to argue that this position escapes Hume's criticism of discourse about God.

In chapter seventeen I will argue that relational predication about the uncaused cause—for example, that it causes—is possible. I agree with Kant that such predication expresses what the uncaused entity is only insofar as it is the *relatum* of the relations of other entities to it. Such relational predicates do not permit one to describe—except negatively—what the uncaused entity is in itself, apart from the relationship, by using predicables which are expressed by empirical language. In saying that the uncaused cause "causes" I do not invoke a concept of analogy such as Kant explicates. The analogy in this case is based, not upon the content of experience, but on the application of the *schema* of causal reasoning to this unique relationship.

The manner in which the uncaused cause is said to "cause" is the basis for other relational predications. Some of these relational predications depend upon a model derived from experience, especially the human person's experience of his own causing. These relational predications are more like the analogous or symbolical predications Kant has in mind. "As if" is essential to the expression of such thinking. But one who thinks of the uncaused cause by analogy with the schema of causal reasoning is not thinking symbolically; one must avoid supposing that the uncaused cause is *like* an agent, *like* a formal cause, and so forth. Either the schema of causal reasoning can be used or not; if it can, there is an uncaused cause. If it cannot, it would be meaningless to say that there is no uncaused cause, but contingent states of affairs obtain *as if* there were one.

Moreover, the theory of relational predication I will develop is unlike Kant's in another important respect. Kant maintains that relational predication "concerns language only and not the object itself." By relational predication one may think the ultimate principle of the empirical world "only as object in *idea* and not in reality." In other words, Kant thinks it is impermissible to suppose that relational predication really *says* anything which is informative except about what is *within* knowledge or language itself.

If one grants that there *is* an unconditioned condition or uncaused cause, Kant's rule is broken. In this case, clearly, one is thinking that whatever the uncaused entity might be in itself, it is whatever it must be to terminate the relationship of contingent things. In other words, the argument in part two concludes to an extrapropositional state of affairs once the applicability of the causal schema is granted. And Kant himself is assuming that there is *something* unconditioned. Thus he is allowing relational predication to indicate what is extrapropositional.

Why does Kant think that relational predication, even though it involves saying that there *is* something unconditioned, nevertheless indicates nothing extrapropositional? The answer is that the unconditioned condition plays a certain role in his whole system. It functions, theoretically, as a regulative principle. The *a priori* forms of sensibility and of understanding constitute empirical objects; they contribute expressions to descriptive language. The ideas of pure reason—which include the self, the world, and God—do not enter into the constitution of empirical objects. But they direct empirical thought. The idea of God, the unconditioned condition, does so, according to Kant, by demanding that the human investigator look at the whole of what can be studied as something absolutely unified, as a perfect system, which has the intelligibility of an effect of a supreme intelligence. In this way one is led to push inquiry onward, always confident that questions—empirical ones about the world—can be answered, that a system will be gradually uncovered, that one will not encounter surds or brute facts.[11]

Thus, Kant's conception of the restriction of the reference of relational predicates to the sphere of the Idea or of language, his refusal to admit that such predications indicate anything extrapropositional, is a consequence of his general theory of human knowledge of the empirical world. I have already argued in the first section of this chapter that this general theory is inconsistent. Therefore, I will not criticize Kant's restriction of the reference of relational predicates insofar as it depends upon his general theory. However, the point which Kant is making here does lead to two important questions which must be considered.

The first of these is a matter of clarification. Kant's regulative principles, obviously, are both similar to and different from the rationality norms discussed in the second section of chapter five. What, exactly, is the relationship between the two? The second question is the ultimate objection which a proponent of empiricism or critique can make to the argument I propose in part two. The objection is: If *obtains* is not a predicable, then all metaphysical statements, including those of empiricists and critical philosophers, *and their supposed contradictories,* are meaningless, not true or false. This objection generalizes the entire thrust of the limiting strategies of these metaphysical alternatives. I next take up the first and then, in the final section of this chapter, the second of these questions.

Regulative principles and rationality norms

Kant introduces the regulative principles of reason when he attempts to explain why one mistakenly supposes that there are extraempirical realities which can be considered as if they were objects. Why, for example, do the questions which lead to the antinomies arise? Kant considers these questions badly formed. What makes people ask them?

Kant's answer is that man by nature has an unrestricted desire to know. This unrestricted desire cannot be satisfied unless the totality of what is to be known can be known. Thus, the ideal of this totality is assumed to be a real possibility, and it is set up as something to strive for. Kant thinks this procedure is natural and valuable. The difficulty comes when the ideal, mistaken for an object, is taken to be an explanatory principle.

In this context Kant states that the principle of sufficient reason is not a theoretical principle. The principle cannot assert that there is a complete explanation for anything, for no such explanation ever is achieved. It instead sets a task. The principle is a rule, prescribing a regress through a potentially endless series of explanations. As a rule, the principle lays down what one ought to do as one regresses through a series of explanations—namely, one ought to keep going. It bids one extend experience and continue inquiry indefinitely. But it does not guarantee that there always really is a reason.[12]

At times Kant speaks of many regulative rules as maxims. For example, he takes a rule of simplicity to be a maxim which urges simplification, but Kant thinks this maxim is balanced by another which urges that distinctions be made. Such maxims he calls "subjective principles"; he suggests that different interests, which are merely a matter of temperament, lead some individuals to prefer one such maxim to another.[13]

Kant also treats theoretical and practical reason as having differing interests, but regards these as common to all men. The interest of practical reason is in the reality of the extraempirical, so that one can act freely and hope for immortality in which God will reward everyone according to his due. The interest of theoretical reason is to extend possible knowledge, but at the same time to unify it. Theoretical reason, thus conceived, is a capacity for building up the edifice of empirical knowledge. Kant says: "Human reason is by nature architectonic. That is to say, it regards all our knowledge as belonging to a possible system," and therefore permits only principles compatible with this interest in system.[14]

When Kant treats the ideas of pure reason as regulative principles, he regards them as theoretical, as common to all men, and as driving in a single direction—toward unity. The ideas of reason guide the work of understanding in the investigation of empirical reality; these ideas also coordinate the methods of theoretical inquiry. They do not arise from experience; rather, they are antecedent to experience. The ideas, as it were, project a plan of completely unified knowledge, and then urge understanding, working upon sense data to fill in the plan.[15]

There is no doubt in Kant's mind that the drive toward unity is necessary. He says:

> The law of reason which requires us to seek for this unity, is a necessary law, since without it we should have no reason at all, and without reason no coherent employment of the understanding, and in the absence of this no sufficient criterion of empirical truth.[16]

Kant elsewhere states that the projected systematic unity of reason is the criterion for the truth of the rules of understanding.[17] The ultimate significance of systematic unity in establishing the criteria of empirical truth gives the ideas which project such a unity a kind of objectivity, not indeed that they are extraempirical entities, but that they point to the totality of empirical knowledge in which all empirical entities would be systematically constituted.[18]

Kant thinks that for the ideas to be effective in directing inquiry toward its ideal limit, one must think of the ideas as if they were extraempirical objects. One must think of the ultimate knowing subject as if it were a capacity to know everything—a kind of metaphysical container of all knowledge—of the world as if it were an infinite whole which could be given in one comprehensive vision, and of God as if he had made the knower and known for each other. The idea of God is most basic, because it leads one to think of what is to be known as an intelligible world; one can seek laws in nature as if one were trying to understand a person's action and work.[19]

The necessity that the ideas be thought of as if they were objects inevitably leads to illusion. This inevitable illusion, according to Kant, is the real source of rationalistic metaphysics. When one sees that the ideas are merely regulative principles, one can avoid positing them as objects. But one still has to think of them as if they were objects; the illusion, although no longer deceptive, remains. Kant uses the analogy of a mirror, which one knows gives an illusion, and yet which one uses to see oneself and objects otherwise invisible behind one's back.[20]

Since Kant thinks of the ideas as really representing ideal limits of inquiry into the empirical world, he maintains that if one makes the mistake of regarding them as objects, they will conflict with the interest which they should further. If one supposes that God is a reality accessible to theoretical knowledge, for example, one is likely to suppose that one has an answer to every question about the world. Thus, the mistake about God leads to abandonment of detailed investigation, which alone builds up real knowledge. Similarly, one who posits the idea of a divine, ordering intelligence in objective reality tends to fill the idea with his own notions and then impose these notions upon nature, rather than carry out the necessary but painful work of empirical investigation.[21]

Why does Kant stress unity so heavily? There are three related factors here, I think. One is that he still has a rationalist ideal of reason. Although he rejects the transcendent metaphysics which Leibniz draws from it, Kant supposes that the ideal is to explain everything, to reduce everything to one perfect insight. This conception of reason's function is coupled with an empiricist notion of experience. Kant, like Hume, thinks of experience as in itself disconnected. The whole functioning of mind from the forms of sensibility through understanding to the ultimate ideas of reason is directed at unifying and harmonizing this multiplicity. Finally, Kant needs criteria of truth. Having denied the realistic conception that one can know things themselves, these criteria must be found in the goal of the mind's own work. The ultimate criterion of truth is that things fit into the system.

One might wonder why the ideas as regulative principles could not be considered mere rules. Why does Kant suppose that it is necessary even to think of them as if they were objects? I think the answer is that Kant thinks of understanding as imposing unity upon sensuous content. At the level of reason a unity of knowledge cannot emerge out of what is known. Rather, one must bring something to the content to serve as a unifying principle. Yet, for Kant all real objects of knowledge are of one sort and stand on one metaphysical level. Thus, to save the objects which are constituted by understanding Kant feels it necessary to deny the reality of the ideas of reason.

In view of Kant's rationalistic ideal it was wise of him to fear the carrying out of the synthesis of knowledge. If the project were carried out in fact, then multiplicity and change in the empirical world would be swallowed up. In many respects one can see in Kant's doctrine of the regulative principles the beginning of Hegel's philosophy of the Absolute Spirit. Kant's reduction of criteria of truth to the ideal of unity of knowledge is adapted and adopted by Hegel. Hegel also accepts Kant's conception of an idea of reason as an underlying principle of the intelligibility of the whole. But Hegel allows Absolute Spirit to be the real totality, not above, but within the whole of the empirical world. In this way Hegel regards reason as a cognitive capacity and carries to completion the project envisaged by the earlier rationalists.

How do the rationality norms compare with Kant's regulative ideas? There are similarities, but also differences.

The rationality norms are not *a priori* principles. Rather, it seems to me, their origin is in the spontaneous functioning of the child's mind, but also in the experience of thinking, making mistakes, and gradually learning how best to question, reason, and judge in order to achieve truth. Thus, I do not admit, even as an ideal, the principle of sufficient reason. This and other rationality norms require limiting clauses.

Again, I do not consider rationality norms to be expressions of various interests. One appeals to rationality norms to support assertions and to exclude counterpositions as unreasonable. Thus, they must not express subjective interests and they must be cognitive, although not theoretical.

I do not think that the rationality norms express any innate drive of reason toward unity. The unity of thought is worthwhile only to the extent that it leads to truth. Sometimes one must accept irreducible distinctions or find oneself in self-referential or other inconsistency. Although the rationality norms express the requirements of love of truth, they are not natural laws or logical necessities. One can choose to be rational or not. One can prefer other values to truth. Thus these norms make a demand which is as unconditional as the value of truth but as defeasible as the appeal of this value when it confronts other, more immediate passions.

The rationality norms lack the quasi-theoretical character of Kant's regulative principles. Although Kant wishes the regulative principles merely to regulate, still he feels one has to think of them as quasi-objects, or they will not work at all. The rationality norms guide questioning, reasoning, and judging only if these acts themselves are competent to realize the intelligibility which is present in experience itself. Thus, one need not think of rationality norms as if they were objects. Undoubtedly, there is a tendency to do so or, at least, to think of them as somehow descriptive of reality. Very likely the reason for this is the general tendency to try to understand everything on the model of common-sense cognition of the world, which is oriented to the practical purposes of daily life, and which therefore takes as a paradigm an object which can be described and dealt with.

Lacking the quasi-theoretical character of Kant's regulative ideas, the rationality norms do not themselves project entities. One uses rationality norms in all cases in which questioning, reasoning, and judging do not occur spontaneously. The rationality norms I invoke in the argument in the second section of chapter five are not a sketch of the uncaused entity itself. Kant's idea of God always includes descriptive content, such as intelligence, omnipotence, and so on. This content is necessary, he thinks, for the idea to function as a regulative principle. The uncaused cause does not have any such content; it simply is, is not caused, and causes.

Finally, there is nothing of the imperialism which Kant feared either in the rationality norms or in the conclusion of the argument in part two which I reach by using them. These norms and this conclusion do not suggest that everything is explained and that investigation can stop. Nor do they provide one with some sort of blank check for imposing one's notions on the world apart from investigation. *D,* the uncaused entity, is proposed as an entity to be investigated.

The status of obtaining and self-referential necessity

It is difficult to strip away everything accidental to kantian critique in an effort to generalize the metaphysical alternative which he tries to formulate. However, P. F. Strawson has suggested the following generalization.

For Kant one cannot separate the significant use of concepts of understanding from the conditions of awareness of objects to which these concepts are applied. Only what is somehow given in experience can be an object of knowledge, since human intuition is sensory. Kant sharply distinguishes the understanding, to which concepts belong, from the faculty of intuition. Understanding is not intuitive. If one attempts to use the concepts of understanding as if they referred by themselves to something, one inevitably becomes involved in transcendent metaphysics—metaphysics of the bad sort.

Strawson suggests that in Kant one finds something faintly echoed which ought to be preserved. There are a number of concepts, which Strawson calls "formal concepts," somewhat like Kant's categories. Formal concepts include *existence, identity, class* and *class-membership, individual, unity, totality, property,* and *relation.* Strawson does not mention *not,* but it seems to me that this concept must be included among formal ones. Formal concepts can be applied or exemplified in empirical propositions, where their use depends upon the availability of empirical criteria for the use of nonformal, empirical concepts. Formal concepts also can be used in purely logical deductions. Just as Kant forbids use of the categories to talk about an extraempirical world, Strawson suggests that

> ... formal concepts cannot be significantly employed in making non-logical assertions without the employment of empirical criteria for the application of other concepts, giving body to the particular applications or exemplifications of the formal concepts involved in such assertions.[22]

Strawson suggests that formal concepts are ultimately derived from experience by generalization. He does not accept Kant's self-referentially impossible position that man does not know things in themselves, to the limits to which human knowledge actually goes. But he thinks that the formal concepts must be flexible enough to be open to new uses; man cannot claim to exhaust the potentiality for modes of experience. This feature of formal concepts, by which they have greater amplitude than already given empirical content, makes it possible for someone to attempt to employ formal concepts in statements which are neither empirical nor logical. Such an employment constitutes metaphysics of the bad sort.

If Strawson is correct, my attempt to develop a philosophical theology is an impossible project. This project depends upon a great many statements which are neither logical nor empirical. For example, I say that since one can know what it would be like for some states of affairs to obtain without knowing whether they do, such states of affairs are contingent. In such states of affairs, which might or might not obtain, for the state of affairs to be the state of affairs *which* it is and for it to *obtain* are not identical. I go on to talk about what is required, unconditionally, for contingent states of affairs to obtain.

In all these statements I use *obtain* neither as a formal concept nor as an accompaniment of empirical concepts. In fact, I use it as a quasi-concept, and use *state of affairs* in the same way. One way of expressing Strawson's point would be as an objection: If *obtains* is not a predicable, then by what right is it used in all of these metaphysical statements? *Obtains* can be employed in empirical statements such as the statement that such-and-such a particular state of affairs obtains, or in logical ones, such as "*Obtains* is not a predicable," but it loses all sense when one attempts to employ it referentially apart from particular, empirical content.

It must be noticed that the forbidding of metaphysical statements would exclude all of them. Anselm's ontological argument depends upon an assumption about meaning and obtaining in the case of a supreme being; the criticism of the ontological argument also always must involve metaphysical statements. Even if one says, as Hudson does in the passage cited above on page 33, that the question "Does God exist" includes within its very meaning a distinction between what is being said and what, if anything, is being said about, one invokes the distinction between sense and reference, and this semantical distinction is neither empirical nor purely formal—that is, syntactical.[23] The empiricist claim that extrapropositional states of affairs always obtain contingently and that there are no necessary truths about them also is meaningless. Hence, its apparent contradictory is not self-referentially necessary, but meaningless. On this theory the same can be said of "One cannot know things in themselves" and "One can know things in themselves."

One might suppose that what Strawson is proposing is simply another version of the verifiability criterion. But his proposal seems to me far more radical, since it would make the verifiability criterion meaningless. Moreover, it is not clear that Strawson's proposal can be condemned without question-begging as self-referentially inconsistent, for it seems to exclude the sort of argument which would attempt to condemn it. To make this point clear I must consider what is involved in self-referential necessity.

As I explained in chapter seven (pages 133-134), self-referential necessity is clearly distinct from other sorts of necessity. In particular, it must not be confused with formal or logical necessity. One can be self-referentially incon-sistent without being logically incoherent, and a self-referential argument is not a *reductio ad absurdum*.

Someone is reading a sentence. The preceding sentence is self-referential and it has a certain necessity. The necessity involved is the inseparability of understanding the state of affairs picked out by the proposition it expresses and knowing that this state of affairs obtains. These are inseparable for the simple reason that the same act of reading gives rise to both. No one can put words together to form a sentence. The preceding sentence also is self-referen-tial and necessary. Any *possible* act which would count as taking the position expressed by this sentence also would provide this or a similar sentence as a counterexample to this position. The first of these two cases clearly is only conditionally necessary. Perhaps no one is reading a sentence; then, since the act is not given, the statement is false. The second example is somewhat different. Only the possibility of using language is required for it to be false. But suppose it were the case that everyone had aphasia. Perhaps then people still could think, but no one could put words together to form a sentence. To the extent that self-referential necessity is concerned with facts, this necessity also is conditional.

The statements of empiricism and of critical philosophy which I have argued are self-referentially inconsistent are not dependent on the possibility of using language. The empiricist claims that there are no necessary truths about extrapropositional states of affairs, and the critical philosopher main-tains that one cannot know things in themselves. The apparent self-referential impossibility of these claims leads to the affirmation of apparent contradic-tories, which seem to be necessary. In both cases, however, both the original positions and their apparent contradictories use what Strawson surely would call "formal concepts"—*states of affairs* and *things*. And these statements are neither logical nor empirical. Thus, if Strawson is correct, these metaphysical positions and counterpositions are neither true nor false, but meaningless.

The question is, Is Strawson correct? He provides no argument in favor of his position. If someone simply lays down a rule saying, "Since *obtains* is not a concept, it may not be used except in empirical or logical propositions," one can answer this challenge easily enough by introducing some additional logical categories. The apparatus I developed in the second section of chapter four is not exclusivistic. Thus, I can say that *state of affairs* is a metaname, that *obtains* is a metapredicable, that such metaconcepts can be used in metapropositions to make metaempirical statements, such as the ones Strawson is ruling out.

This expansion of logical apparatus is not simply an ad hoc device. Or, at least, so I can claim. In propositional knowledge I can distinguish a primary level of empirical propositions in which there are no negations, no metaconcepts, and so on. At a second level one knows a set of entities which one did not and could not know at the primary level These entities are propositions, negation, and other features of propositional knowledge. Inasmuch as one does know such entities, one's cognitional content is not purely empirical. In Kant's terms one has at least this much intellectual intuition. Anyone who takes Strawson's position must grant as much. His suggestion that formal concepts ultimately are derived from experience by generalization cannot mean that they are derived from experience as *body, quality, much, doing,* and so on are derived. These concepts, however general, remain empirical. If the formal concepts did not depend upon knowledge of propositions at the primary level, they also would remain empirical.

Given this expansion of logical categories, the position Strawson is suggesting can be restated by saying that metaconcepts ought to be used only in first-level propositions, where they do not function as concepts, or in statements of logic, where they do not refer to anything extrapropositional. What Strawson's position would forbid is the use of metaconcepts in metapropositions picking out metaphysical states of affairs.

The question remains why Strawson's restriction ought to be accepted. If it is simply laid down as a rule, then one need not pay attention to it. Clearly it is not itself an empirical statement. If someone offers reasons why *obtains* cannot function as a metaconcept in metaphysical propositions, he must say something about *obtains* which is neither logical nor empirical. Thus, it seems that if any theory is proposed for the restriction Strawson suggests, a self-referentially inconsistent position will emerge.

I see only one way in which a proponent of the restriction could try to avoid this difficulty. He might suggest that since the necessity of metaphysical self-referential statements depends upon propositional knowledge, perhaps such statements are valid, not absolutely, but only on condition that someone can know propositionally. There is an inseparability of propositional knowledge from its objects which seems to be unconditional, but this seeming absolute necessity actually is conditional. Propositional knowledge depends completely upon an extra-propositional world, but the relationship is not mutual. If there were no propositional knowledge, one might argue, the world would remain just as it is. If this is true, then it might seem to follow that one cannot use metaconcepts metaphysically; in making reference to the extrapropositional one may only use empirical concepts.

On this theory, it seems to me, one cannot even say that some states of affairs might or might not obtain unless this statement can be reduced to pure syntax. One can imagine a world without propositional knowledge. In this imaginary world one can imagine no negation, thus no might-or-might-not. Everything simply is as it is. States of affairs and their obtaining do not appear at all. These are not features of the world, but projections upon it by the human propositional knower.

I think that this theory comes close to what Wittgenstein had in mind when he wrote the famous sentences at the end of the *Tractatus* which I quoted on page 120. That the world is, is the mystical; in other words, one must simply *see* the world apart from the relational properties imposed upon it by the process of propositional knowledge. If this was Wittgenstein's thought, then his view was more subtle than empiricism. Indeed, the vision of a world free of propositional knowers and what they project is bewitching.

When entertaining this vision, it is important not to confuse the world which is free of propositional knowers with our own world, and then to mix the two. This is the kind of illicit move Kant so often makes by shuttling back and forth between the common-sense and the critical standpoints. In our world, among other extrapropositional entities is propositional knowing itself. Propositions only *are* by being entertained, asserted, and so on. These acts are themselves real and they belong to the world. Hence, in our world one cannot hold an empiricist or critical metaphysics, nor can one suppose that such a metaphysics would be true in a world without propositional knowers. The necessity of self-referential positions which is based upon the inseparability of propositional knowledge from extrapropositional states of affairs holds for all *possible* cases of propositional knowledge. In thinking of a world free of propositional knowers and in talking about it one still considers it an extrapropositional state of affairs which *can* be known by propositional knowledge.

One also must notice that not all of the extraempirical concepts which Strawson mentions—and negation, which I add to his list—work in the same way. I argued in chapter four (pages 43-45) that negation can be reduced to asserting and denying, to believing and disbelieving—in other words, to acts and propositional attitudes of propositional knowers. This reduction eliminates negation from the content of propositions; one is not tempted to think of the world as filled with negative states of affairs nor to make negativity into a metaphysical principle.

Most of the other formal concepts which Strawson mentions—*class* and *membership, individual, property,* and so on—arise mainly because of the relationships established in the inner structure of propositions. Since the structure of propositions need not correspond to the structure of extrapropositional entities—something which becomes obvious when one compares the truths one knows by diverse propositions—these logical entities cannot be directly projected into the world. The case for excluding such projections was made by aristotelians from Aristotle himself to Thomas Aquinas, William of Ockham, and others against platonists, neoplatonists, and scotists.

Since not all extraempirical concepts perform the same function, one cannot automatically forbid the metaphysical use of any of them merely because the metaphysical use of some of them must be excluded. In other words, perhaps *obtains,* used in empirical propositions, signifies something about the extrapropositional which is more than merely a relational property of the known to a knower. To rule out this possibility, one defending a position such as Strawson suggests must show what function *obtains* performs in empirical propositions such that one ought not to use it metaphysically.

Obtains cannot be reduced to the act of asserting. One can assert a proposition which is false. If a state of affairs obtains, the proposition which picks it out is true. Of course, in making this semantical statement one uses *obtains* neither empirically nor syntactically. However, perhaps a defender of the theory can be permitted a certain set of semantical statements. I do not see how he can give any account of what *obtains* does in propositions if he is not allowed to make semantical statements. Moreover, critics of other metaphysical mistakes make semantical statements involving the logical entities which they refuse to accept as part of the furniture of the world—for example, negating does not refer to anything extrapropositional.

Obtains cannot be said to lack any regular function in empirical propositions. The word "obtains" is somewhat artificial, but one uses roughly synonymous expressions with regular meanings in ordinary language. For example, "That is so," "This is how it is," and "It's true that . . ."often are used to express what I mean by "obtains." "It's true that John killed the man on the highway, but it was an accident" is not a statement about the truth of the proposition that John killed the man on the highway; the "it" in "but it was an accident" does not refer to a proposition but to a state of affairs. The sentence could as well begin, "It is the case that. . . ," which is another way of saying *obtains* in everyday language. Of course, *obtains* is not always expressed. If one utters a sentence expressing a proposition in a suitable context, one is assumed to be asserting it, and then one is taken to be claiming that the state of affairs picked out by the proposition obtains. The claim might or might not be justified.

It is tempting to say that *obtains* used in empirical propositions simply means the givenness to experience of what makes the proposition true. This givenness to experience would not be anything over and above what is referred to by the proposition insofar as it is made up of empirical concepts;

the givenness simply would be a relational property, such that the things experienced would remain just as they are even if there were no one present to experience them.

However, *obtains* cannot be reduced to this givenness. There can be true propositions which no one knows to be true; the state of affairs picked out by such a proposition obtains but it is not given in anyone's experience.

But, perhaps, the obtaining of a state of affairs simply is that about it by which, if there were a suitable observer, it would be given to him in experience. In other words, the obtaining of states of affairs is nothing but the potential of entities in the world to affect knowers in such a way that these entities could make themselves known. But notice that on this supposition entities have this potential whether or not there are any propositional knowers. Moreover, if this potential answers to *obtains,* then it either is an empirical property and *obtains* is a peculiar empirical concept, not a logical one, or there is something *about the entities* which can make themselves known to propositional knowers by way of experience that is not reducible to empirical concepts.

The supposition that *obtains* might, after all, be a peculiar sort of empirical concept will not do. If it were correct, *obtains* would be a predicable and it would be part of the content of empirical propositions along with other predicables. Unless such propositions are thought of as formal truths, however, they remain contingent. Something besides their content is required for their truth. If not, the distinction between meaning and reference and the corresponding distinction between entertaining a proposition and asserting it collapse.

One cannot dismiss these consequences by saying that they pose no problem in a world without propositional knowers. In our world there are propositional knowers. A fact which falsifies a proposed interpretation of the meaning of a word which is used in our world cannot be ignored merely because this fact would not be given in some other world.

But the question remains: If *obtains* is not an empirical concept, how is it possible to have this metaconcept unless it is a purely logical concept derived from reflection upon what propositions add to their own empirical content?

The answer, I think, is as follows. One is aware of one's own entertaining of propositions. To be aware of this is to be aware of an act, which is itself an extrapropositional entity. One knows the difference between one's entertaining the proposition and the content of the proposition. To know that a state of affairs obtains is to know that it is neither only the content of a proposition one entertains nor only one's entertaining of this proposition. In other words, to know that a state of affairs obtains is to know that it is in some way *other* than by *being picked out* in one's proposition. To know this is to posit the state of affairs as extrapropositional.

In the case of empirical propositions one posits on the basis of experience. But one also can posit states of affairs which one does not directly experience, provided that reasoning establishes a medium between some experience and the state of affairs one posits. This is how one can posit the uncaused entity.

Obtains thus is a metaconcept; one can have it only insofar as one knows one's propositional knowing. But it is a peculiar metaconcept, for it refers to that extrapropositional factor by which the state of affairs one posits is extrapropositional. One could not know this factor prior to propositional knowledge, yet this factor is not a logical entity mistakenly projected upon the empirical world.

What I am saying is that *in* propositional knowing one knows the world in a way in which one does not know it in the experience and insight which is presupposed by propositional knowledge. The empirical content of propositions cannot be generated by propositions. The self-awareness of propositional knowing brings with it an awareness of the otherness of content from the act of entertaining the proposition. The awareness of the content *as received* is an awareness of this content as having a status apart from one's knowing it. In the reflection involved in propositional knowing, then, one knows oneself as knowing and knows what is known as obtaining.

A defender of the position Strawson suggests might object that on my account obtaining remains a relational property. It is simply the objectivity of the objective world, and this is strictly relative to the subjectivity of knowers. If there were no knowers, then there would be no objectivity. This is undoubtedly true. But there still would be that about the world by which it could make itself known to propositional knowers if there were any. And to the extent that this potential of the world for disclosing itself is not reducible to empirical properties, it is a factor to which one can refer by using the metaconcept *obtains.*

Finally, the defender of Strawson's suggestion might say that even if one can refer to the obtaining of empirical states of affairs, perhaps *obtains* refers to nothing other than that to which the empirical concepts already refer, but in a different way. In one sense, I think, this point is correct. *Obtains* does not posit a different state of affairs; *obtains* still is not a predicable. Thus if "nothing other" means "no other *empirical* content," the point is well taken. However, if this point means that obtaining is not distinct from *what* obtains, then the point is not well taken. It amounts to a metaphysical theory, precisely what the suggestion was intended to eliminate in the first place. There is good reason not to accept this metaphysical theory, the reason I gave in chapter four (pages 43-48) for adopting the contradictory position.

Still, it is not logically impossible that *obtains* for some reason cannot be properly used as a metaconcept to make metaphysical statements. However, if someone is going to argue that this is more than a logical possibility, then he must offer some reasons which make clear why *obtains* cannot be used as a metaconcept to make metaphysical metapropositions. If he offers such reasons, he himself must take some sort of position which will involve more than empirical propositions, syntactical propositions, and even a restricted set of semantical propositions. Directly or indirectly, he must try to say what makes true propositions true.

If no one can offer any theory which makes clear why metaphysical statements are forbidden, then it is speculation against the value of rational discourse to suggest that nevertheless there is a logical possibility that all metaphysical thinking is mistaken. Logically possible positions which no one can give any reason for accepting should not detain a philosopher. If the final sentences of the *Tractatus* themselves *say* anything, they make clear that one need not be silent. What, if anything, one cannot speak about, one must *altogether* consign to silence. Mysticism has no place in philosophy.

10: The Absolute Idealist Alternative

The philosophy of Absolute Spirit

Hume and Kant represent metaphysical alternatives to one side of the philosophical theology I am developing. They maintain that there is no necessary entity or none accessible to human knowledge in which *what* and *that* are intelligibly united. Hegel, on the other side, affirms that there is a necessary being and maintains that man can know this being. The necessary being, for Hegel, is not far from man. In fact, man himself contributes to its fulfillment. For the necessary being is the whole system of reality, completely conscious of itself. Man, more specifically philosophizing man, in particular Georg Wilhelm Friedrich Hegel, has the honor of completing the unification, in a bond of intelligible necessity, of *what* and *that*, of the rational and the real.

Hegel holds that what is usually regarded as the contingent, extrapropositional world really is the content of thought. It seems contingent and external only because thought is not at first completely reflective. However, when the mind for which this seemingly contingent world is content completes the unfolding of it, the world's unbroken intelligibility as a single all-embracing truth appears for what it is. The content of thought is the mind itself, thinking itself. What is thought and the thinking of it are one and the same, and this unity of thought and thinking is reality.

This reality is Absolute Spirit. It is perfectly reflexive. It is the ultimate case of self-referential necessity, for there is no condition apart from itself on which it depends.

In Kant the pressure of reason toward unity pointed toward the coherence

181

of system as a criterion of truth. Hegel regards this unity as realized; truth is coherence. Everything fits into the system without residue.

Kant thought of the thinking self as an underlying subject. At the same time he conceived of God as a perfect intelligence of which one must think as if it were the unconditioned condition of the empirical world. Hegel identifies the underlying subject of knowledge with the unconditioned condition. He rejects the attempt of Kant to limit knowledge to empirical content. Thus, Hegel posits the system which Kant so much desired and so much feared.

Kant kept the principle of sufficient reason as a regulative principle, but he insisted that one should not claim to have theoretical knowledge that there is and always will be a reason for everything. Hegel considers Absolute Spirit to be the sufficient reason of everything. It explains everything by including it all. Kant considered God rationalistically as the most real being, the being bearing in itself the sum of all perfections. Hegel's Absolute Spirit is the totality. It includes all perfections, not in abstraction from the world, but by gathering up all the dynamism and variety of the world.

Hegel rejects many of the presuppositions common to Hume and Kant. They both regarded the data of experience as atomic units, and they thought that connections among these units, as in cause-effect relationships, are imposed by the knower. Thus Hume and Kant both assumed a sharp dichotomy between contingent empirical truths—matters of fact or synthetic *a posteriori* propositions—and necessary propositions based on relationships among ideas themselves. Hegel substitutes for this empiricist starting point the conception of experience as a living process. Experience merges with reason. Necessity is found within experience. At the same time the fully developed idea of reason is identified with reality.

Kant sought to develop a philosophy in which the claims of science would be established and also reconciled with the interests of morality. He wanted to accept the mechanistic picture of the physical world, while holding to a moral world of freedom and a religious conception of God. Hegel also wishes to reconcile the requirements of science with those of morality and religion.

But Hegel's ambitions are even greater. He believes that Christianity, as he understands it, is true, and he wishes to reconcile this truth with a completely rational account of the empirical world. Hegel also is much more interested in history than Kant was. Hegel believes that the concrete process of history can be explained by philosophy. Hegel realizes more fully than anyone before him that becoming is not a secondary category, a form of being inferior to static fixity. And so Hegel wishes to reconcile becoming with stability, time with eternity, the coming to be of creatures with the unoriginated reality of the first principle.

Hegel rejects Kant's unknowable thing in itself. If the thing in itself really were unknowable, we would not know it. For Hegel the thing in itself is not a hidden reality behind experienced objects; it simply is any *thing* at all, considered in abstraction from all its characteristics and relationships. The general and indeterminate conception of "thing" takes shape in the understanding of all the various things man does know. Thus, the thing in itself, far from being unknowable, actually is such that "there is nothing we can know so easily."[1] Not only things, but qualities, quantities, and so on are unknowable in themselves, if "in itself" means in abstraction from a larger whole of which they are only parts. For one knows things only when one grasps them as they really are, and things *really* are, not in isolation but in interrelation.

From another point of view, anything considered "in itself" is taken in its undeveloped stage. Man in himself is the child; a plant in itself is a seed. A fully real man or plant develops into what he or it can be by coming out of himself or itself through a life which involves constant interplay between the self and the other.[2]

One reason why Kant maintained the distinction between objects as they are known and the unknown thing in itself was in order to have something beyond knowledge which could appear in knowledge. Science and history are not make-believe and fairy tales. Kant also needed the distinction to resolve the problems which he believed would lead to antinomies if the objects of the world of experience are taken to be things in themselves.

Hegel does not deny that the scientist and the historian have their own criteria of scientific and historical truth. But he regards the philosophical question about the objectivity of knowledge as a different matter. The philosophical question is: How can one know objective truth when all human knowledge is of things *as man knows them?*

Hegel's solution is at once simple and drastic: Reality as man knows it, once one fully and adequately knows it, precisely is reality as it is in itself. Hegel admits that particular things in the world of experience are only appearances, but he considers them to be appearances in their very reality. The reality of which they are appearances is not unknown and unknowable; it is the whole of which they are parts. If one rationally grasps the parts in their proper places in the unity of the whole, then one sees that the contradictions which are characteristic of the world of experience are really necessary aspects of this manner of being.[3]

The fully real and the fully rational are identical. The ultimate criterion of the truth of knowledge is not that it conform to any object outside itself. How could one possibly compare knowledge to an unknown something outside it to see whether knowledge is correct? The ultimate criterion of the truth of knowledge is the inner coherence of the whole of knowledge. Knowledge is true when it has a place for everything and everything fits in its place. There are no loose ends and no unanswered questions. When knowledge reaches its culmination, what is known is identical with reality, and reality is nothing else but what is known, precisely as it is known.

This point might be illustrated by considering a plausible counterexample. Dreaming involves a sort of thinking. How can this sort of thinking be true? Hegel's answer would be that dreaming is part of reality. It is illusory only insofar as one who is asleep does not realize that he is dreaming. But this illusion precisely is an aspect of the sort of reality which dreaming is. If one takes a dream to be something more than it is, one runs into difficulties. For instance, a person who dreams he has won a million dollars in a sweepstake and who proceeds the next day to begin spending it will find that he does not have the money in the bank. But one does not come to grasp the limitations of dreaming by getting at the things dreamed about in some more direct way. Rather, one becomes aware of the truth of the dream-world by putting it in its proper place in relation to the waking world. When the dream-world fits with the rest of experience with no loose ends, one knows its truth and reality. The knowledge of the truth and reality of the dream-world does not abolish the inconsistency which is characteristic of that world, but the inconsistency of the dream-world is fully explained by its being properly placed in the wider world which one normally regards as "real."

This wider, real world of common sense also has to be seen through, according to Hegel. When one does see through it, one grasps the whole of which it is only a partial aspect. This whole is a knowledge in which the subject-object distinction has its place, but in which this distinction is not accepted as ultimate. Kant's unknown knowing subject merges with his unknowable thing in itself to form in Hegel's philosophy a knowable total reality in which all oppositions are gathered up, explained, and harmonized.

According to Hegel, ultimate truth must be grasped not only as substance but as subject as well.[4] The whole which is reality is not only something thought about—substance—but also is a thinker, a subject. There is no thinking which is not about something real, and there is nothing which is not the content of thinking, which is not *for* thought. The world as one sees it, all experience and history, are harmonized in total reality, which from one point of view is thinking and from another point of view is objective content. Thus, reality is a self-thinking thought, as Aristotle long ago said. But for Hegel this reality which is self-thinking thought is not simply part of reality, cut off from the rest, as was Aristotle's God. It is the whole of reality. Absolute Spirit includes everything else, even the otherness of things other from itself.

According to traditional Christian conceptions God exists eternally as a perfect being in himself. He creates a world as an expression of his own reality and perfection. Human persons are among the creatures in this world, and God reveals himself to them. Mankind is separated from God, but God becomes incarnate in order to reconcile mankind to himself. Human persons thus are enabled to share in the divine life by the gift of the Spirit. The fulfillment of this gift is eternal life in union with God. Thus, creation returns to its source. Hegel accepts this vision of reality as true, but he regards it as a merely symbolic expression of the truth. He considers it the task of philosophy to express this same truth in a literal, conceptual way.[5]

Going beyond what he regarded as imaginative representations, Hegel translates the content of Christian belief into his philosophical concepts. The totality of reality, which is at once all which can be known and the only complete act of knowing, is Absolute Spirit. The Absolute must be understood as a self-realizing process. Beginning with the logical structures of undetermined possibility, Hegel traces this process through its stages.

First the whole structure of possible being in itself is unfolded. The necessary conditions for possible knowledge also are necessary conditions for all possible entities, because the opposition between knower and known has been set aside. Next, being achieves a status outside mere universal possibility by entering upon the course of becoming. The Absolute goes outside itself and in doing so becomes other than itself, assuming the form of a material world, in order that it can *become*—that is, come to be actual. Finally, the development through lower nature to consciousness in mankind reaches the summit of philosophical reflection, in which the whole of things is gathered up. Here, at last, Absolute Spirit, which had come to be other than itself, returns to itself and achieves its full actuality. The Absolute is not merely undeveloped possibility, but fully intelligible reality; reality grasps itself as a self-thinking which also is all which can be thought.[6]

To speak of God existing eternally, for Hegel, is a symbolic way of speaking of the Absolute as mere possibility, as being in itself which is necessary as structure but lacking in actuality. To speak of creation is a symbolic way of speaking of the necessary particularization in which universal and intelligible categories of being are instantiated in material entities, which undergo change in the natural world. To speak of the fall of man is a symbolic way of speaking of the otherness of man, not yet fully aware of his potential divinity, from the full reality of the Absolute. To speak of the Incarnation is to speak of the potential divinity of mankind as such—that the Absolute can realize itself by coming to full self-awareness in man's philosophical reflection upon the totality of reality. The beatific vision of God is a symbol of the philosophical knowledge of Absolute Spirit; this knowledge is superior to religious faith and it is achieved in Hegel's philosophy.[7]

Philosophy, for Hegel, is not simply *about* reality, about God. Philosophy is part of reality, the very culmination of reality, the final self-realization of the possibility of being, which is what religion calls "God." Truth in its final achievement is the whole of reality, not in the sense that everything considered in abstraction is true, but in the sense that the truth of each thing, understood in its proper place, includes its peculiar differences, its particularity, its very otherness from the whole. Absolute Spirit is the product of the process, but it is not a product separated from the process; rather it is the product which is the process, gathering up the whole of the process into itself. Knowledge and reality thus coincide in Absolute Spirit, so that everything is included within the final rational system. The seeming otherness of objects is itself explained. The rational method of investigation, far from being a mere form of knowledge, is grasped as the necessary method of the self-realization of the Absolute, which is not only the known reality but also the knower.[8]

The point Hegel has in mind can be illustrated by analogy with the organism, which is Hegel's favorite metaphor. An organism is not merely an abstract *kind* of thing, a pattern of possibilities. It is a living process. One knows what an organism is not simply by defining it as a fixed species; one must learn about its functions, in which its possibilities are progressively realized. None of the organism's parts nor any of the earlier stages is intelligible or genuinely real apart from the living whole in its fullest stage of development.

Yet a merely organic entity is limited, in that it must give up its various stages as its life progresses. Possibilities which are fulfilled are surpassed, and in a certain sense are lost. Reality is like an organism, but it is one which initiates and shapes its own existence, goes through its own life, and in the process becomes self-conscious. Through this self-consciousness all of the stages of its development are gathered up, united in the living whole, and thus saved and rendered indestructible. For Hegel this salvation, achieved through philosophic knowledge, is the real but hidden meaning of Christian faith. God is not a reality apart from the created world, as a separate and unattainable *Other*. Rather, the Absolute is the true and ultimate actuality of this world; this world is the medium in which the Absolute comes to be.

The significance of Hegel's philosophy of Absolute Spirit for the argument for the existence of an uncaused entity, set forth in part two, is that if Hegel is correct, then the only condition distinct from a particular state of affairs required for it to obtain is the rest of what is, unified in the Absolute. Considered in itself, any particular state of affairs is contingent. One always can understand what it would be like for it to obtain without knowing whether it does obtain, simply because one can think it not as it is in truth, but abstractly and falsely, as mere appearance. As such, the particular state of affairs is isolated and incoherent. It is both something, and yet nothing real. It is finite being, but its finitude—its limitation to being by itself alone— means that it actually is cut off from being.

Yet if all particular states of affairs are taken together in the unified whole which they are, then their reality is established without appeal to any further condition. The condition in virtue of which each part is is the whole of which all the parts are parts. This whole is gathered up in the understanding of it by Hegel's philosophy. This understanding includes not only the unity of the whole and its necessity but also the divisions, the succession of stages found in the parts, and their contingency.

In short, Hegel holds that there is a necessary being, but he denies that this necessary being or uncaused entity is anything apart from the totality of contingent beings.

Proofs for the existence of God

A proof for the existence of God is possible, according to Hegel, but such a proof does not establish the reality of anything separate from entities more directly known to man. Rather, the proofs of God's existence merely articulate the process in which one's mind is "raised to God." The function of the proof is to spell out something which is understood implicitly in knowing every particular entity.

In a full sense the proof of the existence of God is nothing else than Hegel's entire philosophy, which does not demonstrate anything from an unquestionable starting point, but rather renders everything intelligible by putting all things in their proper place, so that the sheer force of insight makes clear that there are no more questions to ask.[9]

Hegel says that "what men call the proofs of God's existence are, rightly understood, ways of describing and analyzing the native course of the mind, the course of *thought* thinking the *data* of the senses."[10] Proving the existence of God is thinking the reality of the world of experience in another form; "true being is another name for God."[11] Hegel is sensitive to the criticism that his approach reduces God to the world. His answer is that in fact he is affirming that only God truly is. People are too attached to the reality of the world, Hegel thinks, and as a consequence they are "more ready to believe that a system denies God, than that it denies the world."[12] However, it is clear that Hegel does not deny the world. He wishes to keep both God and the world, but to identify them with each other.

For Hegel knowledge of God is by no means confined to knowledge that God exists. Man can know what God is, Hegel affirms. It is necessary to the reality of God that he communicate himself. God is not isolated from the world; he does not exist apart from it as if he were not involved in it, as if it were irrelevant to his own being. On the contrary, God gives himself over into the things he creates, particularly to man. Thus, the knowledge of God is not blocked from God's side; God is not "jealous" and does not conceal himself.

The assertion, for instance by Kant, that human knowledge cannot rise to God is a product of false humility and confused thinking. Human reason with its limits might not be able to know God, but that is looking at human reason *as part*, as a thinking which is abstracted and not yet wholly true. It is the "Spirit of God in Man" or "the self-consciousness of God which knows itself in the knowledge of Man."[13] Man's true self is achieved only in a knowledge of all reality, including this knowledge itself, which recognizes itself as complete, as the whole of truth and reality—as God.

Hegel treats the cosmological argument at length and with considerable care. According to Hegel the starting point of the argument is the whole world, as a collection of material things which are finite and contingent. The finitude and contingency of material things are not evident to sense perception; rather, in any adequate understanding of the world one must think it to be finite and contingent. The conclusion of the argument is directly implied by its principle, for in grasping the material things as finite and contingent one directly grasps their unlimited and necessary principle—namely, the whole of which they are only parts.[14]

Spirit, which is revealed in the argument, also is the very knower to which the argument for God's existence reveals Spirit. The philosophic mind becoming aware *is* Spirit, since the "Spirit does not exist as an abstraction, but in the form of many spirits."[15] The argument for God's existence can be expressed in terms of a whole series of categories, for God can be known as the being of things, as the ideal, as the essence or ground from which events follow, as the whole of which particulars are mere parts, as the power which gives actuality, as the cause of all effects. But contingency and necessity are the most adequate categories to use, for they gather up all the rest and provide the fullest résumé of what is involved in the finite and the infinite.[16]

Hegel answers the objections which Kant raised. Yet Hegel is not satisfied with the understanding of the cosmological argument by philosophers prior to Kant. What was wrong with the argument, Hegel thinks, is that finite being was assumed to be an ultimate and real fact, and then the argument had to try to get outside the finite in order to reach the infinite. For Hegel the very fact that finite being is contingent means that in itself the finite is only appearance, not true being. A correct argument need not go outside finite being to reach the infinite. Instead—and for Hegel this solves the problem which he thinks was at the bottom of Kant's objections—one need only see through the pretense of the finite. Then one will see, Hegel is convinced, the infinite which is the real being of the finite:

> The Being of the finite is not its own Being, but is, on the contrary, the Being of its Other, namely, the Infinite. Or to put it otherwise, Being which is characterized as finite possesses this characteristic only in the sense that it cannot exist independently in relation to the Infinite, but is, on the contrary, ideal merely, a moment of the Infinite.[17]

The finite world is only an appearance of the infinite, but this does not mean that the finite is unreal. It is real; it is the infinite; to be the infinite precisely is the reality of the unreal finite.

Hegel explains that contingency in particular things characterizes them to the extent that they are thought in isolation. Any particular entity within experience could just as well not exist as exist. But in the context of conditions in virtue of which these entities do in fact exist, the particular is not only contingent, it also is necessary. This necessity is genuine, although it is only conditional. Thus contingency and necessity, while remaining contradictory, are not mutually exclusive. The dialectical tension of contingency and necessity in particular entities points to the absolute necessity of the unconditioned, of the whole. The whole is not lacking in conditions, but it is not conditioned by anything outside itself. It includes its own conditions, for the conditions of the whole are supplied by its parts. Thus the Absolute is actual in virtue of the parts which make it up. "God" is absolutely necessary because that which is other than the whole is included in the whole as a contributing principle.[18]

Someone can object to the cosmological argument that insofar as it proceeds from the finite to the infinite, it makes the infinite dependent upon the finite. Hegel points out that this objection confuses conditions of knowledge with conditions of reality. To the extent that it attempts to be a proof, the form of the cosmological argument does not correspond precisely to the reality with which the argument is concerned. In its form the argument would treat the finite and the infinite—the beginning and the end of the process of proof—as realities extrinsic to one another. But being is common to both ends of the argument, and if this being is truly real, then the two ends of the argument really cannot be extrinsic to one another. If the two extremes of the argument ever were really extrinsic to one another, Hegel maintains, the argument never could succeed, for finite thought *as finite* cannot grasp the infinite. There is no passing from the merely finite to the infinite.[19]

Yet Hegel does not believe that the gap is unbridgeable or that it must be crossed by a "leap of faith." In reality there is no gap. "Man knows God only in so far as God Himself knows Himself in Man."[20]

Hegel's philosophy makes exalted claims for man. In fact, Hegel is claiming that God comes to be real in man's knowledge; the distinction between this exalted knowledge as human and as divine is overcome. Is this pantheism— namely, an equation between God and creatures? Hegel argues that it is not. Pantheism in Hegel's view errs by absorbing the particularity, the process, and the otherness of creatures in such a way that these are lost in the totality, stability, and self-identity of God. Hegel's position in his own eyes is quite different from pantheism, for he holds that the particularity, the becoming, and the otherness of finite and contingent things are not lost in God, but are gathered up and maintained in the unity, the stable truth, and the conscious and free self-identification of the Absolute Spirit. Mind or Spirit is not a mechanism; it distinguishes things which are united precisely in order to overcome distinction in unity.[21]

Thus Kant's attack upon the cosmological argument is rejected by Hegel, but Hegel himself adapts the argument in such a way that it does not point to the reality of an unconditioned condition which is ultimately other than the sum of conditioned conditions and states of affairs. Hegel regards the cosmological argument as an attempt to articulate the insights which are contained in his own philosophical system.

The significance of Hegel's approach to arguments for the existence of God is clarified further by his treatment of the ontological argument.

This argument, rejected by Kant and by others because it proceeds from the mere concept of a perfect being to an assertion of the existence of such a being, is accepted by Hegel, provided that it is correctly understood. The proper understanding of the ontological argument, Hegel thinks, is that Absolute Spirit necessarily has being as one of its subordinate aspects. One hardly can compare the relation between the concept of a finite entity and the affirmation of its existence with the relation between the concept of God and the affirmation of his existence. Whatever is particular, passing, and contingent is grasped as contingent in itself and as necessary only in virtue of conditions beyond itself. But the whole, which does not itself come to be and pass away, but which is of itself and is absolutely necessary, is grasped as a being which has no conditions outside itself. Its conditions are everything else, for all else—even as *else,* as other—reduces to the Absolute.[22]

If Kant had been able to respond to Hegel, he probably would have pointed out that Hegel was not really answering the objections which Kant had raised. Kant's objections were concerned with proofs for the existence of God as a reality distinct from the empirical world. Kant himself did not deny that reason demands that there be an unconditioned ground of empirical realities. Hegel does not argue that God, as Kant conceived of God, exists. Rather, Hegel holds that the totality of reality exists. Kant never doubted it, nor did he think it needed to be proved. Hegel actually is *excluding* the possibility of the sort of entity which Kant *believed* to be real, but the existence of which Kant thought defied proof.

The importance of Hegel, then, is in his claim that the unconditioned condition is the rational whole of reality, a whole in which truth and being become one and the same. If Hegel is correct, the uncaused entity is not an extraempirical entity which exists apart from the world of contingent beings. In fact, everything finite is a condition for the actuality of this whole, which is absolutely necessary only by including its conditions in itself.

11: Criticism of Absolute Idealism

Unlimited reason and negation as a reality

The metaphysical alternatives proposed by empiricism and by critique attempt to set limits. The former tries to limit reality to the contingent; the latter tries to limit knowledge to the contingent world. The refutation of such positions is achieved by showing that the limitations they try to establish are so narrow that no room is left for these positions themselves.

In the final section of chapter nine I examine what I believe to be the ultimate ideal of such metaphysical alternatives. It is a world free of propositional knowers and of what such knowers project upon extrapropositional states of affairs. It also is a world free of extrapropositional obtaining, to which human thought attains only in propositional knowing.

I argue against these metaphysical alternatives that such a world is not. I try to show that both propositional knowing and reasoning are in some way *original* modes of cognition. *In* propositional knowing one knows the obtaining of states of affairs, and this obtaining is not reducible to the prepropositional content of experience and understanding. *In* reasoning one knows causal relationships, and this order cannot be reduced to anything experienced, understood, or posited by cognitional acts prior to reasoning. Thus, one can ask metaphysical questions about the aspect of the extrapropositional which becomes known only in propositional knowledge, that is, one can ask about the very *obtaining* of contingent states of affairs. And one can answer this question with an answer which first comes to be known in reasoning, that is, with the answer that there is an uncaused cause of empirical states of affairs.

Hegel makes no attempt to limit what is or what can be known. Rather, he rejects all limitations. Far from trying to break the link between human knowledge and extrapropositional states of affairs, he maintains that at a certain point—in his own philosophy of Absolute Spirit—human knowledge and extrapropositional states of affairs merge with one another. Thought and being are one. The need for reasoning and for propositional knowing vanishes as the ability to understand, which is the ultimate principle of being, is fully actualized. Absolute Spirit becomes self-conscious. Spirit thinks its own wholeness to be the thinking which it is. Self-reference, at this limit, is perfect. For Hegel propositional knowing is not banished from the world; it is absorbed into the world and it absorbs the world; an all-embracing insight is achieved by the mediation of reasoning, but not *in* reasoning.

Hegel's absolute idealism is an alternative to the philosophical theology I am developing because if his philosophy is true, the contingency of empirical states of affairs is merely apparent. One can think what it would be like for a certain state of affairs to obtain without knowing whether it does obtain only if one thinks this state of affairs imperfectly, abstractly, apart from its concrete context. In context, Hegel maintains, for states of affairs to be what they are and for them to obtain are—one should say "is"—one and the same. Thus there is no uncaused cause distinct from the contingent, empirical world. Hegel's absolute idealism rejects all the distinctions essential to the metaphysics I am trying to work out.

The absolute inclusiveness of the claim of Hegel's philosophy of the Absolute precludes any attack upon it based on empirical data about which Hegel might have been in error. If Hegel made some mistakes of fact, these can be corrected. The system is designed to accommodate any facts whatsoever. At worst, a defender of Hegel might be forced by particular facts to make certain adjustments in the details of Hegel's account of the unfolding of the Absolute. Perhaps Hegel did not put everything *precisely* in its proper place. But tidying up the hegelian system would perfect it, not refute it. The Idea remains.

Hegel is working out the ultimate implications of rationalism. For rationalism everything in principle has a sufficient reason. All reality would be seen as unified if one could but see it as a whole. The necessity present in any single intelligibility, which cannot be denied without self-contradiction, embraces everything. But Leibniz and later Kant tried to block the fulfillment of the rationalist ideal by pleading the limitations of human knowing. Since Hegel accepts no such limitations, the rationalist ideal is fulfilled in Absolute Spirit. According to the original version of this ideal, individuality, freedom, and contingency as such should vanish completely in the perfect, static unity of a solid block of intelligibility.

Hegel sees the falsity of this outcome and rejects it. Yet he wishes to maintain the rationalist ideal and to fulfill it. In order to do so, he must admit into reality an additional metaphysical principle. The principle he admits is negation.[1] Negation is not in itself anything at all; thus one need not explain it. Yet, admitted as a metaphysical principle, negation does wonders. It keeps individuals distinct although all things are one. It keeps the contingent as contingent as *can be,* although the Absolute, which embraces all things, is a completely unconditioned, necessary entity.

To put the matter in a slightly different way, the alternative to positing contradiction in reality, from Hegel's point of view, is something like Parmenides's One, of which one can say nothing more than: "Is, is; is not, is not." In fact, if Plato was correct in his examination of Parmenides's monism in the dialogue *Parmenides,* one could not say even that. If everything is absolutely one, then one cannot speak. Metaphysics becomes ineffable mysticism. Hegel was not prepared to accept this outcome. For him one can do nothing but speak until one has said absolutely everything. At this point intuition supervenes. One *sees* reality as an intelligible whole, yet not as a solid block of intelligibility. All of the variety and dynamism gathered up by rational discourse is included in the final vision. Discursive reason mediates and terminates in intellectual intuition. Thus differences, which reason incorporates in higher viewpoints, must be as real as the unity in which reason synthesizes these differences. Hence negation must have its place in reality.

Hegel does not mean, however, that one may assert and deny precisely the same proposition.[2] If he allowed contradictory propositions to be true together, the predicables included in the contradictory propositions would lose their boundaries. By saying everything which is logically possible, a pair of contradictory propositions says nothing. Aristotle long ago showed that if one does not say something definite, then one does not say anything at all.[3] How can Hegel admit contradiction into reality, identify reality with thought, yet avoid asserting contradictory propositions?

In speaking of empirical things one avoids contradiction by distinguishing between the subjects, the times, and the respects. "Talking" and "not-talking" are compatible if they apply to different persons, or to the same person at different times, or if "talking" applies to the person as a bodily source of sounds while "not talking" applies to the person as to one who speaks voluntarily. For example, if a person utters words while asleep, one could say he is not really talking.

In hegelian dialectics the *appearance* of contradictions—that is, their showing up in discourse—is recognized as an essential part of the philosophical process and as an important feature of reality. If the contradictoriness were ascribed only to thought and denied to reality, then thought and being would be forever alien from one another, and the whole project of Hegel's philosophy would be undermined from the start. But the appearance of contradictions does not mean that Hegel claims a license to contradict himself. For Hegel truth in philosophy precisely *is* consistency.[4] He sees contradiction as a driving force which makes the process of self-realization of Spirit move along. Contradictory *propositions* must be superceded, and they are superceded by changing the standpoint, by moving from one level to another in the dialectical process. Thus, as I explained in chapter ten, Hegel reconciles necessity and contingency by holding both that the Absolute includes and explains the whole process which reality is, and that each part of this process keeps its own distinctness from other parts and from the whole.

It is important to be clear about what Hegel does with negation. His metaphysical alternative assumes the boundlessness of reason. For him reason cannot come to a point at which there remains something given but inexplicable. Hegel's position is altogether different from the one I take when I reject the principle of sufficient reason in the second section of chapter five. I hold that multiplicity, contingency, and free choice are inexplicable. Therefore, I do not posit negation in reality; I admit limits to reason, without trying—as empiricism and critical philosophy do—to determine the limits *a priori*.

By positing negation in reality Hegel is able to deny that reason has any limits whatever. Whenever a distinction which cannot be rendered positively intelligible must be admitted, Hegel simply attributes the distinction to negation. Since negation is not anything positive, reason does not lack the full explanation of reality although negation remains unexplained. Yet, since negation belongs to propositional knowledge, it is not senseless. With negation one can explain the inexplicable. Negation is a powerful metaphysical principle.[5]

Thus, by treating negation as a metaphysical principle Hegel is able to claim that the rationalist ideal is fulfilled, yet hold that the intelligible whole of reality, Absolute Spirit, includes multiplicity and process. But this metaphysical alternative is only viable if Hegel can avoid falling into self-contradiction, for if he does so, his discourse becomes meaningless.

Initially it might seem obvious that if reality includes contradiction, a philosophy which is true to reality also must include it, and thereby reduce itself to nonsense. But Hegel's arguments that apparently contradictory propositions become harmonious when considered from a higher viewpoint are impressive. In effect, Hegel sees reality in terms of antinomy as Kant explained it. Dialectical contraries appear contradictory, but only because they share a common, erroneous assumption. Once one gains an insight into the common error underlying apparently contradictory positions, one transcends their opposition.

If Hegel's dialectic were open-ended like Plato's, no ultimate claims about reality would be made. But Hegel's dialectic terminates in Absolute Spirit. At this point either all contradictions are overcome in the unity of a single intelligibility or an insurmountable antinomy remains. If the former, Hegel's metaphysical alternative succeeds. Only if Hegel's *final* standpoint is incoherent is his entire metaphysical project a failure. Thus, a refutation of Hegel must deal with his ultimate standpoint.

The following criticism is designed precisely to show that Hegel's final standpoint is inconsistent. The argument is a *reductio ad absurdum*. It is not question-begging to argue against Hegel in this way. The consistency which is a presupposition of meaningful discourse is not a position which others must hold but which Hegel is free to deny.

In allowing, for the sake of argument, that negation can be a metaphysical principle and in granting that Hegel's dialectical logic can resolve all contradictions short of his final viewpoint, one makes all the concessions one can make to his position. To give Hegel a license to contradict himself would be, not to respect his position, but rather to dissolve Hegel's sentences into nonsense, even before seeing what they say.

The inconsistency of absolute idealism

I begin by posing some objections which Hegel can answer satisfactorily. In posing such objections one probes absolute idealism and becomes clearer about the inescapable commitments it includes.

One might attempt to argue against Hegel's system as follows. According to Hegel truth is the whole. But the proposition that truth is the whole is not itself the whole. Therefore, this proposition, like all other propositions short of the whole, is only a partial truth; in other words, if taken as absolutely true, it is false. But Hegel precisely thinks that this proposition is absolutely true. Therefore, Hegel's position is false.

Hegel would answer by saying that no statement about his system, not even the statement that truth is the whole, really conveys the system. In this sense this statement *is* false. The truth which is the whole is the concrete unity of all parts—the complete system itself. One cannot appreciate the meaning of the system except by actually thinking one's way straight through it.[6]

One could take this answer, and again pose the objection which was made against the original statement that truth is the whole. The conclusion of this line of argument is that nothing Hegel says about his work is really true; it always is a partial truth which, taken as complete, is false. For Hegel this is the case with all partial truths. None of the statements Hegel makes about his philosophy is true unless it is understood in its context in the whole philosophy. For Hegel his philosophy as a whole is like one very long sentence; none of it is fully intelligible until one reaches the very end, just as this present sentence is not fully intelligible until one reads to the end of it.

Another way to try to argue against Hegel's philosophy would be to say that the Absolute is related to its appearances, the whole to its parts, completed reality to its passing phases much as Kant's thing in itself is related to phenomena. If this observation were correct, one could argue against Hegel much as I argued against Kant. But an objection of this sort does not touch Hegel. His point is that the Absolute *is* its appearances. The whole is nothing but its parts taken together. The stages of the process, including the final one, are the product.

Another possible objection to Hegel's philosophy is that if the real and the rational are the same in the end, then the system leaves no room for the uniqueness of particular experiences, particular objects, particular events, and particular persons. As I have explained, Hegel makes room by positing negation in reality. However, this kind of objection often has been raised against Hegel by existentialists, by pragmatists, and by others, and it deserves closer consideration. Hegel provides an apparent ground for the objection in many passages, for example, in his treatment of sense-certainty at the beginning of the *Phenomenology of Mind.*[7]

In this passage Hegel examines the claims of immediate experience to attain true knowledge of reality. *This* object is given *here* and *now* to *me*. Hegel does not deny the data on which the claim is based. But he does point out that the emphasized expressions have meanings which are not unique at all. These expressions have regular uses, and they would have no use at all if they meant something different in each case. When one tries to determine what the uniqueness of the particular consists in, one must resort to characterization by qualities which are not unique. The unique has to be located in a context; the sensing subject must function in a normal fashion. From both sides the situation is constituted by meanings and laws of action which transcend sense.

This argument is a refutation of naïve empiricism; as such it is sound enough. Proper names do refer to individuals, and Hegel does not deny the distinction between the sense of a word and its reference. But proper names can refer to particular individuals only by being attached to them by procedures which depend upon a framework of meanings which transcends the apparent immediacy of sensation. The possibility of locating places and times—for example, by latitude and longitude, by dating, and so on—also depends upon a whole system of meanings which is not imposed upon the unique but which inherently attaches to it and which enables one to grasp it. Hegel's point is that the uniqueness of the individual does not provide any basis for regarding sensation as knowledge. Knowledge of the truth is at least propositional; for Hegel propositions are true only insofar as they are properly grounded.

What must be noticed is that while the objection that Hegel leaves no room for uniqueness fails, because his argument admits the data at their own level, Hegel nevertheless cannot be credited in this argument with having provided any explanation for the uniqueness which he correctly shows must be transcended by a consciousness which is to achieve truth. The uniqueness remains, and Hegel is not in a position to allow it to remain unexplained. His philosophy proposes to embrace the totality of reality in a rational system which will overcome all oppositions.

Hegel maintains that philosophy cannot comprehend—positively explain—concrete individuals which occur in the natural world. The incapacity of philosophy to do this, however, is not a failure on the part of reason to attain reality in its wholeness. Rather, reason can explain the concrete singular because particularized objects are *in themselves* constituted by negation. Their uniqueness is not some sort of positive perfection; it is their otherness from one another and ultimately from the unity of Spirit. Materiality generates material multiplicity, which is positively intelligible insofar as it instantiates natural laws, but which in its brute givenness simply is the self-alienation of Spirit which goes out of itself into nature in order to exist over against itself, so that through human consciousness, which develops in the natural world, Spirit can regain itself in full actuality.[8]

Competent and sympathetic commentators find Hegel's solution to this problem disconcerting. A critic had jibed that Hegel's philosophy of nature should "deduce" the critic's pen. Hegel immortalized the unfortunate man in a sarcastic footnote:

> It was in this—and other respects too—quite naïve sense that Herr Krug once challenged the Philosophy of Nature to perform the feat of deducing *only* his pen. One could perhaps give him hope that *his* pen would have the glory of being deduced, if ever philosophy should advance so far and have such a clear insight into every great theme in heaven and on earth, past and present, that there was nothing more important to comprehend.[9]

But the reply does not explain how sensation, which, after all, is something positive, is different from reason, even after reason has located sensation as a stage within the unfolding of rational consciousness. This point is developed at some length by G. R. G. Mure.[10]

What this point makes clear is that Hegel is committed to reducing all differentiation to negation. But his critics think that the determinations by which entities differ are more than negations. Their claim is that one can understand something positive in each of two different entities which one does not comprehend when one understands them together. Hegel is committed to the position that there is no *positive* residue whatsoever when a higher viewpoint comprehends that below it. This commitment is essential to his entire metaphysics. My argument is that when he reaches the ultimate viewpoint, Hegel cannot make good on this commitment.

At the culmination of Hegel's philosophy two things happen at once. The Absolute is completely realized; its progressive coming to be is consummated; reality becomes fully conscious of itself. Also, Hegel's philosophizing, which has been a gathering up of everything into the unity of his system, is completed. At this moment Absolute Spirit and finite spirit, the infinite mind and Hegel's mind, coincide, and the two find their fulfillment in one another. Still, Hegel knows perfectly well that he is only a particular individual; he knows he is not the Absolute itself. Hegel personally is aware that his thought is embodied and contingently located, even as yours and mine.

For Hegel the respect in which he is not the Absolute simply is the fact that he is this particular man. But this particularity, for him, is only a matter of fact which considered rationally has no intelligible content. The otherness of infinite mind and finite mind is not anything one can understand; this otherness is mere negation. And since a negation is not something, there is nothing to be understood; in fact, there is a real unity of infinite mind and finite mind. Still, there is a negation, and so the two are not identical.

I have granted Hegel his use of "negation." Still, he has the difficulty that at the very end of his philosophy there remains the distinction, by the power of mere negation, between the finite and the infinite. This was the sort of distinction his philosophy was supposed to overcome. All through the stages of the process Hegel points to such opposition as a reason for having to proceed onward. At any earlier stage Hegel would have taken the situation he faces at the end of his dialectic as evidence that thought still is inadequate, that the apparent final conclusion is only a partial view.

In the introduction to his lectures on philosophy of religion Hegel maintains that *in religion* the finite and the infinite are united and distinguished in the religious consciousness.

> In thinking I lift myself up to the Absolute above all that is finite, and am infinite consciousness, while I am at the same time finite consciousness, and indeed am such in accordance with my whole empirical character. Both sides, as well as their relation, exist for me. Both sides seek each other, and both flee from each other.[11]

Here Hegel is faced with something more significant than Herr Krug's fountain pen. It should be the work of philosophy of religion to overcome the contradiction. However, philosophy of religion does not do so. Hegel instead describes *other* dichotomies which are solved, he believes, by his philosophic transposition of the content of faith.

Sometimes naive people try to prove the existence of God by laying down as a general principle: "Everything has a cause." To lay down such a principle obviously is a mistake. When one comes to something one wishes to call "God," the question naturally arises, "And what caused *that?*"

Hegel has taken as his project to overcome all distinctions, to reconcile all differences in thought. He sets out to unify everything in a final synthesis, in which all the distinctions nevertheless are preserved. But when he arrives at the end of his effort, there remains a final distinction which thought has not overcome. One naturally wishes to ask, "And what higher unity overcomes *that?*"

To this question Hegel might answer—so far as I can see he never actually considers the question—as follows. At the final moment when the philosophy of the Absolute and the Absolute itself both are consummated, the finite mind and infinite mind are in perfect unity, except that this unity must be recognized as having a double origin. When one distinguishes between Hegel and the Absolute at the final moment, one indicates the relative diversity of origin of one and the same knowledge. The fertilized ovum which is the beginning of a new individual is the offspring of its parents and the child of the universe, but the twofold relation does not remove its real unity, anymore than the relation to mother and to father makes the new offspring two children.

In most cases an argument of this sort is perfectly sensible, as the example shows. But is Hegel entitled to use it? He proposes to arrive at a whole which is absolute truth and absolute reality at once. Moreover, he insists that the product cannot be separated from the moments of the process. The Absolute, he maintains, is not an entity transcending the process, but is this process in its completeness. Truth is not something over and above the partial views; it is the partial views in their systematic unity.

Therefore, if Hegel maintains the distinction between finite mind and Absolute Spirit as a merely relative distinction, based upon diversity of antecedent moments, then the product must in some way be distinct from the process. Once again one meets the problem of negation: the whole either is or is not the sum of its parts. If the difficulty were not at the final moment of Hegel's philosophy, he could solve it easily. But at this point there is no higher view from which to work in an effort to integrate the still unintegrated.

The preceding argument can be expressed more abstractly, as follows.[12] Hegel's position is that the Absolute is nothing but its parts taken as a unity. Truth is the whole; the whole is the Absolute. Still, none of the parts by itself is true. But this position is incoherent. If the Absolute is nothing but its parts taken as a unity, then all of the conditions for the Absolute are given by its parts. If none of the parts is true, then the Absolute is not truth. On the other hand, if the Absolute is truth, each of its parts also must be true.

Someone might object that this argument commits the fallacy of composition. A whole, even one which is nothing but its parts taken as a unity, has properties which are inconsistent with the properties of its parts. For example, the number three, which is nothing but the unity of one plus one plus one, has the property of being one more than two, but none of the units which make up three has the property of being one more than two.

But the example will not work. The number three has the property of being one more than two only by virtue of something distinct from and added to the three units which make up three—namely, the operation of addition by which the three units form the whole number which is three. Without the operation of addition one can consider three units forever and not find anything which is more than two.

In other words, a whole can have a property which is not found in its parts, but this is possible only to the extent that the parts are formed into the whole, and this *forming into a whole* is not itself explained by the parts as such.

One who thinks in terms of Hegel's favorite metaphor—the organism—would point out that the parts of a living body, each taken by itself, lack life; the organs have life only insofar as they are parts of the living whole. Yet the life of the living whole is not some sort of ghostly entity over and above the functioning unity of all the parts.

But this example will not work either. The parts of a living body do not lack life. If "taken each by itself" means considered one by one, then each part is found to be alive; precisely in this consideration one knows the organism itself to be alive. For example, one checks for breathing or for heartbeat or for reaction to some stimulus. If "taken by itself" means cut off from the organism—for example, by surgical amputation—then it is true that what had been a part of an organism lacks life when taken by itself, but it lacks life precisely because it no longer is part of the organism.

Thus, Hegel's position is not saved by the argument that the truth of the Absolute is not part of it nor a property of its parts, but is a property of the conjunction of its parts, or is this very conjunction. If this argument were correct, the conjunction *itself* would be something over and above the parts of the Absolute considered as a unity. But in this case the Absolute would be truth in virtue of something not its parts, not a property of its parts, nor a joint property of all its parts *considered together.* Over and above the parts and their properties would be the conjunction of all the parts; this real conjunction would not belong to the parts, nor would it be a joint property of them. The conjunction would be imposed upon the parts, superadded to them.

In other words, if the Absolute achieves its completeness and its unity by virtue of Hegel's philosophic act, then the Absolute is truth by virtue of a truth which is achieved *in one of its parts*—namely, in Hegel's philosophic act, which is not the Absolute. However, if Hegel's philosophic act arrives at truth because Hegel reaches the truth of the Absolute, which is the *whole,* then Hegel's philosophic act is just as much a relative and incomplete view as any of the others which he transcends on the way to the Absolute.

Generalization of the criticism

If the preceding argument is correct, why did Hegel himself not see it? At least one historian of philosophy has suggested that Hegel did see it, but simply felt that the unity of the final moment *must* be maintained, despite the tension between the opposites which cannot, at this stage, be written off to mere negation.[13] But Hegel surely does not feel the full force of the difficulty.

When a scientist or a philosopher is deeply absorbed in his subject matter and thinks he is reaching the truth about it, his own act of knowing seems to drop away into insignificance. Of course, one wishes to receive credit for one's scientific or philosophic attainments, but one feels that others should accept one's conclusions, as Heraclitus said, not on one's personal authority but on the authority of the suprapersonal truth which they comprehend. Thus it is easy to understand why Hegel, believing he had grasped the ultimate truth which all previous philosophers had been seeking and only partially and inadequately reaching, thought that the culmination of his philosophizing was nothing other than the culmination of the effort of Absolute Spirit to realize itself.

This positing by Hegel of his own thought at the zenith of the whole of reality gives his philosophy an appearance of unmatched arrogance. But from Hegel's own perspective, personal pride and personal humility are equally irrelevant. For Hegel his philosophy is not simply his opinion; it is the truth, which belongs to Spirit as such, and which also is *man's* achievement. "One small step by a man; one giant step for mankind."

The difficulty is that on his own theory Hegel is not entitled to take this modest attitude toward his own work. Scientists and philosophers for the most part think of their work in this way precisely because they make and can maintain a distinction between, on the one hand, their own acts of investigating, learning, knowing, and communicating the results of their research, and, on the other hand, the truth of the reality they are studying. If Hegel keeps this distinction intact, however, his personal act of philosophic thought is not identical with the subject matter of which he is thinking. In this case something remains outside the ultimate whole which philosophy can comprehend, namely, Hegel's philosophic act. If Hegel does not keep the distinction intact, then his act of philosophic thought merges into the subject matter. In this case there is no content of Hegel's thinking which can be detached from Hegel and communicated to anyone else. Discourse ends.

Hegel's general method works best and yields most plausible results when he applies it to specific fields in which human thinking which does involve negation is constitutive. His lectures on history, art, religion, philosophy, and so forth are filled with insights. His method yields least plausible results when he deals with abstract metaphysics and philosphy of nature. These are areas in which human thought is not constitutive. If one reads the works in which Hegel's thought is most plausible, one is tempted to wonder whether his metaphysics might not, after all, be true.

But this wonder itself makes clear that absolute idealism is not true. If it were true, then one could not understand it without *knowing* it to be true. It is a conclusive argument against Hegel's position that almost no one, including those who studied his work most carefully, thinks it is true.

I am not appealing to the verdict of history. My point is much more philosophical. Hegel claims an ultimate knowledge of Absolute Spirit and maintains that this knowledge is communicable by rational discourse. If the proposition which his philosophy unfolds is true, then one cannot understand it without knowing it to be true, because it does not pick out any extrapropositional state of affairs, but claims to *be* reality. If one can understand Hegel's philosophy and ask oneself whether it might not, after all, be true, one can be absolutely certain that it is false, for one should no more be able to doubt the truth of absolute idealism than one is able to wonder whether two plus two equal four.

Of course, someone might suggest that the truth of Hegel's philosophy lies beyond rational discourse, in a kind of vision. The philosophy itself, even taken in its entirety, would only represent the truth in a symbolic manner. Hegel himself surely would reject such a well-meant defense. He claims to translate what he regards as the merely symbolic representation of truth in Christian doctrine into literal, rational discourse. If his own vision is only symbolically communicated by his philosophical works, then it is no better than the poetry in which mystics try to express the inexpressible.

In fact, Hegel's philosophy would be in a worse position than the writings of the mystics, for he would be failing to fulfill a promise which they do not make. To defend Hegel in this manner is to suggest, when all is said, that even though the system as a whole is inconsistent—in strict logic, nonsensical—still it might be true. Such a suggestion would be worse than speculation against the value of rational discourse. It would be playing the metaphysical bear market—staking everything on the complete devaluation of rational discourse.

Yet, despite his own intentions, Hegel perhaps makes most sense if he is read as a poet. "Everything is spirit" cannot express a literal truth. If it did, "spirit" would lose its usual meaning, for besides spirit there is everything which Hegel tries to save by positing negation. If everything truly is spirit, "spirit" merely means "something" and Hegel's philosophy reduces to the trivial identity statement he ridicules: "Everything is something." If the usual meaning of "spirit" is maintained, loose and vague as that meaning is, the statement that all is spirit is patently false. Herr Krug's fountain pen is not spirit.

But if sentences such as "Everything is spirit" cannot express any literal truth, they can be exciting metaphors. They lead one to look at things in a new light. This is the function of poetry. Like many other philosophers, Hegel often is poetical. However prosaic his discourse, it is full of lively metaphor. The distinction between propositional truth-claims and symbolic representation frequently is ignored by Hegel.

Someone might suppose that the failure of Hegel's philosophy to achieve coherence does not imply the failure of any and every philosophical attempt to account for all contingent states of affairs by virtue of their own totality, rather than by an uncaused cause distinct from them. But I think this supposition would be a mistake.

In the first section of chapter five I argue that unless one maintains, as Hegel does, that the contingency of the empirical world is only an appearance, one cannot explain contingent states of affairs without recourse to a necessary state of affairs distinct from them. However, if one maintains that the apparently contingent is itself the necessary, uncaused entity, then one will end in inconsistency just as Hegel does.

One either maintains the distinction between one's own philosophic act and this necessary entity or not. If one does maintain it, something—one's act—is distinct from the whole. If one does not maintain it, one's philosophic act merges with the necessary entity, and thus becomes unique and incommunicable. Moreover, if such a position is true, then understanding a statement of it should be enough to make its truth known. If someone can understand the statement of this position yet still doubt its truth, this fact conclusively shows that it is not true. The only alternative would be to claim that the statement was only a symbolic representation, but to make such a claim is to abandon philosophy for mysticism. Finally, any statement of such a position must attempt to gain plausibility by giving some descriptive characterization of reality as a whole. Hegel's attempt using the concept of *spirit* probably cannot be improved upon. But no matter what metaphor one might choose, either the language one used would be stretched to the point of meaninglessness or the position will become patently false. There is nothing in particular that everything is.

The *reductio ad absurdum* of this metaphysical alternative is the *reductio* of the rationalist ideal as such. One cannot set limits to reason *a priori*, but there are boundaries which are reached and which must be accepted. This does not mean that one should assume that difficult questions are unanswerable. It means that when there is a good *reason* to think that certain questions are unanswerable, one must accept this fact. One should not speculate against the irreducibility of individuality, variety, contingency, free choice, and so forth.

Part of the rationalist ideal was a conception of God as *ens realissimum*—the being uniting in itself the sum of all the perfections of finite entities. The ultimate incoherence of rationalism shows that this concept of God cannot be defended. The entity in which *what* and *that* are intelligibly united is the necessary being which is the uncaused cause of the obtaining of contingent states of affairs. This entity is distinct from what it causes. Far from gathering up the perfections of the contingent, whatever is characteristic of any contingent state of affairs must be denied of the uncaused entity. Negation belongs to metaphysical discourse; it is misplaced when it is posited in necessary being itself. I explain this point in chapter fifteen.

Someone might argue that Hegel's final, unresolved contradiction is no more mysterious than some of the doctrines of Christian faith. Christians, for example, believed that Christ is true God and also true man. This objection is interesting; it perhaps throws light upon the frame of mind in which Hegel himself confronted the outcome of his own philosophy. Hegel perhaps was more a Christian than is often supposed.[14] But this objection cannot rescue Hegel's philosophy from incoherence. Christians believed in mysteries, such as the Incarnation of the Word, but they did not claim to understand these mysteries in the form of rational reflection. Hegel has made the latter claim.

Christians could maintain the truth of that which they did not claim to understand, because they supposed that such truth is known by a divine understanding which surpasses human knowing. Hegel rejected such a theological articulation of Christian faith in favor of his own philosophy which made—or claimed to make—the mysteries of symbolic faith into the insights of conceptual reason. Hegel is not entitled to flee into mystery, not even at the end of his philosophic quest.

Finally, one might suppose that perhaps Hegel has erred only by being overly ambitious. If he had recognized that there is no Absolute Spirit, that meaning and necessity are present only in limited, closed segments of reality, perhaps he might have succeeded in his project. Undoubtedly there is something realistic and attractive about Hegel's dialectical method, which takes reason seriously, which overcomes the dichotomy between knowing subject and known world, and which seeks to uncover the ultimate principles of reality without resorting to any transcendent uncaused entity.

This metaphysical alternative has been developed in various forms of post-hegelian relativism. In chapters twelve and thirteen I expound and criticize this approach, in which finite minds are regarded as the constitutive principle of reality.

12: Relativism
as a Metaphysical Alternative

Relativism as a reaction to absolute idealism

In the previous chapter I argued that Hegel's philosophy of Absolute Spirit is inconsistent because at its consummation finite spirit and the Absolute find their fulfillment in one another, yet still remain alien to one another. If Hegel's philosophic act is withheld from the Absolute, his finitude and his interpersonal relationship with other men is preserved, but at the cost of denying the completeness of the Absolute itself. If Hegel's act is not withheld, but is permitted to merge into the Absolute, the Absolute is preserved, but Hegel's own finitude and his interpersonal relationship with others is lost.

This hegelian dilemma, articulated in the form of abstract argument in the previous chapter, unfolded itself historically soon after Hegel's death. Hegel's followers and students divided into two camps—the Old Hegelians and the Young Hegelians (or the right and the left). The Old Hegelians defended the reality of the Absolute, and they attempted to vindicate Hegel's philosophy as a transposition of Christian faith. The Young Hegelians accepted much of Hegel's thought, especially his analysis and critique of previous philosophy and religion, and some version of his dialectical method. But they rejected the Absolute; they denied that there is any spirit transcending the particular minds of particular men, unless it be the minds of many individual men united in social solidarity.

Hegel's philosophy was sufficiently ambiguous that both camps could claim to develop his true thought. The Young Hegelians, however, were ready to attack Hegel's thought in the interest of the unique, the historically given, the material, the sensuous, and the still-to-be-realized future. Hegel had imagined his philosophy to be the last stage of a dialectic; the Young

Hegelians accepted it as a stage to be transcended. The Absolute itself thus became an unreal appearance, and Hegel's philosophy of the Absolute a point of view which, if taken as final, was seen to be illusory. This reaction to Hegel could call on his own authority and claim to be the true fulfillment, by negation and sublation, of his thought. The "materialism" of Marx's dialectic emerged as a reversal of Hegel's idealistic dialectic; the existentialism of Kierkegaard's faith emerged as a reversal of the essentialism of Hegel's philosophic transposition of Christian faith.[1]

It is important to notice that the young Hegelians, despite the vigor of their attack upon the hegelian right wing, still take for granted the soundness and the adequacy of much of Hegel's interpretation of previous philosophy and religion. This fact simplifies their task of criticizing claims to knowledge about God or faith in him. Many post-hegelian philosophers think that they are dispensed from the need to examine the history of thought about God; Hegel has already done that. He has gathered up in the Absolute everything which can be said on behalf of God. Thus, the destruction of Hegel's Absolute spells the death of God. It hardly occurs to anyone that this particular execution perhaps terminates a case in which the conviction is based on mistaken identity.[2]

In Hegel's own philosophy, at least as it was understood by the Old Hegelians, the reality of the Absolute has certain implications. The philosophy is a reflection, a turning back of thought upon consciousness and history, a gathering up of all the stages, an arrival at a final self-consciousness, the achievement of which is its own purpose and justification. Thus Hegel's philosophy is oriented toward the past. His thinking is speculative, not practical. He specifically rejects the proposal that philosophy should teach the world how it ought to be. The task of philosophy is to understand the world, not to reform it.[3] Particular facts are essential conditions for the realization of the Absolute, but the unity and universality of the whole is more important, because only the whole is truth and full reality. Sensation and sensuousness have their place within the Absolute, but reason completely incorporates these lower forms of consciousness. The objective reality of the Absolute subject is superior to the subjective existence of the finite object— and any human person is one among many finite objects.

These aspects of hegelianism are not accidental to one another; they fit together as necessary characteristics of the sort of philosophy Hegel develops. If the Absolute is to be real, it cannot be a future possibility; if it is to be true, it cannot be a fiction of Hegel's productive imagination; if it is to be perfect self-consciousness, it cannot require completion in outward action; if it is to be a universal whole, it cannot admit its parts to equality; if it is to be realized by philosophic reflection, it has to be rational rather than sensuous; if it is to be objective and valid for the whole world, it cannot be personal and have the unique value of that which is peculiarly for me or for thee.

The Young Hegelians, in denying the reality of the Absolute, deny all these implications of Hegel's philosophy. Indeed, in many cases it is because they are determined to avoid these implications that they deny the reality of the Absolute. Thus those who react to Hegel tend to stress the responsibility of philosophy for future possibility: philosophy must not only understand the world but also change it. The full reality of human spirit, the achievement of man's own possibilities, should be imagined by the philosopher, projected into the future, and made into a practical objective. For most of the Young Hegelians the actual accomplishments of particular persons and particular societies at particular moments of history are the ultimate reality, the only final meaning and justification of history. Either the universal whole is impossible, or, at any rate, it is yet to come. Reason has some role to play, but passion, sensuousness, will, need and satisfaction, and the like also have a role which is even more important. The subjectivity of the individual, the interest of the class, the depth of the immediate interpersonal relationship of thee-and-me outwit the cunning of reason and reassert the dignity of the individual person.

Hegel's Absolute is *absolute* precisely because, being the whole, there is nothing beyond itself to which it could be relative. If one continues to think of reality more or less in Hegel's fashion, but maintains the distinctiveness of human action as a principle apart from the rest of reality, then man's finitude can be preserved. But the Absolute is finished. Reality which has man standing outside it no longer is the whole and therefore no longer is absolute. It is relative, relative to man who stands outside it. If one also holds to Hegel's conception that man contributes to the realization of the Absolute, then the reality which remains when the Absolute is finished is relative to man in the sense that it depends upon human thought and human action for its own meaning and completion.

In this way the *reductio ad absurdum* of absolute idealism generates post-hegelian relativism. Considered from the perspective of human action, which endows it with meaning and value, the world apart from man is relative to man. In this perspective reality is not a whole in which man finds himself a small and dependent part. Rather, the massive, amorphous *other* which stands against man is mere negation until human words and deeds make it into a world. Reality depends upon man. If there is no Absolute Spirit to make the whole meaningful, the human spirit must wrestle with the negation which man encounters on every side as he tries to make sense of that which in itself is nonsense, as he tries to act purposefully in a world which is indifferent to human concerns.

Since hegelianism is the fulfillment of the rationalist ideal, the *reductio ad absurdum* of hegelianism also spells the end of rationalism. Post-hegelian relativism is marked by its vehement rejection of the overinflated claims of rationalistic reason. Not everything can be reduced to intelligibility; not everything can be explained. The assertion of the priority of human meaning-giving is accompanied by an endorsement of aspects of reality which Hegel tried to write off to negation: individuality, variety of kinds, contingency as such, free choice, and so on.

Rejecting the *reality* of rationalistic reason, post-hegelian relativists never-theless often keep the rationalistic *definition* of reason, with the result that sometimes irrationalism is endorsed. To the extent that this irrationalism is merely an assertion of aspects of reality which rationalism fails to respect adequately, it is a legitimate and necessary reaction. However, if one supposes that the principle of sufficient reason is the primary law of reason, yet believes that this primary law can be violated in some situations, then one is likely to suppose that *every* rationality norm can be violated in some situations. In this way post-hegelian relativism fosters a new morality in questioning, reasoning, and judging. In general, of course, one ought to be reasonable. But since total rationality is an absurd ideal, one is not altogether irrational if one permits oneself to be as irrational as one must to make the best of each situation as it arises.

The preceding explanation suggests how post-hegelian relativism originates as a dialectical antithesis to Hegel's philosophy of the Absolute. But if the Absolute is thesis and post-hegelian relativism is the antithesis, one need not assume that the truth lies in a higher synthesis. What is more important, one should not assume that the whole philosophical world since Hegel has been totally absorbed in the widespread reaction to him. Other developments have occurred.

Among these developments, of course, has been the reformulation of other metaphysical alternatives. But there are other important options open to post-hegelian philosophers. Without trying to solve ultimate metaphysical questions, one can attempt to make an inventory of the various types of entities which reality includes. Perhaps most important, philosophers can do worthwhile work without *claiming* to solve metaphysical questions by detach-ing from the wreckage of metaphysical systems the methodological devices which made them work—to the extent that they did work—refining these methods, and employing them both critically and constructively. The critical employment of such devices keeps clear of metaphysics provided that no *a priori* limits are set upon what there is, what can be known, and what can be said. The constructive employment of such devices keeps clear of metaphysics provided that no claim is made that the results achieved are definitive for reality.

The dialogues of Plato can be understood as a paradigm for philosophical work which uses a variety of methods, both critically and constructively, but abstains from the intoxicating adventures of metaphysics. A post-hegelian philosopher can use philosophical methods critically and constructively, as

Plato does, without making metaphysical commitments. One can reflect upon the history of philosophy, notice mistaken descriptions of phenomena, and return to the things themselves by providing more accurate descriptions. One can notice that apparently insoluble problems about reality actually are rooted in linguistic confusions; by clearing up these confusions one can dissolve the seemingly insoluble problems. Moreover, these methods can be applied to human thinking in general, both theoretical and practical.

In areas in which critical reflection is at a low ebb, philosophers can provide a valuable service by clarifying prevalent misunderstandings, bringing relevant data into focus, and facilitating communication among persons who are cut off from one another by inarticulate metaphysical or other assumptions. Such work is particularly important when it is applied to political, social, and other practical thought; in these areas the philosopher's work can facilitate not only communication but also the cooperation which is impossible without communication.

Description of relativism

None of the modes of philosophical work which I have mentioned is included in what I call "post-hegelian relativism." Post-hegelian relativism is a metaphysical alternative which poses an obstacle to the philosophical theology I am proposing. Philosophies which truly and completely abstain from metaphysics do not pose any such obstacle. One who does not make any metaphysical assertions whatsoever also does not exclude metaphysics. The most one can show without making any metaphysical commitments of one's own is that certain *specific* attempts at metaphysics fall into some sort of inconsistency. Post-hegelian relativism, however, attempts to exclude other forms of metaphysics altogether. Thus, it itself takes a stand and becomes a metaphysical alternative.

In many cases, it is hard to tell where a philosophy which is metaphysically abstinent ends and a relativistic metaphysics begins. The confusion is compounded because "metaphysics" often is used to signify only certain kinds of metaphysics, especially rationalistic metaphysics of which Hegel's philosophy is the paradigm. For this reason philosophical methods which in themselves can be employed by a philosopher who abstains from metaphysics also can be exploited quite inconspicuously to articulate a metaphysics.

The metaphysics of post-hegelian relativism focuses upon *human action* as a principle. If a philosopher merely observes that human action sometimes links *what* and *that*, meaning and obtaining, he is not taking a metaphysical position. However, if one maintains that human action somehow is constitutive of reality in general and that the necessity to which it gives rise is the only extrapropositional, intelligible unity between meaning and obtaining, then one is taking a metaphysical position. This metaphysical alternative to the philosophical theology I am proposing denies—at least implicitly—that there is an uncaused entity distinct from contingent states of affairs. It asserts that the only necessity which must be acknowledged is immanent in the empirical world. In making necessity immanent such a metaphysics agrees with Hegel. In distinguishing between human action and that of which action is a principle, post-hegelian immanent metaphysics rejects the Absolute Spirit and posits in place of it a multiplicity of immanent states of affairs, each endowed with a relative necessity by human words and deeds.

The common properties of post-hegelian relativism form a syndrome which is protean. It is impossible to define this syndrome by working from a single paradigm. I therefore list the following characteristics shared by the many positions which implicitly or explicitly assert this metaphysical alternative.

1) They consider experience to be a continuum; whatever one experiences as distinct one also experiences in relation to a wider context; in this respect they agree with Hegel against the atomistic conception of experience shared by empiricism and critical philosophy.

2) They regard human knowledge as an active interchange between the embodied knower and the environment, situation, or condition; they agree with Hegel in rejecting the sharp dichotomy between knowing subject and object of knowledge.

3) They hold that experience and reason are dynamically related, that facts and values cannot be isolated from one another, that meaning and existence can be intelligibly linked; in these respects they agree with Hegel in rejecting the ultimacy of distinctions considered ultimate by empiricism and critical philosophy.

4) They consider human knowing to be an open-ended process which unfolds itself dialectically but which does not attain a final, absolute standpoint; in the dialectical conception of knowledge they agree with Hegel; in the exclusion of an absolute viewpoint they agree with empiricism and critical philosophy.

5) They stress pluralism or polymorphism by insisting upon irreducible diversity; they reject the reduction of all being, or all knowing, or all language to a single system united by a single principle.

6) They consider philosophy to be practical and describe philosophic work in terms of its activity and method rather than in terms of its product; they reject any metaphysics which attempts to produce a general theory of reality.

7) They consider human activity, operation, behavior, use, praxis, or something of the sort to be the principle which accounts for whatever

intelligible unity there is between *what* and *that;* they reject any superhuman principle of meaning and value.

8) They consider philosophy to be a means to human values other than knowledge itself; they reject the ideal of theoretical wisdom as a value in itself.

9) They regard classifications and definitions as provisional and alterable, but not wholly arbitrary, devices which emerge in the human process of knowing; they reject the supposition that there are fixed essences, determinate objects, defined states of affairs which human knowing in no way constitutes but only finds and accepts.

10) They hold that human intelligence or intentionality or use of language introduces meaning into things and thus constitutes facts and truths; they reject the view that a predetermined truth necessarily emerges from the process of inquiry.

11) They tend to assume that if there were a god, it would be something like Hegel's Absolute; they usually hold that such a superhuman principle would be incompatible generally with the full reality of finite entities, and especially with the freedom and dignity of man. Preferring the reality of man and of this world, they usually reject such a god. If they do admit the possibility of a superhuman principle of meaning and value, they deny that man can reason to the existence of such a principle.

The varieties of post-hegelian relativism which share these characteristics include the exploitation for metaphysical purposes of methods perfected by post-hegelian philosophers whose work has shaped the leading contemporary philosophical movements: pragmatism, linguistic analysis, nontheistic existentialism, and marxism. The methods can be used without metaphysical commitments. But they also lend themselves to metaphysical exploitation.

A post-hegelian relativist works toward establishing intelligibility in one limited area at a time. In dealing with each problem or case or situation or region he works the materials he finds into a coherent and complete system, something like a small-scale hegelian absolute. But instead of supposing that the intelligible unity he unfolds depends upon a transcendent Absolute Spirit, he assumes that this intelligibility is man's own actualization of the possibilities afforded by the situation. The intelligible unity which is discovered is attributed to human action, behavior, use, or something of the sort. The method becomes a metaphysics at the moment one asserts that there is *no other* principle of intelligibility—that is, when one says that meaning *wholly* originates in use, that existence *completely* precedes essence, that *nothing* is seen rightly except in the perspective of revolutionary action, and so on.

A miniabsolute unfolded by a post-hegelian relativist can be viewed as a set of conditional propositions which interlock with one another to form an integrated and satisfyingly complete whole. The consequents of all the propositions in the set are posited categorically when one relates the whole system to a proposition which is the antecedent of one of the conditionals. This antecedent is a self-referentially necessary proposition; one who understands the proposition also knows that the state of affairs it picks out obtains. In chapter nine (pages 172-174) I discussed such self-referential necessity which is contingent upon human action.

The following are further examples of propositions which have self-referential necessity. If one knows what it is like for a certain word to be able to function in a certain way in a particular context, then one knows that one meaning of the word is this particular *use* of it in this context. If one knows what it is like to fall in love with a certain person or to fear one's own death, then one knows that one *has* fallen in love with this person or that one *does* fear one's own death. If one really knows what it is like to be a member of the downtrodden masses, one knows oneself *to be* a member of the downtrodden masses—class consciousness has been achieved. If one knows what it is like to solve a particular problem, one must *have solved* that particular problem.

In all of the preceding examples the state of affairs is particular and the cognitional act is more than theoretical. The understanding of such propositions and the obtaining of the states of affairs which they pick out are inseparable because one only grasps the meaning of the proposition in an experience in which one also is involved in the actual state of affairs.

By contrast with such cases the following questions can be considered. Are there at least one thousand distinct languages in use in the world today? How many divorces and how many deaths were there in the United States in 1973? What is the present average family income in Canada? How old was Albert Einstein when he died? One can understand these questions and one can entertain propositions which might answer them—for example, by guessing—without knowing whether the states of affairs picked out by such propositions obtain or not.

But a relativistic philosopher probably would not admit this distinction to be as sharp as it initially seems. He might point out that one who does not know two languages cannot really know how distinct they are—distinctions between languages are not clear-cut but are a matter of more-or-less. He might say that there are divorces and divorces, that there are deaths and deaths; statistical tables really are not informative. In some cases a so-called divorce is recorded, but the marriage was merely a legal device to facilitate immigration; should such a case be counted among *real* divorces? Does one include the deaths of aborted fetuses—that is, those which die after live birth—in *human* mortality tables? What does a statistic about average family income tell one if one does not know what the cost of living is, what social services are available, and--most important of all—what are the incomes of the poorest families? The proper answer to the question "How old was Albert Einstein when he died?" will be determined by the context in which it is asked. For some purposes a suitable answer might be a very rough approximation, but for other purposes one might wish to have his age not only in years but also in months and days.

Some examples of relativism

Obviously, I cannot survey the many instances of post-hegelian relativism. There are dozens, perhaps hundreds, of important examples. As I have explained, the line between a metaphysically abstinent method and an instance of relativist metaphysics often is not clear. Moreover, many works which are clearly metaphysical are mixed cases, not pure cases, of post-hegelian relativism. What I mean by "mixed case" is that a philosopher might maintain a relativistic position up to a point, but at the same time he might lean upon or fall back upon empiricism, critical philosophy, or absolute idealism at times, perhaps without realizing that he is doing so.

For example, many philosophers who practice linguistic analysis and who explicitly reject the verification criterion nevertheless fall back upon that criterion surreptitiously by means of other devices—for example, by an exclusivistic use of the categories of "science" and "grammar" or by invoking the criterion criterion. Many who claim to do pure phenomenology without presuppositions fall back upon cultural "structures" which are remarkably similar to kantian categories. Many existentialists and marxists use the notions of Nothingness and Destiny, history and liberation, or the like, very much as if these represented personified transcendent principles—Hegel's Absolute sojourning incognito. Pragmatists at various times have fallen back on all of the metaphysical alternatives.

Some pragmatists would say that philosophy must concern itself with solving problems. Problems arise when situations are unsettled, confused, unsatisfactory, or unbalanced. The objectively doubtful situation gives rise to a felt need; the situation becomes problematic. Intelligence is used to define the problem, to work out possible solutions, to think of ways of putting the possibilities to the test. The test comes in practice. Judgment is found to be sound if the need is satisfied, the problem solved, the situation transformed toward dynamic equilibrium. Such judgments are true, not in the sense that they conform to something absolute, but in the sense that one has a warrant for asserting the judgment relative to the situation. Pragmatism becomes a relativistic metaphysics when a general theory is proposed—for example, that existence and intelligibility coincide *only when* needs are satisfied by the solution of problems through a process of inquiry in which the inquirer and the problematic situation interact and both are transformed.

Some linguistic analysts would say that philosophy must concern itself with dissolving pseudoproblems, with clearing away the puzzles or muddles which develop because of the odd uses to which linguistic expressions sometimes are put by metaphysicians, theologians, and others. The process of clarification is a sort of therapy, which exposes the root of the difficulty, which shows the fly the way out of the flybottle. The outcome of a properly conducted analysis is the dissolution of the original question. The general theory behind such a method might be that one's world is shaped (or various worlds are shaped) by linguistic frameworks, that the expressions constituting these frameworks have meaning *only because* of their use—in a full-blooded sense of "use"—that uses belong to forms of life, and that forms of life are simply given or are arbitrarily adopted by decisions of principle.[4]

Some existential-phenomenologists would say that philosophy should concern itself with existentially significant experiences which must be interpreted by careful analysis in order to uncover the truth concealed in these experiences. The general theory might be that facts are constituted by human meaning-giving, that meaning-giving in particular cases is a function of one's life world, that one's life world *altogether depends* upon one's perspective on reality, and that this in turn is a function of one's fate or one's existential project.

Some dialectical materialists might say that philosophy must remove ideological camouflage in order to allow the real structure of social conflict to appear; this revelation transforms the situation by creating consciousness which establishes the meaning of the situation as an instance of alienation to be overcome. The theory behind this approach might be that any interpretation of facts is *merely* a superstructure, the superstructure is determined by interests, interests are a function of one's class, one's class is a function of the means of life, and these are a function of the evolving relationship of man-in-society to the environment.

The first thing to be said about these various forms of relativism is that, setting aside their exclusivistic claims, each of them is valid with respect to some parts or aspects of reality. None of them is dealing with mere ideas or with a world of pure illusion. The fact that contemporary philosophies are dealing with something real makes them plausible; they usually can throw new light upon some set of data. Moreover, the fact that philosophies of this sort can say something important without the ponderous apparatus of many classical philosophies makes them attractive to nonphilosophers.

Practical problems, though not all problems, are solved by the mutual modifications of ideas and facts which lead to the formulation of a practical intention capable of satisfaction; the method of pragmatic inquiry can be profitably employed in many situations. The meaning of some expressions, though not of all, is their use in particular contexts; many skillful examples of linguistic clarification can interest and enlighten a thoughtful person. The limits of one's discrimination of the multiple intelligibilities in reality are a function of the existential conditions under which one's world is shaped; becoming aware of these limits is necessary if one is to avoid making exaggerated claims for his own interpretation. Perhaps more of our thinking is ideological than we realize (although all little children can ask the same naive questions with the same disinterested wonder); the unmasking of ideological sources of opinion, the uncovering of rationalization in general, is necessary to overcome bias which prevents one from confronting reality as it is.

Moreover, each of these forms of relativism has seized upon and developed—often with great ingenuity—some important part of the methodology which is essential for any adequate philosophical theory. Theoretical inquiry often is blocked by practical problems; a pragmatic approach is necessary to end frustrations and to open the way to fruitful investigation. Analytic clarification is necessary; without it pseudoproblems so clutter the philosophical scene that real problems cannot be discerned. Arid theory out of touch with the things themselves must be set aside by careful attention to the immediately given, considered precisely as it presents itself to us. Self-knowledge gained by an insight into one's own bias is necessary to gain objectivity.

Insofar as the various forms of relativism exploit philosophical methods which also can be used without any commitment to a relativistic metaphysics, such metaphysics is easily confused with the valuable work of metaphysically abstinent philosophers. The respectability of such valuable work, carried out in a manner genuinely open-minded with respect to metaphysics, lends plausibility to metaphysical relativism.

However, explicitly or implicitly, sometimes perhaps almost without realizing it, a practitioner of a metaphysically neutral method can slip into a relativistic metaphysics. The taking of such a position can be unobtrusive since relativism is the antithesis of most of what has been called "metaphysics" prior to the present century.

The general form of the metaphysical position is that philosophical knowledge is *impossible* except in particular situations, cases, regions, and so on. Insight into the particular grasps an intelligible unity between facts and meanings, since the particular in its uniqueness cannot be other than it is. The only uncaused cause about which it is relevant to ask is the principle of human action—the need, drive, interest, feeling, will, or whatever—which by means of the action generates both a certain state of affairs and the understanding of the proposition which picks out this state of affairs. General theoretical propositions are not, strictly speaking, true or false. They are useful devices for a practical cognitional process which begins and ends in the concrete. Abstractions always lie, but some lies are more useful than others.

Obviously, this metaphysical position is an alternative to the philosophical theology I am developing. If relativism is sound, the argument proposed in part two is worthless. However, few relativists seriously entertain an argument of the sort I propose. If they do entertain it, they often offer objections derived from Hume and Kant, or they assume that the argument must be understood as Hegel understood it. In the latter case, the *reductio ad absurdum* of rationalism will be thought to have invalidated any other argument for the existence of a superhuman metaphysical principle.

13: Criticism
of Metaphysical Relativism

Relativism is inconsistent

Unlike empiricism and critical philosophy, post-hegelian relativism maintains that there is an intelligible unity between *what* and *that,* and that this necessity is not inaccessible to human cognition. The necessity, in fact, arises from human action itself. A deliberate human act both generates a state of affairs and includes an understanding of the meaning which is immanent in this state of affairs. One who acts cannot help knowing that the state of affairs which he is bringing about does obtain. Here, meaning and existence are integrated.

This observation in itself does not constitute a metaphysics. Relativism as a metaphysical alternative only arises when the necessity which is generated in human action is claimed to be a constitutive principle of reality as such. In general, metaphysical relativists deny that there is any superhuman principle of meaning and value. If they admit the possibility of such a principle, they nevertheless exclude the possibility of theoretical argument to any extra-empirical uncaused entity, and allow at most that one can posit such an entity by one's own fiat—linguistic, pragmatic, existential, or other.

Since human acts obviously require many conditions distinct from themselves to obtain, metaphysical relativism lacks initial plausibility when it is articulated as a straightforward metaphysics.

The only theoretical position I know of which would lend support to metaphysical relativism is philosophical fatalism. Philosophical fatalism is the theory that one can deduce the truth of particular, factual statements from logical truths alone. Although relativists do not appeal to fatalism, they might well do so, for if fatalism were true, each human act would be in itself a necessary state of affairs.

Hardly anyone takes philosophical fatalism seriously, however, because it conflicts with the generally accepted view that there is an important distinction between logical truths and matters of fact. Philosophers have been perennially fascinated with arguments for fatalism, and there have been many ingenious attempts to give this theory some plausibility. Since the fallacies in a typical argument for fatalism are exposed in another work, I will not pursue the matter here.[1]

To the extent that a relativistic metaphysics rejects abstraction, insists upon the intelligible unity of *what* and *that* in limited situations, and asserts the uniqueness of each situation, such a metaphysics implies that one cannot ask a meaningful question without already knowing its answer. This position is not immediately plausible, but it can be given some plausibility.

A relativist can argue that the difference between knowing what it would be like for a state of affairs to obtain and knowing that it does obtain is nothing but the difference between a general and inexact knowledge and a precise knowledge of the state of affairs. On this theory, when one asks whether a certain state of affairs (SA) obtains—for example, "Does John love Mary?"—the meaning of the question is indeterminate. As one looks at SA more carefully, one discerns precisely what is involved in it. But when this is known, the question itself gives way to a precise knowledge in which SA is seen either to obtain or not, and whichever is the case is necessary to SA in its unique reality: "John could not help loving Mary."

This theory, which would make the meaning of any question about SA indeterminate, cannot mean only that in asking the question to which one does not have the answer there always are some details about the particular state of affairs which one does not take into consideration. Ignorance of some details is compatible with knowing what SA would be like, yet not knowing whether SA does or does not obtain. Therefore, those whose positions imply that, when the question is asked whether SA obtains, the meaning of the question is indeterminate must intend something more—namely, that the abstract knowledge of what it would be like for SA to obtain is not really applicable to the unique reality of SA, which either obtains or does not obtain. The only reality which is intelligible is the concrete reality; this concrete reality is through-and-through unique; therefore, questions to which one does not already have answers are not about realities. Such questions might be mere heuristic devices.

One might suppose that this theory is nominalism and that its development leads directly back to empiricism. But such a supposition would be a mistake. Nominalism denies that there is any necessary, extrapropositional state of affairs. It restricts clarification to the field of ideas or linguistic expressions. The present theory admits intelligibility to the content of experience. It also can admit that there are formal truths. But it is different from empiricism in maintaining that the ultimate fount of truth about reality is contained in the unique moments of lived experience, that this content is intelligible, and that insight into the particular grasps necessity, because what obtains in its uniqueness could not be anything other than what it is.

Again, it would be a mistake to argue that the extrapropositional in its uniqueness must remain unintelligible, or that necessity is altogether excluded from particular entities. There certainly is a sense in which a state of affairs generated in a deliberate human act is both intelligible and unique.

Furthermore, there are instances in which abstract knowledge is as the theory says it is. Sometimes the meaning of a question is not determinate when it is asked in its abstract form; the question only clarifies itself as one proceeds toward knowledge of the particular. This is the case, for example, when one is entering upon a certain vocation, such as marriage, and asks himself or herself what sort of life this will be, what the implications of the present commitments will be, what, in short, the future has in store. A person getting married never knows what he or she is doing; the future is hidden from one's eyes. One's insight into the reality grows only as one tries to live the commitment, and one's understanding of the commitment itself develops continuously. If it does not, one regards one's own marriage as if it were merely an objective state of affairs to be studied by sociologists and other scientists. The objective appraisal misses and perhaps even falsifies the existential reality.

Another example in which abstract knowledge functions as the theory proposes is in the questions one asks oneself in the course of creative activity and answers for oneself by a genuine, creative effort. The poet begins with a vague question; the meaning of the initial question is defined as the poem takes shape. Only when the work is perfected is the poet in a position to understand precisely what he was seeking. At this point the intelligibility, which is unique, is achieved in the work itself. The question is transformed and dissolved in the reality to which it inadequately pointed.

But when one asks whether someone is reading a sentence or has written a book—the states of affairs used as a point of departure for the argument in part two—this question is not open to development in the way in which some other questions are. Indeed, the question "Do you, John, take this woman, Mary, to be your wedded wife?" must have a predetermined meaning. One does or does not commit oneself; one would not have this choice if the meaning of the question were not settled before the answer to it is given. In this sense, when one is about to act one understands what one is going to do *before* the state of affairs obtains. Similarly, a person who begins to write a poem must grasp the definite meaning of the question "Shall I try to write a poem?" or his creative effort could never begin.

If one tries to maintain, as a general philosophical position, that although particular states of affairs are intelligible, abstract thought about them never grasps their reality, one is taking a position which is self-referentially inconsistent. The position itself is general and abstract. Therefore, according to itself it does not touch the reality of *particular acts* of abstract thought. Nor does it touch the reality of particular states of affairs; it talks about the unique abstractly.

If a relativist protests that he does not intend his abstract statement of relativism to be more than a pointer to the unique particular, then he admits that his general philosophical position does not come to grips with the unique reality of someone's reading a sentence or writing a book. What is more, he admits that his general philosophical theory does not touch the unique reality of the argument I propose in part two.

If a relativist says that he is considering the argument proposed in part two and objects to it, then either he claims to see something wrong with the argument peculiar to its unique reality or he claims there is something in principle wrong with the argument. If the trouble is supposed to be peculiar to the argument in its unique reality, then one simply must *see* this difficulty; no one can communicate it to one who does not see it. Such an objection amounts to a claim to an intuition which cannot be rationally articulated.

If the argument in part two for the existence of an uncaused entity is supposed to be defective in principle, then one who objects to it must *say* what is wrong with it. Reasons must be given for regarding the argument as inadequate. The reasons given must bear upon this particular argument, of course, but insofar as they are reasons they would apply to any similar case. Not all fallacies are formal fallacies, but all fallacies violate some rule or rationality norm, and any rule or norm applies to an indefinite set of cases.

Empiricism and Kant's critical philosophy seek to draw boundaries to the possibilities of human knowing. Hegel rejects all boundaries and claims to have actual knowledge of the whole of truth. Relativism *seems* to be a modest compromise. Human knowledge at any given moment is limited, but the limitations are not absolute. One can transcend them. No one can quarrel with relativism about this point.

The difficulty begins when the relativist assumes that the only alternative to empiricism, critical philosophy, and absolute idealism is to treat each limited situation, case, structure, muddle, horizon, or whatever as a mini-absolute—that is, as a closed system which contains within itself answers to all the questions which can be meaningfully asked within it.

Metaphysical relativism means that all truth—that is, whatever is rationally accepted as true—is a function of *a* or of *b* or of *c* or of . . . , where "*a*" and "*b*" and "*c*" and ". . ." stand for irreducibly diverse and untranscendably limited principles. But if this position is true, then either the position itself is a function of one (or of a definite, but limited, set) of these principles or the position itself is not a function of such a principle. If the position itself is a function, say, of *a*, then either the position admits *b* and *c* and . . . as equally reasonable or the position excludes *b* and *c* and . . . as not true or as less reasonable. If the position excludes the alternatives to *a*, then the position does not really mean that all truth is a function of *a* or of *b* or of *c* or of . . . ; what the position really means is that all truth is a function of *a*. If the position admits the alternatives, then it has comprehended *a* and *b* and *c* and . . . in a single view, and in this unified view the limits of each of these principles (and of any set of them) are transcended.

In other words, the relativist implicitly claims that his own position is different from nonrelativistic ones. Relativism is better. Other positions are only relatively true, but the relativist regards his own relativistic position as absolute. Either it excludes alternatives as false or it relativizes them into positions less adequate and less reasonable than relativism. The relativist thinks of his own position as pluralistic, nondogmatic, and tolerant. In fact, relativistic positions are as monistic, dogmatic, and exclusivistic as any metaphysics. Indeed, a sincere relativist is more monistic, dogmatic, and exclusivistic than most metaphysicians, because he is quite unaware that he is taking a metaphysical position. A sincere relativist is metaphysically naïve.

The relativist's unification of the many principles of intelligibility which he posits and his transcending of their limitations can be looked at in either of two ways. Considered in one way, relativism is a restrictive strategy, not unlike empiricism and critical philosophy. The relativist claims to have absolute knowledge that it is true that all claims to have absolute knowledge are false. Considered in another way, relativism is a strategy of total comprehension. The relativist thinks his position can transcend and unify what he sees as many merely relative points of view. If the relativist's superior knowledge can relativize every alternative metaphysics, however, it must embrace the whole of reality. The knowledge required to ground a relativistic metaphysics would have to comprehend the meaning of all the propositions which pick out states of affairs which obtain. Otherwise, the relativist could not know that *all* knowledge-claims are only relatively valid.

Hegel, of course, thought he had the required knowledge. For Hegel all "truth" short of the Absolute is necessarily relative—a mere moment in the Absolute, a mere point of view to be transcended. However, once Hegel's Absolute is reduced to absurdity, the relativity of partial truths to the "truth" which is the whole also is undercut. Each particular truth thus tends to become a miniabsolute. The attempt to *legitimatize* this tendency is relativism.

Relativism and other metaphysical alternatives

A reader who has followed the exposition and criticism of empiricism, critical philosophy, absolute idealism, and metaphysical relativism to this point might object that I give little credit to the achievement of modern and contemporary philosophy. A reader who notices my considerable debt to ancient and medieval philosophy might suggest that I seem to assume that philosophy reached its zenith centuries ago and has made little progress since.

I could respond to a defender of modern and contemporary philosophy *ad hominem*. The assumption that there is cultural progress in a fairly straight line comes from a certain metaphysical perspective—one exemplified by Hegel. Moreover, Hume attacked his rationalistic predecessors; Kant severely criticized Hume; Hegel's reproaches against Kant often are harsh; post-hegelian philosophers have frequently ridiculed the philosophy of Absolute Spirit. Contemporary metaphysical relativists of each variety sharply dismiss or coldly ignore all who do not use the proper method and speak the proper philosophical language.

But a response *ad hominem* would not do justice to empiricism, critical philosophy, absolute idealism, and metaphysical relativism. Those who worked out these metaphysical alternatives, with tremendous ingenuity and labor, have made clear many errors which must be avoided, many problems which must be solved, and many truths which must be preserved. The philosophical theology I am proposing could not have been developed in the middle ages, although ancient and medieval philosophy also includes many forgotten truths, poses many important problems which are ignored today, and indicates errors which a philosopher is still likely to commit if he neglects the history of ancient and medieval philosophy.

Hume made several important points clear. First, there is no logical necessity uniting distinct extrapropositional states of affairs, and the intelligible link between any extrapropositional state of affairs and its own obtaining is not logically necessary. Second, the obtaining of extrapropositional states of affairs and the causal ordering of them cannot be discovered by the analysis of ideas. Hume saw clearly that rationalism is mistaken. However, Hume oversimplified the metaphysical problem by assuming that logical necessity is the only mode of necessity. He also overlooked the originality of propositional knowing and reasoning, and thus failed to see that one knows the obtaining of states of affairs *in* propositional knowing and one knows causal order *in* reasoning (see above pages 177-179 and 126-129).

Kant also made important contributions. First, not everything can be explained. The principle of sufficient reason is not a law of being, but a rationality norm. Second, human knowledge of the extraempirical is very limited; the extraempirical can be known only relative to the empirical. Kant saw the dangers of carrying the rationalist ideal to its limit. He suggested that the extraempirical ground of empirical states of affairs must be spoken of by means of negative and relational predications. However, Kant excluded theoretical knowledge of the extraempirical; he also deprived empircal knowledge of its realism and objectivity to such an extent that he prepared the way for absolute idealism.

Hegel's insight cannot be disregarded. He asserted that there is an intelligible link between *what* and *that;* he rejected scepticism and romanticism. Hegel was the modern champion of man's ability to know what all men by nature desire to know. He also brought into focus, for the first time, the metaphysical significance of history and the metaphysical vocation of man. However, Hegel claimed too much for human reason. Attempting to overcome false dichotomies, he missed the significance of irreducible, positive differences.

Post-hegelian relativism rightly agreed with Hegel in recognizing that there is an intelligible link between *what* and *that.* At the same time metaphysical relativism rightly differed from Hegel in recognizing both the irreducible positive differences among individuals and kinds, and the *positive* reality of contingency and freedom. Post-hegelian relativism, in its various varieties, paid serious attention to the relative necessity which arises in human action; in attending to this conditioned intelligible link between meaning and existence post-hegelian philosophy contributed much to man's self-understanding. However, in denying the legitimacy of theoretical philosophy relativism itself became an untenable theory. It excluded or rendered inaccessible to human inquiry any necessary entity, distinct from the empirical world, which would intelligibly and unconditionally link *what* with *that.*

The bitter and irresolvable conflict among varieties of contemporary relativism suggests the sectarian character of each of them. A post-relativistic philosopher must try both to speak to man as such and to listen to men in all their diversity. There is an alternative to metaphysical relativism, which preserves much of what is attractive in it.

The limitedness of human knowledge can be admitted while *a priori* restrictions on knowledge are rejected. The philosopher need neither confuse himself with the Absolute nor resign himself to the confines of the relative. The reality of an unconditional intelligible link between *what* and *that* can be admitted, while the identification of this necessity with any or all empirical states of affairs is rejected. The philosopher can remain a *lover* of wisdom; he need not claim to possess the ultimate science.

If there is an uncaused entity, such as *D,* then the obtaining of contingent states of affairs *can be* explained; if human knowledge of *D* is achieved indirectly, by way of reasoning from empirical states of affairs, then man cannot claim to *have* an explanation of a sort which would displace the many relative intelligibilities which originate in human action.

An uncaused entity such as *D* does not compete with immanent principles of being and value. Rather, to grant the possibility of theoretical knowledge of such a transcendent entity is to prevent any immanent principle from covertly taking its place. Plato long ago suggested that the best way to preserve openness is to assert the reality of a transcendent Good, while being careful not to define it. Aristotle failed to recognize the usefulness of such an ideal. He did not see that it has a considerable indirect value. If one accepts the reality of a transcendent principle which one does not claim to understand as it is in itself—that is, apart from the relationship of immanent entities to it—then one is protected from domination by any particular and limited principle which might be invoked as an ultimate and exclusive source of meaning and value.

A metaphysics based upon any particular, immanent entity will be as spacious and as confining as the intelligibility of that definite entity. Many miniabsolutes are not better than one big Absolute. Much better than either is an uncaused entity which one can claim to know about without claiming to comprehend. Kant sensed the point which Plato had made, but Kant paved the way to absolute idealism and to metaphysical relativism rather than turning modern thought from this way. Kant's regulative "as if" is not enough to limit the excessive claims of reason; the residue of rationalism in Kant's thought prevented him from seeing how to posit an ultimate principle of explanation without employing it illegitimately in place of immanent explanatory principles.

Any relativist can easily enough brush aside the argument I have given against metaphysical relativism. Relativistic theories have at their disposal plausible responses to any theoretical criticism. Because the various forms of relativism are oriented toward practical concerns, their attacks on metaphysics tend to be *ad hominem.* A pragmatist can suggest that anyone who considers a metaphysical question, such as whether God exists, is trying to bolster his own sagging faith or is seeking an escape from the real problems of life in this world. A linguistic analyst, after noting that the language used in theoretical metaphysics is puzzling, odd, and not reducible to ordinary language, can put the metaphysician in his place by seeing what he is doing as a strange language game belonging to a *peculiar* form of life. An existentialist can accuse the theoretical metaphysician of trying to escape the anguish of facticity, the burden of freedom, the inevitability of death and nothingness. A marxist can point out that the arguments of theoretical metaphysics are mere ideology.

No such attack is relevant. Even if a person proposing a metaphysical argument is raving mad or completely dishonest, the genesis of what he says is irrelevant to its truth. If the argument is not sound, then one who rejects it should be able to point out something specifically wrong with it.

As I have explained, one who truly asserts no metaphysical position cannot put any obstacles in the way of the metaphysics I am attempting to develop, unless he can show that it is somehow inconsistent. Usually metaphysical relativists do not take seriously theoretical arguments, such as an argument for the existence of God, and criticize them. Many recent works begin by saying, "Of course, everyone agrees that the old rationalistic arguments for the existence of God are useless."

Such works then proceed to attack the position itself, rather than the argument. God cannot exist because there is evil in the world, because I could not stand not being God if there were a God, because man cannot be free if God stands over him, because God is useless and distracts one from worldly concerns, because the existence of a perfect being would make human progress toward perfection pointless. These are serious issues, to be discussed in part five.

Transition to part four

W. Donald Hudson says that the question "Does God really exist?" is meaningful, but he holds that the proof of the existence of God is "systematically elusive." Hudson states the basic reason for this elusiveness:

> Reality, in a final or absolute sense, is not something which we can discover. In the last analysis what we take to be 'real' is a matter of choice. We have to make our own ultimate ontological decision; we have to make up our own minds what criteria we will use for the application of the word 'real'.[2]

This statement is only an example picked at random. Dozens or hundreds of equivalent statements could be gathered from contemporary philosophical writings.

One might be tempted to answer this sort of claim by saying that if one is free to choose the criteria for using the word "real," one will choose criteria according to which this position is unreal. If it is unreal, then one of course need not consider it.

But Hudson does not mean that one can make words mean anything one wishes. Some criteria are more rational than others. It seems, then, that someone who holds that the proof of the existence of God is not as systematically elusive as Hudson suggests has the burden of articulating and defending the criteria according to which he uses the word "real."

A request to articulate such criteria and to justify them seems reasonable. But is it? If one thinks of the uses of words in a language on the analogy of plays in a game, one might suppose that the criteria for using words should be as easy to articulate as the rules for making plays. The rules of chess or football, for example, are clear enough. One can define castling in chess or making a forward pass in football with sufficient precision that instances of castling can be distinguished from other moves and that instances of making forward passes can be distinguished—in most cases—from other plays.[3]

However, I doubt that there are rules for using words similar to rules in games such as chess and football. It seems to me that the criteria for using words are considerably more subtle and that they resist attempts to articulate them. Obviously, if one cannot articulate the criteria, one cannot show them to be rational. But this does not mean that one's uses of words are irrational.

The United States postal service has been attempting for some years to introduce the use of more machines and automatic devices in the sorting and handling of mail. Much mail carries a zip-code in the address. If an optical scanner could pick up the digits of the zip-code and feed the information to a computer which could distinguish tokens of the ten digits from one another, mail sorting could be done very rapidly by machines. I am not certain whether this project has achieved success. When I last read about it, the engineers had encountered serious obstacles.

They were not even trying to program the computer to distinguish tokens of the ten digits written by hand. They were only trying to write a program which could distinguish printed or typewritten tokens of the digits. The problem might seem easy, but it requires that the criteria for taking a given blob of ink to be a token of one or another of ten digits must be articulated. The articulation of these criteria turned out to be almost impossible. After considerable work, if I recall correctly, something like eighty-five percent accuracy was achieved.

The odd thing about this problem is that a child rather easily learns to distinguish not only the blobs of ink which are tokens of the ten digits but also those which are tokens of the letters and other signs used in a written language. And the child fairly quickly learns to distinguish such tokens not only within the rather narrow limits of print but also within the much wider variations of handwriting.

There certainly are criteria for calling something a token of a particular letter or a digit. But what are they? These criteria are not like the rules of a game. They govern a use without one being conscious of them; one does not make an intellectual judgment in applying these criteria. The discrimination is a matter of recognition at a subconscious level of experience.

Someone might suggest that there is only a family resemblance among the tokens of a letter or digit. The point would be that there is no single defining characteristic, but only overlapping sets of similarities. Thus, two individuals belonging to the family might not resemble each other in any characteristic at all. This situation would account for the difficulty of articulating criteria. The project would, in fact, be impossible, for on this theory there are no universal criteria.

I find this use of the expression "family resemblance" puzzling. If I look to see whether the expression ever is actually used in this way in the language in which it is at home, I find that it is not. Ordinarily, one only calls a likeness among a set of individuals a "family resemblance" if one knows that they do have a common characteristic, namely, relationship to at least one common ancestor. Perhaps the puzzles which are caused when "family resemblance" is used in a philosophical *theory* of language can be dissolved if one recognizes that here too there must be something besides the sign itself which gives unity to a set of uses of a word, but the unifying principle might not be so obvious as to appear on the face of things at a glance.

What I am suggesting is that the difficulty of articulating criteria for using a word like "reality" does not mean that there are no criteria. One does not make up one's own mind what criteria he will use for the use of the word "real" unless he defines it stipulatively. One can define some words, but one cannot define one's whole vocabulary, by stipulation.

In most cases, though not in all, the criteria for using a word are quite definite, just as the criteria for discriminating blobs of ink as tokens of various letters and digits are quite definite. If one sometimes cannot tell of which letter or digit a given blob is a token, the difficulty does not arise because all letters and digits form a continuous series with no sharp boundaries. There are fixed essences, but some individuals are so abnormal as to be unrecognizable. One cannot tell *what* the essence of such an individual is. The difficulty could not arise if there were no essences.

The word "reality" seems to me to be one of those for the use of which the criteria are not very definite. I think this word does express several concepts which are unified in a peculiar way. In the argument I proposed in part two, however, I did not use the word "reality." As a matter of fact, I do not think that many people ask, "Does God *really* exist?" More often, I think, people ask, "Does God exist?"

I am not suggesting that one who attempts to do metaphysics has no special obligations with respect to his use of language. His uses of words are bound to be extraordinary. I have tried to build up a technical vocabulary, beginning in the second section of chapter four. However, it must be admitted that language is used in an irregular way when I say, at the conclusion of the argument in chapter five: "There is an uncaused entity, which necessarily obtains, and which causes contingent states of affairs to obtain."

If the way in which this irregular use of language is derived from regular uses can be clarified, then my extension and stretching of ordinary language and bending of linguistic rules can perhaps be justified. I attempt to provide some clarification in part four. However, I do not pretend to articulate and justify the criteria for the use of the words I use.

IV: The Meaningfulness of God-Talk

14: Limits of Reductionism

The four orders

In parts two and three I have tried to show that there is an uncaused entity, *D*, which is distinct from contingent states of affairs. In the present part I assume that the arguments developed in parts two and three are sound. I do not here try to add to the proof *that* there is an uncaused entity. Instead, in the present part I try to clarify how talk about *D* is meaningful. However, in doing this I also try to show that what already has been established implies a good deal more about *D* than I have explicitly stated up to now.

The present chapter is preparatory to the next three. In the present chapter I am concerned not with *D* but with what is *not D*. It is important to be clear about what is not *D*, because everything one can say of *D* somehow gains its meaning from what one knows and can say about what is not *D*. What is not *D* includes everything contingent, everything which falls within the field of man's experience. I use "experience" here in a wide sense which I will clarify.

What I said of *D* in part two can be distinguished into three closely related points: 1) that *D* is *uncaused*, 2) that *D* *obtains*, and 3) that *D* *causes* contingent states of affairs to obtain. In chapter fifteen I consider how *D* is said to be *uncaused* and show what else can be *denied* of *D*. In chapter sixteen I consider how *D* can be said *to obtain* and show that some other metapredicables can be *affirmed* of *D*. In chapter seventeen I consider how *D* can be said *to cause* contingent states of affairs and show that some other relational predications can be made involving *D*.

In the fourth section of chapter seven I explained how one knows causes

230

and effects *in* reasoning. Such reasoning works with experience, of course, but the cause-effect relation, as Hume correctly argued, is not itself an object of unreflective observation. *In* reasoning—not prior to reasoning nor as a product of reasoning—one understands the two states of affairs, which are cause and effect of one another, precisely insofar as they are united together in a cause-effect state of affairs which includes them both. In criticizing absolute idealism and in criticizing rationalism in general I argued that reason must accept certain irreducible limits. The multiplicity of individuals and the variety of kinds, freedom of human choice and contingency as such, cannot be explained. If everything could be reduced to an intelligible unity, this would mean that there was only one something. For example, Hegel's Absolute Spirit was considered by him to be the one and only reality.

Everything there is, then, cannot be reduced to a single intelligibility. No one predicable can be affirmed of everything man knows, for, as I said in criticizing absolute idealism, there is nothing which everything is. However, many things within experience can be reduced to one or another of a small number of intelligibilities. Reasoning reduces multiplicity to unity, and reasoning is a continuous process which links cause-effect states of affairs to one another. But, as I explained in chapter seven (pages 126-132), not all cause-effect relationships are of one mode. If the states of affairs united in various cause-effect states of affairs are linked by distinct modes of causality, they cannot be reduced to a single intelligibility.

For example, many cause-effect states of affairs which are constituted by physical causality can be embraced in a more inclusive cause-effect state of affairs homogeneous with them, that is, one of physical causality; many cause-effect states of affairs which are constituted by formal causality can be embraced in a more inclusive cause-effect state of affairs homogeneous with them, that is, one of formal causality. But a system based on physical causality and a system based on formal causality can be united neither in a more inclusive *physical* cause-effect state of affairs nor in a more inclusive *formal* cause-effect state of affairs. Systematization comes to a limit. Beyond this limit one can unify only by using metaconcepts—for instance, as one does in using *cause-effect state of affairs* to think about the distinction between physical and formal cause-effect states of affairs. *Cause-effect state of affairs* is a metaconcept based on the common schema of causal reasoning; to say that something is a cause-effect state of affairs is not to describe the content of experience but only to indicate that this content is organized.

I use the word "experience" in the following way. I say that whatever man can know prior to all causal reasoning is "given in experience." Whatever can be known only in or on the basis of causal reasoning is not given in experience. *D* is not given in experience. However, many entities which are not perceived by the senses are given in experience. One's own acts of propositional knowing, the intentions informing one's outward acts, and the meanings of words are not perceptible to the senses. But all of these are given in experience.

There are various ways of classifying the diverse kinds of entities which are given in experience. The making of such an inventory requires some principle of division. One can make an interesting and useful classification without claiming that one's principle of division is better absolutely than any other and without claiming that one can demonstrate the completeness of the inventory. Such work is descriptive; it depends upon induction. One can call the making of an inventory of everything given in experience "ontology." The remainder of this section is an attempt at such ontology, which is part of *descriptive* metaphysics.

Causal reasoning, as I have explained, provides very comprehensive intelligibilities. A distinction of modes of causality, then, can serve as a principle for ontology. What is known in causal reasoning is one state of affairs insofar as it includes other states of affairs or, to put the matter conversely, two or more states of affairs insofar as they are united in a single, more inclusive state of affairs. A unity of many, a multiplicity unified—this is called "organization" in a very wide sense of the word. The physical world is organized; logical thinking is organized; a person's life and a society are organized; artificial and symbolic entities, such as the parts of a technological system and the expressions of a language are organized. I call a whole set of entities considered insofar as they are organized an "order."

Thomas Aquinas distinguishes four orders.[1] Of the various acts of human cognition, he says, the act of reasoning is especially concerned with order. Understanding is concerned with *what* something is and with meaning; propositional knowing is concerned with *that* something obtains and with truth. Reasoning is concerned with *why,* that is, with the explanation of the unity of distinct entities which consists in the relation of one entity to another. The unity of distinct entities is order; thus it is peculiar to reason to know order.

Since reason is especially concerned with order, orders can be distinguished by the diverse ways in which reason itself is related—ordered—to its subject matter.

There is an order which reason does not bring about but only considers; this is the *physical* order studied by the natural sciences. Whether the order studied by mathematics also belongs here is a difficult question which I will not try to answer.

There is another order which reason by its own consideration introduces into its own acts; this is the *intentional* order of thought-entities studied by logic. Thomas also includes language here, but I think he is mistaken in doing so.

There is another order which reason by reflection and deliberation constitutes for possible choices; this is the *existential* order of human acts which make up personal and interpersonal life—one's own life and the life of society. This order is studied by ethics in one way, by biography and history in another way, and by some parts of psychology and social science in still another way.

Finally, there is another order which reason by invention or planning or habits of using induces in or imposes upon what is in human power; this is the *cultural* order, which includes works of art, products of manufacture, the results of engineering and technology, and also all sorts of symbols, including linguistic ones. This order is studied in various ways by many arts and applied sciences, by linguistics, criticism, and so on.

Thomas includes the relationship between contingent states of affairs and an uncaused cause in the order which reason does not bring about but only considers. I am concerned here only with entities given in experience, and thus do not include this relationship in any of the orders I distinguish. It seems to me that reason can be said to "consider" both the physical order and the metaphysical relationship of the contingent to *D* only if "consider" is used in different senses in the two cases. In parts two and three as a whole I discussed not only the contingent and *D* but also how reason is related to this metaphysical subject matter; later chapters of the present part may further clarify the nature of the metaphysical order.

Thomas does not develop to any extent the ontology implied by the metaconcept of *order*. But in chapter fifteen I will argue that no predicable which is descriptive of anything given in experience can be affirmed of *D*; the four orders include many—perhaps all—entities given in experience; thus it will be helpful at least to begin to unfold the ontology implied by *order*. If I did not do this, I might make clear that *D* is distinct from the entities included in one order—for example, the physical—but leave unclear that *D* is distinct from the entities included in the other orders. The following exposition of the distinction and relationship of the four orders also will be referred to at many points later in the book.

The four orders can be distinguished within a single experience; this is perhaps the best way to begin to clarify them. Suppose one goes to a lecture which presents an explanation of something. One listens to the lecture. In listening one *hears* in four diverse ways. 1) One hears sounds, which belong to the physical order. 2) One hears the explanation, which belongs to the intentional order. 3) One hears a person who wishes to communicate, to share something; his act belongs to the existential order. 4) One hears spoken language, a discourse, which belongs to the cultural order.

Hearing *sounds* is a function of the sense of hearing. Waves in the air—which a physicist studies—affect one's ears and thus one's nervous system—in ways which the biologist and psychologist study. One hears sounds because one is an organism enmeshed in the natural world. The physical order also includes other kinds of organism, inorganic entities, and many processes and events. Entities in the natural world are neither isolated atoms nor a homogeneous mass; they make up a continuum of process but this continuum, like a language, has distinctive features which stand out. Quantity, qualities including dispositional properties, physical space and time—all these are also aspects of the physical order.

Hearing *an explanation* is a function of understanding or interpreting. Distinctions are made and examples examined. Insights are gained and affirmed as insights into extrapropositional states of affairs, and truths are unified into a systematic knowledge of the subject of the lecture. One hears an explanation only because one is a thinking subject engaged in reflective thought. One keeps such thought straight only if one is aware of its inner conditions and limits. These conditions and limits establish the order of questions to answers, of insights to experiences, of parts of propositions to one another, of propositions to other propositions, and so on. Instances or examples and classes; problems and solutions; proofs and evidence; affirmations and denials and contradictions; sciences and other systems of knowledge—all these belong to the intentional order.

Hearing a person *communicate* something is a function of cooperation, of sharing in a common life together. Parents and children at some point usually begin to experience a barrier to communication. "Children simply do not listen," says the frustrated parent; the young person says, "My parents never hear anything I try to tell them." Hearing a person depends upon a commitment to a common cause; one who hears must appreciate the value which the speaker intends to communicate. Hearing is an aspect of a personal relationship. In such a relationship persons become a community. The existential order includes virtues and vices, customs and laws, institutions and unique moments of ecstasy, offenses and reconciliations, and a great deal more.

Hearing *discourse* is a function of belonging to a form of life or to a cultural group, the group of those who use a certain set of sounds or marks to communicate explanations, to express feelings, to make promises, or to play various other language games. The set of uses which constitute a language blend into other uses which ordinarily are not thought of as linguistic. For example, geometrical constructions or laboratory demonstrations; smiles, kisses, and gifts; arrowheads, pots, machines, factories, and garbage—all these are uses of natural entities for purposes in which significance is put upon what is used by the human intention which *appropriates*—makes into human property or possession—nature and puts it at the service of man. The cultural order is the residue of past human thought and action; the existing cultural order also makes it possible that future thought and action will go on within a human world with means already at hand. Human beings are culture makers; in a very broad sense of "symbol" one can say that in all transforming uses human beings make symbols. Some anthropologists use "symbol" as a verb and say that man is an animal who "symbols"; this expresses the role of man as *homo faber*.

The four orders are similar in that each of them is a unity made up of a multiplicity of things organized by a certain set of relationships. As Plato pointed out, "one" and "many" do not have a single meaning. "Order," which is based upon unity and multiplicity, also has many meanings. The relationships which constitute order in each of the four orders are not of the same sort as those which constitute order in the other three orders. Because reason is related to each order in a different way, the mode of causality known *in* reasoning in respect to each order is irreducibly different.

An example of a relationship which constitutes physical order is the connection formulated in any scientific law—for example, that a certain force accelerates a certain mass at a certain rate. Or, a certain amplitude of sound waves brings about a certain response in the nervous system of an organism having the sense of hearing. An example of a relationship which constitutes intentional order is any law of logic—for example, that one cannot both assert and deny the same proposition or that one can gain insights into kinds by studying examples. An example of a relationship which constitutes the existential order is any of the conditions of a free choice which follow from the values presupposed by all human acts—for example, the requirement that an act be directed to something understood as a good or the requirement that one accept a person's plausible explanation of something if one sees no reason to reject it. A relationship which constitutes cultural order is exemplified by the fitness of a technique to the goal it is intended to achieve, or by the aptness of linguistic expression to communicate the explanation of a subject matter.

Relations among the orders

Each of the four orders includes in its own way what is included in the others. At the same time no one of the orders comprehends the whole reality—the very ordering principle—of any of the others.

The physical order includes the human organism. The bodily person knows, acts, symbols (makes use). Knowledge begins from sensation and experience. But human knowledge also includes the *negation* which excludes the truth of a proposition and the reasons which are sufficient to prove a given conclusion. These are not physical relations; they are not formulated in natural laws. Human acts presuppose emotions and desires, natural interests and capacities. But human acts occur only if one has a capacity to make free choices, to shape one's personal life, and to form communities by commitments. Symboling presupposes materials and powers and goals which ultimately are natural. But symboling also presupposes inventiveness or creativity or established usages by which nature is appropriated and subdued, possessed and made to serve.

The intentional order includes reasoning in respect to all four orders; this was the fact, observed by Thomas, from which this ontology begins. But reason does not establish and cannot explain the uniqueness of the particular—for example, that this body is my body. Reason by itself does not bring about any human act; it articulates a variety of possible acts, but choice is the principle by which one possibility among others is realized. Reason plans and guides work, but culture is constructed only by human trial and error, concretely engaged with the stuff which is to be subdued.

The existential order also includes the others. One can choose to eat, to sleep, and the like. One can choose to think. One can choose to express oneself, to work. But one cannot choose his own body, nor can one choose not to die. One can choose neither that a proposition be true nor that an argument be sound. One cannot choose that a technological process succeed or that linguistic expressions mean what one wishes them to mean.

The cultural order also includes the others. Languages contain symbols for the entities of all the orders; art can serve natural needs, and it can be a way of gaining knowledge and a help in improving personal communication and community. But no one can do any symboling if there is not a natural world with given properties and possibilities, or if he lacks insight into the manner in which what is given can be transformed and ordered to a purpose, or if he cannot make choices and elicit the cooperation of others.

The four orders are irreducibly distinct from one another. To reduce them to a single system, reason would have to relate them all to a single principle; reason would have to be related to the various entities in all of the orders in a uniform way. Thus, any attempt to unify the four orders into a single order amounts to relating every state of affairs included in all of them to a principle located in some one of them, and to following the relationship by only one of the modes of causal reasoning. In other words, the orders are themselves related and unified, but not in only one way; each of them unifies by the special way in which it includes the states of affairs which are included in the others.

At the same time the orders really are united with one another. One finds them together in experience, and one can know that they are distinct and related. Their distinction is shown by the diverse ways in which they mutually include one another's content. But the unity is real. The entities of each of the orders can be said to be the same as—in diverse senses of "same"—the entities of any other of the orders.

The relationships which constitute the various orders are formulated in physical laws, logical principles, existential requirements, and cultural exigencies of aptness, suitability, or the like. States of affairs complete one another in causal orders; a state of affairs lacking its complement is abnormal, absurd, unreasonable, or inadequate in some way. Thus causal reasoning articulates norms for states of affairs which are known in such reasoning to be included in larger systems. A state of affairs without its complement is not as it ought to be. As Plato held, reason's first principle is the Good—that is, the complete or perfect whole in which the incomplete or imperfect parts are completed or perfected.

However, the normativity of each of the four orders is different. I briefly indicate the differences and provide a few examples.

The normality of the physical order is conformity to natural laws. "The sun ought to be rising soon," one says, expecting this instance to fulfill the laws of a known order. Looking for purposes in natural processes is a mistake; one imports into the physical order a normativity which belongs to the existential. Conversely, to try to apply the normativity of the natural to human action is confused; an example of such confusion is the view that unjust action is simply "abnormal behavior."

The correctness of the intentional order is conformity to logical principles. "One ought not to draw a syllogistic conclusion from two negative premises," one says, pointing out that there is no principle which would render intelligible such an inferential step. One who tries to build logic on psychological laws of association mistakenly supposes that logical correctness is merely a matter of normality. If one merely described human thought, one might find that certain logically incorrect modes of thinking are normal. On the other hand, to try to apply the normativity of logical principles to one of the other orders is to regard as logically impossible deviations from other sorts of norms which nevertheless sometimes occur.

The rightness and reasonableness of the existential order is conformity to love of human values. "One ought not to discriminate against anyone on the basis of race, sex, or some other irrelevant factor" and "One ought to accept the testimony of a person whom one has no reason to think dishonest or incompetent" point out that certain ways of acting are or are not in line with values such as justice and truth. To regard violations of such norms as nothing more than mistakes, resulting from ignorance or confusion, is to suppose that wrongful acts are like errors in logic. However, one can choose to violate existential norms, because human values are many and in themselves incommensurable; one basic value can be used as mere means to some other.[2] On the other hand, to regard the innocent mistake of a small child as if it were the violation of an existential norm is to suppose that the child could have chosen otherwise, when in fact he could not.

The aptness or adequacy of the cultural order is conformity to the implications of a particular purpose. "One ought to change oil after driving in a dust storm" and "One ought to use words which one's audience can understand" indicate what is necessary if one's purpose of keeping the engine running or of making oneself understood is to be achieved. To suppose that violations of technical, artistic, linguistic, and other rules are always undesirable is to ignore the creative dimension which must be allowed for in this order. Sometimes the only sensible thing to do is to shift one's purpose slightly, to compromise, to adapt means and ends to one another as well as possible. On the other hand, to employ the same strategy in dealing with a matter of correctness of reasoning or justice is to suppose that logical principles and existential norms are merely relative to subjective purposes. This supposition is one of the false implications of metaphysical relativism.

The distinction of the four orders from one another also helps to explain why there are diverse philosophical approaches. There is some room for a legitimate diversity of disciplines, each illuminating in a distinctive way, each focusing on a distinct order. However, when an approach centering upon one order becomes imperialistic, so that the distinctness and irreducibility of the others is denied, then an oversimplified model is projected and the misfit between the model and its subject matter generates insoluble problems.

Hegel, for example, tried to reduce nature to the intentional order. In place of the individuality and facticity which is distinctive of the natural he posited negation. The real is the rational; truth is the whole. Everything is the content of a self-referential act of Absolute Mind. Post-hegelian relativists take the cultural order as a base of operations from which to reconstruct other orders—for example, by treating them as mere projections of linguistic categories.

A naturalist such as Mill reduces logical principles to the status of generalizations from experience; a naturalist tries to explain moral and social reality in terms of psychological laws, evolution theory, and so on. Radical existentialism maintains that human freedom creates everything, beginning with its own situation. Kant tended to subordinate everything to the noumenal realm of practical reason and freedom; the inconsistency of his metaphysics follows from his existentialist project of limiting reason to make room for faith.

The various forms of reductionism cannot succeed. The stubborn irreflexivity of the human body and its unique relation to the thinking subject whose body it is argues against any form of idealism. One who denies the irreducibility of the physical order cannot give meaning to egocentric particulars, without which assertion and denial are impossible.

The indispensability of negation in the intentional order and its irreplace-ability by any sort of extralogical opposite argues against any theory that thinking is *nothing* but a physical process. "Nothing" means "*not*-anything." The word "not" can be used in some senses such that affirmation and negation can be represented by contrary physical states—for example, by positive and negative electrical charges in a computer. But "not" cannot be reduced to a physical analogue in every case. When the physicalist says that thinking is *nothing but* a physical process, he opposes everything physical to any possible nonphysical entity. The possible nonphysical entity must be in the "mind" of the physicalist if it is to be excluded, and it can be there—on his theory—only as something physical. But the physicalist does not wish to exclude this physical characteristic. He wishes to refer to what the physical is *not,* and to exclude it.

But how can one refer to what absolutely is *not?* Reference is a relation; for a physicalist it ultimately must be a physical relation; but physical relations only hold between physical states of affairs. What absolutely is *not* is not a physical state of affairs. The physicalist can shift his ground by denying the very meaningfulness of "nonphysical." However, if an expression is not empirically meaningful, neither is its contradictory. If the expression "physical" is not empirically meaningful, then the physicalist, on his own theory, cannot be saying anything about the real world.

Someone might object to this argument that one can and does refer to what is not, at least in one sense of "refer." But this objection misses the point. I maintain that the intentional order is not reducible to the physical order; therefore, I admit reference to what is not. First-level propositions do not include negation, but concepts based on the denial of first-level proposi-tions are used in second-level propositions, and in this way one makes reference to what is not.

However, a physicalist must somehow dispose of every instance of nega-tion, and he can dispose of it only *in* the physical order, since this order is the only one he admits. In *some* instances he might seem to be able to dispose of negation. However, my argument is that a physicalist cannot dispose of an instance of negation except by presupposing some other instance of it. Thus the physicalist falls into self-referential inconsistency when he says that thinking is *nothing* but a physical process; in this case the reference to negation cannot be disposed of in the physical order.

The preceding argument, of course, is only a sketch. I do not claim it to be compelling as it stands. Working in collaboration, Joseph M. Boyle, Jr., Olaf Tollefsen, and I have developed a self-referential argument for human free choice. The basis of this argument is simple, but its full development required a whole book.[3]

The argument for free choice begins by noticing that since determinism is neither a matter of fact nor a logical truth, a determinist must give a deterministic account of the phenomena of choice; in doing so he implicitly appeals to a rationality norm of some sort. The rationality norm to which he appeals is not reducible to the physical order, since it is not merely a matter of normality; not reducible to the logical order, since one can choose to disregard it; and not reducible to the cultural order, since the determinist claims that his position is more reasonable philosophically, not merely preferable for some particular purpose. Thus, the determinist claims that one *ought* to accept determinism, and the normativity implicit in this *ought* is such that the determinist's claim implies that one can respond by making a free choice.

One who denies the irreducibility of the cultural order deprives himself of language, without which he cannot communicate and defend his position. A linguistic sign can be developed creatively; hence language is more than a natural, behavioral phenomenon. Language is distinct from logic, because in using language one always does more and less than one intends; logic orders intentional entities just to the extent that one is aware of the conditions of propositional knowing. Language resists arbitrary choice; one can decide whether one wishes to speak and what one wishes to say, but one cannot by *fiat* make an expression do a job for which it is inadequate.

This outline of an ontology of the four orders could be filled out at considerable length; the arguments in respect to irreducibility, as I already mentioned, are merely sketched here to give the reader some idea of the way in which the distinction of the orders can be defended.

15: What the Uncaused Entity Is Not

The principle of negation

States of affairs pertaining to the various orders obtain in different ways.

Physical states of affairs obtain only if certain entities exist or events occur or processes go on in the natural world. One attempts to verify a proposition picking out a physical state of affairs by making an observation of the right kind and at the right place and time to gather evidence that the state of affairs obtains if it does.

Intentional states of affairs obtain only if intelligibilities are conceived, propositions are entertained, or reasonings are carried out. In other words, the obtaining of intentional states of affairs is contingent upon acts of thinking. Even a formally true proposition is not entertained and asserted simply by being the proposition which it is; rather, a formally true proposition which *is understood* is known to be true if it *is entertained.* The necessity of a formal truth is conditional; there is no formal truth if there is no proposition which is formally true, and there is no such proposition unless someone entertains it.

Existential states of affairs obtain only if choices are made. Human acts depend upon choices and upon habits which are established by commitments and maintained by one's willingness to keep these commitments. Societies depend upon personal communication and cooperation. Complex institutions may seem to have a life of their own, and in a certain sense they do, but they originate in choices—perhaps many choices which are not consciously coordinated. Moreover, institutions are only sustained by continuing willingness to live with them.

Cultural states of affairs obtain only if persons have purposes which they attempt to realize by making use of something which is available.

No matter how a state of affairs pertaining to one of the four orders obtains, it is contingent. Every state of affairs included in any of the four orders might or might not obtain. It follows that one can understand the predicables in propositions picking out any state of affairs pertaining to one of the four orders without thereby knowing that any particular state of affairs obtains. I use "*F*" as a symbol for any such predicable. If one entertains a proposition that something is *F*, one might happen to know that the state of affairs which the proposition picks out obtains—for example, if the proposition is self-referentially necessary. Still, one knows that the state of affairs is contingent; the state of affairs might or might not obtain.

The uncaused entity (*D*) is a state of affairs included in that which is the uncaused cause (*Dc*) of the obtaining of other states of affairs. *Dc* is contingent although *D* is not. When throughout the present chapter I say "contingent state of affairs" and "contingent proposition," I do not include *Dc* and the proposition *Xc*—that an uncaused cause causes other states of affairs to obtain. How "causes" is said of *Dc* will be considered in chapter seventeen.

Many states of affairs in each of the four orders are included in wider states of affairs. In all such cases, if one knows that the state of affairs obtains and the proposition is true, one can still ask, "Why is anything *F?*" An answer to this question is provided by causal reasoning of an appropriate mode. The state of affairs about which one asks is understood, along with its complement, in a wider, cause-effect state of affairs.

The states of affairs which are constitutive of the four orders cannot be reduced to a single order by any intelligibilities based directly upon what is given in experience. The modes of causality appropriate to the diverse orders reach a limit when causal reasoning uncovers constitutive states of affairs. In one sense, states of affairs which constitute the four orders are not caused— that is, they are not caused in the way in which anything within an order is caused. For example, if space and time are basic conditions of physical entities, then there is no physical explanation of the spatiotemporal character of nature, although *space* and *time* are involved in causal reasoning about any state of affairs included in the physical order. The same will be true of the constitutive principles of each of the orders.

However, as I showed in the first section of chapter five and in my criticism of absolute idealism in chapter eleven, even if there were a proposition which picked out a state of affairs constitutive of an order which included *all* contingent states of affairs, such a proposition would be contingent. I also use "*F*" to symbolize any predicable in any proposition picking out a constitutive state of affairs. Since such a state of affairs remains contingent, one can ask, "Why is this *F*?"

As I argued in part two, this question is only answered by positing an uncaused entity which requires nothing to obtain except to be the state of affairs which it is. Whatever *D* is in itself—that is, apart from the relation of contingent states of affairs to it—one could not know the truth of a proposition picking out *D* and still ask, "Why is this true; why is *D* such-and-such?" Thus, if one knew what *D* is in itself—that is, if one knew *D* directly, not as the term of a relation which something else has to it—one would know any proposition picking out *D* to be necessarily true and one would know that any predicable which applies to *D* could not apply to it for any reason other than *D*'s being what it is.

If one forms a proposition that *D* is *F*, one cannot know that the proposition is true merely by considering what it means. *F* is an intelligibility which can be used in contingent propositions; it could not be used in contingent propositions if states of affairs in which something is *F* obtain simply because something is *F*. A proposition that *D* is *F*, if known to be true, would be knowledge of what *D* is in itself. However, what *D* is in itself is all that *D* requires to obtain, while whatever is *F* requires something besides *F* to obtain. Therefore, a proposition that *D* is *F* cannot be true.

"*F*" stands for any predicable which can be applied to anything in a proposition picking out a state of affairs within any of the four orders or constitutive of them; no proposition of the form *D is F* can be true. Thus one must deny any statement which describes *D* positively in language used for describing anything involved in the four orders, unless this language is used in a sense different from its usual one. Moreover, if the four orders do not include all contingent states of affairs, any predicables in propositions picking out other contingent states of affairs—whether within other orders or constitutive of them—likewise can be applied to *D* only in false propositions.

Another way of reaching this conclusion is as follows. In the argument in the final section of chapter four I concluded both that there is a necessary entity, *D*, and a necessary truth, *X*. *X* is a proposition picking out the state of affairs which *D* is. I have said nothing thus far about the content of *X*, except insofar as *D* has been characterized through the argument as a necessary entity which is an uncaused cause of contingent states of affairs. If one could formulate a proposition picking out *D* in which the predicable would be an intelligibility of *D* in itself—not a relational or other metapredicable—one could not understand the proposition without knowing that the state of affairs it picks out obtains. One can understand propositions in which predicables derived from experience are applied without knowing that the states of affairs such propositions pick out obtain. Thus, the proposition *X*, as a necessary truth picking out *D,* neither can be replaced with nor can be supplemented by any proposition formed with predicables which also can be applied in propositions picking out contingent states of affairs.

The point can be put more briefly as follows. Whatever *D* is in itself, it requires nothing to obtain other than to be what it is. Whatever anything contingent is, it does not obtain by being what it is. Therefore, whatever *D* is in itself, it cannot be what anything contingent is. Hence, whatever anything contingent is, *D* is not.

Someone might suggest that while *D* cannot be characterized by any single predicable also applicable to a contingent entity, a sufficient set of such predicables might provide an adequate characterization of *D.* This is the rationalistic position which Kant criticizes. The rationalists suppose that a most real being, an *ens realissimum,* would be a sum total of perfections. But one cannot derive necessity from any combination of perfections belonging to contingent entities. Hegel tries to do so and fails.

One argument I propose against absolute idealism in chapter eleven (pages 202-203) is that if such a philosophy were true, one could not understand it without knowing it to be true. Hegel, in effect, proposes his philosophy as a replacement for proposition *X.* The fact that one can understand the metaphysics of Absolute Spirit without knowing it to be true conclusively shows that it is false. Similarly, inasmuch as *D* could not be understood without being known to obtain necessarily—if *D* were known in itself, not merely by the relations of other things to it—it is impossible to describe *D* in itself by using predicables which do not apply necessarily to that to which they do apply.

What *D* is not

Any proposition which cannot be affirmed as true must be denied. Thus, in speaking of *D* all of the expressions which cannot be used to say what *D* is—since they signify predicables which can be used in picking out contingent states of affairs—should be used in saying what *D is not.* In this use these expressions keep precisely the same meaning they have when they are used to express contingent propositions which are true.

Thus *D* is not a body, nor is it matter or energy, nor does it evolve or change in any way, nor is it spatial or temporal. *D* is not numerically one, it has no size or shape, it is neither a whole nor a part. *D* has no sensible properties, no dispositions or capacities such as are found in natural things. In the precise sense in which entities in the world can be self-identical, equal, like, above, or outside, *D* is none of these. *D* is not doing anything; it is not undergoing anything.

As mentioned already, it must be kept in mind that all of these negative predications are made in such a way that the expression used to say what *D* is not is used in exactly the same sense in which it would be used to say what something contingent is.

Moreover, the exclusion of any predicable does not mean that its contrary can be applied to *D*. This point is not easy to keep in mind consistently, because normally if one says of something that it is not *F*, one supposes and often suggests that it is *G*.

Such a supposition is one obstacle to an initial grasp of the irreducible distinction of the four orders. For example, naive naturalism results from the difficulty of overcoming the common-sense view that to be is to-be-out-there-now, an entity in nature. It is less naive, but equally erroneous, to suppose that the negation of physical characteristics in respect to *D* implies that *D* should be characterized in a positive way by what applies to entities in one of the other orders—for example, the existential.

Thus, if *D* does not change, it does not follow that *D* is standing still, fixed, inert, or rigid. If *D* is not a substance, it is no more a process or an event. However, if *D* is not a body, it does not follow that *D* is a mind. If *D* is not an individual, it is not a class. If *D* is not above or outside, this does not mean it is the ground of being or that it is immanent in everything as power or life. Furthermore, *D* does not know, love, act justly, or become angry as human persons do; still, one should not infer that *D* is ignorant or lacking knowledge as something subhuman lacks it, nor that *D* lacks love as a stone lacks it, nor that *D* is unjust or immoral or amoral, nor that *D* lacks feeling and concern.

None of these negations should be taken as indicating that *D* itself is a mere idea, nor that it is a negation, nor that it is a logical entity of any sort—all these also fall within experience. The exclusion of these, at the same time, does not mean that *D* is unintelligible, or false, or irrational. *D* is not an action, a community, or an institution; but this does not mean that *D* is an omission, an autonomous individual, or something spontaneous and lawless. *D* is not a symbol, a tool, or a product; but neither is it useless, pointless, or raw material.

There is a sense in which a human person knows in experience of himself what it is to be a subject, a moral person, a creative principle; *D* is none of these, nor any of their contraries which come to mind.

Someone might object that if one cannot affirm of *D* some of the contrary opposites of predicables which are denied of it, then one has no knowledge of *D* at all. To say of something that it is *nonred* is informative if one means that it is some other color. But to say, simply as a contradictory opposite of something's being red, that *whatever it is,* it is *not* red is altogether uninformative. One does not know whether what is being talked about is the virtue of justice, the number two, or the assertion of a proposition. None of these is red. Something of which one knows only that any proposition which tries to describe it is false is an unknown entity.

In one sense this objection is correct. The denial of all the propositions of the form *D is F* does not provide any positive description of *D*. But in another sense the objection is mistaken. Since one must deny every proposition which applies to *D* any predicable applicable to a contingent entity, a conjunction of all these negative statements forms a description of *D* which distinguishes *D* from each and every entity given in experience. However little one knows of *D*, one knows that it is not like anything contingent. *D* is something wholly diverse from all the entities with which man is familiar.

This conclusion is relevant to the new theism. The new theism has arisen at least partially because of dissatisfaction with traditional views which did not include a complete statement of what *D* is not. If one says that *D* is changeless and fails to add a negation of the contraries of "changing," one suggests that *D* is static and inert. If one says that *D* is not a particular, limited entity and fails to add a negation of the contraries of particularity and limitation, one suggests that *D* is abstract and indefinite. If one says that *D* is not affected by man's sufferings and stops with this negation, one strongly suggests that *D* is cold and unconcerned about evil.

One must negate of *D* *everything* descriptive of entities given in experience. One must not reserve a certain set of descriptive predicables, thinking that *D* is like contingent entities in a few respects, which can be included in a minimum description of *D*. Any such minimum description is not only inadequate to *D*—which is what is usually admitted—but is altogether false of *D*.

Kant imagines that although one cannot speak of God theoretically, it is possible to speak accurately of him in the language of practical reason. This position is erroneous. Descriptive language drawn from the existential order is no more adequate for talking about God than is descriptive language drawn from the physical order. Both languages are suited for talk about what is not *D*. What is not *D* need not obtain. *D* is a necessary being. Much contemporary theology follows Kant's lead and attempts to translate talk about God into existential language. But this language only appears to be better suited for discourse about God. In reality, an existential description of a necessary entity is informative only if it is either negative or relational—that is, if it indicates how other things are related to *D*.

Finally, metapredicables such as *obtains* and *causes* are usually limited, so that they signify the obtaining or causing appropriate to one or another of the four orders. *D* does not obtain and does not cause in any mode in which any contingent entity obtains or causes. To the extent that "exists" suggests one or another mode of contingent obtaining, one ought not to say that D exists.

In other words, if D is God, then God does not exist, unless "exist" is used in a sense quite distinct from the senses it has when one speaks of objects existing in the physical world, of human persons existing through freedom, and so on. Those who believe in the reality of God yet say that God does not exist seem to me to be making this point. However, if they go on to claim that one should say that God is present or that he is eternal instead of saying that he exists, they offer a suggestion which easily creates further confusion. An uncaused entity is no more present than absent, no more everlasting than evanescent. Of course, "eternal" not only means everlasting; it also means "nontemporal." In the latter sense D is eternal, for D is neither past, present, nor future. Yet D is not timeless as truth and love are timeless.

16: What Can Be Affirmed of the Uncaused Entity

An uncaused entity obtains

The argument of the preceding chapter shows that no expression can be used in an affirmation about D in the same sense in which it is used in a descriptive statement about a contingent entity. All too often, attempts to talk about D—God, a first principle of reality, or whatever—stop short of a full statement of what must be denied of D for fear that a complete way of negation would leave nothing whatever to talk about. However, only a thorough-going way of negation compels one to make clear how one can affirm anything of D.

One can correctly affirm something of D if the expression one uses takes on a special sense, one proper to D. Expressions which can be used in affirmations about D take on a special sense because their meaning shifts to accommodate what D is. But what is D? No positive description of it is possible. How can the meaning of expressions used to make affirmations about D shift to accommodate what D is if one does not know what D is?

What D is in itself—that is, apart from the relations of contingent states of affairs to D—is unknown. But the conjunction of all the negative statements one can make about D does provide a definite description of D. D is not bodily, not mental, not changing, not static, and so on—in short, not-like-anything-within-experience. This description distinguishes D from everything contingent, allows one to refer to D, and serves in place of a proper name of D. Thus, there is something to which expressions used in affirmations about D can and must conform—not to what D is in itself, but to what D is *not*.

Sometimes D is said to be the "wholly other," the "transcendent," and

248

"the holy." Such expressions might be proposed as ones suited for use in affirmations about *D*. If "wholly other" means that *D* *cannot* be said to be whatever contingent entities are said to be, this expression is appropriate, but nothing is affirmed.

The same is true of "transcendent" if it is used to mean that *D* is *not* given in experience and *cannot* be described in the language used to describe experienced entities. "Holy" has a richer meaning than the other expressions, but part of what it seems to mean is the otherness of *D*. That is said to be "holy" which is set apart from immediate concerns centering upon experienced entities. Thus "holy" also can express what *D* is not.

However, "wholly other," "transcendent," and "holy" are expressions which can be used in *affirmations* about contingent entities. If one uses these expressions in affirmations about *D* in the same sense as they are used in affirmations about contingent entities, then the propositions involving *D* expressed by such affirmations should be denied. It is a mistake to suppose that some special set of expressions, even ones used in religious contexts, can be used to give a minimum description of *D*. Man is wholly other than the rest of creation; what is unknown is transcendent to understanding; the sacred dimension of human existence is holy. Using these expressions as they are used in the preceding statements, *D* is not wholly other, is not transcendent, and is not holy.

No linguistic expression which signifies a predicable which cannot be applied to *D* in a true proposition can take on a sense suited to making an affirmation about *D* merely by shifting its meaning to accommodate what *D* is not. Such a shift in meaning would be total; nothing of the original meaning would remain. For example, if one says that the entity which is not-like-anything-within-experience is a body, either the word "body" loses its meaning altogether or else it takes on a sense in some other way than by shifting its meaning to fit that of which it is said.

However, metapredicables do not have meaning in the same way predicables do, and so metapredicables can take on sense by shifting to accommodate that to which they are applied. Metapredicables do not provide any descriptive content for propositions picking out states of affairs within experience. Hence, expressions signifying metapredicables need not wholly lose their meaning if one uses them in affirmations about *D*. *Obtains* and *causes* are metapredicables; the former a nonrelational and the latter a relational metaconcept. In this chapter I consider only nonrelational metapredicables. I consider the relational type in chapter seventeen, for these not only raise special problems but also open up additional possibilities for forming true propositions referring to *D*.

I explained above (pages 241 and 246) that the meaning of "obtains" partly depends upon that of which it is said. Physical states of affairs obtain if something exists or happens in the world; the obtaining of the intentional is in something *being thought;* the obtaining of the existential is in something *being chosen;* the obtaining of the cultural is in something *being used.*

However, the meaning of "obtains" is not reducible to any or all of the various modes in which states of affairs belonging to each of the orders obtain. As I explained in chapter nine (pages 177-179), the obtaining of states of affairs which do obtain is a factor—distinct from what they are—by which propositions which pick them out are made to be true. Of course, a state of affairs can obtain without being picked out by any proposition; if a proposition did pick it out, its obtaining would make the proposition true.

Thus obtaining is a counterpart of truth, but obtaining must not be confused with truth. One can say that a state of affairs which obtains *holds true,* but "true" in this case does not refer to propositional knowledge; "holds true" simply means "obtains." The obtaining of states of affairs is not experienced; one knows obtaining *in* propositional knowing, when one posits as other than one's knowing the state of affairs picked out by the proposition which one affirms.

Thus when one says that an entity which is not-like-anything-within-experience obtains, "obtains" takes on meaning from that to which it is applied by shifting its sense to accommodate what *D* is. The description of *D* by way of negation does not evacuate the sense of the metapredicable *obtains,* because this metaconcept is not directly based upon the content of experience. The way of negation denies of *D* all the properties which one normally thinks of as conditions for the obtaining of something, because one *normally* thinks of contingent entities which only obtain in one or another of the orders. But these conditions are alternatives to one another. Physical entities, for example, exist somewhere and at some time; propositions and negations do not. Thus, the conditions which must be satisfied for any contingent state of affairs to obtain do not wholly determine what *obtains* signifies.

Still, if one is to say meaningfully that *D* obtains, one must be in a position to posit the content of a true proposition which refers to *D.* One gets into this position precisely by a reasoning process, since *D* is not given in experience. The argument proposed in part two is such a reasoning process. Therefore, the very meaning of "obtains" used in affirmations about the uncaused cause (*Dc*) and the uncaused entity (*D*) depends upon and emerges from the argument.

The argument proposed in part two begins from the obtaining of states of affairs which are given in experience. These are contingent; they also have contingent causes. Contingent causes are themselves caused. It is possible and reasonable to ask why these cause-effect states of affairs obtain and to expect an answer which does not simply raise the same question once more. At this point the argument concludes to *Dc,* which requires nothing to obtain except what is included in itself, and to *D*, which requires nothing to obtain except to be the state of affairs which it is.

All of the propositions in the argument up to the conclusion have meanings which were clarified either in the second section of chapter four or in the second section of chapter five. However, prior to the conclusion of the argument "obtains" is not used in the precise sense in which it is used in the conclusion. How can a new meaning be generated *in* an argument?

This objection might seem formidable, even insurmountable. Critics of reasoning toward God often implicitly assume or explicitly state that reasoning does not generate any knowledge which could not in principle be achieved without reasoning. If reason is as limited as such critics suppose, no meaning which one did not have at the beginning of an argument could emerge from the argument—except, perhaps, to the extent that meanings might be divided or combined without being transformed. This view of reasoning belongs to empiricism and to critical philosophy; I criticized it in the fourth section of chapter seven, where I explained how one knows causes *in* reasoning.

Hegel and metaphysical relativism accept an opposite assumption—that reasoning can transform every meaning. My criticism of these positions in chapters eleven and thirteen indicates that reason must accept limits; not everything can be reduced to unity, since some incompatible positive intelligibilities cannot be wholly preserved in the synthesis of a higher view.

When the argument of part two reaches the conclusion that an uncaused cause (*Dc*) obtains, the words in which the conclusion is expressed already have been used in the argument. "Cause," "not caused," and "obtains" are not new words, but "obtains" and "cause" do have new senses, because they are being used in a peculiar context—the context of the argument and of "not caused." The way of negation further clarifies this context by making clear that *D* not only is not caused but also is not-like-anything-within-experience. Thus, the word "obtains" takes on new meaning, which emerges from the argument, when it is used to affirm that an uncaused cause obtains.

One ought not to be surprised that when expressions are combined in a new way, they mutually modify one another's meanings. The meaning of at least some expressions is a function of their use in particular contexts. Words constantly gain new meanings in this way. If they did not, language would be much poorer than it is. English would lack "genes," "quanta," "infinite numbers," "no-fault insurance," "superego," "astronauts," "fem-lib movement," and so on. In reasoning one knows causes; language is extended to express what one learns in reasoning, just as it is extended to express what one learns by experience.

In reasoning one knows what one could not know otherwise; one puts two and two together and comes up with something unexpected. Poetry also depends upon this fact. If words could not change in unexpected ways and take on surprising new meanings by being put into novel contexts, they would have no poetic use. But it would be a mistake to think that only poetry generates new meanings by putting existing expressions into novel contexts. Living language in general is poetic; many expressions yield more or less easily to the pressure of reason.

Normally one does not say that anything obtains except to point out the contrast with what one supposes might have been: it might not have obtained.[1] "Obtain" cannot be used with this usual connotation in an affirmation about D. Why, then, might one not say that D does not obtain? As I explained at the end of chapter fifteen, one can say that D does not obtain if "obtain" is used in any of the senses it has in affirmations about contingent entities. D does not obtain as a physical, intentional, existential, or cultural state of affairs.

However, the context of the argument through which D is posited alters the meaning of "obtains"; the usual connotation of *obtains—might not have obtained*—is altered. I say "altered," because *might not* remains relevant as a function of the argument and of its contingent starting point. The argument might not have been thought out. If it had not been, "obtains" would not acquire the meaning which emerges from the argument. Of course, this fact bears not upon D but only upon human knowledge of D. What is more important, the argument begins from a contingent state of affairs—someone's reading a sentence. This state of affairs might not obtain. If it does not, then the conclusion of the argument remains hypothetical.

When I formulated the argument in chapter four (pages 53 and 58), I stressed this point by using a future contingent state of affairs—someone's reading a sentence tomorrow—during the course of the argument, and re-placing it with a past state of affairs—someone's having written the book—only at the very end of the argument. Beginning with a possible state of affairs, the argument proceeded exactly as it would if one began with a state of affairs which does obtain. The *meaning* of the conclusion emerges from the argument in either case. But if the contingent starting point obtains, then Dc and D also are posited. The extrapropositional beginning of the argument leads to an extrapropositional state of affairs at the conclusion.

Thus the understanding of the meaning of "uncaused entity" and the assertion that there is an uncaused entity remain distinct. Although D is a necessary being, this necessity is not logical necessity, as I explained in chapter seven (pages 129-133). One can say that D *might not* obtain, provided that "might" expresses only logical possibility.

Other affirmations and some comparisons

One can make certain other affirmations about D by using expressions which take on new meaning in much the same way "obtains" does. Such expressions, including "something," "one," "true," and "good," can be used of entities in all four orders. All of them express a contrast which is constant in schema but variable in content, depending upon that to which they are applied.

"Something" and "one" are closely related. "Something" contrasts the distinct with the merged, the part with the larger whole. "One" contrasts the undivided with the divided. Something is one considered in contrast with what it includes; one thing contrasted with another thing is something. Two somethings become one thing if they are not distinguished from each other.

The physically one is an individual; it is something since it is one of many individuals. One bee is something in a beehive which unifies the somethings within it. One mountain is something in one range, which also is a larger something.

The intentionally one is not an individual. To be sure of one thing is to know the truth of a certain proposition, if no more; to know something about a certain matter is to know one proposition or another about it, but to seek more. General understanding is something, while more adequate knowledge unites partial insights. "Something" contrasts with "everything" as particular with universal.

The one of the existential world is neither an individual nor a universal. A person does something rather than do nothing; one can't do everything. But the something one person does is a contribution to a wider cause which is accomplished in the course of a whole life or by a whole community of persons working together.

The world of culture uses "one" and "something" in yet another way. A single word is a sign, not a token; thus one can use the same word over and over. Each token is something. Again, a new invention is "quite something"; many copies of the same design are one product.

"One" and "something" can be used in affirmations about *D*.

Whatever can be said of anything else must—in the sense in which it is said properly of other entities—be denied of *D*. *D* is distinct from everything else man knows. For this reason *D* is eminently something; it is a distinct knowable entity. Apart from knowledge, *D* and contingent entities are not reducible to a single principle distinct from *D* itself, since *D* is uncaused. One might be tempted to say that *D* is part of "reality," but *reality* also is a metapredicable which shifts its meaning to conform to that to which it is applied.

"One" also can be used in affirmations about *D*. The description of *D* built up by the way of negation is definite. As I will explain in chapter seventeen, *D* also can be called "one" by relational predication.

What satisfies expectations is called "true." A true oasis is not a mirage. A true proposition is not false; experience verifies it, or it generates no incoherence, or it opens the way to the unfolding of knowledge, or it enables one to do things. A true husband or wife is faithful; the love for which one hopes is not refused and one's own love is not betrayed. A true dollar bill is not counterfeit, and a true leather binding is not cheap plastic; the true gives the service one expects.

D also can be said to be true. *D* does not *appear* at all; thus *D* cannot appear to be other than it is. One begins an inquiry expecting to find a principle; *D* satisfies that expectation. The proposition (*X*) that *D* obtains is necessary and cannot be false. Moreover, since *D* itself is necessary, it must *hold true*. *D* cannot lack what it needs to provide what contingent entities require to obtain. *D* satisifes the expectation of contingent entities; it is a true cause.

Whatever meets the norms of its order is as it ought to be; what is as it ought to be is called "good." As I explained in chapter fourteen (pages 237-238), normativity is closely linked to reason, to order, and to causal necessity. To be good is to be complete, to be in order, and to be fulfilled by whatever complement the order provides. "Good" does not have its usual sense when it is affirmed of *D;* the contrast implied by "good" must be altered. *D,* being unique, is its own paradigm; it cannot fail to be what it should be. Since *D* requires nothing to obtain other than to be what it is, *D* cannot be incomplete. The causal necessity contingent entities share in by being in order, *D* does not need; it is necessary in itself.

Moreover, if one must deny all propositions attributing the perfections of contingent entities to *D,* one also must exclude every imperfection—every lack and limitation—of contingent entities from *D.* Thus one can say that *D* is perfectly good.

It would take me too far afield if I were to compare and contrast the preceding account of affirmations about *D* with various other theories of God-talk. However, a few remarks might be helpful.

A common formulation of traditional thomism, but not of Thomas Aquinas himself, is that existence belongs to God by proper proportionality: God's existence is to God as the creature's existence is to the creature. A common objection to this formulation is that since God and his existence are unknown, the proportionality is uninformative. In the context of reasoning toward *Dc,* however, one reaches a conclusion which makes reference to a theoretical entity which a believer might wish to identify as God, and in this context both "cause" and "obtains" take on new meaning. Thus, a supporter of proper proportionality might defend his position by proceeding as I have in the present chapter.

One of the objections to analogy of proper proportionality is that such analogy is not clearly distinct from metaphor. Metaphor does involve shift in meaning which is somewhat similar to that which I have been describing.

Interestingly, some recent work in philosophy of science stresses that new meanings do emerge in theoretical argument. Mary Hesse, for example, remarks that

> ... rationality consists just in the continuous adaptation of our language to our expanding world, and metaphor is one of the chief means by which this is accomplished.[2]

However, what is usually called "metaphor" arises in the stretching of the meanings of *descriptive* expressions. Therefore, metaphor is not involved in the use of the expressions with which I am concerned in the present chapter. Metapredicables are not descriptive to begin with; expressions signifying metapredicables cannot be used to indicate a way of seeing things, since ways of seeing have to do with what is describable.

Dr. Ian Ramsey develops the idea of disclosure models in discourse concerning God.[3] There are many parallels between what he says and what I have been saying, especially in respect to the relationship between the way of negation and the shift in the meaning of expressions used in making affirmations about *D*. Dr. Ramsey's theory has been criticized in respect to several points which I also consider unsatisfactory.[4] I think that his idea of disclosure models is a valuable insight, but I would wish to articulate this insight by reference to argumentation from which meaning emerges. Otherwise, the meaning of talk about God cannot be shown to be reasonably derived from ordinary langauge used to talk about experienced entities.

17: Relational Predications about the Uncaused Entity

Relational predications about experienced entities

In this chapter I try to clarify the least understood and probably the most important of the ways of speaking of the uncaused entity (D). The argument in part two arrives at D as a state of affairs included in the uncaused cause (Dc) of the obtaining of an experienced, contingent state of affairs—someone's having written a book. But the argument could begin as well from any contingent state of affairs other than Dc itself. Thus, the primary question to be answered in the present chapter is, What does it mean to say that D—by way of Dc—causes any and every other state of affairs? But before explaining how this relational predication can be made of D, I must try to make clear different ways in which relational predications are made of experienced entities. Also, after I explain what it means to say that D causes, I will indicate how this predication opens the way for others, including some in which descriptive expressions shift meaning so that they can be used in making affirmations about D.

Some relationships are based upon a real unity between two distinct entities. Each modifies the other; there is mutual dependence and neither can be thought of or spoken about without implying the other. Examples are the physical relationship between male and female, the intentional relationship between name and predicable, the existential relationship between friends, or the cultural relationship among parts of the system of objective culture—for example, lock and key, the lock-key combination and a door, the locked door and a wall, and so on. Relationships of this sort obviously are diverse in the diverse orders; in fact, these diverse relationships in part *constitute* the orders

256

in their diversity, since each order is a unity made up of a plurality of states of affairs related to one another.

Yet despite the diversity of such relations all are alike in one important respect. In each of these cases there are two entities which are unified in the following way. In some respect the two are very like each other; each is something by itself; they can exist apart. Male and female diversify individuals of a single organic type; each individual is a distinct organism; their births and deaths need not coincide. Similarly, one term of a proposition contains an insight distinct from the other; perhaps in the first instance one is gained apart from the other, but they are alike in being concepts. Friends must be similar in commitments; each must be a person who lives his own life, and could do so without the other. Parts of objective cultural complexes are produced or developed by similar processes; each part has its own design and character, and parts often are replaceable.

In another respect two entities related in the manner under consideration have definite differences which they can be seen to have even apart from the relationship itself. For example, a child sees that boys and girls are built differently and wonders why. For a concept to be able to be a name it must be formed in such a way that it can *stand for* what is; for a concept to be a predicable it must be able to characterize what is *such* (concepts may have both capacities, just as individuals of some species are bisexual). Those who are to be friends must differ in temperament or ability or the like; these differences allow them to give something to each other. The parts of complexes of objective culture also are different; the key, for instance, not only is shaped differently from the lock, but the key is a rigid unit, while the lock has many parts, and some parts of the lock move while others are firmly attached to one another and to the door.

The similarity and the difference together set up a situation in which the two entities can be fully themselves only to the extent that they become a single principle. Male and female organisms can exercise all of their functions only if they become a single principle of generation. Name and predicable are knowledge of that of which they are concepts only if they become elements of a proposition in which a state of affairs is known. Friends can fully develop their individual personalities only by sharing in community with each other. The lock and the key serve their purpose only by being used in the same act.

Because the full reality of both terms of such relationships depends upon their unity with each other, the full understanding of either depends upon a simultaneous and equal insight into the other. Up to a point one might know and refer to an entity involved in such a relationship without becoming aware of its relativity or mentioning that aspect, for there are nonrelative aspects which can be considered by themselves. But in considering any experienced entity a point is reached at which certain characteristics which have been discovered are not wholly intelligible by themselves. Such characteristics become fully intelligible only if they are found to belong to the entity insofar as it is, or is suited to be, included in a larger unity.

The unity in diversity of that which is ordered, together with the possibility and limits of knowing the relata in distinction from one another, is the foundation for reasoning. One can and does come to know *in* rational discourse, because one grasps at once the distinctness, the disposition to one another, and also the unity of the relata. One makes new discoveries in *reasoning* because one relatum points to the other, and in cases such as those now under consideration one relatum even indicates some of the characteristics of the other.

Let us imagine that the fem-lib movement ends in the elimination of males, not only from personkind but also from all other animal species. Reproduction could be carried on by cloning—an artificial technique by which females can reproduce themselves in individuals like younger identical twins without male interference. In this gentle new world let us also imagine that the previous existence of males was stricken from every book and record, was never mentioned, and eventually was forgotten. Still, a brilliant biologist might observe that there were certain peculiar features shared by all those organisms which could reproduce only by cloning. Looking for an explanation of these features and reflecting on the facts of evolution, the biologist might be able to develop a fairly conclusive demonstration that there must at some time in the distant past have been a different type of person. The characteristics of that other type could be worked out in some degree of detail. The vanishing of the type would be something of a mystery, perhaps, but its extinction might be explained by its natural inferiority.

This bit of science fiction can be paralleled by examples in the other orders. If an anthropologist of the future—after locks are no longer necessary and their use is forgotten—were to discover a lock without discovering any key, a study of the lock could lead to a hypothesis as to what it was for, and to the prediction that very likely another item would be discovered; this item could be described with considerable accuracy. If one discovered a bundle of letters which a historically well-known person wrote to a friend about whom nothing is otherwise known, one could guess many characteristics of the friend from the letters, even if they never said anything directly about the person to whom they are written. If one knows certain properties of a concept which can serve as a predicable, one can infer properties of the concept which could serve with it in a proposition as a name. For example, if the predicable is the determination of a precise time—at 7:20 p.m. on November 23, 1963—then the name must be of a particular event; if the predicable is a fixed measure of continuous quantity—six feet, seven inches—the name must be of an object which is more or less a solid.

Relations such as I have been describing are extrapropositional and irreducible to what is not relative in respect to both terms; in reasoning one can come to know such relations. These are points it would be unnecessary to argue were there not philosophical positions to the contrary. These positions, empiricism and critical philosophy, have been examined in chapters six to nine. But another difficulty must be noticed here. There is a natural but mistaken tendency to suppose that all relations are of the type already described—that is, mutual-dependence relations. Thus, children at a certain age seem to suppose that what they do not see is invisible; they enjoy playing peek-a-boo, some psychologists think, on the assumption that what they do not see cannot "see" them.

But, as the example of seeing suggests, not all relations involve mutual dependence. Seeing depends on what is seen; one who can see requires the visible to fully realize that capacity. But the visible does not seem to gain or lose anything by being seen. Similarly, an animal which is looking for water depends on the water which it seeks; the water *which is sought* does not depend on the animal. Again, thought as such is related to something thought about, but what is thought about is not in any respect fulfilled by this fact. Commitment to a value depends on the worth of that to which one is committed, but the value does not become worthwhile because one commits oneself to it. Even use does not necessarily transform what is used. One uses the North Star to steer by, but this means of orientation is not affected by one's use of it.

In each of these relations one term of the relationship—the functions of seeing, seeking, thinking, committing, steering a course—is relational through and through, although each of these functions or acts belongs to something, such as a human person, which is not purely relational. At the same time the other term of the relationship—the visible, the sought, the thought about, the value, the means of orientation—is not correspondingly relational through and through. As with the other relations, two entities are necessary for unity and fulfillment, but the need and the realization are on one side; the other neither needs nor is fulfilled. It must be noticed, however, that the nondependent terms of relations such as these must have certain characteristics; the visible has certain physical properties, the sought after can satisfy a need if it is found, the thought about must have what it takes to make itself known, the value must have what makes it worthy, and the means of orientation must be accessible, stable, and so on.

Relational words and concepts always work in complementary pairs. Male and female, name and predicable, friend and friend, lock and key—the expressions are used as complements and defined together. The same is true of expressions of the other sort of relations: seeing and visible, seeking and the needed, thought and object, commitment and value, steering and guiding star. But the second set of pairs differs from the first to the extent that the two sorts of relations differ. The first set of pairs of expressions indicate mutual dependence; the second set of pairs of expressions indicate a one-sided dependence.

One must think of both terms of any relation as reciprocally related, and linguistic expressions of relations indicate as much. But the relational predicable applied to one term in relations of one-sided dependence does not indicate relativity in the nondependent term itself. If one says that a certain comet is visible, one posits a potential relation of seeing to it, and one indicates that the comet has what it takes—sufficient output of light—to be an object-term of the relation of the seeing. But the comet has that characteristic in itself; if no eye existed as yet, the comet could streak through the universe, in all respects just as it now does, but it could not be called "visible." Yet as soon as one thinks of seeing the comet one must think and say that it is "visible."

"One must think and say"—does this phrase indicate a sort of illusion? No, to be an object-term of a relationship of one-sided dependence is an aspect of the reality of such entities, but it is not anything other in them than what they would be if they were not involved in the relationship. For example, whatever the visible requires to be visible is an aspect of its reality. However, this aspect is not affected in any way by the fact that there are eyes to see.

The need for each other of the relata in a relation of one-sided dependence is not mutual. The visible, the sought, and so on are not completed and fulfilled in relationships of this sort as seeing, seeking, and so on are. Moreover, causal reasoning proceeds from the dependent side in *discovering* such relationships, although once they are discovered one can learn more about the dependent term of the relation by studying the nondependent term.

A clear distinction between the two types of relational situations and the two modes of relational predication is vital in metaphysics. The ignoring or misinterpretation of dependence in relational states of affairs is an important aspect of empiricism and critical philosophy. The assumption that all relational states of affairs involve mutual dependence is characteristic of idealistic philosophies, such as Hegel's, and also appears in all forms of contemporary relativism, with respect to the inner structure of any regions of intelligibility they admit. This is why idealism tries to save the objectivity of knowledge and value by identifying knowing and choosing with the whole of reality. This also is why all the forms of metaphysical relativism fail to save the objectivity of knowledge and value; the relativist holds that thinking and willing both determine and are determined by what is thought and willed within some limited situation, and no two situations are really alike.

How the uncaused entity is said to "cause"

Causes is a metapredicable just as *obtains* is; hence, much of what I said in chapter sixteen with respect to *obtains* also applies to *causes*. "Obtains" does not express a descriptive predicable based on direct experience; neither does "causes." "Obtains" shifts its meaning to adapt to that of which it is said; so does "causes." The obtaining of entities in the diverse orders differs; the modes of causality constitutive of the various orders also differ. Obtaining is an extrapropositional counterpart of the knowledge of the truth of propositions; causing is an extrapropositional counterpart of the reasoning in which the order of things is known.

Neither "obtain" nor "cause" can be used in the same sense in affirmations about an uncaused cause (Dc) as they are in affirmations about other contingent states of affairs. However, the common schema of both metapredicables can be detached from the variable content. The argument developed in part two can be understood precisely as detaching the common schema and ultilizing it in an attempt to render intelligible the otherwise unintelligible obtaining of contingent states of affairs which do obtain. The second section of chapter five argues that there is a *rational* necessity, although there is no *logical* necessity, to make this extension. If the argument is sound, as I now assume, just as "obtains" emerges from the argument having taken on a new meaning, so does "causes."

Without repeating the argument of part two, I recall that the application of the causal schema rested on the following considerations. Contingent states of affairs within experience do obtain although they need not. Their obtaining is not identical with what they are; thus there is a gap of the sort which leads to a demand for explanation—that is, for finding an intelligible link which would close the gap. The obtaining of contingent states of affairs cannot be explained by saying that all such states of affairs together are self-sufficient. An explanation is possible only if there is something distinct from experienced, contingent states of affairs. It is reasonable to demand and to expect an explanation; the objections of empiricism and of critical philosophy do not show otherwise. Therefore, one must posit a factor which would explain the obtaining of contingent states of affairs. The explanatory factor must be an uncaused cause (Dc); causing what is contingent, Dc itself is contingent; however, being uncaused, Dc obtains because it includes D, a noncontingent state of affairs—a necessary entity—which obtains merely because it is the state of affairs which it is.

The application of the causal schema through the argument can be summed up either from the side of Dc or from the side of the obtaining of the contingent states of affairs which Dc is posited to explain, although the causal relation is discovered in arguing from effect to cause. One can express the relationship, considering it from the side of the effect, by saying that contingent states of affairs which do obtain rather than not require something other than themselves to obtain, and this requirement is fulfilled by Dc. Conversely, one can say that Dc satisfies what other contingent states of affairs require to obtain, assuming that other causal conditions are given—but the obtaining of the latter also must be referred to Dc.

There is some analogy between Dc's causality and that of other causes, for the schema of causality is common. There is always a danger that the analogy will be overextended. For example, physical causes bring about effects which are or involve changes, and physical causes always presuppose something to work upon. A flame heats the water in the kettle; this is a change; moreover, the flame does not heat water unless someone puts water into the kettle. Physical causes themselves also are effects. In terms of the distinction developed earlier in the present chapter physical causality is a mutual-dependence relationship. Dc does not bring about changing as such, but Dc causes contingent obtaining, which of course includes the obtaining of states of affairs involving change. Dc does not presuppose anything to work upon, for what does not obtain cannot be presupposed by the causing of its obtaining. Finally, the causality of Dc cannot involve mutual dependence or Dc itself would be caused.

One could carry out similar analyses of analogies drawn between Dc and causes according to modes other than the physical. In each case similarities projected on the basis of what is proper to any particular mode of causality are misleading with respect to Dc and must be denied of it. This is an essential part of the way of negation. The analogy between other causes and Dc only holds to the extent that the causal schema applies. Many objections against the causality of Dc proceed in one of the two following forms. Sometimes it is argued that if Dc is a cause, then it must have properties F, G, and H, where "F," "G," and "H" signify properties of causes of a certain mode; Dc cannot be admitted to have these properties; therefore Dc is not a cause. The answer is to deny that Dc must have the properties stated—for example, *being prior in time, being mutually dependent, being a merely possible value*, and so on. Sometimes it is argued—with more sophistication—that if Dc truly is a cause, it must have one of two or more disjunctive sets of properties; Dc cannot consistently have any of these sets of properties; therefore Dc is not a cause. This approach at least recognizes that there are many modes of causality, but it erroneously assumes that modes of causality are restricted *a priori*. Of course, the very fact that there are various modes of causality argues against the *a priori* restriction of the causal schema to the modes which are recognized. The answer to arguments of this sort, which arise mainly from empiricism, is that *Dc* is a cause without fulfilling the criteria for being a cause in any mode of causality other than that proper to itself.

These considerations help to make clear why to affirm that *Dc* is a cause is not to describe *Dc*. But one might suppose that knowledge of the effect of *Dc* must make possible some description of *Dc*. Ordinarily one can discern some characteristics of a cause by examining its effect. But the case of *Dc* is different, since the effect of *Dc* simply is the obtaining of other contingent states of affairs. Because *obtains* is not a descriptive concept, knowing that *Dc* causes other states of affairs to obtain does not provide a description of *Dc*.

Of course, one does know that whatever *Dc* is like, it has what it takes to make contingent states of affairs obtain. One also knows that for *Dc* itself to obtain, nothing extrinsic to *Dc* is required. If *Dc* needed something else to obtain, then *Dc* would not be uncaused.

In chapter four (pages 56-57) I pointed out that since the obtaining of contingent states of affairs is contingent, *Dc* also is contingent. If *Dc*'s causing were not contingent, then *Dc*'s effects also would be noncontingent. Cause and effect remain correlative, or the schema of causal reasoning is altogether abandoned. I also pointed out that *Dc* can be uncaused only if it requires nothing not included in itself to obtain. Therefore I posited *D*, an uncaused entity included in *Dc; D* requires nothing to obtain other than to be the state of affairs which it is.

This conclusion of the argument naturally leads to the following important question: If *Dc* is contingent because it is the cause of contingent states of affairs, then why is *D* not likewise contingent, since *Dc* requires this included state of affairs, *D*, to obtain?

The solution to this problem is that *Dc* is contingent *only because* it is involved in cause-effect states of affairs such as that by which one comes to know *Dc*. As a cause of contingent obtaining, *Dc* must be contingent, because *Dc* might not have effects and without effects *Dc* would not be a cause. To be *what* it is in the causal relation, *Dc* must have something other than itself—effects. But to obtain as cause of these effects, *Dc* requires nothing not included in itself; otherwise it would not be uncaused. The relationship between *Dc* and the contingent states of affairs which *Dc* causes to obtain cannot be one of mutual dependence; both terms of a relationship of mutual dependence are caused as well as causing.

Dc's causing of contingent states of affairs to obtain is contingent, since there is no cause without its effects. But *Dc* also is uncaused. *D*, the necessary entity posited in *Dc* to account for *Dc*'s uncaused obtaining, must not be regarded as a state of affairs distinct from *Dc* apart from the causal state of affairs in which Dc is involved. If Dc and D are really distinct apart from the causal relationship, then D causes Dc, there is another causal state of affairs including both D and Dc, Dc is not uncaused, and the contingency of Dc will be transitive to D. In other words, to assume a distinction between Dc and D apart from the causal relationship in which Dc is involved would be to reject the conclusion of the argument in part two and to posit instead an infinite regress of contingent states of affairs, with no unconditional explanation of the obtaining of anything.

Therefore, D and Dc are not distinct from each other aside from the causal relationship in which Dc is involved. If D is a necessary being and Dc is an uncaused cause, the only difference between these two states of affairs is Dc's relation of causality. This relation cannot be grounded in some factor in Dc which is distinct from D. Thus, the *relation* of Dc must be grounded in some factor which is not included in Dc. This factor, however, does not make Dc mutually dependent; it adds nothing to D itself. If it did, Dc would not be an uncaused cause.

The relationship of Dc to the contingent states of affairs which Dc causes to obtain must be a one-sided dependence relation. Dc does not depend upon its effects; they depend upon it. Dc really causes these effects, just as the object of knowledge really causes one to know it. But Dc's causing is nothing in it other than D—its being as a necessary entity, just as an object's making itself known is nothing in it other than its being what it is.

In other words, the relationship between other contingent states of affairs and Dc makes all the difference to contingent states of affairs—they would not obtain but for this relation. But this relation makes no difference to what Dc is apart from the relation. Dc would not be an uncaused cause if the relation made any difference to it. D in and of itself has whatever is necessary for it to be the cause in this cause-effect relation; it acquires nothing new in being so; but considered as cause, D is Dc. D is distinct from Dc only inasmuch as contingent states of affairs require Dc; just as light is visible only inasmuch as there are eyes to see. Visibility adds nothing to light over and above what it is if there are no eyes; causing adds nothing to a necessary entity over and above what it is if there are no contingent states of affairs.

The statement that the causal relation of Dc to its effects makes no difference to what D is aside from this causal relation can be misunderstood. The expression "makes no difference" has many uses in descriptive statements about states of affairs within experience. For example, someone says, "What you want makes no difference to me." The property of *making no difference* is contingent in such cases. All such concepts, if applied to D, form propositions which must be denied. The nondependence of D upon the effects of Dc does not mean that D is unconcerned, detached, indifferent, and so forth. All these concepts also are descriptive. New theists are correct in rejecting the mistakenly drawn descriptive conclusions of *D*'s metaphysical nondependence; however, it is equally erroneous to use the *contrary* expressions to formulate a description of *D* as "involved," "concerned," "struggling alongside his creatures," and so on.

Thus, the relation of *Dc* to contingent states of affairs is not one of mutual dependence; the relation is a one-sided dependence of contingent states of affairs on *D*, which is *Dc* only insofar as it is the term of the relation. However, another false supposition must be avoided. The one-sided relationships given as examples in the first section of the present chapter have a property which the relationship of *Dc* to its contingent effects cannot have.

Ordinarily the causality of the nondependent term of a one-sided relationship is exercised simply by its being what it is, while other states of affairs change so that the nondependent cause sometimes causes and sometimes does not. Light illuminates simply by being light, while reflective objects come and go from its vicinity. What is sought after naturally has the properties for which it is sought, but changes in the conditions of an organism make these properties relevant and desirable.

Dc's causing of the obtaining of other contingent states of affairs should not be understood on this model. Aristotle's God, which is self-thinking thought moving other things by attraction, and the neo-platonic One which emanates automatically—as well as many other versions of gods and metaphysical first principles—are understood in this way. All such models imply a metaphysical dualism; the world of contingent entities or the receptacle of the emanation must exist in their own right. *Dc* as an uncaused cause cannot depend as cause upon whether certain states of affairs happen, because of some other cause, to obtain.

Thus, although *Dc* adds nothing to *D* except the one-sided dependence relation of contingent states of affairs on *Dc,* this relation is not precisely like other one-sided dependence relations. Nothing apart from *Dc* brings about states of affairs which then obtain or not by reference to *D*. If *Dc*'s causing were dependent, it would not be an uncaused cause. Apart from their relation to *D,* the contingent states of affairs *Dc* causes are nothing; states of affairs which do not obtain cannot be brought within range of *Dc*'s causality, as reflective objects can be brought into the light and thus be illuminated.

Consequently, the relation of *Dc* to the contingent states of affairs *Dc* causes to obtain is similar in one respect to a mutual-dependence and in another respect to a one-sided dependence relation of the familiar sort. Like the one-sided dependence relation, *Dc* is distinguished from *D* only by the relation of something else to *Dc*. Like the mutual dependence relation, *Dc* makes a difference to its effects without anything other than *Dc* itself making it be the case that *Dc* makes this difference.

However, the relationship between *Dc* and the contingent states of affairs

Dc causes is not the same as either of the usual types of relationship. This conclusion should not be surprising; both of these sorts of relationship are discovered in reasoning about states of affairs within experience. Moreover, both of these sorts of relationship allow one to project something about the cause from one's knowledge of the effect. One knows, at least, *how* the cause is a cause in the usual sorts of relationships. A cause in a mutual-dependence relationship realizes a capacity it has; a cause in a one-sided dependence relationship brings about effects only under conditions it has no part in causing. The way of negation requires that both of these initial descriptions must be denied of *Dc*.

Additional relational predications

The meaning of *Dc* and the assertion that *Dc* obtains emerge from the argument in part two. The argument begins from a particular, contingent state of affairs—someone's reading a sentence or writing a book. However, the peculiarities of the starting point are completely irrelevant to the argument. What is important about the starting point is that it is extrapropositional and contingent. States of affairs in all four orders are contingent. Moreover, the differences in the meaning of "obtains" at the beginning of the argument also make no difference to the outcome.

The point of the argument is to proceed from some contingent state of affairs, of whatever sort, to an uncaused cause which is a necessary being. As I have explained, the meaning of "uncaused," "obtains," and "causes" in the conclusion of the argument depends on the context of the argument. But the meaning of these expressions in the conclusion is independent of what is nonessential to the argument. Thus, no matter what the starting point, the conclusion of the argument has the same meaning. Since one refers to *D* only by way of this conclusion, the argument posits only one *Dc*, not as many uncaused causes as there are contingent states of affairs, modes of contingent obtaining, and so forth.

But "one" here is predicated relationally. "One" has many senses—for example, numerical unity—which are used in affirmations about entities given in experience. As part of the way of negation, one must deny that *D* can be called either "one" or "many" in any of the senses in which these words are used to describe empirical states of affairs.

Still, a relational predication of "one" of *D* is not insignificant. The intentional, the existential, and the cultural orders depend upon man, since intentional entities are by being thought, existential entities are by being chosen, and cultural entities are by something's being used. Man is part of nature and depends upon the rest of it. Nature itself is an order in which nothing is altogether independent of anything else. Of course, some of the relations of physical causality are indirect and remote; moreover, perhaps there is no one relationship which pervades all of nature. However, nature is one order—the physical order.

If *Dc* causes *any* state of affairs to obtain, then *Dc* must cause all states of affairs which do obtain other than itself to obtain. If *Dc* did not cause some state of affairs to obtain, *Dc*'s causing of a state of affairs dependent on the one which *Dc* did not cause would require something distinct from *Dc* itself. In this case *Dc* would not be an uncaused cause.

Thus *Dc* is not merely the uncaused cause of the obtaining of some particular state of affairs, assuming that other conditions are given independently of *Dc*. *Dc* is the cause of the obtaining of every other state of affairs which obtains. Nothing apart from *Dc* itself is presupposed by *Dc*'s causality, or *Dc* would not be an uncaused cause. As the cause of the obtaining of *everything* other than itself, *Dc* is called "creator."

There are two standard objections to the position that there is a creator. The first is that the conception of creation is unintelligible, since it is nonsense to talk about making things out of nothing. The second is that if the created world is really distinct from the creator, then creation does not totally depend upon the creator, while if it is not really distinct, it is not contingent.

The answer to the first objection is that in one sense the notion of creation is unintelligible, in another it is not. Creation cannot be explained; if it could, *Dc* would not be uncaused. Moreover, very often the charge of unintelligibility simply means that what is called "unintelligible" cannot be placed in some familiar category. Creation, being unique, cannot be placed in any of the other modes of causality, and so creation is not intelligible by assimilation to anything else. However, I have tried to show how "creator" is defined by reference to the argument for the uncaused cause. Assuming the clarifications I offer to be adequate, they show the reasonability of stretching language and bending linguistic rules to the extent that the argument in part two requires. If this is admitted, then "creator" also becomes intelligible through the argument. The popular expression "make something out of nothing" has not entered into any argument I have proposed. However, one can define this expression, in terms of the preceding argument, by saying that *Dc* causes all contingent states of affairs to obtain and that *Dc* requires nothing extrinsic to itself to do so except—in most cases—other states of affairs which *Dc* also causes to obtain.

One can answer the second objection by making distinctions. The created world is really distinct from the creator in the sense that the creator is necessary and the world is not. The created world is not really distinct from the creator, however, in the sense that the created world is in a relation of one-sided dependence on the creator; this relation involves the world with the creator; and this relation is inseparable from the very obtaining of the contingent. The created world does not *totally* depend upon the creator in the sense that within creation contingent states of affairs also depend upon each other, and these dependences are not identical with the dependence of all creatures on the creator. The created world does totally depend upon the creator in the sense that no cause within creation causes unless it obtains, and nothing else obtains unless Dc causes it to obtain.

The second of the two preceding objections perhaps arises from a confusion caused by the assumption that properties of other modes of causality can be attributed to Dc.

One confusion—a very common one—is to think of creating as if it were a type of physical causality, a tremendous push given the world at the beginning. However, obtaining, which is the proper effect of Dc, is tenseless. Dc is not as such a cause of movement, although Dc causes the obtaining of physical states of affairs involving movement. The obtaining of *all* contingent states of affairs is equally dependent upon Dc; thus all physical states of affairs, insofar as they obtain contingently, depend equally and immediately upon Dc for their obtaining. Creation is not an initial push indirectly transmitted to subsequent states of the universe.

Another confusion is to think of the universality of the causality of Dc on the model of the generality of the fundamental causes in other modes of causality. One erroneously supposes that Dc causes other causes to cause as they cause one another to cause. But Dc does not cause in the way in which any cause within experience causes. Dc causes all causes of other modes to obtain, for causes of other modes are themselves contingent states of affairs. In causing causes of other modes to obtain, Dc in no way competes with the causality of these other causes. Causes within experience are intelligibly related to their effects in their own proper ways; the causality of Dc, in making these relationships obtain, cannot preempt them. If Dc did not cause the obtaining of causes and effects according to all other modes of causality, then they would not obtain. However, what is contingent and merely possible does not *lose* anything in becoming actual. When Dc causes other modes of causality to obtain in certain instances, Dc does not displace these other modes of causality, but gives them their place in reality.

A model for the uncaused cause

The argument in part two concluded that D must be posited as a theoretical entity. To say that D obtains does not fully explain the obtaining of contingent states of affairs, but the positing of D does open the way to explanation. To refuse to posit *D* would be to say that contingent states of affairs obtain, ultimately, for no reason at all. The clarifications of the present part have fulfilled their purpose if they have shown that the language of the conclusion of the argument in part two is reasonably derived from ordinary language. However, these clarifications seem to move the inquiry no nearer to a positive, comprehensible explanation. In fact, the pervasive way of negation seems to block completely such an explanation.

However, I do not think the situation is as hopeless as it seems. There is something within human experience which is somewhat similar to *Dc*'s causing—a human person making a free choice. In a free choice a person determines between alternatives in such a way that under the very same conditions he could have done otherwise. All of the conditions for the obtaining of either alternative are the same, except the choice itself. Similarly, in *Dc*'s causing, *D* remains the same whether *Dc* causes or not. All of the conditions for contingent states of affairs either obtaining or not obtaining are the same, except for the very obtaining of contingent states of affairs which do obtain.

I do not suggest that the analogy is precise. A human person making a free choice is not an uncaused cause. Human choices are contingent upon many conditions other than the person himself; to begin with, one does not make choices if one is not alive, conscious, and so on. Moreover, human choices are self-determining; a person making a choice constitutes his own life, existentially speaking.[1]

However, there is some similarity. Insofar as human persons make choices, a whole order of entities comes to be. The person as free transcends the existential order to which his freedom gives rise. The same can be said of the person as knowing subject and as culture maker. Except in the physical order, entities are by being objects of *human acts* of thinking, choosing, using. Similarly everything given in experience is by being caused by *Dc*. Human choice, mysteriously creative as it is, bears some analogy to the causality of *Dc*, by which everything comes to be out of nothing.

To suggest this analogy is not to retract anything I have said previously. In chapter fifteen I made clear that the way of negation demands that attempts to describe *D* using language *in the same sense* in which it is used to describe entities within experience must be rejected. I also argued that descriptive language cannot take on meaning merely by a shift of sense adapting it to fit the negative characterization of *D* as something not-like-anything-within experience.

But what I now suggest is that descriptive language can take on meaning appropriate to *Dc* and *D* by a shift which is conditioned by the relational predication of *causes* of *Dc*. The present chapter has clarified how "causes" can be said of *Dc*, what "*Dc* causes" cannot mean inasmuch as *Dc* is *uncaused,* and also what *"Dc* causes" cannot mean inasmuch as contingent states of affairs either obtain or not, as the case may be, wholly because *Dc* either causes them or not. All I suggest now is that a causing which is uncaused and which determines between contingent possibilities is analogous to human free choice. A pattern of metaconcepts is the locus of the similarity.

Because the similarity on which I would base an analogy is in a pattern of metaconcepts, I do not suggest that one can predicate "free" of *Dc*'s causing by the symbolic anthropomorphism admitted by Kant. As I explained in chapter nine (pages 165-166), Kant is willing to permit for practical purposes the use of descriptive language in its usual sense to help man establish a moral and religious relationship to God. Kant suggests, for example, that one might take the orderliness of the cosmos as an occasion for thinking of God *as if* he were an all-powerful and wise ruler of the universe. I do not suggest that anything in the *content* of experience is relevant to the analogy between free human action and the causality of *Dc.* Rather, I observe that there is an analogy between the two *modes* of causality, neither of which holds between states of affairs *within* any order.

This analogy does not warrant the drawing of any firm conclusions about *D.* Yet the analogy does permit one to project a hypothesis, using man as model. The model will be an analogue model. It permits talking about *D* not only practically but also theoretically. A procedure of this sort often is used in the natural sciences.[2] One can hope to dispense with a model if other, more direct knowledge becomes available; at present, however, only a model will permit description of *Dc* without contravening the way of negation.

Using man, considered as free agent, as a model for talking about *D* can lead to absurdity. But the working out of the model can be controlled to some extent by what is already established with respect to *Dc*'s causality, the relationship of *Dc* to *D,* and so forth. Implications of the model which are incompatible with anything independently established can be denied; the model is adapted to fit its new subject matter. As a step in theoretical inquiry, the proposal of such a model is justified, even though it is not at present clear whether one can find independent evidence to check the validity of the model and the deductions one can make from it.

One value of a model precisely is that a conceptual apparatus already developed in work on another subject matter is made available for use in an inquiry into a subject matter for which one has no adequate conceptual apparatus. It seems to me that much of the speculation about God's attributes in scholastic philosophy and theology can be understood as the working out of the implications of a model based on human free choice for thinking about divine causality. Here I only summarize a few of these implications.

If *Dc*'s creative causality is thought of on the model of human choice, then *Dc*'s creating is an *act*. This free, creative act presupposes that the alternatives be presented for choice in another mode than that in which they will be realized or not realized. In human free choice the alternatives are presented by being entertained as propositions. Therefore, *Dc*'s free, creative act pre-supposes knowledge.

However, *Dc*'s knowing and its free creative act cannot be thought of in a way which would make *Dc* a caused cause. If *Dc*'s knowing and free creative act were distinct from *D* otherwise than by the relation of what is known and caused to *Dc*, then *Dc* would be a caused cause. Therefore, *D* must be its own knowledge and freedom.

If *D* is its own knowing, *D* must know itself, since only in knowing itself can *D*, while remaining uncaused, know what is other than itself. If *D*'s knowing is identical with *D*, *D*'s knowing cannot fail to be adequate; thus *D* knows infallibly, and the truth of *D*'s infallible knowledge also is *D* itself.

Similarly, free acts presuppose a value which is not chosen. In *D*'s case this value cannot be other than *D* itself, for if the value were other, *D* would be caused in this respect. The value which is not chosen is the ultimate good to which all acts of choice are directed. Since in *D*'s case this value must be identical with *D* itself, *D* is its own ultimate good. Moreover, *D*'s love of this good cannot be distinct from *D* itself, or *D* would be caused in this respect. Therefore *D* not only is its own freedom and its own ultimate good; *D* also is love.

Dc's free act of creating cannot depend upon any purpose apart from *D* itself. An extrinsic purpose would be a cause; since *Dc* is uncaused, *Dc* must create all things for *D* itself. However, for *Dc* to create can be of no benefit to *D;* if it were, *Dc* would not be uncaused. *Dc*'s act of creating cannot be pointless. The only point seems to be in the created world, considered not as an acquisition of *D*, but rather as an outward expression or communication of the obtaining, the knowing, and the loving of *D*. A creative act which brings about an orderly result not to satisfy a need but to express oneself is an act of play. Therefore, *Dc*'s free creating is a form of play (cf. Prov. 8:30-31).

Since *D* knows, acts freely, and plays, *D* lives, since these are forms of life. Moreover, the functions which are characteristic of this life are spiritual ones; therefore *D* is a person.

The way of negation remains. The model is suggestive; it indicates a direction that further inquiry into *D* might take. However, considering the model philosophically, one cannot be certain whether the inferences are sound. The extent of isomorphism and the actual meanings of the concepts used in the model in application to *D* cannot be settled without some other access to *D*. At this point, I think, many Jews and Christians would be willing to say that *D* is a partial and inadequate concept of what they would call

"God." Such believers think they have another access to D by which to criticize the model.

In part six I shall consider the possible meaningfulness of religious claims. However, before proceeding to this topic, I consider in part five several existential objections to belief in God.

V: Existential
Objections to God

18: Human Freedom
Is Compatible with Creatureliness

Two problems distinguished

In this part I examine several problems which are probably more important to anyone who is not a philosopher or theologian than are the more
technical problems considered in parts two, three, and four. As I mentioned
in chapter thirteen, many post-hegelian thinkers brush aside theoretical arguments about the existence of a creator. Instead of theoretical objections to an
argument that an uncaused cause exists they propose existential objections to
God. These objections are important, because they tend to block a consideration on their merits of the theoretical issues and because they pose major
obstacles in the way of persons who seek God.

The following seem to me to be the most important existential objections
to God. First, if God exists, how can man be free? Second, how can one make
sense of the evil in the world if there is a good, wise, and omnipotent God?
Third, doesn't human concern with God and religion distract men from their
real, earthly concerns? Fourth, does not the supposition that there is an
eternal and all-perfect being detract from the meaningfulness of finite process, development, and progress? The present chapter deals with the first of
these problems. The other three will be treated in the next three chapters.

To some extent these questions present a challenge to the reality of the
uncaused cause which, through the preceding argument, has been characterized as a personal entity who knows, chooses, and creates. These questions
pose an additional challenge if the personal creator is believed to have all the
characteristics attributed to him by traditional Jewish and Christian faith. I
wish to keep these two challenges as distinct as possible.

Of the four problems the questions about human freedom and about the presence of evil in creation are the most difficult. Of these two problems the question about freedom can be considered independently of the question about evil, but not vice versa. Thus, the problem of the compatibility between man's action being free and its being within the scope of the creator's uncaused causing takes first place.

The word "freedom" is used in several senses; a distinction among them is essential to this problem. The general schema for meanings of the word "freedom" includes as elements someone's acting, the action, and someone or something else which could be in opposition to the action, but which in fact is not in opposition to it. The meanings of the word "freedom" are filled out by diverse ways in which the opposing factor is specified, both as to what it is and as to how it could oppose the action.

Thus, one sort of possible opposing factor is a physical force or constraint imposed upon the action from without. One who is raped does not have intercourse freely; one who is tied up cannot move freely. A quite different sort of possible opposing factor is regularity and routine, whatever is established beforehand—the dead hand of the past. One who lacks originality cannot create freely; what works according to a set formula leaves no room for the free emergence of novelty. Still another sort of possible opposing factor is an obstacle to the fulfillment of a norm, a block to being and doing as one ought. In Freud's psychology a neurotic is not free; in St. Paul's theology a sinner is freed from sin only by the grace of God.

The three senses of "freedom" already distinguished, as well as the two senses to be distinguished in the next paragraph, all enter into the meaning of "freedom" as it is applied in political and social contexts. Political and social freedom is not so much a special mode of freedom as a complex of other sorts of freedom mixed in varying proportions and applied to groups of persons instead of to individual persons.

The two sorts of freedom most relevant to the present problem are freedom to do as one pleases and freedom of choice. Freedom to do as one pleases excludes the subjection of a person and his action to the demands of another; freedom to do as one pleases means that one is not blocked by the authority or by the power of another person from acting in accord with his own desires. An obedient child is not free to do as he pleases; a rebelling adolescent demands precisely this freedom. Free choice is a very different matter, although it often is confused with freedom to do as one pleases. Free choice excludes the complete determination of a person's action by antecedent factors. One has free choice only if he deliberates about possibilities genuinely open to him, chooses to realize one of these possibilities, but—all the antecedent and concomitant conditions other than his very choice remaining the same—could also have realized some other possibility.

Human free choice and freedom to do as one pleases both seem to some people to be incompatible with the existence of a creator.

If one's choice and all its causal conditions are caused by an uncaused cause, how can one choose otherwise? Does it make sense to say that the creator causes a person's freely doing what he chooses to do, as well as *all* the causal conditions of that choice? In other words, can God cause one to make a choice, and still have it be the case that there was a genuine alternative open to one? If the answer is negative, then either there is no uncaused cause or there is no human free choice.

Traditionally, the problem of divine causality and human free choice was the chief problem in reconciling the reality of a creator with human freedom. Contemporary philosophy is less concerned about free choice. Many contemporary philosophers are content to allow that human actions are altogether determined by heredity and environment, by nature and nurture. But few contemporary philosophers are content to accept the idea that man is not the supreme *mode* of being if not *the* supreme being. Very many contemporary philosophers who are proponents of various forms of metaphysical relativism maintain that all meaning and all value arise from human thought and decision. For them God is unacceptable because they feel that he restricts man, makes the human person into a slave or, at least, into a permanent underling. If God is Father, man is infant; since man has come of age, Father must retire. Humility, traditionally regarded as a virtue, has become a vice. One sees this transformation not only in Nietzsche's forceful attack on the "slave morality," as he calls traditional Christian morality, but in almost all nontheistic post-hegelian philosophy.

The two problems must be considered separately. I first consider the traditional problem about the compatibility between divine causality and free choice, then the contemporary problem about the compatibility between divine authority in giving meaning and establishing values, and human freedom to do as one pleases.

Divine causality and free choice

One argument for fatalism is that since propositions about the future are true or false now, the future already is settled. Part of the plausibility of this view arises from a tendency to confuse "true" in an objective sense with "known to be true." No doubt any proposition about the future is either true or false at present; the state of affairs it picks out, which includes temporal specifications, obtains or not. But not all propositions about the future are known to be true at present. Moreover, if some future events depend upon factors which are really at present indeterminant—for example, the free choices of persons—then no one could know at present whether propositions about such events are true or not.

One way to introduce the problem of the creator's causality and human free choice is to pose a dilemma. Either the creator knows all possibilities and which of them will be actualized, and then the future already is settled, and there is no room for free choice; or the creator lacks knowledge about some possibilities and the conditions which will or will not actualize them, but then the creator somehow is dependent and is not an uncaused cause.

A more popular way of putting the question is, "If God knows beforehand what a person is going to do, and if God's knowledge cannot be mistaken, then how can the person choose freely?" One answer to this question is that the time reference (beforehand) characterizes entities within experience, but must be excluded from God in the way of negation, and applies to God if at all only by way of relational predication. Thus, for God man's action is not future. God knows all things at all times without his knowledge being conditioned by time.

Still, how can God's knowledge of one's action be eternally and infallibly true and one's action at the same time be free without God's knowledge being conditioned by what he knows? This question can be answered in part by explaining that God does not know what is so by seeing that conditions sufficient to bring about a state of affairs are given; rather, he knows in the mode of practical knowledge. Thus, God does not know things because they are so; they are so because he knows and causes them. God's knowledge is not caused; he remains an uncaused cause.

This answer is compatible with the position that there is an uncaused cause, but this answer merges the problem of divine knowledge and human freedom into the problem of reconciling human freedom with a universally efficacious creative causality.

It is worth noting that the difficulty which must be resolved originated within Judeo-Christian thought. Outside this religious tradition no one developed any very clear conception of human free choice. The notion of freedom of choice for human persons is related closely to the conception of God as a free creator, of man as made in God's image, and of God confronting man with the Covenant or the Gospel, and demanding that man freely respond by a commitment of faith or by a rejection. Thus, paradoxical as it may seem, the doctrines of free choice and universal divine causality tend to go together historically.

Another point is that the alternative metaphysical approaches considered in part three do not offer plausible theories which would save human free choice. Both Hume and Hegel exclude human free choice; they insist that human persons are really free, but in senses of "free" such that every human choice is completely determined by factors extrinsic to the choice itself. Kant tries to defend free choice for the human person, but he does so by cutting human free causality away from the natural world, and attributing to the human person in his transempirical reality an initiative which is wholly unconditioned. Kant speaks as though the human person is distinct from God, but Kant never invokes God as an ultimate principle of the reality of human free acts. Causality of one thing by another is limited by Kant to the empirical world. Some who now hold that human persons are free assume that if human freedom is to be real, it must exclude all other causal conditions—such is the position of Sartre, whose concept of human freedom is influenced by Kant.

The traditional Jewish and Christian conception of human free choice did not hold that a free act is uncaused. The position rather was that an act is done by free choice if a person could have done otherwise under the very same set of conditions with the sole exception of the choice of the act itself. In this conception the choice makes a difference between which of two or more possibilities is realized, but one can only choose among antecedently shaped possibilities, and all such possible actions are conditioned by factors other than one's choice. This conception of free choice conforms to the Jewish and Christian belief that man is not a creator, that man is limited, that his causality always is situated in a given context over which he has no control, and that human action really occurs in the natural world, is subject to its physical order, but also makes a real impact there. In other words, traditional religious thought regarded the physical order as not wholly deterministic; nature was considered to be loose-textured enough to allow events which are not determined *wholly* by natural causes.

A common solution to the problem which has won acceptance even with many Christians is that human acts, to the extent that they are free, escape from being caused by God. But this solution will not do; the creator's causing of what is caused by human free acts cannot itself be caused by human free choice. If the transcendence of the creator—the fact that he is altogether uncaused—is to be maintained, then no cause of his action can be admitted. If any cause is admitted, then the creator is included in the contingent order of things; in other words, the ultimate principle of intelligibility becomes immanent. This outcome is unacceptable, because it is radically incoherent. Divine transcendence must be maintained; the creative act of an uncaused cause can in no way depend upon human free choice.

The only possible solution to the difficulty begins by recalling that one cannot understand what the creator's action is in itself. If one says that the creator causes *x,* and assumes that "causes" is to be taken here in any sense which one understands on an empirical basis—that is, in any sense appropriate to any other mode of causality—then *x* could not be replaced by "someone to make a free choice." Almost inevitably, when one says that the creator causes *x,* one imports into the meaning of "causes" some property of some other causality, for example, of causality through freedom. But there is no justification for doing this; the way of negation, which underlies the relational predication by which one calls the uncaused cause "creator," excludes the importation of any such property. Once one sees that "causes" in "the creator causes someone to make a free choice" says nothing about *what* this causality—which in reality is identical with the creator—is in itself, then one also sees that the assertion in question is not and *cannot* be incoherent.

The whole ground for predicating causality of the uncaused entity is the need of the experienced world for a principle transcending itself. Free choice follows upon deliberation, and deliberation depends upon knowing what a choice would be like before one makes it. Thus, the very conception of a free choice involves a real distinction between what might have been chosen and what actually is chosen. At the same time the very conception of free choice implies that no proportionate, immanent principle can account for the fact that one alternative actually is freely chosen. The very fact of free choice therefore requires the reality of a condition which can account for the *obtaining* of the free choice, without detracting from the freedom of the choice. Within experience there is no causality which can fulfill this requirement.

This conclusion explains why the doctrines of human free choice and of divine creative causality are parts of one perspective, and why the denial of creative causality entails either the denial of human freedom or the affirmation for the human person of a causality which is really creative. If God is thought not to exist, the human person either must be reduced to the status of a function within the whole organism of the universe or must be granted the status of an uncaused cause of his own free choices. No post-hegelian philosophy which excludes God can regard man both as superior to the natural world and as subordinate to a still higher principle of meaning and value.

As to the creator's own being, his causing a person to make choice *A* and his causing a person to make choice *B* (an alternative to *A*) make no difference to him in himself. If this difference made a difference to the creator, then he would be a caused cause. The only reason there is for saying that the creator causes someone to make one free choice or another is that one knows from experience that someone has in fact made one free choice or another. Thus, while it is correct to say, "John makes free choice *A* because the creator causes John to make free choice *A*," this relationship does not warrant an argument from the attributes of the creator to the characteristics of the choice. One must say that the creator infallibly knows what he knows and that his causality always effects what he freely chooses to cause. But these affirmations concerning the creator cannot be made conditions of his effects by way of the relational predications concerning the creator, for the relational predicates acquire their meaning *from what is related to the uncaused cause,* not from anything affirmed of the creator in himself.

This point may become clearer by reflection upon an effect other than a free act—for example, Fido chases a rabbit at a certain time. Since the cause of all the causes of this event is the creator, one can say that the creator *at this time* causes Fido to chase the rabbit. The tense of the relational predicate applied to the creator must shift with the event; thus, the next day: "The creator caused Fido to chase a rabbit yesterday." But the temporal specification cannot characterize the creator in himself. Therefore, one cannot argue: "Since the creator is timeless, and his causality is not really distinct in him from his reality, he causes timelessly; cause and effect are correlative, and therefore the effect is likewise timeless." As soon as "cause" is said of the creator as a relational predicate, it is false to say that the creator causes timelessly.

If one recognizes the general difficulties of speaking about creative causality, which cannot be spoken of in the same way as any causality *within* human experience, then one feels less difficulty about human free choice. How can a creature be other than the creator, yet wholly caused by the creator? How can a creature be what it is in itself in any respect if all that it is in every respect is caused by the creative act of the uncaused cause? The mysteriousness of such creative causality is not limited to special instances of it—for example, the causing of free choices.

Nor should it be supposed that the creator's causality of free choices must impose upon them alien conditions. The uncaused cause is no more outside things—alien from them—than within things. Moreover, there is no imposition upon that which does not resist. Since the creator is the cause of all causes, creative causality presupposes nothing; nothing does not resist.

To sum up. Relational predicates said of the creator do not describe what he is in himself. All one knows by way of relational predication is that whatever the creator is, he is what he must be to account for the fact that he is the term of the relationship to him of the entities which require him as cause. Thus, since everything, including temporal events and free acts, requires the creator as transcendent cause, one knows that he has what it takes to be such a cause. Whatever is characteristic of entities within the orders of human experience—in other words, whatever could be incompatible with the facts one is trying to explain—must be denied of the creator as he is in himself.

The real mystery is not the creator's ability to cause someone to make a free choice. The real mystery is his ability creatively to cause anything at all. If the creator can cause Fido to chase a rabbit and to do it at a certain time, he can as well cause John to make choice *A* and to make it freely. Both temporality and freedom belong to the effects insofar as they are entities distinct from the reality of the creator's causality, and this reality remains concealed by the transcendence of the creator, a transcendence made clear by the way of negation.

The seeming cogency of arguments against the compatibility between creative causality and human free choice arises, as I said above, from an almost irrepressible tendency to suppose that one understands what creative causality is in itself. It is extremely difficult to keep clear in one's mind that "cause" said of an uncaused cause is said in a unique sense. One keeps importing the idea of one thing pushing another, or of a producer and a product, or the like. These relations hold between entities bound together in one of the orders within experience. The creator *really* is transcendent. The creator is not Hegel's Absolute.

The possibility of thinking about the creator's act on the model of the human person's free choice—a possibility I explained in the final section of chapter seventeen—intensifies the temptation to suppose that one understands creative causality. Clearly, if one person chooses that another should act in a certain way, the action of the second is not free if the choice of the first is efficacious. If the creator's causality of human action is modeled closely on human free choice, it seems to follow that if the creator chooses that human persons act in certain ways, then these persons have no choice in the matter.

However, to draw this conclusion is to press the model too far. Human acts of free choice are given in experience. Being contingent, their obtaining must be explained. For one human person to make another do something is not really a matter of making the other's own choice occur—no man can cause another's free choices. Thus, in human relations one either respects another's freedom or attempts to circumvent it; one does not cause it. The creator's relation to human free choice is quite different; the creator causes the obtaining of the human person's free choice precisely as such.

Some have suggested that the relationship of the creator to the human person is somewhat like that of a dramatist to the characters in his play. However, I think that this analogy is seriously misleading. The characters do not make free choices; they are imaginary. Man's creatureliness does not detract from his reality; there is no reality to detract from apart from this creatureliness. Moreover, fictional characters can have some reality—that of the sources in experience which suggest them—even prior to the playwright's work.

Divine causality and human autonomy

If one thinks of divine causality and human choice using human free choice as the model for understanding divine causality, it is easy to see why

the two modes of causality seem to put the creator and the human person
into competition. If both are choosing in somewhat the same sense with
respect to the same acts, then the choices of one or the other must prevail.
This way of looking at matter, even if it is recognized as a confusion when
one considers the problem with respect to the obtaining of *free choice*, easily
gives rise to the other, related problem of divine causality and human
autonomy—man's freedom to do as he pleases.

How can a transcendent creator give meaning and establish values without
infringing upon the autonomy of the human person? How can man be free to
do as he pleases if he has an all-seeing and omnipotent Father standing over
him? As the double formulation just offered suggests, the problem has two
quite distinct forms. Only in the first form does the issue turn on the
compatibility between human freedom and the creator's grounding of meaning and value. In the second form the issue rather turns upon the authority of
the Judeo-Christian God and the desire of man neither to submit to that
authority nor to be punished for ignoring it.

I consider the first form of the problem first. How can one reconcile
creatureliness with freedom to do as one pleases?

In one conception of such freedom I think there is no solution. If one
supposes that the human person is not truly free unless he creates all
meanings by his own interpretations and all values by his own decisions, then
the reality of a transcendent creator precludes this sort of freedom.

A human person does not create his own possibilities as a human person.
One must discover these possibilities. Each person can shape his own life in
many ways, but the distinction between actualizing possibilities which fulfill
a human person as such and actualizing possibilities which mutilate a human
person as such is not up to man. Still, the limitation indicated by this
distinction is not imposed upon man by the creator, as if one could better
exist without being anything at all, and could have it open to oneself to be
whatever one pleased.

The creator imposes nothing upon the creature in making the creature
what it is, for apart from being created, the creature is nothing at all.
Fundamental moral limits—the distinction between what is good for human
persons and what is destructive of human persons—follow from man's being
what he is. Many specific moral obligations do follow from one's own
commitments.[1] Hence, moral limits are never imposed upon a person.

Moreover, moral limits are not so much a consequence of creatureliness as
of the dignity with which human creatures have been endowed by the
creator. Subhuman entities can do no moral wrong. Human persons have
moral boundaries because of their freedom of choice, and because of the
broad field of possibility upon which that freedom opens. Man can do moral
wrong only because he has it in his power to be less than he might be, to fall

short of the greater possibilities open to him. Moral limits limit man only from limiting himself to being more limited than a created person needs to be.

Post-hegelian relativists have reacted strongly against the threat of the Absolute. In rejecting the Absolute contemporary philosophy stands up for man's dignity as a person who is not merely a part of an all-encompassing whole. This stand is correct and important.

Yet the appeal of contemporary relativism partly arises from the fact that it does not wholly exclude the Absolute. Man himself—massed in totalitarian society or standing in existential isolation—becomes the sole source of meaning and value in reality.

Relativism allows one to feel that incompatible moral judgments are not necessarily contradictory; either incompatible moral judgments can both be true for those who think them so, or no moral judgment is true or false. For the relativist the difference between right and wrong is not the difference between doing what one believes is truly good and doing what one believes is truly evil. Rather, the difference between right and wrong is redefined into a difference between being "tolerant," "open," "well-adjusted," "authentic," "realistic" (in short, being a relativist) and being "fanatical," "narrow," "out-of-step," "phony," "idealistic" (in short, not being a relativist).

If I am immoral, then I limit *the* good to *my* good. Since this limitation is not in accord with reality, I must redesign reality so that what-is becomes what-is-*for-me*. To openly narrow reality—that is, to deny values most people recognize—would obviously be absurd. I hardly can present myself as a reasonable person demanding impartially that everyone accept as a criterion of meaning and value my peculiar self-limitation. If I am not careful, everyone will see that I am claiming to be the creator, and this claim will elicit a negative reaction. I therefore propose—without fully intending to act on the proposal—that everyone enjoy the same right; I suggest that reality is nothing but what is for each one of us.

The trouble is that each person is included in the reality which every other person confronts. Either there are other people, real people, and that is hell, according to Sartre's famous line in *No Exit*, or there really are no *other* people. In the latter case either everyone merges into a mass society or I emerge as Overman while everyone else sinks to the level of the human, all-too-human (which is Nietzsche's transposition of the Christian conception of the "mass of perdition"). In other words, if one holds that man is the measure of *all* things, then he must admit himself to be a nonman according to the measure others would impose, or he must decide that others are nonmen according to his criteria.

The ultimate unsatisfactoriness of a relativistic conception of human freedom to do as one pleases can be grasped by a simple thought-experiment.

Let us imagine two possible worlds, world A and world B. In both of these worlds, let us suppose, there is no suffering, no pain, no sickness, no accidents, and no death. There is no need to make a living. The ordinary problems of life are fully taken care of and one enjoys immortality.

In world A one can begin from scratch and have anything one wishes. One can build, furnish, and equip the whole world precisely to one's own standards and specifications. There is only one catch. In this world there can be no other real people. One would not be the measure of *all* things if there were others who could measure differently. One knows that there are no real people and can never forget it. As compensation, however, one can have robots which in all respects look and act like real people. One can have as many of these robots as one likes and can make them do anything one wishes. If one cares to engage in orgies, the robots will oblige, and will seem in all respects like real people—but one will know that they are not. If one cuts them, they bleed. If one hurts them, they react. But one knows they are only robots, that they can impose no meaning and value. Over and over and over again, forever and ever and ever, one can do just as one pleases. But one cannot die.

In world B one cannot begin from scratch. The world already is built, furnished, and equipped. One must accept things as they are. There are real people in this world. A good feature of world B is that everyone is friendly; no one wishes to harm anyone else, nor to benefit at the expense of others. People have different interests and abilities. They must work to accomplish things. But they do work together. Within limits everyone can do his own thing. But there are limits, because one has to consider the rights and interests and sensitivities of others. One has to put oneself at the service of others, in the sense that one has something to give, and must work to give it and to share it with others. One cannot die in world B either. But who would wish to die in such a world?

The moral is that freedom to do as one pleases is not an unqualified good. No one wishes to be exploited. No one wishes to be absorbed in the Absolute. But there is no reason I can see to suppose that the fact that human persons are created means that the creator is an exploiter. And there is good reason, already stated at length, for maintaining that the creator is not the Absolute.

This brings up the second form of the problem respecting the compatibility of human autonomy with human creatureliness. How can the freedom of the human person to do as he pleases be reconciled with the authority of a God who hands down categorical imperatives and who threatens with eternal misery those who do not fulfill them?

This question certainly is difficult. But it is a real question only if one believes traditional Judeo-Christian doctrines. If one did believe such doctrines, then he would not consider this question, or any other difficult question raised by his faith, in abstraction from his whole religious understanding of reality.

Thinking within his religious conception of reality, an orthodox Jew or Christian would point out that God's law should be regarded as a gift rather than as a burden. The same psalm which began, "The heavens declare the glory of God," added to its meditation on creation a meditation on the law of God, according to which this law was a blessing rather than a burden.[2] Whether traditional doctrines on human dignity and on God's authority were compatible with one another is a difficult question which I am not going to consider. But they certainly seemed compatible to those who believed them.

Undoubtedly the reason was that the religious believer hoped for something beyond mere obedience to law. He looked upon the obedient acceptance of what he regarded as God's will as a means of liberation, of salvation.[3] But the reality for which he hoped was something higher. In the New Testament the Christian hope was for redemption from death and sin, for life everlasting in an eternal community of persons in some ways like world *B*.[4] Hell, as Christians understood it, was less pleasant than world *A*, but in many respects very like it.

In sum, if one does not accept traditional religious beliefs, then there is no reason for supposing that the creator gives laws or that he punishes anyone for disobeying them. If one did accept traditional religious beliefs, one presumably would take seriously the whole, not only the parts, of that set of beliefs. One would regard divine law as more precious than gold, because one would see the will of God as one's own sanctification, and one would hope for sanctification, seeing it not as something dehumanizing but as something infinitely ennobling to the human person.

Orthodox Christian faith maintained, in fact, that the relation of human persons to divine persons was to be familial. This was the import of the doctrine of the Incarnation: the Son of God, a divine person, became man so that human persons while remaining creatures might become by adoption members of God's immediate family.[5] Whether such a belief is true is beyond the scope of the present work, if not beyond the competence of philosophy, to say. A related philosophical question is what such a belief might possibly mean, if anything. I shall treat that question among others in chapter twenty-four.

19: Evil Is Real but Is Not Created

Introduction

A person touches a hot stove and experiences a painful burn. Animals, caught by other animals, suffer pain when they are wounded. An infant struggles for breath and feels as if its lungs will burst of suffocation. People starve and feel terrible hunger pangs as they do so. These are *felt* miseries. Pain is a modality of consciousness which no animal or person likes, which all animals and people fear, hate, and try as much as possible to avoid.

One's eyes are burned and one goes blind. An animal loses part of its body in a fight and survives in a mutilated condition. The struggling infant dies of suffocation. Starving people are weak and sick. These are *physical* lacks or harms. An entity is missing, or it loses, something suitable to it which it normally would have.

A person is burned by acid thrown at him for revenge. Animals are tortured and mutilated by people who enjoy doing so. People are allowed to starve while many other people give pets much food which could keep starving human beings alive. The baby is suffocated by its parents, who do not wish to take care of it, who regret that they did not have it aborted, and who decide that the fact that the infant now is a few weeks beyond birth will not prevent them from getting rid of it, as they could have done legally up to its birth. The vengeful act, the sadistic act, the negligence toward hungry fellowmen, the murder of the helpless child—these are *moral* wrongs. Such acts and omissions involve an abuse or a guilty nonuse of human freedom to choose and to act.

All of these—felt miseries, objective lacks or harms, and moral wrongs—can be called "evil." One could add to them confusions and errors of thought, failures and mistakes in cultural activities. Each of the four orders—the physical, the intentional, the existential, and the cultural—has norms which indicate the full being of entities in that order. And in each case entities can exist while falling short of the wholeness and the goodness appropriate to them. Thus there are various modes of evil.

As with the question of freedom, the problem of evil presents a challenge to one who maintains that there is a creator—an uncaused cause which causes all the other causes of every state of affairs—and that this creator is God. The challenge can be formulated in two ways. First, as a challenge to the reality of a creator, the problem of evil is how there can be a single, ultimate cause of everything given in experience, inasmuch as experience contains the radical opposition of good and evil. How could the same ultimate principle be responsible for such a fundamental discrepancy as that between these opposites? Second, as a challenge to Jewish and Christian faith, the problem of evil is how one can believe there is a loving and almighty God when one considers the evil one finds in the world.

These two distinct questions usually are mixed together in philosophical discussions. I regard this mixing as a prime source of the confusions and difficulties usually considered as "the problem of evil." Therefore, as with freedom, I shall deal with the two questions separately.

There are three unsatisfactory ways of dealing with the first question. First, one can maintain that reality, after all, does not have a single, ultimate principle. The universe is regarded as a product of two or more distinct and conflicting factors. Second, one can deny the reality of evil and maintain that it is an illusion. Third, admitting that evil is real and denying that there are many ultimate principles of reality, one can treat evil as merely relative—as a partial or lesser good.

Materialists generally accept the first solution; they deny that there is a creator and they consider evil to be the interference of the parts of the world with one another, especially the interference of accident and nature with human interests and desires. Much Eastern philosophy and religion denies the reality of evil, and this denial often leads to the position that the whole world of experience is illusory. Hegel and many post-hegelian relativists regard evil as a characteristic of parts which are taken out of the context of a larger whole to which they belong. Evil is merely immaturity, lack of full development, a stage in evolution which will be transcended.

The difficulties involved in each of these three approaches should be obvious.

The universe certainly does depend upon many and conflicting principles, but all of these factors are caused by the creator. Any cause not caused by the creator would cause it, and then it would not be uncaused. Assuming, as I do in this part of the work, that the reality of the creator is established, the first solution is ruled out.

The notion that evil is an illusion also must be rejected. The examples given at the outset of the present chapter certainly are not of illusions in any ordinary sense of the word "illusion." Moreover, any attempt to reduce everything given in experience to illusion is bound to end in inconsistency. Thus the second solution also is ruled out.

The third fares no better, because the arguments developed against Hegel's philosophy and against post-hegelian relativism remove the foundation for regarding evil as a merely relative factor in reality. On the one hand, human knowers have no place to stand from which they would be able to view all the parts of reality as functions of an all-inclusive whole. On the other hand, the very practical interest of any relativistic philosophy depends upon some universal value which is controlling in all particular cases or situations. Problems, muddles, and so forth *always* are unsatisfactory; pragmatism, analysis, and so forth *constantly* seek to overcome these unsatisfactory—that is, evil—states of affairs.

One step toward a resolution of the first question is to distinguish between sensible evil and what is understood to be evil. Felt miseries, pain and sense suffering in animals and human beings, are repulsive. But in what sense is pain evil?

If one accepts the theory of evolution, it is clear that one must regard pain as a useful adaptation. Painful sensations are very acute; they call attention to themselves and evoke a strong emotional reaction. This emotional reaction—which is not a mere reflex—generates avoidance behavior. If one did not feel the pain of a burn, one would not be so likely to avoid hot stoves, and one might burn oneself without noticing it. As Roger Trigg remarks, one's dislike of pain leads one to regard it as an evil, but this is not to say that pain itself, apart from the attitude one has to it, is evil:

> It may well be true that dislike or distress at a pain is a necessary condition for its being judged an evil. However this may not be the only considera-
> tion. There are such points as the undoubted biological value of some pain.
> If pain did not distress us, or if we were congenitally insensitive to it, our
> failure to remove ourselves from pain-producing situations could injure us,
> perhaps fatally. It seems that our dislike of pain might even further our
> good sometimes.[1]

Even after the initial pain-producing stimulus is withdrawn or avoided, the continuing painful sensation has a value to the extent that it makes one favor or protect the injured part and conditions one to avoid injuries from similar causes in the future.

It must be admitted that like any other adaptation which is generally useful, the sense of pain sometimes serves no purpose. Evolution selects what usually is of value for survival, but such selection can be wasteful and it also can leave behind structures and functions which seem to have lost their point—such as the appendix. However, it is clear—especially from the experience of the few individuals who lack normal sensitivity to pain—that pain is useful.[2]

Considering pain from the standpoint of this insight into its function, one can regard it as a useful good. But it is not understood to be good in itself. Pain is a positive reality. But as a sensation it is peculiar in that it has no content of its own. One sees color, one hears sounds, and feels warmth and hardness, but pain has no objective correlate. It is not of something else. This fact about pain helps to explain the inadequate ways previously discussed of dealing with the problem of evil, for pain tends to be regarded as the paradigm of evil.

The causes in virtue of which pain and satisfaction are felt clearly must be distinct principles, for one is as much a positive reality as the other. But the principle in virtue of which the opposites are felt is not to be confused with the principle of their being. "Being felt" and "being" without qualification are not identical, even in the case of pain. The same creator can account for the fact that states of affairs of diverse sorts *obtain*. Moreover, the fact that pain and felt satisfaction are not *of* something in the way that other perceptions are might lead to the erroneous judgment that they are illusory. However, to be real is not necessarily to be an *object* of sense experience. Finally, the evil of pain is relative, and its level of reality only is appreciated properly when it is understood from the higher viewpoint of its function in life. This superior view of pain does not eliminate its character as a perceived evil, but it does transform one's experience of pain.[3] However, not all evil is relative in the way that pain is.

One who points out that pain as such is not absolutely evil—that, in fact, it has a certain intelligible value—is in danger of being misunderstood. I am not suggesting that one should ignore the human misery caused by immoral acts and omissions. Nor am I saying that one should put up with pain or expect others to put up with it if there is a way to ease it. I merely point out that while pain is a *felt* evil, it has a function which is important biologically and perhaps in other ways for the good of animals and of human persons. Nor should anyone say that the only value of pain is that it leads one to avoid pain. It leads one to avoid damage which might easily be fatal if one were not warned and guided by pain.

Physical lacks or harms and moral wrongs are not sensed. One does not, in a literal sense, see blindness or death or negligence or murder. One grasps these only by understanding a certain standard or norm which one judges is not satisfied in a given case. Unlike pain, objective harms or lacks and moral wrongs are not sensible evils; they are understood to be evil. Understanding and judgment are concerned with the world, not merely with certain contents of experience. Thus, evils which are *understood* present the real challenge to the concept of a creator. How can the same created universe include radical opposites—understood goods and understood evils?

Some authors deny that it is necessary to clarify what evil is before dealing with the problem. The coauthors of a recent book, for example, assert that a definition of evil is irrelevant, for the problem remains the same however one defines evil, provided that one specifies what is to count as evil.[4] But the authors then go on to lump together pain and suffering, physical and mental deformity, and moral wrong. They also postulate a mystical experience of an all-powerful, all-evil god, which, they say, a theist would wish to argue against on the ground that there is much good in the world. They themselves demand the same consideration—to be allowed to argue against the existence of an all-powerful, all-good God on the ground that there is much evil in the world.[5]

This tactic seems plausible, but it is fallacious. It is fallacious, in the first place, because these authors ignore the basic distinction between sensible evil and intelligible evil.

The tactic is fallacious, in the second place, because no experience—even if it be called "mystical"—is capable of defining its own content as an extraempirical, all-powerful, all-evil god any more than any direct experience is capable of defining its immediate content as an extraempirical creator. As I pointed out in chapter three (pages 21-24), if one has no ground for maintaining that there is a transcendent reality which could be presenting itself in a particular experience, one has no ground for assuming the content of the experience to have an objective transcendent referent.

The tactic is fallacious for yet a third reason. If the coauthors had troubled to clarify the meaning of "evil," it would have become evident that evil does not need an explanation in the same way that good does. A full-fledged treatise on good and evil would take us far afield, but a brief excursion into value theory is necessary at this point.[6]

Good, evil, and creative causality

"Good" and "ought," "bad" and "ought not," are closely related. Anything is good if and only if it is as it ought to be; a person is good morally if he is habitually disposed to do as he ought to do. People have different standards for many useful things, but a good item of any sort meets one's standards. A good argument, likewise, reaches the conclusion an argument ought to reach. Good exercise is the exercise one ought to have. Good parents care for their children as they ought to.

Some theories of value suggest that there are ideals, existing by themselves, which establish standards. This suggestion is not helpful, because it leaves unclear the relationship between good entities and these ideals, and it leaves unanswered the question why these ideals themselves are good. Other value theories make positive values (goods) relative to desires or positive interests and make negative values (disvalues or evils) relative to aversions or negative interests.

This approach merely pushes the issue back a stage, because it leaves unanswered the question: What makes the difference between the two sorts of attitude or interest? Still other value theories deny the objectivity of values altogether, and suggest that human attitudes toward things lead men to use value-language by relational predication of the objects of their thoughts and feelings. Those who take this approach do not explain why human beings have the two kinds of thoughts and feelings which differentiate the subjective psychological data. However, the values projected upon things can be distinct, relationally understood aspects of a value-free objective world only if the subjective principles are somehow distinguished.

It is interesting, and ironical, that the theory of value last mentioned finds its main supporters among philosophers who, also, are the main proponents of the view that evil in the world is incompatible with, or argues against, the reality of an all-good, all-powerful God.[7] Of course, such philosophers usually defend a subjectivist theory of value in discussing ethics, while they keep arguments regarding God and evil in a different compartment. It does not occur to them that if values are not independent of human thought and feeling, then there is a problem as to why people cannot get rid of evil by changing their thinking and altering their attitudes. If, as is obvious, this cannot be done, there must be some objective reason why it cannot—and the subjectivist theory of value collapses.[8]

An adequate account of value must begin from the fact that existing entities often are incomplete. Something is, but it is not all that it might be. *What* the something is and to what order of entities it belongs must be taken for granted in distinguishing between the extent to which it already is, and the extent to which it is still short of its full possibility. If one looks at certain works of art, one cannot tell whether they are finished or not, since one does not know what they are supposed to be. If one does not know whether a certain field is to be regarded as cultivated or not, one does not know what standards to apply to the plants growing there—are they healthy specimens or are they obnoxious weeds?

While one has to categorize anything to be in a position to distinguish between the extent to which it already is, and the extent to which it is still open to unrealized possibilities, the distinction is not merely subjective. Nor are the unrealized possibilities mere figments of an observer's imagination. A living person can starve; a child can grow up. Both are real possibilities. As this example of possibilities—starving and growing up—suggests, I do not maintain that realizing possibilities is always good and not realizing them is always bad. Such a position would be oversimplified. A person fulfills himself as a potential murderer by committing murder as truly as a person fulfills himself as a good parent by taking care of his children.

A helpful example of the distinction between good and evil, in terms of possibilities, is health and disease. Organisms have many possibilities; an individual of any species of living entity both is what it already is, and might be what it is not yet. Fulfilling some possibilities is healthy; fulfilling others is sick. What is the difference? A healthy function realizes a possibility or set of possibilities such that the organism functioning in this way can continue to function in many other ways; a sick function realizes a possibility or set of possibilities such that an organism functioning in this way has its other possibilities blocked.

Healthy functioning is a way of living which opens the way to further and fuller living; sick functioning is a way of living which more or less seriously blocks further functioning. The limit of sickness is death—no possibilities left at all. What is good for the organism is that by which it is able to have life and to live more abundantly; what is bad for the organism is that which fulfills its possibility for reduction in functioning up to the limit of complete nonfunctioning.

Health and disease distinguish certain goods and evils in the physical order. This same schema can be used to distinguish good and evil in the other orders. In the intentional order, clarity, consistency, certitude, and explanatory power are desirable traits for an inquiry or an argument. Their opposites certainly are possible, but thought is blocked when the possibilities of confusion, inconsistency, lack of proof, and failure to explain are fulfilled. Inquiry expands under the one set of conditions; its possibilities are limited under the other set. John Dewey understood this point, and much of what he says in his logical works is a development of it. Good logic and good method make knowledge grow.

In the cultural order—art and technology—one assumes the same sort of distinction. Originality and inventiveness are valued because they open up new areas for artistic or economic exploitation. Economy and efficiency are valued because they make the most of resources, to preserve a greater basis for realizing further possibilities.

In chapter eighteen I briefly indicated a similar distinction between good and evil in the existential (moral) order. Immorality is the use of freedom in a self-limiting way. Morally right choices preserve the basis on which free choice can expand its work of realizing the fullness not only of the individual person but also of the person as a member of a wider human community. Morally wrong choices prefer *this* good *here-and-now for me,* and sacrifice something of the full ambit of human possibilities which could be realized in the ever-expanding life of mankind as a whole.

If this theory of value is correct, it follows that good and evil are not related to each other symmetrically. Both involve the realization of possibilities. But good is on the side of further and fuller realization; evil is on the side of delimitation. Things are not bad, however, merely by being limited. They are bad to the extent that they have possibilities which might have been realized, but which are now blocked, because a certain possibility was realized which blocks further and fuller realization. Evil is the nonfulfillment of what the entity or person might have been. The sad state of lack or wrong is compared with the entity's or person's wider possibilities which have been frustrated. Intelligible evil, in contrast with sensible evil, is mutilation or shortcoming.

As I explained in chapter fourteen (pages 237-238), the laws, principles, requirements, or rules which constitute each of the four orders are normative for entities in their respective orders. In different ways in each case an entity can be in a certain order yet not wholly be *in order* according to the constitutive principles of its order. Whatever is in an order is partial and incomplete by itself; reason points to a wider context—eventually to the order as a whole—for the complement of each entity in the order. Thus, an entity is evil to the extent that it is out of order; being out of order, an entity lacks the completeness it would receive if it were in order.

Evil thus has a negative character. It is in itself, not a positive something, but a lack of something. Yet not all lack is evil. The person who could murder another is not evil for remaining unfulfilled in this respect. Doughnuts are not evil merely because they really do have holes in them. But a person who attacks the foundation of other goods in another person by killing him does something wrong, because the choice to act in this manner narrows the scope of one's own freedom to an arbitrarily selected subset of all the possibilities a human person can wish to further. A hole in one's gas tank, which allows the gasoline to leak out, also is something missing; the lack of integrity of the metal is a privation in this case, since there ought to be metal where the hole is.

Likewise, lack of sight in a stone is a negation; blindness in a man is lack of sight, but it is a privation because the man is missing something he ought to have. Not knowing the answer to a problem is as such merely a negation; not knowing the answer to a question on a test for which one is supposed to have studied is a privation. For an infant not to have fed the hungry is only a negation; for an adult who has the means and the opportunity to feed the hungry not to do so is a privation.

To the extent that a privation is negative, that it is a lack of something, it does not obtain. What does not obtain as such does not demand any explanation. To the extent that privations do need to be explained, they can be understood either as incidental to something positive, which is good so far as it goes, or as a consequence of the causality of something which already suffers from some privation.

Thus, one animal eats and another is destroyed, or a reproductive process which has been interfered with by radiation leads to a monstrous birth. An individual pursuing a certain good violates some other as a means to his end, thus doing moral evil, or a person proceeding on a previous immoral commitment perverts his own understanding, his society's institutions, or his religion to conform with this wrong disposition. A machine wears out in doing what it was built to do, but as it loses its original perfection it spoils materials to which it is applied. In each case the initial evil is incidental to some good, and the train of consequent evils follow as privations in effects which are proportioned to the privation in their immediate principle.

As I explained in chapter seventeen (pages 264-268), the causality of the creator is according to a unique mode. Creative causality does not displace any other mode of causality. Nothing is totally dependent upon the creator if "totally dependent" excludes dependence upon other causes according to the various modes of causality which obtain among entities given in experience. The creator causes the obtaining of all contingent states of affairs, including all other cause-effect states of affairs, without interfering with the relationships within such states of affairs. As a privation, evil is explained to the extent that it needs to be and can be explained by the defects of causes within each of the orders which fail to achieve or to keep open the possibilities of completeness in their respective orders.

Thus, the answer to the first of the two questions formulated at the beginning of this chapter is clear—the question how the creator can be the ultimate cause of everything given in experience, which includes the radical opposition of good and evil. The answer is that the creator causes states of affairs which involve evil, but does not cause evil, since evil does not require a creative cause. Evil is the nonobtaining of what might have obtained and ought to have obtained but does not obtain. What does not obtain does not require a cause of its nonobtaining as such.

This conclusion can be stated in another way. Evil is a defect in any entity according to the norms of the order to which it belongs. Evil in any order can be reduced to principles within that order. States of affairs which are subject to privation do obtain, but not precisely insofar as they suffer from privation. Creative causality accounts for the obtaining of contingent states of affairs which *do obtain.* The norms of particular orders are not norms for the creature-creator relationship as such. Therefore, the creator accounts for contingent obtaining which, as such, is good. Nothing transcending a particular order is required to account for that nonobtaining which is evil. Moreover, no norms which define nonobtaining as evil transcend a particular order; the creator's causality, if subject to norms, must be under a "law" which transcends every particular order.

Each of the erroneous solutions to the problem of evil has an aspect of truth which can be fit into the preceding explanation.

First, evil does not exist by itself. It always exists in and mutilates a good. To the extent that the entity which is subject to the privation is real it remains good. But the working and effects of such an entity often are contrary to the working and effects of a perfect example of its type, which is free of privation. For example, health and disease are contraries. One thinks of disease as simply evil. In fact it has two aspects. In one aspect the organism is deprived of some of its necessary or normal conditions for full functioning. In another aspect, however, it is still alive and functioning. Disease is not pure evil; it is a way of being alive. Just and unjust people struggle with one another. Injustice as such is privation. But the unjust opponent still is a person, who has human dignity, who is acting by free choice, who is pursuing a certain good. Similarly, a misunderstanding is contrary to correct understanding, but the error itself presupposes some grasp of what one was trying to understand.

These examples indicate that evil is found in a good, and various goods and evils appear as contrary, positive realities. But the opposites here are the good without qualification and the good subject to privation. The privation as such is not *contrary* to anything. This is the reason why it is necessary to overcome evil with good; all that could be attacked and destroyed directly would be the residual good. Evil as such must be hated, but it can be overcome only if the damaged good can be restored to the integrity it has lost.

Second, some, at least, of what one considers evil is so only because of a mistake in one's perspective. In such a mistake there is a real evil, namely, misunderstanding of what is truly good and evil. But what one thinks evil need not really be so. Most people, for example, regard pain as such as an evil. The standard of judgment is emotion; one operates here at the subintellectual level. Sense perception does not grasp the privation involved in understood evil.

Intelligible evil is a real privation. Sometimes, possibly quite often, one thinks something evil when there is no real privation. One is dealing in such cases with an unreality, with the contradictory opposite of what is real and good, with something merely unreal and self-contradictory. One has an illusion that material and organic existence, with its susceptibility to pain, is evil, because one imagines one should exist with complete freedom from such conditions, perhaps even that human persons could do without bodies. Or one imagines that one should be unlimited, which is an illusion, since a creature must be limited and there is no privation in its being so. One who can imagine not being limited in certain ways erroneously judges that the mere fact of limitation is somehow a cosmic injustice, and then rebels against limits which in no way indicate privation. Insight and resignation are necessary to overcome such illusions, and the religions and philosophies of the East are not altogether wrong in teaching the need for such attitudes.

Third, many conditions which are appropriate to entities at a certain stage of development imply privation if they are not surpassed. To have the emotional makeup of a two-year-old is suitable for a two-year-old; it is a privation in an adult. Likewise, the sort of obedience or even the sort of innocence which is appropriate in a small child is unsuitable in an adult. A good technique—for example, for surgery—at one period is very poor technique when better methods are developed. There is a relativity, not in good and evil as such, but in the possibilities of entities under different conditions. Evil is privation; privation is a lack of what should be present; what absolutely cannot be given under certain conditions is no privation under those conditions.

The foregoing account of the meaning of "evil" makes clear why one could not have a mystical experience of an all-evil, all-powerful god. Since evil as such is privation, an all-evil god would be total privation. But total privation would eliminate that which is deprived.

Someone might object that the clarification of evil as privation only solves a theoretical problem. The existential question remains. The creator must bear the responsibility for knowingly and willingly bringing about states of affairs in which privation is an important feature. The creator causes the obtaining of states of affairs which are far from what they ought to be; he causes people to make free choices which lack what they should have to be morally good. Thus, the creator is somehow responsible for evil.

One wonders: "How could the creator, if he is good, bring about a state of affairs such as this world, including so many and such great evils?" The question is understandable, but it depends upon the assumption that one knows precisely what "good" said of the creator means, and that it means what it means in other cases. But the meaning of the word is not the same when it is said of the creator and of his creatures. Said of the creator, "good" excludes moral goodness, kindness, benevolence, sensitivity to the feelings of others, and so on.

This answer may be frightening. One has no philosophical assurance that the creator is "on our side." Restricting oneself to the results attained by the argument that there is a creator, one finds little reason to admire and love him. The world obviously is beset by many evils. Of course, there are certain goods in it too. If one is not unduly pessimistic, one might feel that the creator is not to be hated, but is to be regarded with a certain wary wonder. Undoubtedly he is great. But is he not also cruel or, at least, lacking in sensitivity? No, this also is excluded by the way of negation.

It is tempting, but erroneous, to suggest that the relation between the creator's knowledge and human understanding of good and evil is like the relation between human understanding and sensibility in respect to pain and felt satisfaction. The analogy suggests that the creator grasps everything on a higher level, from which the judgments men make of evil are relativized. I do not accept this analogy because it attempts to treat the transcendence of the creator on the model of an otherness within our experience. No such immanent otherness is adequate to express the disproportion between creator and creature.

Therefore, it seems to me that the last word of metaphysics with respect to the responsibility of the creator for creation is that the creator does not cause evil as such, but does cause to obtain states of affairs which involve evil. Since the norms, if any, of creative causality are not known, it makes no sense to talk about the creator's responsibility if "responsibility" suggests shortcoming on his part. If the norms which are known—those of the various orders according to which judgments of evil are made—were applicable to the creator, then his creation might be judged evil to the extent that there are evils in the effects. But these norms are not applicable to the creator.

Evil and the God of faith

The second of the two questions which I distinguished at the beginning of this chapter is how one can believe that there is a loving and almighty God in view of the evil one finds in the world. This question is a challenge to Jewish and Christian faith. Believers did wish to say that God loves mankind much as a father loves his children. They also held that God is all-knowing and all-powerful. Thus sceptical opponents challenge believers with a dilemma. If God is all-good, he must be willing to prevent evil. If he is all-knowing, he must foresee evil and know how to prevent it. If he is all-powerful, he must be able to prevent it. Yet evil exists. Therefore, God must lack one or more of the attributes believers attribute to him.

One traditional response of believers to this dilemma is that a great deal of evil in creation, if not all of it, results from the wrongdoing of human persons and other rational creatures—devils.[9] God created such free beings, but the evil of their action was their own fault.

Sometimes this line of argument has been developed as a free-will defense of God's goodness, with the suggestion that the free choices of creatures are in no way caused by God.[10] This way of developing the argument is incompatible with Christian tradition.[11] It amounts to saying that some contingent states of affairs obtain without being dependent upon the creator. However, I think that the traditional explanation of evil in terms of the freedom of creatures can be understood without denying the universality of divine causality. As I have explained already, human free choice and the moral evil in it belong to the existential order; divine causality transcends this order. Whatever obtains, insofar as it obtains, is good; the privation in a morally evil act does not require ultimate explanation.

Still, the challenge proceeds, why does God create states of affairs in which evil is present? Jews and Christians believed that God allowed evil in creation in order to draw greater good from it. The presence of evil in creation would show lack of love on God's part only if it were shown that God ought to prevent evil and fails to do so. This point, which is implied by the conclusion of the immediately preceding section, has been further explicated in a very effective way by several recent authors, so I will not dwell upon it here.[12]

I think that it is important to point out, however, that much of the attack upon the view of believers that God allows evil for the sake of greater good proceeds on questionable assumptions. Surely, it is argued, an all-knowing and omnipotent creator could find a better way of accomplishing good than one which involves all the misery one finds in the world. For example, Edward H. Madden and Peter H. Hare confidently assert: " . . . it is clear that there are many possible universes other than the present one with much less interference and much less evil which God could have created."[13] Similarly, Terence Penelhum takes for granted that there are possible alternatives to pain which would fulfill the same function yet be preferable to it, and that God could have created one of these alternatives.[14]

But how does one know that there is a better way? If one views some evil in its immediate context, one can perhaps imagine some way in which certain relevant goods could be achieved without this evil. But no overall judgment can be made unless one has an overall comprehension of creation. What, after all, does it mean to talk about "many possible universes other than the present one?" Unless one knows perfectly how a state of affairs is related to every other state of affairs, one cannot know what difference it would make to the remainder of the universe for any single state of affairs to be other than it is.

I think the possibility of alternative universes is perhaps too easily accepted because of an oversimplified conception of divine omnipotence, a conception in part propagated by believers themselves. Thomas Aquinas, for example, maintains that God can do whatever is logically possible.[15] But divine omnipotence must not be taken to mean that God can do precisely what created causes as such can do. God cannot act in a creaturely and defective way. He cannot do anything incompatible with what he has done; thus he cannot change the past. According to believers he cannot fail to keep his promises. Clearly, this last point was extremely important to believers, precisely because it is *logically possible* for God to renege.[16] According to Thomas Aquinas himself God cannot annihilate what he has freely chosen to create, since he could have no reason for changing his free decision once it is made.[17]

So far as I can see, metaphysics cannot demonstrate that the uncaused cause is omnipotent. Believers certainly held that God is omnipotent: "We believe in God, the Father almighty. . . ." But what does "omnipotent" mean here? It surely means that God can do what he has done and that he acts freely. It means that no other power exists unless it is created by God. It means that no created power can set itself in opposition to God, as an antigod which might defeat him. It means that God will fulfill his promises; there is no danger that he might try to keep his word and fail. However, so far as I can see, nothing in traditional religious faith required one to believe that God could create all sorts of possible worlds other than the one he has created. Traditional Jewish and Christian doctrine—I distinguish *doctrine* here from *theology*—was notably reserved about such speculative questions.

I suspect that a great deal of confusion in this matter arises from hidden rationalistic assumptions. Leibniz held that God needs a sufficient reason for creating, and that his reason is that this is the best of all possible worlds. As I argued in the second section of chapter five, this rationalism would eliminate contingency. If my argument in chapter seven (pages 131-133) is correct, logical possibility and necessity do not have the ultimate metaphysical status attributed to them by rationalists and empiricists alike. God's existence is not logically necessary; his necessity is more basic than mere logical necessity. There is good reason to suppose that the necessity of God's own being precludes his causing various logical possibilities, beginning with his own nonexistence.

The free-will defense and the position that God permits evil in order to draw greater good from it made sense within the Christian perspective. However, those who do not accept Christian faith point out that even if it is logically possible that God has an adequate justification for each and every evil he allows, still this logical possibility is not a great probability. Moreover, the critics charge, if a Christian attempts to defend himself by appealing to his faith, then he is invoking a source of argument which is not acceptable in philosophy and which cannot be invoked without begging the question.

However, Christians were the ones who gave the reality of evil its sharp cutting edge, just as they were the ones who made a serious problem of the compatibility between God and human freedom. If one does not believe that God reveals himself to be one who loves human persons, to be one who hates the evil which afflicts mankind, and to be one who has taken up the human cause against this evil, then one has no reason to expect God to prevent this evil or to overcome it. Evil, surely, was a mystery for Christians; to those who only *half believe* in Christian faith, it is an unanswerable scandal.

To one who fully believed, the mystery remained but the scandal was removed.

In the first place the suffering of the innocent and the misery of the just were seen in a certain perspective.[18] Limitation of one's view to this life was incompatible with the same faith which made so acute the paradox of God's permitting evil. Suffering was considered a mysteriously necessary initiation, like the birth trauma an infant must undergo, squashed in the birth canal and pushed into a cold, overstimulating world—where life really begins.

Second, the sincerity of God was believed to have been shown by his willingness to send his only Son, who shared the least pleasant aspects of the human condition. Christians believed that God did not ask anything of mankind which he was not willing to share himself.

The question of evil, as it arose in the context of Christian faith, cannot be resolved, so far as I can see, outside that context. Within the context of faith, believers did not really think that they possessed a rational solution to the question. The book of Job taught that human explanations for evil are vain:

> I know that you can do all things,
>   and that no purpose of yours can be hindered.
> I have dealt with great things that I do not understand;
>   things too wonderful for me, which I cannot know. (Job 42:2-3)

To sum up. Whether possibly meaningful or not—a question still to be examined—Christian faith regarded evil as a mystery more than as a problem. Christians did not believe that evil falsifies faith; they agreed with St. Paul: "I consider the sufferings of the present to be as nothing compared with the glory to be revealed in us" (Rom. 8:18). Christians did not regard the experience of evil as evidence of a lack of love on God's part; they believed that by suffering they were somehow united with Christ. For those who believed in traditional Christian doctrine the evidence of God's love was not to be sought in the contingencies of life so much as in God's past deeds. That he gave his only Son was the essential evidence of the Father's love: "Is it possible that he who did not spare his own Son but handed him over for the sake of us all will not grant us all things besides?" (Rom. 8:32).

The argument against Christian faith based on evil began to have its effect during the Enlightenment of the eighteenth century. In the background was rationalism, which had presumed to explain God and to justify his ways, that is, to make God intelligible in philosophic terms and to show him to be a morally upright sort of individual. The favorite argument from reason for the existence of God at the time was one based upon the wonderful orderliness and design one finds in the world—for example, the complexity and beauty of the plan of the organism or of the mechanics of the heavens.[19]

I do not think that the argument from design or orderliness in nature is cogent. I do not appeal to such considerations. The whole approach, it seems to me, is based on a misleading analogy between divine creation and human making, in fine art and in technology. Not design and order in the world but the mere fact that there is a world is the ground of the argument I have proposed.

It is worth noting that anyone who rejects or doubts the reality of God because of the presence of evil in the world does not thereby mitigate or overcome this evil. Christians did not deny evil, as if possessed with blind and stupid optimism. Traditional Christian faith was very much concerned with evil; in fact, evil was one of its fundamental themes. Christians thought they had standards for recognizing evil and they hoped that they had been granted salvation—the overcoming of evil. From their religious perspective Christians would have regarded the rejection of the reality of God as a *normalization* of evil in the world, as an endorsement of its inevitability.

It may be said that the argument offered here is a fine argument, but what good are arguments against the reality of evil as it is experienced—for example, the pain of one, poor innocent child being murdered by its parents? The answer is that arguments can only meet arguments. The death of the innocent child and the hunger pangs of the millions of innocents who are starving unjustly cannot be answered by arguments. They must be answered by works of love. Father Damien answered for the evil of leprosy. If we care to, we can contribute to such a reply to evil; if we do not, then it is hypocrisy for us to talk about the inadequacy of rational and theological arguments to meet the existential reality of evil.

20: Religion Need Not Conflict with Humanistic Values

The dignity of man

Religion and humanistic values can conflict. Religious persons can be fanatical. They can be ready and willing to lie, to cheat, to torture, to kill, to disrupt valuable social institutions, to arouse hatred, to practice hypocrisy, and to motivate people by fostering unnecessary anxiety—they can be and have been ready and willing to do all these things for the sake of religion. At the same time, some humanists regard the overcoming of all religious belief as itself a humanistic value; such humanists classify all religion as superstition, illusion, or worse. Clearly, religious fanaticism cannot be reconciled with any set of humanistic values, and a humanism which defines itself in opposition to religion cannot be reconciled with religion.

Thus, admitting the possibility of conflict between religion and humanistic values, I attempt in this chapter only to show the *possibility* of their reconciliation. In other words, I try to show, against several arguments to the contrary, that religion and humanistic values are not necessarily incompatible.

What are the considerations which are thought to indicate a necessary incompatibility between religion and humanistic values? There are four main arguments. First, religion subjects man to the will of God; religion reduces the human person to the status of an instrument of divine purposes. Second, religion teaches that human nature is corrupt; the ideals of human personhood are detached from mankind and projected into an alien and transcendent being—God. Third, religion necessarily is fanatical, because it considers its peculiar interest to be identified with the Absolute; when the value at stake is infinite, everything merely finite must give way or be obliterated.

Fourth, religion evacuates meaning and importance from this present life by promising happiness and glory in a future life.

A full response to these arguments would require the statement of a complete ethical theory. Since I have articulated an ethics in another work, I refer the interested reader to that book, and limit myself here to summary replies to these arguments.[1]

In chapter eighteen (pages 284-285) I touched upon the objection that religion subjects man to the will of God. A human person, being a creature, does not have absolute freedom to do as he pleases. But such freedom is not an unqualified value. Because man does not create his own possibilities, human life has meaning and value which man does not himself invent. The value theory sketched in chapter nineteen (pages 290-293) clarifies the relationship between the givenness of human possibilities and the objectivity of moral values. Moral goodness is a manner of choosing and acting which preserves and enhances the field of possibilities in which free choice operates.

Nothing I have concluded about the creator would restrict man or require human individuals and societies to adopt particular ways of acting. The conception that the will of God is expressed in the form of a law which should be adhered to in human life derives solely from religious faith—in Western culture almost altogether from Jewish and Christian faith. Traditional religious faith maintained that the commands of God were not arbitrary decrees imposed upon man by an exploiting deity, but were a form of loving guidance, given mankind for the benefit of human life. Jews and Christians believed that God had nothing to gain from human obedience and was not really harmed by human disobedience.

This theme pervades the whole New Testament. It is particularly clear in the parables which compare God to a loving and forgiving father and in Jesus's self-characterization as "good shepherd":

> The thief comes only to steal and slaughter and destroy.
> I came that they might have life and have it to the full.
> I am the good shepherd;
> the good shepherd lays down his life for the sheep.
> The hired hand—who is no shepherd nor owner of the sheep—
> catches sight of the wolf coming and runs away,
> leaving the sheep to be snatched and scattered by the wolf.
> That is because he works for pay; he has no concern for the sheep.
> I am the good shepherd. I know my sheep and my sheep know me
> in the same way that the Father knows me and I know the Father;
> for these sheep I will give my life. (Jn. 10:10-15)

One might resent the implication that God regards one as a sheep, but such resentment would miss the point of the analogy. The point was not the sheeplikeness of man, but the care and concern of God. Jesus is represented here as excluding altogether any supposition that the relation of God to man was one of master to slave. The inferiority of sheep to shepherd was ruled out by comparing the mutual relation between shepherd and sheep to that between Jesus and the Father. The latter point is developed in the discourse attributed to Jesus at the Last Supper, in which he stated that he loved his disciples as the Father loved Jesus himself:

> All this I tell you that my joy may be yours
> and your joy may be complete.
> This is my commandment: love one another as I have loved you.
> There is no greater love than this:
> to lay down one's life for one's friends.
> You are my friends if you do what I command you.
> I no longer speak of you as slaves,
> for a slave does not know what his master is about.
> Instead, I call you friends, since I have made known to you
> all that I heard from my Father. (Jn. 15:11-15)

The point of quoting these passages here is not to claim that what they say is true or even meaningful. The point is to show that Christians who took seriously the idea that their lives were subject to divine commands also believed that those commands were nonexploitative. Resentment against divine commands and the sense that obedience to them would be servile submission to an alien will arose when believers, having lost confidence in the integral content of their faith, remembered only its moral demands. Defective religious instruction no doubt played a part in this development, since negative commandments and the threat of eternal punishment often were stressed more heavily than the positive promise of everlasting life in a community of friendship among human and divine persons.

Some Christians have supposed that God's will defines "good"; this position is voluntarism. Those who hold it think that acts are not commanded by God because they are good for man, but acts become good for man only because they have been commanded by God. But Christians did not necessarily hold this position. Thomas Aquinas, for example, maintained that nothing offends God which is not contrary to human good. He quoted St. Paul, "Let your service be reasonable" (Rom. 12:1), in support of the position that divine law demands of man only what is rationally required. For Thomas, conformity to the divine will was required of man because divine goodness could be shared in by human persons, and a free commitment to this goodness—loving God above all things for his own sake—was regarded as the principle of the community of friendship among divine and human persons.[2] If the goodness of the creator is the source of every good, then the love of the creator's goodness—if that is possible—does not preclude but rather implies the love of every good, including one's own good and that of one's human neighbor.

The second argument—that religion teaches that human nature is corrupt and that it detaches human ideals from mankind and projects them into an alien transcendent God—also involves theological assumptions and draws them from a theological position which not all Jews and Christians share.

Obviously, the philosophical argument I have developed in respect to the creator does not indicate that human nature is corrupt. The theory of value I have outlined excludes the possible meaningfulness of "total depravity," since evil is a privation of good in a state of affairs which remains good, insofar as it obtains at all. The mere fact that a human person is created does not make him evil. Being caused is not itself evil in a creature, since there is no alternative to it except nonbeing. Hegelianism, which identified evil and falsity with partiality and which identified goodness and truth with wholeness, nurtured the view that the objectification of the Absolute in a natural world was itself an evil which must be overcome. But Hegel's transposition of traditional religious doctrines altered the distinction Jews and Christians made between the creation and the fall.[3]

The conception of the creator which emerges from the argument I have presented differs greatly from Hegel's conception of the Absolute. One of the most important differences is that the creator is not dialectically related to creatures as the hegelian Absolute is related to particulars. Hegel's Absolute is whole, real, good, and true; the particulars, taken in themselves, are only parts, appearances, evil, and false.

Further, it should be clear that the creator is not a composite of perfections abstracted from human personality and absolutized. Kant and Hegel worked from the rationalistic concept of the divine as a sum of perfections; Feuerbach considers the personality of God to be

> ... the means by which man converts the qualities of his own nature into the qualities of another being—of a being external to himself. The personality of God is nothing else than the projected personality of man.[4]

Feuerbach's point has been echoed by Marx, Freud, Dewey, Sartre, and many others. This point is not well taken in reference to the creator, the definite description of which is gathered from the way of negation. This description by negation underlies all affirmative and relational predication concerning the uncaused cause. Clearly, then, the creator has none of the qualities of man's own nature.

Whether the Christian doctrine of the Incarnation might be meaningful is a question still to be considered. However that question is resolved, one must admit that traditional Christian doctrine did not present God as a superhuman personality formed of absolutized human perfections. Anthropomorphic language was used by Christians about God, but the anthropomorphism also was cancelled out by insistence upon the mysteriousness of God in himself. The Incarnation of the Word was believed to climax God's self-revelation. In Jesus, God was believed to have made himself present to mankind, not by forcing human persons to give up their proper nature, but by himself accepting the conditions of human nature. The alienation, if any, was thought of as on God's side, not on man's; the Word of God was believed to have "emptied himself" in assuming human nature and suffering a humiliating death (Phil. 2:5-8).

Feuerbach, working out of the background of Hegel's thought and from a version of Christianity in which man's sinfulness was stressed, assumed that whatever religion attributes to God, it must take away from man: "To enrich God, man must become poor; that God may be all, man must be nothing."[5] God's holiness must be compensated for by denigrating human nature, by treating it as corrupt.

Not all Christians accepted the idea of man's total corruption. True, Christians believed that the Godlikeness of mankind was damaged by man's sin, but most Christians also believed that human nature remained good, and that it was really redeemed by Christ. Thomas Aquinas repeatedly asserted that grace—the Christian life—presupposes and builds upon nature.[6] He maintained that the fulfillment proper to human nature would be included within man's supernatural destiny.[7] He also held that the principles of human morality are formed by reason on the basis of the innate propensities of the human person.[8] This same view was articulated by Vatican Council II:

> He who is "the image of the invisible God" (Col. 1:15), is Himself the perfect man. To the sons of Adam He restores the divine likeness which had been disfigured from the first sin onward. Since human nature as he assumed it was not annulled, [note omitted] by that very fact it has been raised up to a divine dignity in our respect too. For by His incarnation the Son of God has united Himself in some fashion with every man. He worked with human hands, He thought with a human mind, acted by human choice, [note omitted] and loved with a human heart.[9]

Once more, I do not claim that this Christian doctrine is true or even meaningful. I only point out that Feuerbach's position is not verified in respect to every theistic conception of the relationship between God and human values.

Fanaticism and otherworldliness

The third argument for the position that religion and humanistic values are necessarily incompatible is that religion is necessarily fanatical. Feuerbach also put this argument clearly:

Faith left to itself necessarily exalts itself above the laws of natural morality. The doctrine of faith is the doctrine of duty towards God,—the highest duty of faith. By how much God is higher than man, by so much higher are duties to God than duties towards man; and duties towards God necessarily come into collision with common human duties. God is not only believed in, conceived as the universal being, the Father of men, as Love:—such faith is the faith of love;—he is also represented as a personal being, a being by himself. And so far as God is regarded as separate from man, as an individual being, so far are duties to God separated from duties to man:—faith is, in the religious sentiment, separated from morality, from love.[10]

Feuerbach goes on to cite the doctrine that faith alone justifies, and to argue that faith demands in its service immoral—that is, unloving and intolerant—acts of coercion and persecution.

Once more the hegelian residue causes part of the difficulty. The conception of the creator which emerges from the argument in part two does not allow one to suppose that he is an individual being separated from and a rival to man, as Feuerbach assumes the God of faith must be. Yet I do not think Christians and Jews would deny the possibility of identifying what I call "the creator" with what they mean by "God." Moreover, in opposing justification by faith and the good works of love to each other, Feuerbach treated as essential to Christianity a theological position peculiar to a certain group of Christians.[11]

St. Paul, who teaches the importance of faith (Rm. 3-7), also teaches the primacy of love (1 Cor. 13:13). And love, throughout the New Testament, is said to manifest itself not in doing good to God—it was assumed that God does not need anything—but by doing good to one's neighbor.

Religious fanaticism, of course, is a historical fact. Immoral means were used to further religious ends, and those who used such immoral means thought they were justified in doing so because of the absolute importance of the end. This is the reality to which Feuerbach and others refer when they assume that faith must make demands incompatible with morality.

It is important to notice, however, that not all fanaticism has been religious. The wars of the twentieth century have been ideological conflicts, but the basis of the hatred is humanistic ideology—Marxist, liberal, Nazi, and so on—not religious faith. The justification of mass murder for the sake of a cause—one cannot make an omelet without breaking eggs—depends only incidentally upon the specific content of that cause. This point is important, for it indicates that the principle of fanaticism is wider than the content of religious faith.

One might argue that religion is especially prone to fanaticism inasmuch as religion is directly concerned with God, and the importance of God is believed by religious persons to transcend every human value. I admit that this view has been taken by some persons, and it supplies a premise on which one can argue that acts otherwise immoral can be justified by their religious purpose. But I think that this view is confused.

Religion is extremely important to the religious person, but religion is not identical with God himself. A religious person should regard religion as itself a *human* good, a good which is created and which is realized in human persons. If there were no created persons, there would be no religion, since religion is the relation of harmony or friendship between created persons and God. This harmony or friendship does not add anything to the creator; he is an uncaused cause. Therefore, religion is *man's* relation to God.

According to traditional Jewish and Christian doctrine the right religious relation of man to God was inseparable from the right relation of human persons to one another, and from a harmonious inner relationship of the person in himself. Inner integrity was believed to be necessary for sincerity of life, and both were regarded as inseparable from love of neighbor, which was considered essential to love of God. Moreover, respect for such human goods as life itself, justice, and faithful marital love was considered essential to the carrying out of love of one's neighbor.

The fact is that Jews and Christians did not regard religion as the sole human good. Both Jews and Christians believed that the religious commitment itself is a free choice on man's part. Freedom in choosing a good implies its nonabsoluteness, for if one believed that one good included everything of value in another, then it would be impossible to choose the second in preference to the first. Thus the belief that religious commitment is a free choice implied that the religious good is not absolute, that it is only one good among others, that other goods in some respects include aspects of human value which are not present in the religious good itself.

Of course, once a person made a religious commitment, he did not see religion as one particular good among others. The religious orientation shaped life as a whole, animating and harmonizing all particular goods. For the devout Jew or Christian a religious concern was the most basic concern of life, yet it was not exclusive of other human concerns. It endorsed other values and sanctified them. An inclusivistic attitude was compatible with traditional theism precisely because God was conceived of as a creator who had made all things good, and man was believed to be made in the image of God and appointed ruler of creation:

> You have made him little less than the angels,
> and crowned him with glory and honor.
> You have given him rule over the works of your hands,
> putting all things under his feet. (Ps. 8:6-7)

Jews and Christians believed that God's creative love does not displace but makes a place for every mode of causality within creation; similarly, they believed that man's love for God does not displace but makes a place for every human love which is not mutilated by evil.

Morality, from a Jewish and Christian theistic perspective, did not mean loving God instead of loving creatures. Morality for traditional theism was based on love of God, but it also meant loving *every creature as a creature,* loving no creature as if it were God. Theists thought that every other good must be understood as a reflection and participation of divine goodness. Thus, God was loved in every love which was open to the whole ambit of created goods. Moral evil, in a theistic perspective, precisely consisted in a disordered affection by which a person closed himself against some human good, by foreshortening love to treat some other finite good as if it were God. Such a disordered affection did not detract from the goodness of God in himself, but Jews and Christians believed that it did offend God by detracting from the full value he wished man to place on created goods other than the one sinfully idolized. Thus, theistic morality could regard fanaticism of any sort, including religious fanaticism, as a sin. Religious fanaticism is a form of idolatry in which the created good of religion is wrongly exalted to the position of divinity.

If this position is correct, then the notion that religion necessarily leads to fanaticism and the denigration of secular values is mistaken. The historical facts are not in question. But a theist could argue that only by referring all human goods to their transcendent principle—God—can they be understood in their full dignity, which is nevertheless finite. Moreover, Jews and Christians believed that confidence in divine providence is necessary if man is to overcome the temptation to use humanly destructive means in a desperate effort to save himself.

A Jew or a Christian could argue that without trust in God, secular humanism tends to oscillate between selfish noninvolvement (rationalized as individual freedom) and obsessive commitment.[12] Either everything is merely finite, merely relative, and merely transitory—the selfish mind-set prevails—and then nothing is worth getting excited about, dedicating one's life to, or dying for; or something is transcendently valuable, absolute, the final solution to mankind's problems—ideology prevails—and then that is the only thing of importance to mankind, it is the cause in which everyone is obliged to submerge himself, and it justifies any necessary means including mass murder. The believer could argue that only hope endorsing and elevating mankind's estimate of the value of *all* human goods can call forth dedication combined with detachment—dedication to the dignity of the human person in all his aspects combined with awareness of the relativity of each aspect, including the religious itself.

The fourth argument for the necessary incompatibility between religion and humanistic values is that religion evacuates the meaning and value from this present life by promising happiness and glory in a future life—"pie in the sky when you die." Hegel made the fulfillment of the Absolute immanent in the historical process, opposing the traditional belief in a transhistorical culmination of the plan of providence. The post-hegelians have not reacted against Hegel in this matter. Rather, they have adopted his position as part of their own substitute for traditional views.

Christianity had promised mankind the possibility of sharing in divinity by adoption into the family of God; Hegel claimed that mankind shares in divinity by nature, that divinity realizes itself only in and through the human spirit. The post-hegelians hope that the human condition can be transformed to such an extent that mankind can achieve absolute perfection without this fulfillment involving any God beyond man himself. Socialistic theories proclaim the coming of the heavenly kingdom on earth; individualistic theories promise personal freedom from guilt and a life of happiness in doing as one pleases. All agree that human nature can be transformed so that mankind can achieve a level which will liberate human persons from their present, all-too-human limitations.

Obviously, nothing in the argument I have presented regarding the creator demands an otherworldly goal for human life. Moreover, it is worth noticing that Jewish faith does not stress, even if it admits, the idea that the fulfillment of this life is in a more perfect existence after death.[13] This belief and its problems are more central to Christian faith. Christian faith proclaims a kingdom which is yet to come, a consummation of history beyond history, "resurrection of the body and life everlasting."

There is no doubt that otherworldliness was essential to traditional Christian faith. In popular teaching, Christianity often was represented as holding life on earth to be a mere means to heaven. Christians, considering this world little more than a place of struggle and temptation, were tempted to apply themselves to their daily work in a lazy and mediocre way. Some of them placed little value upon originality and creativity, feeling that Christian life required only that one avoid sin and do one's duty—for example, by taking care of one's own family.

The Christian hope of everlasting life easily was used to defend injustice and to excuse the maintenance of inhuman socioeconomic conditions. It is easy for the rich to say that poverty is always with us; it is easy for individuals who are devoting their energies to improving the standard of living for themselves and their families to say that radical changes in society are unnecessary, because this life is transitory and saving one's soul is all that matters.

But such abuses do not demonstrate that Christian faith in an afterlife necessarily undermines concern about human well-being here and now. Many Christians devoted themselves unselfishly to the poor, the sick, the imprisoned, the ignorant, and the spiritually impoverished. And the motive of this devotion was religious. Christians believed that Christ would judge each person according to his deeds, that everyone was required to feed the hungry, to give drink to the thirsty, to welcome the stranger, to clothe the naked, to care for the sick, to visit those in prison (Mt. 25:34-40). By contrast, the rich were warned repeatedly in the New Testament, for example:

> As for you, you rich, weep and wail over your impending miseries. Your wealth has rotted, your fine wardrobe has grown moth-eaten, your gold and silver have corroded, and their corrosion shall be a testimony against you; it will devour your flesh like a fire. See what you have stored up for yourselves against the last days. Here, crying aloud, are the wages you withheld from the farmhands who harvested your fields. The shouts of the harvesters have reached the ears of the Lord of hosts. You lived in wanton luxury on the earth; you fattened yourselves for the day of slaughter. You condemned, even killed, the just man; he does not resist you. (Jas. 5:1-6)

Such statements, and there are many of them, gave little support to those who used Christian otherworldliness as a rationalization for lack of social concern.

Deeper, perhaps, than these considerations, however, is the fact that Christian faith did not have to be understood as putting exclusive emphasis upon the future kingdom. Certainly Christians did hope in the future, and their perspective was not limited to the present life. But they also believed that the kingdom of God somehow had already begun in this world. This belief was not mentioned in much popular preaching and teaching, in which there was a tendency, going back at least to St. Augustine, to emphasize the means-end relationship between the present life and the heavenly kingdom which Christians expected would be fully realized only at the end of history.

Two quite different attitudes can be taken toward an action which is related to a future hope. A student, for example, can view his studies as a pure means to getting a job and earning money later on. But he also can take a positive attitude toward his present studies; he can see what he is doing as worthwhile in itself, while also hoping to make his work as a student a basis for later employment. If in the first case the student does not see the necessity of a course for his occupational goals, he will not wish to take it. It will seem irrelevant. If he does not think he is likely to obtain a good job by getting a college degree, he will drop out. If he knew he were going to die shortly, he certainly would not continue to be a student. In the second case a student can regard what he does while he is a student as a worthwhile part of his life. He will enjoy his studies for their own sake, and he will more likely develop genuine interest in the subjects he studies. Even if he is not motivated by hope of a better job, he may continue his studies; he might continue to study even if he were certain he was going to die in a year or two.

These two different attitudes also can be taken toward the life of a Christian in this world. Perhaps many Christians regarded life in the world very much as does a student who has no taste for study. Such an attitude toward this life is antagonistic to any humanism. However, Christians also were able to regard this life as the beginning of the eternal life for which they hoped. In that case the hope for the future did not detract from humanistic concerns. In fact, one who felt that his present efforts would have eternal significance probably was more inclined than other people to take life seriously at every moment.

Christians were able to draft a charter for an inclusive humanism working from various aspects of St. Paul's teaching. For example, Paul commends all truth and every good (Phil. 4:8). He holds that the redemptive act of Jesus initiated the gathering together of all things in Christ and their reconciliation with the Father (Col. 1:17-22). This restoration was a work to which Christians were called to contribute; they were to work to build up the "body" of Christ (1 Cor. 12-14). All things belonged to Christians, and they to Christ, and Christ to the Father (1 Cor. 3:22-23).

This sort of humanism was endorsed by Vatican Council II: "Christ's redemptive work, while of itself directed toward the salvation of man, involves also the renewal of the whole temporal order."[14] The continuity between humanistic concerns in this world and the Christian hope for the eternal was stated by the same Council as follows:

> ... after we have obeyed the Lord, and in His Spirit nurtured on earth the values of human dignity, brotherhood and freedom, and indeed all of the goods of our nature and fruits of our work, we will find them again, but free of stain, burnished and transfigured. This will be so when Christ hands over to the Father a kingdom eternal and universal: "a kingdom of truth and life, of holiness and grace, of justice, love, and peace" [Preface of the Feast of Christ the King]. On this earth that kingdom is already present in mystery. When the Lord returns, it will be brought into full flower.[15]

Again, the Council said: "God's plan for the world is that men should work together to restore the temporal sphere of things and to develop it unceasingly."[16]

Once more, then, the evidence indicates that religion need not eclipse the humanistic values which can be realized only by activity in the present life. However, in respect to otherworldliness I think it must be admitted that the positive appreciation of the values to be achieved in this life was a muted theme in traditional Christianity. Nevertheless, I take it that the contemporary treatment of this theme by many traditional theists, exemplified by the statements of Vatican II, is sufficient to show its compatibility with traditional theistic faith. One could cite numerous parallels to the position of Vatican II in modern Jewish and Protestant teaching on the believer's responsibilities in this world, particularly in respect to social justice.

My general conclusion in this chapter, then, is that there is no necessary incompatibility between traditional Jewish and Christian religious faith and humanistic values. Conflicts have occurred, but conflict is not inevitable. The greatest sources of difficulty have been the influence on contemporary humanism of Hegel's immanentization of the Absolute, and the tendency of Christianity to regard everything short of the heavenly kingdom as mere means. But there can be a humanism which is more modest than that influenced by Hegel. There also can be a form of Christian life, compatible with traditional beliefs, which would endorse and enhance the significance of this present life, by regarding it as the beginning of eternal life, rather than as a merely disposable first stage for launching oneself out of this world.

21: Developing Creatures and a Perfect Creator

Stability is not prior to change

If there is a creator who is altogether uncaused and nondependent, how can there be real meaning and value in the development which creatures undergo? If the creator, the first principle of being, is perfect and immune from change, must not the processive aspects of creatures be regarded as defects? If the created universe must go through a long process, in which much evil is permitted for the sake of greater eventual good, would not the creator have done better to have created things in their final state?

Hegel identified the process of creation with the self-realization of the Absolute. By making this identification Hegel emphasized the importance of development. Much post-hegelian thought, which has rejected Hegel's Absolute, has kept with various amendments his insight into the importance of development. Hegel's influence is supplemented by the impact of evolution theory, which first achieved scientific status in biology, but which was quickly—and not always cautiously—extended by analogy to the whole of nature, to human life and society, and to thought and culture. Many contemporary philosophers consider development or change to be a mode of reality at least as basic and as important as perfection or stability.

The first point to be noticed is that stability and change, perfection (in the sense of completeness) and development, must be excluded from the creator. Any sort of change which man understands, any kind of process which pertains to anything in human experience, must be denied of the uncaused cause. But the way of negation also demands the exclusion from the uncaused cause of any sort of changelessness and any form of perfected development which is a sort of changelessness or perfection of anything within human experience. Thus, the creator is not changeless in the way in which laws of nature, including the laws of evolutionary process itself, are changeless. The creator does not preclude development in the way in which true propositions preclude development. The permanence of fundamental human values—such as truth and justice—is not a permanence which can be affirmed of the creator. Human history has an open future but a closed past; what has been, cannot be undone; the past is complete and perfect. The creator is not complete and perfect as is the past.

The proposition that there is a creator is a necessary truth; this truth can never be false. Since the uncaused entity requires nothing to obtain except to be the state of affairs which it is, it cannot fail to obtain, but this fact does not mean that stability is a more basic category than change. "Stability" and "change," "development" and "perfection," mark differences within the world of experience. Empirical knowledge can be scientific only to the extent that the world is considered to be unchanging in some respects. But the necessary truth of the proposition that there is an uncaused entity does not depend upon the presupposition that the uncaused entity is immune from change. Rather the exclusion of change or development from the uncaused entity is required by a principle which also demands the exclusion from it of stability and perfection. The principle in question is that of the way of negation, which I attempted to clarify in chapter fifteen.

For a creature to be created is not for it to change. There is no "it" to undergo change antecedent—that is, logically prior—to all the causal conditions of the obtaining of any state of affairs, and the creator is the cause of all the causal conditions of every other state of affairs. The creator, as such, is the principle of created entities, in which stability and change are correlative aspects. Therefore, the creator must not be considered the static principle of created entities, as if the fact that the created universe is caused meant that it is somehow unstable and in need of a *static* principle to sustain it.[1]

That change and stability are correlative aspects of entities within experience is easily seen so far as the natural order is concerned.[2] If there were no stability in nature, there would be no order; laws of nature, or lawlike statements about the natural world, would be impossible. But the order of nature has the stability of a regular process.

The world of living things evolves; the inorganic world can be said to "evolve" in another sense of the word. Life adapts and develops more complex forms; inorganic entities seem to be degenerating into less diversified and less complex structures. Both living and nonliving things develop according to their proper laws of development; the two domains also mesh in a manner which makes clear that the laws of the development of both domains are coordinated. The most general aspects of the natural order as a whole are stable.

One might assume that the whole process of nature comes about by chance. Chance does seem to play a role in nature, but the play of chance itself is lawlike. Moreover, what is chance in relation to some causal factors is an aspect of an orderly process in reference to a wider context. Chance has its place *in* all evolutionary processes; the evolutionary process as a whole, considered from a scientific point of view, cannot be regarded as chance. Chance as such is not intelligible; laws of nature are sought in scientific inquiry with confidence that they can be found. However greatly organisms evolve, for instance, their evolution is conservative in the sense that it is a dependable way of maintaining the peculiar reality of organic existence. Evolution sacrifices individuals to maintain their species and sacrifices species to maintain life itself. Organic life—what it is to evolve in the organic mode—is as permanent as the evolutionary process.

An analogous analysis can be made of the relationship between stability and change in the intentional, the existential, and the cultural orders. "Evolution" and other process words are not used in precisely the same sense in the diverse orders. In biology "evolve" has a definite meaning which includes organic reproduction. Organic reproduction does not belong to anything apart from the biological domain. To use the word "evolve" as if it could have a single meaning in all its uses leads to many muddles, for example, in cultural anthropology and in ethics.

To regard evolution in morality as if it were natural evolution, for instance, is to exclude the constitutive role of human reason and freedom from individual and social existence. The result is that the properties of existential norms, which are both cognitive and nonnaturalistic, become inexplicable.

Within the moral or existential order stability and process, in a sense appropriate to this order, are correlative. Free choice is a capacity of self-realization; human persons, as individuals and communities, constitute themselves and work out the possibilities open to persons in the human condition. But there is an order appropriate to this process too; it is an order which does not necessarily obtain, but which ought to obtain. Fundamentally, this order is the ordination of human acts to an ever-more-adequate fulfillment of the specific possibilities of the individual person and the human community. The possibilities in question are values such as life, truth, justice, love, and peace. If history is not understood by reference to the *possibility* of progress in realizing such values, there is no interpretative framework adequate to make sense of history, for human history is not simply a series of natural events, but is a sequence of disasters and of fulfillments in a struggle toward goals which all men can recognize as humanly significant.

The conclusion which follows from the preceding argument is that stability and change are correlative aspects of the orders of entities within human experience. Neither of these aspects of nature, of morality, and the other orders—which in their own ways are stable unities of many entities in continuous processes—is more basic than the other. Neither aspect can be affirmed of the creator in any of the senses appropriate to entities within any of the four orders which can be distinguished within experience.

Traditional Jewish and Christian religious faith stressed the changelessness of God:

> Of old you established the earth,
> and the heavens are the work of your hands.
> They shall perish, but you remain
> though all of them grow old like a garment.
> Like clothing you change them, and they are changed,
> but you are the same, and your years have no end. (Ps. 102:26-28)

The changelessness of God also is taught in the New Testament (Jas. 1:17).

To the extent that such passages simply negate change of God they do not conflict with the conclusion for which I have argued. Such passages also present no difficulty to the extent that they emphasize the dependence of creatures on the creator. To the extent that such passages suggest that God is changeless in an immanent sense—"Your years are unending"—they could be interpreted as metaphorical expressions of the creator-creature relationship.

But Jews and Christians also had another reason for stressing God's changelessness: they believed that God is faithful and dependable. The fidelity of God was stressed throughout the Bible; traditional theists were strongly committed to the permanent truth of their faith and to the dependability of what they took to be the divine promises in which they put their hope.

My point is not that the creator is in process. Process must be denied of him; to assert that the creator is in process would be to say that he is not really uncaused after all. But any changelessness of a sort intelligible on the basis of experience also must be excluded from the creator. This exclusion prevents one from drawing mistaken conclusions about the relative priority and importance of stability and change as one finds these two modes of being in entities within experience. I think that the philosophy of Plato and Aristotle, together with confusion between fidelity—which is attributed to God by relational predication within religious discourse—and metaphysical changelessness led many Christian thinkers to the conclusion that stability is prior to, and better than, change. I do not think that this conclusion is correct nor that it was essential to traditional religious faith.

One of the insights of the new theism is the irreducible reality and importance of process. In this emphasis new theists have performed a service; the views held by traditional theism about process were too rationalistic. The assumption that change must be reduced to stability is merely a special instance of the assumption that multiplicity must be reduced to unity. Getting rid of this instance of rationalism will help to remove obstacles to theological coherence, provided that one does not fall into the trap—which the new theists unfortunately do—of asserting that the creator is himself in process.

Why is creation in process?

Once the assumption that stability is prior to and better than change is set aside, the problems stated at the beginning of this chapter resolve to the questions why the creator creates a universe at all, and why he creates this universe, which includes process.

Any philosophical attempt to answer questions such as these must be highly speculative. Nevertheless, provided that one bears in mind the speculative character of this attempt, it is a legitimate extension of the model described at the end of chapter seventeen. The implications of the model can be drawn out; however, the language used in drawing them out cannot be tightly controlled. Therefore, while I think that what follows is meaningful, I by no means claim that its meaning is as clear and definite as is the meaning of the conclusion of the argument in part two.

Why does the creator create? The answer cannot be that he must create in order to realize his own potentiality, nor can the answer be that he creates in order to acquire anything for himself. Both of those answers are ruled out, for either of them would imply that the creator is fulfilled by his work, that he is not the uncaused cause. If the creator must create in order to be himself or if he stands to gain anything by creating, then he is caused by his creation. This is excluded.

According to the model proposed at the end of chapter seventeen the creator creates freely. Since he is uncaused, no cause whatsoever limits his freedom in creating. Since he is uncaused, he can stand to gain nothing whatsoever by creating.

Following out the implications of the model, the creator's freedom in creating and his independence of his creatures does not imply that the creative act is purposeless. The creator in creating somehow expresses himself and to some extent communicates his own goodness—*that is, his having what is necessary to make* all *caused states of affairs obtain.* Therefore, one must say that the creator creates not to gain anything for himself, but still because of his own goodness—that is, to express himself and to share with others that by which he can cause them.

No doubt the sharing or communicating accomplished in creation is limited. No expression is total. The creator does communicate himself in creating, although the communication is short of what is expressed by it.

Sometimes Christians said that all things are created by God for his own glory. If they meant by this that God creates everything with no selfish purpose, but simply to share his own goodness, then it makes sense to speak of God's "glory" as a reason for creation. But it would be a mistake to suppose that God creates because he needs or can benefit from the admiration and praise of creatures. God does not need a cheering section.[3] If God wills that creatures admire and praise him, this could only be because it would be good for creatures to do so.

The creator need not cause anything. Everything within human experience is contingent; whatever obtains in any of the orders also might not obtain. Given the fact that the creator does create, the contingency of creatures indicates the freedom of their creator; if he had spun out the universe by some sort of natural impulse, then he would be involved in the universe. The Absolute of Hegel could not create. The world of experience bears witness to the fact that it might not be, that it is created, and thus that it need not have been created.

If one assumes, with Leibniz and others, that the created universe is the best of all possible worlds, and that the creator could not help but create what is best, then his freedom in creating is denied. If one accepts the assumption that the creator can bring about anything not contradictory in itself, then one must hold that possible worlds make up an infinite set. None of the members of this set could be a total expression of the creator; a perfect expression of the uncaused in a creature is impossible. All worlds of the infinite set would be good, each in a different way, but since the set of possibilities is infinite, none of the possible worlds could be the best. "The best of possible worlds" is nonsensical in the same way as "the largest of whole numbers."[4]

Rather than taking an *a priori* approach, one must proceed from what is in fact created if one wishes to speculate—so far as such speculation is possible—about the creator's purpose in creating. In other words, the attribution to the creator of a purpose in creating is a relational predication, which must be grounded in the way the created universe actually is found to be.

One need not claim to know all the variety and complexity of creation to be certain that all the creatures one does know or can know are somehow related to one another. The whole set forms a single order—the order of creation—even if one cannot comprehend this order, as one can each of the four distinct orders, in a single system. Within any order the lack of order is a defect—a falling short of the paradigm of that sort of thing. If the purpose of creating is the self-expression of the creator, then no defect can be permitted by the creator in what he does create except insofar as he can bring from it something positive which would otherwise be impossible. But a defect in the order of the whole of creation could lead to no ulterior good. Thus, an avoidable defect in the order of creation as a whole is excluded. This conclusion agrees with the religious belief that divine wisdom reaches "from one end of the earth to the other, ordering all things for good" (Wis. 8:1).

In what part of the created universe is to be found the greatest good intended by the creator? In no *part* of it. The good of the whole order of creation includes whatever is positive in all of its parts. The whole of creation is that self-communication which the creator has freely chosen. The greatest good of creation, the order of creation as a whole, includes all created entities and all their relationships with one another. This is what Thomas Aquinas meant when he said that "the greatest good in things created is the perfection of the universe, consisting in the order of distinct things, for the good of the whole always has precedence over the perfection of individual parts."[5]

Within the created universe there is order. The entities of the material world which lack intelligence are used by man; such use does not detract from nature—man cannot violate natural laws—but transforms it into a world of culture. In other words, nature has possibilities which can be fulfilled only by culture-making human reason, freedom, and work. In human life particular abilities and efforts find their highest fulfillment in building and perfecting a community of all human persons, cooperating in peace and friendship, sharing in work and in enjoyment. These observations about the order within the created universe agree with traditional religious belief. Believers held that man is set over the works of creation, with a mandate to perfect and govern the physical universe (Gen. 1:28-29; Ps. 8:5-7).

A human person is not above the rest of creatures as if the human were separated from and opposed to subhuman creation. No, persons and communities possess what is less than human as property; mankind gathers up the rest of creation to fulfill human possibilities in it. In so doing, mankind rejoins the rest of the natural world by means of culture. Similarly, the human community is not greater than its individual members and their works, in the sense that the whole community is an independent totality—a totalitarian society—opposed to individual persons and their works. The whole community should gather up its members; its greatness is in its inclusion of their individuality as well as in their contribution to the completion of the whole.

Christians believed that Christ is a "body" who includes Christians; they believed they were called to contribute themselves and their work to the building up of the fullness of Christ (Eph. 4:15-16). The fullness of Christ was believed to include the whole of creation. All creation suffers birth pangs, according to St. Paul, waiting for the revelation of the glory of God's children (Rm. 8:19-23). God's plan in creating, according to Paul, is to "bring everything together under Christ, as head, everything in the heavens and everything on earth" (Eph. 1:10).[6]

These considerations with respect to the purpose of creation provide the foundation for explaining why the creator chose to create a universe including process. Could the creator not have brought about the same ultimate result more simply and more directly, and thus avoided much evil present in the universe as it is? The question takes a more specific form for the believer. Can the believer reconcile the belief that human works are necessary for salvation with the belief that God does not need sinful men to accomplish the work of salvation, which traditional Christian thought considered wholly a result of grace?

Thomas Aquinas did not discuss these precise questions, but he did consider a closely related problem: Why does God not produce all created effects without their created and proportionate causes? He says that it is not

> . . . superfluous, even if God can by himself produce all natural effects, for them to be produced by certain other causes. For this is not a result of the inadequacy of divine power, but of the immensity of his goodness, whereby he has willed to communicate his likeness to things, not only so that they might exist, but also that they might be causes of other things.[7]

The greatest good in creation is the order of the whole; exclusion of causality from the created universe would remove this order. If no creature had any active role in the production of any effect, creation would lack much of the reality it has.[8] If the purpose of God in creating is self-expression, this purpose would be less fully achieved in creatures which were like God in existing, yet not like him in causing something else to be like themselves.[9]

From this point of view it seems clear that a universe which includes the prerogative of causing—the actual universe—is better than one made up of otherwise similar entities—if this is intelligible—which did not have this prerogative. If the creator had chosen to create a universe as similar as possible to what the actual universe eventually will be, but without the process this universe is going through, that other universe would have been no more nor less than the actual universe a free self-expression of the creator. But such a universe would have expressed the creator *less well.*

The creatures of that universe would not have had the character of ones who overcame, who achieved, who arrived at a goal. The real relations which make up the dynamic order of the actual created universe would have been missing. The process of the development of the created world is not a mere means to its consummation. The process is part of the product; the outcome could not be what it will be if it were not to be the outcome of the process which is going forward. Moreover, passing time does not mean total annihilation of the past; the past lives in the present. A dialectical conception of change, like Hegel's, is valid at least for some change—that involving the intentional, the existential, and the cultural orders. Hegel's mistake of identifying the world with God does not invalidate his insight into the world.

If one supposes that one gives more credit to the creator by attributing less to creatures, one is mistaken. Thomas Aquinas points out: "To detract from the perfection of creatures is to detract from the perfection of divine power."[10]

For Hegel otherness as such is negation. However, once one rejects the rationalistic prejudice in favor of unity, one is in a position to accept the very otherness of creatures from the creator as a positive aspect of their obtaining. The self-expression of the creator does not fall short of what is to be communicated precisely because it is *other* than the creator; this otherness is an important aspect of *what is expressed.* Creation can be said to "fall short" of the creator only in the sense that for any contingent state of affairs to be, it must be in a certain mode, which precludes its also being in other positive and incompatible modes, while all lack and limitation must be denied of the creator as part of the way of negation.

If creatures express the creator precisely in being other than the creator, then the causality of creatures as distinct from the causality of the creator must be regarded as an aspect of the self-expression of the creator, not as a principle interfering with this self-expression.

When I was a small child, my parents used to buy each of us children a kite in the spring. One of my early memories is the first time I received my own kite. I took it with great satisfaction and went to my room to unwrap it. But when I had removed the wrapping, I found I had only sticks. The "wrapper" was part of the kite itself. I did not make that mistake the next year. But if one thinks that the development of the created universe by the causality of created causes is a mere means to the final product, a mere wrapping of the reality, one makes the same sort of mistake.

Thus, it is a large part of what is positive about the created universe that effects come about by way of created causes, that the eventual purpose of creation be achieved in a way which to man seems inefficient, and that seeming deviousness be admitted into the unfolding of creation. The purpose of the creator is, not simply to bring about a certain final state of things, but to bring about effects by the causality of creatures themselves, for this created causality also is valuable. The fact that eventual fulfillment is reached by such a process contributes positively to the "product." If one attends only to the outcome of the process, the creator's method seems inefficient. Thus, one can call the principle which renders this aspect of creation intelligible "the principle of the creator's inefficiency." The creator is not inefficient as if he were incapable of getting results more easily than he does; apparently he is not interested only in results.

The act of creation can be called "playful," not in the sense that the content of creation is unimportant, but in the sense that the creator is not a laborer and creation is not a product of alienated labor. The whole of what is created, its multiplicity and change as well as its unity and stable features, its development as well as its achievement, expresses the creator. As in a play, the whole play, not merely the last scene or the falling of the final curtain, is the purpose of the playwright.

The principle of the creator's inefficiency does not imply that the creator creates evil. However, if evil is permitted only to the extent that it contributes to the whole order of creation, the value of the process helps to suggest—at least in some cases—what might be the meaning of permitted evils. As I explained in chapter nineteen, evil as such is privation; as such it does not require to be created. Still, the good which suffers privation remains good, is created, and must be worth creating for its contribution to the order of creation as a whole.

The specifically religious question of the compatibility between salvation by grace and by works perhaps also finds an answer in the principle of the creator's inefficiency. The Christian could believe that the history of salvation, from the faith of Abraham to Mary's consent to be the mother of God's Son, expressed the generosity of the Father in making men and women fellow workers in the redemption. The Christian also could believe that his own sanctification, which does not come about instantaneously, is more a matter of God's grace the more it is a matter of his own work. Moreover, the Christian could see this work, not as an arbitrary imposition or a meaningless test—as Christians sometimes regarded it—but as a beginning of the participation in divine life which Christians believed to be the purpose of redemption.

Once more I do not here assert the Christian doctrines to which I refer. Thus far I have not even claimed them to be meaningful. I only suggest that if these doctrines are meaningful, certain seeming inconsistencies are not insoluble. The next four chapters will take up the question of how religious doctrines which purport to depend upon divine revelation might be meaningful.

Conclusion to part five

Before proceeding to the consideration of this question, a last word may be in order about the problems considered in this and the preceding three chapters. These problems are serious because of their great personal implications. They touch the existential nerve. Neither believers nor unbelievers find it easy to think about such problems with open minds. Believers find in these difficulties some of the gravest threats to their faith. Unbelievers find in them some of their most plausible reasons for not believing—which also, I think, is a matter of faith.

Still, it is important to think as clearly as possible about these problems. I suspect that many people today take the worst of both worlds—that is, the worlds of faith and of unbelief. Faith presents God as a loving but demanding Father; it raises expectations of special care but creates a sense of sinfulness. Unbelief promises man freedom to shape his own universe of meaning and value, but presents him with an indifferent and cold universe. To experience evil as an outrage, to feel it necessary to resent moral law, and yet also to think oneself abandoned—"thrown"—into an indifferent and perhaps hostile universe, is to take the worst of both worlds. One ought, at least, to enjoy the advantages of one or the other consistent position.

VI: The Meaningfulness of Christian Beliefs

22: Miracles as Signals
from the Creator

Introduction to this part

Up to this point I have neither asserted the truth of Christian beliefs nor considered their meaningfulness. In this final part I deal with the question of meaningfulness. I do not deal with the question of truth, because this question is not within the competence of a philosopher. Whether Christian beliefs ought to be accepted as true can be decided only after one considers three distinct sorts of questions: 1) philosophical questions concerning their possible meaningfulness, 2) historical questions concerning certain alleged matters of fact, such as the life, death, and subsequent appearances of Jesus, and 3) a moral question as to whether one is either permitted or obliged to assent to Christian teaching. An answer to this last question would presuppose answers to the philosophical and historical questions and some standards of moral judgment.

The question of the meaningfulness of Christian doctrine is twofold. Christians claim that the creator has opened a conversation with mankind and that in this conversation he has communicated certain truths about himself which otherwise would be inaccessible to human inquiry. Examples of such alleged truths are the doctrines of the Trinity and the Incarnation. The first question regarding meaningfulness is whether it can be meaningful to say that the creator has communicated to man some otherwise inaccessible truths about himself. This question again has two aspects. One aspect is the possible meaningfulness of the alleged *communicating*—in other words, does it make sense to say that God has spoken? The other aspect is the possible meaningfulness of the alleged *content* communicated—for example, does it make sense to say that God is three persons, one of whom has become man? The second question regarding meaningfulness is concerned with the possible existential meaningfulness of the alleged communication: Would there be any *point* in a communication from the creator to creatures? This second question is important, for even if Christian doctrine is not logically absurd, it might be wholly pointless and irrelevant to man, and so belief in it would be existentially absurd.

In chapter twenty-four I will consider the first and in chapter twenty-five the second of the two questions distinguished in the preceding paragraph. There are two prior questions. Can some particular event within human experience be regarded as a signal from the creator? I take this question to concern the *possibility* of miracles; I discuss it in the present chapter. The other prior question is what "person" and "community" mean when these expressions are used of human individuals and groups. This question will be treated in chapter twenty-three.

In taking the question of the possibility of miracles to be equivalent to the question whether any particular event within human experience can be regarded as a signal from the creator, I set aside two concepts of *miracle* which are irrelevant to my present concern. First, there is the concept of *miracle* according to which some specific happening might demonstrate the existence of God or might conclusively prove the truth of religious claims to someone who as a matter of principle took a sceptical attitude toward such claims. I set this concept aside, because a signal requires interpretation, and it is at least a necessary condition of interpreting some occurrence as a signal from the creator that one supposes that there is a creator and that receiving a signal from the creator is not regarded as impossible. Second, there is the concept of *miracle* according to which unusual happenings, even mere coincidences, might count as miracles if they are regarded by believers as striking examples of the general self-expression and communication of the creator which pervades all of experience. I set this concept aside, because *signal* implies one segment of experience clearly distinct from others; a signal must stand out from background noise.

The question of whether some particular event in human experience can be taken as a signal from the creator becomes acute in the context of the argument of parts two and four, for that argument concluded that every positive reality is altogether caused by the creator. In chapter twenty-one I drew the conclusion that creation as a whole can be regarded as the self-expression of the creator or as a communication of his goodness. If this conclusion is correct, why should any one event more than any and all other events be regarded as a signal from the creator?[1] Before I attempt to answer this question—which emerges from my own position—I must clear the ground by considering Hume's objections to the possibility of miracles either happening or being known to have happened.

Hume's critique of miracles

Hume includes a treatment of miracles in his *An Enquiry Concerning Human Understanding* (Section X). Presupposed by what he says on miracles is his general theory of causal knowledge, according to which knowledge of cause-effect relations is built up by repeated experiences. Sometimes the connection between two events is observed in all cases; sometimes only now and then. Hence, a wise man proportions his belief—his degree of expectation—to the evidence. If a connection is constant, one expects with absolute confidence that it will hold. If a connection holds only sometimes, one expects it to hold with a degree of confidence proportionate to the times it has been found to hold.

Now, Hume continues, the connection between the testimony of witnesses and the truth to which they testify is a cause-effect relation. The only reason to expect testimony to conform to reality is that it often does. But this relationship is not one which holds in all cases. Sometimes witnesses disagree; in such cases their testimony cannot be altogether true. Sometimes witnesses are few and possibly mistaken; sometimes witnesses are biased and dishonest.

When direct experience of the course of nature provides ground for one belief while the testimony of witnesses provides ground for a different belief, a wise man must weigh the conflicting evidence. If the experience of the course of nature is not a constant one—for example, if it is the experience of the weather in a certain place at a certain season—and if the witness has been found to be reliable in statements of fact of this sort—for example, the weatherman talking about *the past*—then one can reasonably believe the witness against one's expectation based upon experience. For example, if the weatherman reports that the temperature in Miami in June dropped below freezing for a short time, one might reasonably accept the report; however unreliable weathermen are as predictors, they are usually honest and competent reporters, and with respect to the weather one must be ready to expect the unexpected.

However, if the testimony of witnesses is on one side of the scale and all direct experience of the course of nature is on the other, then it is reasonable to believe the direct experience instead of the witnesses. Hume mentions the case of an Indian prince who doubted what Europeans told him about frost and its effects. The prince was reasonable, Hume says, although the phenomenon of frost and its effects is not "*miraculous,* nor contrary to uniform experience of the course of nature in cases where all the circumstances are the same."[2]

A miracle for Hume is not simply an unusual event, such as a coincidence, nor is it merely an unexpected event, which nevertheless turns out to occur more or less regularly under suitable circumstances. A miracle is an event which either in itself or in its mode of happening is contrary to the laws of nature. A dead man coming back to life is proposed by Hume as an example of an event in itself contrary to the laws of nature; a sick person becoming well or a healthy person falling dead at the command of someone claiming divine authority would be examples of events contrary in their mode of happening to the laws of nature. Thus Hume defines miracle as "a transgression of a law of nature by a particular volition of the Deity, or by the interposition of some invisible agent."[3]

It is worth considering carefully why a coincidence or an unexpected but explicable event cannot count as a miracle. (I think Hume is correct about this point, although I do not accept his *definition* of miracle.)

A case in which a skydiver's parachute fails to open but he survives unhurt, because just before he hits the ground a truck loaded with feathers passes under him and breaks his fall, is a good example of a coincidence. Some people might say that the skydiver was "saved by a miracle," but they would not need to assume there was any special causal principle at work. Both the skydiver's fall and the manner in which it was broken would be explicable by ordinary causal factors. Even a religious believer might deny that the happening was attributable to God in any special way, particularly if the skydiver ridiculed such a suggestion and boasted that he intended to take advantage of the additional years given him by "lady luck" to live a dissolute life.

A case in which a primitive man first encounters black rocks which do not merely become hot when placed in a fire but which themselves catch fire and burn, contrary to all his previous experience with rocks, is a good example of an unexpected but explicable event. The primitive man might at first regard the black rocks with considerable wonder and awe, but his wonder and awe would recede when he discovered that similar rocks left in a similar fire for a similar length of time regularly catch fire and burn. The experience of burning coal, at first extraordinary, becomes accepted as part of the ordinary course of nature, no more nor less intelligible than all the rest of nature.

Thus, Hume concludes, if any event is to count as a miracle, it must be more than unusual and more than unexpected on the basis of past experience. The event must be inexplicable as a coincidence and it also must be unique— that is, not a member of a set of events which regularly can be observed or made to happen under certain definite circumstances. Unusual but lawlike happenings will not do; the appearance of a comet is not a miracle, even though it is unusual.

To this point I agree with Hume's position; I think he is right about what *cannot* count as a miracle. I disagree with Hume's definition of miracle as an event *contrary to the laws of nature,* contrary to all the direct experience one has of the actual course of events in the world.

Given this definition, Hume is in a position to compare the evidence in favor of miracles—which he takes to be limited to the testimony of witnesses—with the evidence against. By definition all direct experience counts against. By the common canons of assessing the testimony of witnesses, no testimony can be absolute evidence in favor of the truth of that to which testimony is given. Hence, testimony always must be assessed as having less weight than direct experience when a purported miracle is at issue.

Hume's statement of the argument deserves to be quoted; I omit the examples:

> A miracle is a violation of the laws of nature; and as a firm and unalterable experience has established these laws, the proof against a miracle, from the very nature of the fact, is as entire as any argument from experience can possibly be imagined. . . . Nothing is esteemed a miracle if it ever happen in the common course of nature. . . . There must, therefore, be a uniform experience against every miraculous event, otherwise the event would not merit that appellation. And as a uniform experience amounts to a proof, there is here a direct and full *proof,* from the nature of the fact, against the existence of any miracle, nor can such a proof be destroyed or the miracle rendered credible but by an opposite proof which is superior [note omitted].
>
> The plain consequence is . . . that no testimony is sufficient to establish a miracle unless the testimony be of such a kind that its falsehood would be more miraculous than the fact which it endeavors to establish.[4]

Hume's observation on this conclusion—an obvious allusion to the Christian doctrine of the resurrection of Jesus—is that if anyone says he saw a dead man restored to life, one should consider which would be the greater "miracle": that the witness was mistaken or lying or that the purported event had actually occurred.

Having built this foundation, Hume proceeds to argue that no miraculous event ever was established with the sort of evidence he regards as necessary. His argument partly depends upon assertions of historical fact; it is not my business to consider these matters. But Hume's argument also involves the assertion of some general rules of criticism. First, he holds that the number and reliability of witnesses is important for assessing the value of testimony; he claims that no miracle is attested by many reliable witnesses. Second, he holds that people are naturally gossipy and credulous about reports of highly unusual events; he claims that these psychological characteristics account for the propagation and acceptance of miracle stories. Third, he holds that reports which originate among distant and long-past "ignorant and barbarous nations" cannot be checked and ought to be regarded with scepticism; he claims that reports of miracles are of this sort. Fourth, he holds that conflicting witnesses render one another incredible; he claims that all different religions conflict and that all religions abound in purported miracles.[5] Hume adds to these four points a further one. A person who is interested in a certain cause must not be trusted too far in matters which bear upon that cause; Hume claims that religious believers are motivated by vanity to consider themselves witnesses to the divine, and that they are motivated by fanaticism to use pious frauds to promote their faith.[6]

From this argument Hume draws the general conclusion that no human testimony can have sufficient force to outweigh direct experience of the laws of nature, and thus establish a miraculous event and so provide a basis for any system of religion. Yet Hume admits that "miracles"—extraordinary and unrepeatable exceptions to natural laws—might occur in nonreligious contexts. He offers the example of an imaginary report attested by unanimous historical evidence of total darkness on earth for eight days, beginning January 1, 1600. He thinks such a report, if so attested, could be accepted, because general experience admits the possibility of decay, corruption, and dissolution in nature. On the other hand, if Queen Elizabeth I were supposed to have died and then risen again, Hume thinks any testimony to that purported fact would have to be discounted, since people often are dishonest and foolish, and since the appearances might be explained as error or fraud. With respect to purported religious miracles Hume concludes:

> As the violations of truth are more common in the testimony concerning religious miracles than in that concerning any other matter of fact, this must diminish very much the authority of the former testimony and make us form a general resolution never to lend any attention to it, with whatever specious pretense it may be covered.[7]

Hume's final comment is ironic: Christian teaching is totally irrational, and thus anyone who believes it should be directly aware of a continuing miracle in his own person.

Recent followers of Hume have taken a harder line than Hume himself. Hume seems to be saying that miracles are not logically impossible, but they are never to be accepted, particularly not as a basis for religion. Some of Hume's recent followers try to rule out the logical possibility of miracles or the methodological possibility of confirming their occurrence. For example, it is suggested that purported miracles involve the conflict between a particular past event—the miracle—and a general law of nature. The past event cannot be verified; the law of nature can be verified whenever one wishes. Therefore, the law of nature always has the advantage.[8] Again, some argue that since laws of nature say what happens, either the purported miracle did not occur or the supposed law of nature is not really a law. This amounts to saying that any supposed miracle, if it actually occurred, is merely a counter-example to a generalization.[9] A third suggestion is that if the miraculous event were explicable by the action of a god, this fact would only show that the factor called "god" would have to be included in the natural world. Thus, a miracle would not show the reality of any transcendent entity.[10]

Defects in Hume's critique

The first point to notice about Hume's position on miracles is that he and his followers assume that any event must be natural—that it must be according to the laws of nature or contrary to those laws. Recent followers of Hume make this point clear by excluding the possibility of anything *really* contrary to the laws of nature; the alternative becomes: according to the laws of nature thus far known or according to laws of nature as yet unknown. Hume, because he regarded natural laws as nothing more than generalizations based upon repeated experience, was not in a position to be quite so exclusivistic. He had to admit the logical possibility of an inexplicable unique event, such as an eight-day eclipse. Yet, even in this case he suggested that the event would conform to the general character of nature known by many analogies as liable to "decay, corruption, and dissolution."

This suggested account of the imaginary unique event has an odd metaphysical ring. The metaphysics it implies is a closed naturalism. I suspect that in the back of Hume's mind—certainly in the back of the minds of his present-day followers—is a picture of nature as a huge machine, grinding away inexorably and regularly, every event locked into the whole. Only some such picture as this would warrant the assumption that every event must be either in accord with known or discoverable natural laws, or else—and how *obviously* absurd!—contrary to them.

The assumption is false. Consider a unique event: Hume wrote an essay on miracles. I see no reason for saying that it occurred either in accord with or contrary to any law of nature. Doubtless, the psychological processes of thinking out the essay, including the deep emotional factors which led Hume to take an interest in this subject and to write about it in the way in which he did, occurred in accord with certain natural laws. The physical behavior involved in writing also occurred in accord with certain natural laws. But Hume's act of writing this particular essay, while not contrary to any natural law, hardly seems to follow from any natural law or any set of such laws.

A follower of Hume who is a determinist would argue that there are natural laws of such complexity that no one yet understands them, but that if someone eventually does come to understand them, Hume's authorship of this essay could be fully accounted for. However, I assume here a point I believe has been argued successfully in another work, namely, that determinism is self-defeating.[11] Human persons can make free choices. In chapter fourteen I outlined a descriptive metaphysics of the orders of reality within experience—taking "experience" in a broad sense. The physical order is one of these, but if free choice is possible, the existential order is distinct from and irreducible to the physical. The physical order of nature, understood as one of several orders, must be open or loose-textured enough to admit the effects of thinking, of choosing, and of symboling. Hume's physical and psychological behavior in writing his essay on miracles was within the physical order and was not exempt from the causal factors which condition what occurs in that order. But in virtue of the irreducibility of thinking, of choosing, and of symboling to natural processes and events Hume's writing of this essay, considered as an integral human act, was a unique event neither contrary to the laws of nature nor in accord with them.

The loose-textured character of the physical order of nature permits testimony to count for more than Hume allowed. If one were compelled to regard every witness as giving testimony either for or against a natural event, and if one also were compelled to regard the giving of testimony itself as a natural event, then Hume's theory of the relationship between testimony and expectations based upon past experience would be plausible. However, very often witnesses testify to happenings such that neither the giving of the testimony nor that to which testimony is given either agrees with laws of nature or is contrary to them. A simple example is the happening to which testimony is given when an individual says to a friend of the opposite sex: "I love you. Believe me, I will love you no matter what." A person who hears such a declaration hardly regards either the love or the declaration of it as happening in accord with any natural law; neither, however, is it contrary to any law of nature.

Hume admits that someone might deny that reasoning based on testimony is founded on a cause-effect relation. He says, "I shall not dispute about a word." He regards it as sufficient to note that belief grounded in testimony is based on the principle that the reports of witnesses and the facts usually agree.[12] The trouble is that more than the meaning of a word is at stake. Hume bases his argument on his own theory of cause and effect. But something more than past experience of the relation between testimony and facts is involved in one's belief in another's declaration of love. In this example, in fact, the only access to the facts is by way of the testimony, because the facts to which testimony is given are existential, not physical.

Even when a person bears witness to facts which could be empirically verified, the interpersonal relationship enters into the rational criteria of evaluating testimony. One trusts witnesses or does not, not only on the frequency with which their reports have been verified or falsified but also on one's appraisal of their character, of their desire to be careful and accurate in this particular case, and of the conviction and sincerity which they communicate *as persons*.

Moreover, it is not unreasonable to trust others somewhat further than Hume's criteria would allow. If one does not extend trust, others are unlikely to act in a way which will compel trust in them. If one does extend trust, one runs a risk of disappointment, but one also takes the only possible opportunity for developing a relationship closer than *common* criteria of trustworthiness would admit. No new depth of intimacy can be achieved unless one is willing to venture beyond the limits of caring and sharing reached in one's previous experience.[13]

Hume assumes that when testimony and laws of nature seem to conflict, all past experience stands against testimony. This assumption is faulty on several counts.

In the first place, knowledge of laws of nature is based largely on testimony. I know no one personally who has verified the principle of inertia for himself. In all my experience objects in motion seem to slow down and stop by themselves. If one accepts Hume's example of resurrection from the dead as a miracle, the law presumably violated would be that dead persons do not come back to life. I do not see any way of verifying such a law for oneself. I think it is true in general only because I know of no dead person among my immediate acquaintances who has come back to life, and I have the testimony of many witnesses that their experience is like mine. Insofar as the proposition is a universal negative, I can imagine an experience which would falsify it but can conceive no experimental method for verifying it.

In the second place, one can confirm or disconfirm testimony by indirect methods and by direct ones. One can inquire into grounds for regarding a witness as credible; one also can seek other evidence, including various sorts of traces. By "traces" here I mean the sort of evidence which might be admitted in a criminal trial, such as fingerprints, bits of skin, and the like. In a historical investigation traces might include subsequent, independently knowable occurrences which would be difficult to explain if the testimony were rejected.

In the third place—and this point is very important—Hume fails to take into account the experience of learning by experience. One important factor which makes one accept reports of events contrary to previous experience is that one has had the experience of having other empirical certitudes undermined by fresh evidence. Thus, the certitude of no "law of nature" is as great as Hume makes out for the purpose of his essay on miracles.[14] In rejecting reports of frost and its effects the Indian prince was not as reasonable as Hume suggests.

My reference to this example is not intended to suggest that Hume is wrong in distinguishing between miracles and natural events hitherto foreign to one's experience. Events of the latter sort cannot count as miracles. Yet if Hume's theory of evidence and testimony is correct, the Indian prince ought not to have yielded to *any* testimony. Hume himself points out that the manner in which water must be described as freezing is contrary to analogies of experience. Yet, paradoxically, he suggests that it only "requires a pretty strong testimony to render it credible to people in a warm climate."[15]

If a reputable scientist were to announce tomorrow that he had discovered and carefully tested a remedy for leukemia, and that the remedy had worked successfully in one hundred cases, people would very likely believe what he announced, even if his testimony were supported only by a few close colleagues, and despite the fact that the new remedy, if genuine, would reverse all previous experience of this disease.

I do not say that the fact that one accepts such testimony against past experience shows that stories of miracles also are acceptable. What I do say is that if Hume's argument against accepting the testimony for miracles were correct, one would have no reasonable basis for accepting much of the testimony which almost everyone does accept.

The possibility of miracles

Much of the plausibility of Hume's theory of miracles arises from the fact that he treats the entire subject in the framework of a legitimate, but very special, question: Can the testimony of witnesses to miracles serve as a foundation for religious belief? Dealing with this question, Hume has no occasion to ask himself what his attitude would be if he himself were to experience a happening which might be regarded as a miracle.

My main objective in the present chapter is more limited than Hume's. I wish to clarify what a miracle would be like and how one could know that a miracle had occurred. In other words, my question is whether a happening could reasonably be regarded as a signal from the creator and, if so, what sort of happening it would have to be and under what conditions it could reasonably be accepted as a signal from the creator. For the limited purpose I have in view it will be sufficient to consider first-person situations and imaginary states of affairs, setting aside the problem of evaluating the testimony of others with regard to purported historical events.

Suppose an individual has a personal experience of a peculiar sort. While he is writing at his typewriter, the machine suddenly rises a foot above the tabletop, hovers in the air for some seconds, and then drops back in place with a loud "plop." One having such an experience might suspect that he was hallucinating. However, if he knew no reason to doubt his own perception, he might well look for some hidden cause of the strange happening. He might suspect the presence of a magnetic effect, or an invisible fine wire, or a strong jet of air under the machine. If inquiry closed off these possibilities, the possibility of hallucinating might be considered, even with no special reason in favor of it. But suppose that the individual's wife had heard the "plop" of the machine falling, and had come running from another room to see what the trouble was. Suppose further that a glass top on the desk had cracked when the typewriter hit it.

Any reasonable person faced with this set of data—admittedly a product of pure fantasy—would admit that the typewriter had risen, hovered, and fallen. He would admit that he had no explanation for the event. The interesting question is: Would he think that the event violated any laws of nature? More precisely, would he think that his typewriter had defied the law of gravity?

He might say so, but he might also think that *some unknown factor* brought about this queer happening. On this supposition—which is very likely the one a person would accept, even if he *said* that his typewriter had "defied gravity"—gravity would no more be violated than it is when a magnetic field, an air current, or something of the sort suspends a heavier-than-air body in thin air.

If one were herding sheep in a desert countryside, where there was little brush, and if one thought he saw a bush burning for a long time, one might go to see why the fire was not burning out. If the flames seemed to shoot up from the bush as if it were on fire, but without consuming its branches, one might suppose that some hidden fuel supply was keeping the fire going. But if investigation revealed no hidden fuel supply, one would be faced with an unexplained event. If one observed no factor which might cause the peculiar event, he would not know how to try experimentally to bring it about again. Although all one's past experience supports the generalization that whatever burns is consumed, one would not necessarily suppose that a law of nature was being violated. One might well suppose that *some unknown factor* was causing the flame and protecting the bush from being burned by it.

If one were a member of a revolutionary group whose leader announced one evening to all his companions that in a few days he would be captured, machine-gunned to death, and disemboweled by a bayonet, but that a few days afterwards he would rise from the dead and return to the group, one might reasonably be sceptical that these predictions could be fulfilled. If the capture and death occurred as predicted, one probably still would be sceptical about the promised resurrection. If another member of the group telephoned a week later and said that the group's leader had shown up, alive and well—though still full of holes—one would have reason to remain sceptical. But if one then saw the person himself, if one put one's finger into the holes left by the machine-gun slugs and put one's hand into the cavity left by the disemboweling bayonet, then one hardly could deny that *some unknown factor* was at work.

Of course, someone might wish to say in the last example that the happening would be contrary to the laws of nature. However, even here it is not easy to say precisely what law of nature would be violated. A person having such an experience would be faced with a fact contrary to his previous experience; one never has seen a dead man come back to life. But which natural law would be violated by it?

Werner Heisenberg points out that in its beginnings modern science made statements about limited relations and thought these statements were valid only within limitations. However, eventually the modesty was lost:

> Physical knowledge was considered to make assertions about nature as a whole. Physics wished to turn philosopher, and the demand was voiced from many quarters that all true philosophers must be scientific.[16]

Today, according to Heisenberg, physics is returning to self-limitation. Its focus is on individual properties of phenomena; questions about the ultimate nature of body, matter, energy, and so on are left open.

If Heisenberg is correct, one should not assume that the physical order is a rigid mechanism, every aspect of which could be fully described by an interlocking set of natural laws. Rather, one should assume that known laws of nature are partial accounts of phenomena. To the extent that these partial accounts are sound one assumes that certain factors are involved in a situation. If something unexpected happens, one need not assume that the usual factors are excluded; one simply assumes that some other factor is operative.[17]

In reading theological discussions of miracles one often observes the excessive alacrity of theologians conceding that a miracle such as a resurrection from the dead is "scientifically impossible." Sometimes no reason is given for the alleged impossibility; sometimes a reason which sounds scientific is given—for example, that physicochemical processes which are *irreversible* begin at death. The question is: What is irreversibility? A process is said to be "irreversible" in a strict sense if it occurs in a closed system, and if the occurrence of the process so alters conditions within the system that the initial state of affairs cannot be restored. In a looser sense many observed processes are said to be "irreversible." For example, if one throws a stone in a pool, the impact makes ripples. The reversal of the process is not strictly impossible, but no known physical causality would bring it about.[18] Obviously, in neither the strict nor the loose sense of "irreversibility" does the irreversibility of the physicochemical processes which begin at death show that a miraculous resurrection from the dead is "scientifically impossible." Those who believed in such a miracle did not assume that the physical order is a closed system nor did they suppose that the causality involved was of any usual sort.

Still, none of the imaginary examples I have proposed thus far—not even that of the revolutionary leader who returned from the dead—would count as a miracle, although any of these imaginary occurrences would be incredible on empiricist principles. Strange things happen, and normally one writes off strange things to *some unknown factor,* and lets the matter drop. In some cases one might suspect that there were spirits or demons, ghosts or invisible persons at work. Certain peculiar phenomena are investigated at present by parapsychology; its findings suggest that perhaps mind has immediate power over matter other than one's own body. Such possibilities do not indicate anything miraculous. They merely point to previously unknown aspects of nature—or of the other orders of entities within experience.

I do not see why one would ever consider any happening a miracle unless one had an independent ground for thinking that there is a creator. I proceed now assuming that the previous parts of this book have supplied a ground for thinking there is a creator. On this assumption I think that under certain conditions one might suppose that the *unknown factor* in virtue of which the typewriter levitated, the bush burned without being consumed, or the friend came back from the dead was not an unknown created factor.

What are the conditions under which such a supposition would be reasonable? I do not think that the supposition would be reasonable merely because one had to admit that some unknown factor was at work, even if one also accepted the conclusion of the previous chapters. After all, events which initially seem unique and inexplicable often are eventually explained. If one is confident that no immanent explanation will be forthcoming, there must be a special reason for such confidence.

A few years ago there was a proposal—I do not know whether it was carried out—that radio waves be beamed in a certain pattern at some nearby stars in the hope that if rational beings lived on possible planets of such stars, they might receive the message and answer it. If this project were carried out and a signal were picked up which included creative variations on one's own theme, one might reasonably—after any earthly explanation was ruled out so far as possible—suppose the message had been answered.

Analogously, if one who has read the previous chapters and accepted their conclusions were to say to himself, "If the creator can do so, I wish he would cause my child who is suffering from leukemia to get well," and if the child shortly afterwards actually recovered completely, and if the condition before and after was documented by the clinical records made by two different specialists on the disease, and if there was no recurrence during a five-year period, then one would have some reason to think that the creator had *responded* to one's wish.

The wish that the creator might cure one's sick child would not be wholly irrational if the arguments of the preceding parts of this book are sound. One would have ground for thinking that the creator causes the obtaining of all other states of affairs; one might reasonably think of the creator on the model of a human person; one might therefore suppose that the very idea of appealing to the creator is itself caused by the creator. One also might suppose that this idea is not obviously evil. Thus one might think that making an appeal to the creator either would be a good thing to do or at least was permitted by him for the sake of some ulterior good. A person making an appeal in this frame of mind would be disposed to interpret a seemingly inexplicable cure as a response.

Similarly, if we add to the example of the burning bush the additional detail that a voice seems to come from the bush, claiming to be the creator, and if examination reveals no hidden speaker or electronic source of the voice, and if the voice gives directions for seemingly impossible deeds which one succeeds in carrying out as directed, then one would have a warrant for saying one had heard from the creator.

Likewise, if the group leader who rose from the dead had claimed to be the "son" of the creator and if he asserted that he had been restored to life by the power of the creator, one who experienced the whole happening would have ground for saying that in a special sense the creator *had acted* in this case.

In these examples one who regarded the cure of leukemia, the burning bush happening, or the resurrection event as a signal from the creator would not exclude that in all other cases the creator is the cause of all the causes by which anything whatsoever obtains. The understanding of the special character of the miraculous events would depend upon interpreting them not only as requiring an *unknown factor* but also as pointing directly to the creator himself as that factor—"pointing directly" because no suitable immanent cause is discovered or can even be projected with a general description on the basis of the evidence, while the existential relations of appeal/response or hearing/speaking provide content for the supposition that the required unknown factor is no created cause.

It is worth noticing that on this definition of "miracle" the possibility of knowing that a miracle has occurred is part of the possibility of the miracle. For a miracle is defined, not as an objective event contrary to natural law, but as an event which can be taken as a signal from the creator. Without the signal aspect the possibility that the happening is merely an unexplained natural event could not be ruled out.

Malcolm L. Diamond argues that it is reasonable to reject *a priori* the supernatural explanation of "miracles" because to admit the possibility of such exceptions to scientific laws would force scientists to sacrifice their autonomy. In some cases they would hold for an ultimate scientific explanation, but in others they would have to accept a nonscientific judgment that no immanent explanation would ever be forthcoming. Diamond makes the loss of autonomy appear particularly unacceptable by sketching a fictional situation in which a scientist would have to subordinate his personal as well as his scientific judgment to that of a religious authority—the Pope.[19]

Diamond's view obviously is shaped by the assumption that scientific laws are all-embracing. I have criticized this assumption already. But what about the question of scientific autonomy?

The interest of Dr. Alexis Carrel in the allegedly miraculous phenomena at Lourdes, France, and the manner in which Carrel reacted to these phenomena shows that Diamond's concern about the autonomy of science is misplaced. Carrel, as a young physician around the turn of the century, became interested in the supposed cures at Lourdes. In 1903 he went to see for himself. Impressed with the facts, he did not set aside his scientific objectivity. Instead he observed and later described the conditions under which miracles occurred:

> The miracle is chiefly characterized by an extreme acceleration of the process of organic repair. There is no doubt that the rate of cicatrization of the anatomical defects is much greater than the normal one. The only condition indispensable to the occurrence of the phenomenon is prayer. But there is no need for the patient himself to pray, or even to have any religious faith. It is sufficient that someone around him be in a state of prayer.[20]

Carrel was certainly a competent scientist; in 1913 he won the Nobel Prize for his work in surgery. He did not assume a supernatural explanation of the phenomena which he described; he instead supposed that there are as yet unknown relations between psychological and organic processes. Only near the end of his life did Carrel come to a *personal* conclusion that "everything happens as if God listens to man and answers him."[21] In reaching such a conclusion Carrel did not yield his scientific autonomy to a religious authority. Rather, he admitted the limitations of the physical order; he claimed for himself the right *as a person* to think beyond the limits of scientific method. As Charles A. Lindbergh wrote:

> Most men of reputation are cautious in discussing phenomena which lie beyond science's accepted frontiers, knowing the argument and criticism that such discussion brings. On these subjects, as on others, Carrel spoke and wrote more freely than many scientists can think.[22]

Lindbergh observed that Carrel's extrascientific thinking was often sweeping and undisciplined. However, Carrel's honesty and scientific integrity remain beyond question, despite his attitude toward miracles. He observed the facts, including the *factual relationship* between the phenomena of healing at Lourdes and prayer.

Diamond also raises the question why miracles, if genuine, are so infrequent. Why does God not cure everyone at a shrine such as Lourdes who seeks his miraculous intervention?[23] One can answer this objection along the following lines.

A miracle is not primarily a personal favor. It is rather a signal, a special communication from the creator. Yet, according to believers miracles were not only signals of a further communication to come and of a further relationship to be established; they were statements *in* a communication and gestures *in* a relationship. Believers held that one who did not get his cure at once would get it—or something better—later on. The motto of believers was: "Persistence always pays." Those who believed in the future resurrection of the body as a sure hope for all who love God tended to regard miracles which they believed in as mere samples of that much greater miracle yet to occur. Thus, believers maintained that all sincere prayers are answered—in due time.

Believers also considered miracles such as healings to be a divine example of the works of love which they themselves were asked to undertake on behalf of others. That not all diseases are cured miraculously thus could be regarded as an instance in which the principle of the creator's inefficiency—discussed in chapter twenty-one—is operative.

Whether miracles as I have defined "miracles" do or do not occur is not under consideration here. However, I think it worthwhile to conclude this chapter with some remarks on the criteria for evaluating alleged miracles.

First, all of the grounds for probability should be taken into account. These include the independently established conclusion that there is a creator, that this creator can reasonably be thought about through using the model of a human free agent, that creation is a self-expression of the creator, and that any attempt on man's part to communicate with the creator or any alleged communication from him is a state of affairs which would not obtain unless the creator caused it to obtain.

Second, Hume's criteria for accepting evidence for miracles, though not sound in all respects, are near enough to the mark that one should take them quite seriously. Stories of miracles are not to be accepted lightly, and most such reports probably are false. It must be noticed that not everyone is as credulous as Hume makes out, and not all reported miracles are alleged to have happened in the distant past in barbarous and ignorant nations. Moreover, not all religious differences are a matter of conflict, and not all religions abound with *well attested* miracles.

Finally, if there is a place at which miracles are reported to happen in our own day; if the alleged miracles include cures of cancer otherwise regarded as incurable, cures of organically caused blindness with restoration of the function of vision even prior to the healing of its organic cause, and cures of other diseases such as tuberculosis with otherwise unknown rapidity; if all serious scientific researchers, including medical specialists who are sceptical of the whole affair, are welcomed at this place and provided with facilities to examine those who claim they have received miraculous cures; if many cases in recent years are well documented, including clinical records made both before and after alleged miraculous cures; if some researchers, so outstanding as to rank among the leading medical men of the world, have had their initial scepticism overcome by the facts they encountered at this place; if this place is associated with a religious body which maintains the possibility of miracles in the sense previously defined, but at the same time discounts and rejects the majority of miracles alleged by her own members to occur; then that place surely deserves to be investigated by anyone who wishes to assess the facts with respect to miracles.[24]

23: The Human Person
and the Human Community

The human person

This chapter clarifies concepts which will be used in the following chapters dealing with divine persons and human persons. These chapters also will deal with communities of such persons, including communities made up of persons of both sorts. Throughout the present chapter I am speaking exclusively of *human* persons and *human* community. First, I clarify the concept of *person*, then the concept of *community*.

The human person is complex. Both predicables ascribing outward corporeal characteristics and predicables ascribing states of consciousness can be applied to any normal person. For example, "John is touching something hot; John's hand is moving rapidly; John's hand is blistered" ascribes corporeal characteristics to John. The same sort of predicables can be applied to any primate; somewhat similar characteristics can be ascribed to certain plants and even to inanimate bodies. "John senses heat; John is frightened; John's hand hurts" ascribes certain states of consciousness to John. Similar states of consciousness might be ascribed to any primate, but they cannot be ascribed to a plant or a nonliving body. "John thinks that the problem is badly defined; he is committed to arriving at a solution; he is working out a model for developing a better answer" also ascribes certain states of consciousness to John. The behavior and activities of subhuman primates do not lead us to ascribe similar states of consciousness to them. Moreover, these peculiarly human predicables are both noncorporeal and different from other states of consciousness. One's thoughts, commitments, and projects do not cease to exist when one goes to sleep; unconsciousness of these entities during some

343

time is compatible with them continuing to exist as dispositions for later specifically human experiences and acts.

This complexity of the human person poses a classical philosophical problem. How is one to interpret the relationship between body, consciousness, and self? Usually the problem has not been formulated as clearly as this question, for often the distinction between states of consciousness and specifically human dispositions is ignored. If so, the tendency is to ask about the relationship between body and mind, or about the relationship between body and soul (self). In the former case consciousness is emphasized and specifically human dispositions generally ignored. In the latter case the dispositions and the self to which they seem somehow to belong are emphasized, while consciousness is considered only peripherally. Ancient and medieval thinkers emphasized the self; modern, especially recent, philosophers emphasize mind or consciousness.

I know of only three main approaches in previous philosophical works to the body/mind or body/soul problem.

One approach is to set up a model in which the two are regarded initially as distinct entities, one material and the other immaterial. Given this model, one asserts that either there are two entities such as the model suggests, or one of these two is irreducible while the other is reducible. Thus, the first approach to the problem gives three solutions: dualism, physicalism, and idealism. The dualist says that body and soul (or mind) are distinct entities somehow tied or glued or mixed together. The materialist says that the body is real and the mind is only an appearance or a corporeal quality or a disposition for bodily behavior. The idealist says that the mind is real and the body is only an appearance or an objectification or a projection of mind.

The second approach to the body/mind or body/soul problem is to set up a model in which the two are related as coprinciples of a single living and personal whole. To prevent the coprinciples from becoming distinct entities, a solution based on this sort of model must make the relationship of the coprinciples nonsymmetrical and make them depend upon each other to exist. This approach has been followed in some major philosophical reflections, perhaps the most important of which was that of Aristotle in *De anima*. Aristotle regards the soul as an actualizing principle which unifies and makes to live and to act in a human way the materials which are formed into a human, living body.

An analogy—but only an analogy—is a running machine. The parts which make up the machine are matter; they *are* the machine only potentially. In other words, the parts are the machine when it is taken apart and not running. The way the parts are put together and its running also *are* the machine; these give the machine its actuality. The soul organizes the materials which make up a human body; the soul makes these materials a body capable of living. Conscious states and dispositions are the working of the body and its adjustment to work in certain specific ways.

The third approach to the body/mind problem is to set up a model in which the two are related as different moments in a single, continuous process. The body can be regarded as the residue of this process; the mind as its unfolding toward an open future. Sartre's analysis of the person in terms of the in-itself and the for-itself uses a model of this sort.

None of these ways of dealing with the body/mind or body/soul problem is satisfactory.

Dualistic attempts are at odds with the facts of human experience precisely to the extent that a dualist sets up a dichotomy between two entities. When John carries on an inquiry to which he is committed (dispositions which characterize the self), he does various things such as seeing (state of consciousness) by opening his eyes and focusing them (bodily behavior). How all this fits together if the elements are attributed to diverse entities is inexplicable.[1] Dualists propose various accounts of the relationship—for example, that the two things interact, or that they work parallel to each other, or that the states of one entity are reflected by the states of the other. None of these accounts is plausible; all suffer from the fatal defect of having to link together disparate entities with links which always remain either too mental to tie into the body or too bodily to tie into the mind.[2]

Idealistic attempts are unsatisfactory because they must reject the reality of the body, and this reality is part of the data of the problem. Moreover, the idealist has no criteria by which to convict the body of nonreality, because in principle he cannot explain the standard of reality from which his own body—and any body as such—falls short. What *is* a body if no body is *really* a body?

Materialistic attempts are unsatisfactory because they cannot make sense of the specifically human dispositions which are characteristic of most persons. These dispositions are related to certain characteristically human acts and states of consciousness. For example, the materialist cannot admit the possibility of free choice. But this possibility is real.[3] A person can make a free choice. In such an act one is aware of determining himself to one of two or more alternative possible courses of action. The commitment is a disposition; it does not go away when one is not conscious of it. Yet it is not, as disposition, located anywhere in one's body; it has no corporeal characteristics at all. Moreover, it is a disposition to action, and human action, while it often includes bodily behavior, is not reducible to such behavior.[4]

Some contemporary versions of the materialistic account of the complexity of the human person are called "the mind-body identity thesis." Proponents of this thesis devote most of their attention to states of consciousness which might be ascribed to any primate; they pay little attention to specifically human dispositions. Although the thesis concerns mind-body *identity*, proponents of it make clear that they do not mean that the body is nothing but a state of consciousness. Frequently the position that mind and body are identical is dignified with the title "identity hypothesis" or "identity theory," although it is unclear how the thesis would *explain* the data. The data are the distinct sets of corporeal characteristics and corresponding states of consciousness. To assert that these sets of data are not after all distinct—even assuming this assertion to be intelligible—hardly seems to explain anything. Since facts are irrelevant to the mind-body identity thesis, arguments about it concentrate on attacking and defending the logical coherence of the "theory." This debate seems to me a case of speculative inflation of the sort I criticized in chapter five (pages 80-82).

In the final section of chapter fourteen I sketched an argument against the position that thinking is nothing but a physical process. There are other, more developed critiques of materialism and arguments for the irreducibility of thought to physical processes.[5]

Aristotle's attempt to clarify the unity and complexity of the human person is initially more plausible than any of the attempts based on the dualistic model. However, if the soul or self really is nothing but what organizes the body and makes it function, then the acts and dispositions of the self would be limited by the materiality of the body. Aristotle does not seem to have been aware of freedom of choice, but he was aware of the nonphysical character of propositional knowing, which is revealed by the human ability to distinguish between the material and the immaterial. Aristotle seems to have realized that such a capacity and its dispositions could not belong to a human self as he conceived it, and so he suggested that a nonhuman agent also was involved. With this suggestion Aristotle avoided materialism, but at the cost of slipping into dualism—a position he desperately tried to avoid.[6]

An attempt to clarify the unity and complexity of the human person which regards body and mind as different moments in a continuous process has to give an account both of the process and of its continuity. The process must be such that bodiliness is a residue, that the mental can be transformed into the corporeal. The continuity must be such that either the body or the mind or something else undergoes the process. If one denies that the process belongs to anything, the two moments become alienated from each other, since they are defined by their opposition, and dualism breaks out afresh. If what undergoes the process is the body or the mind, then either dualism or a one-sided reduction recurs. If what undergoes the process is neither the body nor the mind, one escapes dualism, but at the cost of introducing a third factor, which an approach of this sort tries to avoid. The self which is creating and the self which is created cannot be identified and yet must be identified if one wishes to regard the body and the mind as two aspects in a self-generating process.

In chapter fourteen I proposed a descriptive metaphysics of four orders of reality within experience—taking "experience" in a broad enough sense to include everything of which man has direct knowledge. These four orders are the physical, the intentional, the existential, and the cultural. The four orders are distinguished from one another; they are not reducible to one another; however, they are not separated from each other; each includes the content of the others *in its own distinctive way.* My view of the person presupposes this ontology.

Many philosophies treat the person as if he were primarily or even exclusively limited to one of the four orders. The fact that the four orders are distinguished *within* experience—"hearing another" has four meanings—indicates that human persons are related to one another in all four orders. Hence, human persons must be understood as belonging to all four orders and somehow embracing them all. The consequence is *not* that the person is four realities—quadralism instead of dualism—but that the person is a complex reality whose unity is other than the unity of entities which are limited to any one of the four orders.

The person considered as pertaining to the physical order is a plurality of vital and psychic functions, integrated into the personality which psychology studies. Psychic life gradually emerges in the course of evolution. The human organism is the product of a long process of differentiation and complexification by which organic nature achieved this level of fulfilling the potentialities of matter. Psychic functions realize potentialities of a biological substructure—the nervous system. The biological structure and vital functions of the human organism depend upon and integrate physiochemical processes.

I think that Aristotle's account of the unity of the sentient organism is plausible for animals other than persons and for persons as natural bodies. Aristotle takes care of the body/mind problem to the extent that this problem is a question of the unity of the body and sense consciousness. The fact that states and functions of sense awareness are not reducible to vegetative functions of organisms, and *a fortiori* not reducible to the characteristics of inorganic bodies, does not mean that sentient mind is not an aspect of the organism. The transcendence of sense-consciousness to bodies lacking it—for example, that sense consciousness is *of* all sorts of bodies and that consciousness itself is not outwardly observable—does not argue against the natural and material character of sense consciousness; all life is remarkably different from merely inorganic matter.[7]

P. F. Strawson provides arguments which I consider sound for holding that the concept of "person" is primitive, and that the ascription of both objective bodily characteristics and conscious states to one and the same individual depends upon recognizing the indivisibility and irreducibility of the "person."[8] The only difficulty with Strawson's theory is that it is not a theory of persons but of sentient organisms in general, including both persons and brute animals. Strawson deals effectively with the mind/body problem but he does not touch the self/body problem.

The person considered as pertaining to the intentional order is a self-conscious subject for whom things known are objects. The person can know anything, including himself; what is other than the person is known as belonging to—but does not know—a world of objects. As Hegel pointed out, the subject is reflexive; the subject can think of himself as other and then recapture himself in this very thinking.[9] The person as thinking of himself and as thought of by himself is one as person but two as subject and object of thinking. Negation originates in such knowledge; negation belongs to the world of thought and not to the world of nature.

As I explained in chapter nine (pages 178-179), it is only because human persons are self-conscious subjects that human knowledge of the world is an objective knowledge of things themselves, not merely an indirect relationship with things *as known.* A person in knowing understands his own knowing; he grasps what his knowing itself contributes to knowledge. In understanding his own knowing he adjudges the content to be other than the knowing; the content is not reflexive. The content known thus can be posited in a proposition (*pro-positio*) or projected (*ob-iectus*).[10]

The person considered as pertaining to the existential order is a self-determining agent, a principle of his own action by free choice. The person acts; the world is a scene in which one creates and plays the role of his own life. Choice depends upon and involves understanding. The reflexivity and negation characteristic of propositional knowledge also condition choice. In choosing, one proceeds upon prior deliberation regarding objective possibilities, one excludes at least one real possibility which therefore never will obtain as an empirical state of affairs, and one proceeds toward the realization of another possibility with which one partially identifies one's self. In the chosen possibility one finds some degree of self-fulfillment.[11]

The person considered as pertaining to the cultural order is man symboling, man the maker and communicator. By thought and freedom man engages in a creative interplay with his environment. But this environment is not merely a natural world; it is a human situation. Man builds his home in nature and continues to build his cultural home as he lives in it. In using symbols and tools man becomes aware of himself as master of the things he uses; he also should become aware of his dependence upon these things, of his finitude, and hence of his obligation to respect and to wonder at the subhuman world even as this world comes under subjection to human persons.

Each of these four considerations focuses upon an important aspect of the complex unity of the human person. However, if one takes any one of these considerations and sets it up as *the* model of the person, something important will be downgraded or omitted. The discussion of various formulations of the body/self problem indicates the consequences of taking any of these considerations in isolation as an adequate model. A naturalistic consideration grounds Aristotle's model; the consideration of man as knowing subject grounds a dualistic model which tends toward idealism; an existentialist consideration grounds a moments-in-a-process model; the consideration of man as culture-maker grounds an operationalistic dualism which tends toward materialism.

A better model can be developed by beginning from the fact that the person is not limited to one of the four orders. A person is in all four of the orders, and he embraces all of them in himself. In the person the four orders are distinct, irreducible, yet normally inseparable. The unity of the person is unlike the unity of any entity which is enclosed within one of the four orders. The unity of the person is mysterious and must remain so. This unity is immediately given in human experience, and it cannot be explained discursively, since reason cannot synthesize the distinct orders in a higher positive intelligibility. One can reason from any order to the others only insofar as all the orders are included in any one of them.[12]

A preliminary suggestion of the model of the person I propose can be given by means of an example in which certain important aspects of the person are reflected. The example is a statement (*S*): "This set of marks can be used to express a proposition the assertion of which can serve as a point of departure for articulating and communicating a new model of the person."

Like any other statement, *S* unites the four orders in itself. First, *S* is a set of ink marks—or a succession of noises—entities in the physical order. Second, *S* expresses a meaning and it has a logical structure. Third, to assert the proposition *S* expresses is a human act, and this act is oriented to the social purpose of communicating something. Fourth, *S* is a use of natural objects to express meaning, and this use has a creative intent inasmuch as I am attempting to work out a new model for understanding the complex unity of the human person.

Unlike many other statements, *S* is peculiar in that the proposition *S* expresses is self-referential. Thus, *S* refers to *S,* and *S* says of itself that it has the four predicables mentioned in the preceding paragraph. This fact makes clear that the four orders which are present in *S* are not so distinct that they are not also united. Still, the physical marks on the paper, the assertion, the act of asserting it, and the creative effort are distinct; confusion of any one of these with any of the others would make it impossible for one to understand *S,* since each of them is referred to by different propositions—namely, by the four propositions set out in the preceding paragraph.

Unlike many other statements including many self-referential statements, the act of asserting S, insofar as it is a human act, also has a reflexive aspect. The act of asserting S promises to articulate and communicate a model of the person, and that very act itself is the first step in carrying out what it promises. The human act itself involves the use of physical objects which are ink marks or sounds; the act gets its meaning from what one is doing; part of what one is doing precisely is asserting this proposition; and the act aims beyond what one does in it to the ulterior purpose of creating and communicating the model set out below.

Again, unlike many other statements, including many self-referential statements, the creativity projected in S also involves reflexivity. If the effort made here to set out a new model of human personhood is creative, then S is a step in that creative effort. The creative effort uses the material objects, the proposition, the act of asserting—but the creative effort to develop a model of the person also uses the creative effort of formulating S and setting it out. And, in aiming to go on from S, as I am now going on from it, the creative effort of S also aimed toward producing a certain experience, developing a model (which is an entity in the intentional order), affecting human action, and completing the work of this chapter.

The statement S, considered precisely as a set of marks or sounds—natural entities in the physical order—makes possible but also limits the other aspects of the reality of S. The meaning, the human act, the creative attempt—all depend upon the physical reality of S and none could exist without it. These aspects of S are limited by the characteristics of its natural reality, characteristics which must be accepted as they are and respected for the possibilities they offer. The physical aspect of the reality of S is not isolated from the other aspects, although it is distinct from them as they are from one another. What is peculiar about the physical reality of S is that this aspect is not reflexive; it provides a fixity and a self-containedness which the other aspects lack. What is physically, is other than the reflexive self; physical objects cannot be transformed dialectically; a bodily entity is what it is in its *self*, regardless of what one thinks or chooses or makes of it.

The model for understanding the complex unity of the human person now can be proposed. In contrast with any model which would confine the person to one of the orders, the model I propose is that there are four distinct and irreducible aspects of the person. A person is a physical body; a person is a propositional knower in whose world of meaning logical entities exist in being thought; a person acts by free choice; a person is a maker and user who puts things to work for new purposes and brings into actuality values which are otherwise only ideal possibilities.

These four aspects of the person are united, as the four aspects of the statement S are united. This unity is unlike the unity of any entity which is limited to one or another of the four orders. The unity of the person is not an intelligible principle of a fifth order, distinct from the four, nor is it something like an entity belonging to one or another of the four orders hidden behind all of them. The four aspects of the person all involve and in a way include one another, as the four orders always do. Moreover, the four aspects of the person are mutually irreducible to each other, as the four orders always are. If it were not for both the unity and the irreducible diversity of these four aspects of the person, the distinct sorts of reflexivity belonging to one person as thinker, doer, and maker, and the irreflexivity of the same person as body, would be impossible. The person is the self who *unifies* these four distinct and irreducible but normally inseparable aspects. The self is a unifying principle; various aspects of the person are unified by the self but not identified with it.

The unity of the person, by which the person is one self, is evidenced, first of all, by the compenetration of the four orders. Each of the four unifies itself, in its own way, with the others. The person includes these four modes of unity. The body thus includes the other aspects of a person; the other three aspects of the person each includes the body; the bodily aspect of a person is not one *thing* divided against the rest of the person as another *thing.* Indeed, on this model the soul or self is not part of the body or something hidden within it; it would be better to say that the body is one aspect of the person, united with the others by the soul or the self. But this statement must not be taken in an idealistic sense, as if the body were not a material object—a sentient organism in the physical order.

The body of a person differs from the material reality of a statement in an important respect. A human body as such has a mind; a person's body is capable of sense consciousness. Sense consciousness, like materiality in general, is not open to dialectical transformation. But sense consciousness provides an imperfect reflexivity, as is evidenced in the guidance of perception by perception (noticing, paying attention), learning by experience, and the like. Reflexivity in such cases is imperfect, for the two terms of the relationship are distinct moments in a process. In other words, though both ends of the relationship are within the unity of a human organism, the feedback of sense consciousness cannot of itself establish a relationship which distinguishes its own terms.

The reflexivity of propositional knowing, in contrast with that of sense consciousness, is complete. Knowing, insofar as it is reflexive, distinguishes itself into subject and object; when knowing itself is known, the two terms are other only as opposite terms of the relation. If such reflexivity did not occur, one never could know his very knowing, something one does in any true self-referential proposition, for example: that any proposition is either true or false. It is worth noticing that this reflexivity, while complete in its single instance, is not total. The proposition has other instances which are not self-referential.

One could carry out an analysis of the reflexivity of choice and of symboling parallel to the preceding analysis of the reflexivity of propositional knowing. In making commitments a person determines himself; in using anything a person uses his own abilities. But the reflexivity in each case while complete is not total; one commits oneself to a value which is not wholly identical with oneself and one uses something other than the abilities immanent in oneself. Thus self as knowing subject, self as existential agent, and self as culture-maker are open to and dependent upon what is not self. For this reason the self which unifies the bodily aspect of the person and these three reflexive aspects of the person is easily distinguished from the creator.

However, the self which is the principle of the unity of a human person is not identical with the knowing subject, the existential agent, or the culture-maker. All of these are included in the self; they are aspects of it. But the constitutive self of a human person is revealed in the *unity* as well as in the distinction and interrelationship of the four orders.

As I argued in chapter twenty-one (pages 319-320), the created universe does have unity—that of being created—which transcends the diversity of the four orders. This unity cannot be reduced to a rational system, as can the order proper to each of the four orders. The unity of the human person somehow embraces the community of everything man experiences. The unity of the human person is the image within creation of the unity of the creator. The unity of the creator is the unity of the term of all arguments toward an uncaused cause; these arguments begin in the diverse orders. These arguments have nothing in common at their starting points except the contingency of everything which is experienced and the unity of the person who experiences.

Thus I conclude that the complex unity of the human person is a fact for which one ought not to expect an explanation. Nothing else within experience is precisely the same sort of complex unity, although a statement can serve as a model for the person as the human person can serve as a model for the creator.

When death happens to the bodily person, is the self totally destroyed? I do not think any conclusive rational answer can be given to this question. It is difficult, if possible at all, to know to what extent the other aspects of the person need bodily life and to what extent the self depends upon the distinct aspects of the person which it unifies. The statement, S, could have none of its other aspects without the physical reality of sounds or ink marks. But S is not a person; S is only a model of the person. The person has an additional unifying factor, namely, the selfhood which is the common principle of reflexivity in thinking, choosing, and using. The statement, *S*, participates in this unity only insofar as this statement is embraced within a person. Thus, one can think it possible that when death happens to the bodily person, the self is not utterly destroyed but perhaps survives, although, as it were, in a mutilated condition.[13]

The very possibility of disembodied survival has been under attack in recent years.[14] Believers, of course, were far more heavily committed to the resurrection of the body than to the immortality of the soul.[15] However, I am not convinced by the arguments that disembodied survival of a self is impossible. Many of these arguments rest upon the impossibility of satisfying a demand for a criterion of personal identity after death. The demand for a criterion often involves covert verificationism, as I explained in chapter seven (pages 119-120); in this particular case those who argue against disembodied survival frequently seem to assume that only a criterion exactly like continuity—which more or less serves as a criterion for the identity of an organic individual—would be acceptable.[16] Moreover, many arguments against disembodied survival reject various proposed criteria of personal identity on the ground that these criteria might—mere logical possibility—be met by two or more distinct individuals.[17] Such arguments presuppose a rationalistic theory of individuation—that is, identity of indiscernibles and intelligible difference between any two individuals.

On the theory of the person which I have proposed, it is in principle impossible that one should provide a criterion—that is, a logically sufficient one—for the self-identity of a *person,* but this impossibility does not show that persons are not self-identical. It merely shows that one cannot have a criterion for everything. Of course, each self which survives—if any do—in a disembodied condition is distinct by being the mutilated self of a person who began to be when a certain organism was conceived at a certain place and time. But this unalterable fact—which might be known only to God—is not what is demanded by those who ask for a criterion by which a "disembodied spirit" could be identified as the "soul" of a particular dead man. They are asking for a statement of the criteria by which one could recognize mutilated selves existing under conditions of which we have no experience. Obviously, there is no way to satisfy this demand.

The human community

"Community" is a narrower concept than "interpersonal relationship." Some relationships among persons are not very different from the relations of animals to one another or of persons to nonpersonal entities. A community is a unity of many persons, achieved in all four orders of reality, which transcends the unity of any multiplicity of entities within any one of the four orders, just as the unity of a person transcends the unity of any entity within any one of the orders.

The natural unity of distinct persons is chiefly their biological relationship. In sexual reproduction a man and a woman become a single principle of a new human person. Human life is not caused in a child by any nonpersonal principle; rather, life is transmitted in a continuous stream. The sperm and the ovum live by the life of the parents until they unite to form a new human individual. All human persons are blood brothers, or at least blood cousins.

Mankind is an interbreeding population. Apart from this complex biological society no individual human person could exist. In this bodily community individuals do exist in distinction from one another. One does not die whenever any human person dies. Still, "humanity" not only signifies abstractly what is common to all human persons, in virtue of which one can say of each, "This individual is *human*"; it also signifies the concrete, living process of human bodily life, which is a natural species, a whole to which all individual human persons belong as parts.

Human persons also know together. Two persons think of the very same proposition; they agree or disagree about its truth. (If anyone disagrees with this position, he must be thinking of it, and this fact confirms the position stated and falsifies the disagreeing position.) In this way inquiry proceeds as a dialogue—as an argument which is free for all.

The unity of diverse persons as knowing subjects in the world of thought also becomes clear when we ask the question "Who, today, knows physics or any other field of study?" The answer cannot be the name of one person. No person, not even the most able, knows the whole of any science. The physicists know their subject matter, but only the whole group have all the knowledge which pertains to the discipline. Individual scientists must be specialists; even the scholar who is interested in general questions must specialize in them. His special field of interest is questions which bear upon principles of the whole subject matter, but these questions are specific in that they are only a few of the questions which must be asked about the subject matter.

The unity of distinct persons in common action is a very important aspect of community. Of course, two or more persons may be common agents in the sense that their behavior happens to conduce to a single outcome—for example, their carelessness in driving causes an accident—without uniting as persons. Again, persons can cooperate in a purely contractual relationship without sharing a common commitment. But common action also can originate in a unified principle of specifically personal action. Only such unity constitutes community.

For example, two persons who both have their hearts set upon some one value which they both regard as superior to their individual wishes, desires, or satisfactions can come to appreciate each other's judgments of value. They not only make similar judgments, but each knows that the other shares his view. They not only make similar commitments, but each knows that the other endorses the same value to which he commits himself. Moreover, the two individuals approve and encourage one another's judgments and commitments; in this way each includes the other within his own concern. In such a case the two persons will unite their efforts if they can.

The common good which binds them together cannot be some defined goal attainable by obvious and readily specifiable means. Such a goal would not take a person outside himself to a purpose he could recognize as superior; only an open-ended value can provide the content for a common commitment. The commitment of two or more persons to a single value sometimes is expressed in a community constituting act, such as the adoption of a national constitution.

Derivative from the basic commitment which constitutes a community of action is a set of institutions. These distinguish roles and shape behavior in accord with the basic commitment. The action of each individual person becomes in this way a contribution to a common good to which all alike are dedicated. Each person does his own work, not for himself alone, but as a share in serving the good cause to which all are committed. Each person's dedicated action thus becomes less exclusively yet more truly his own; it becomes his share in what all do together. Each person's contributions are accepted by all as "ours." In a true community members even take responsibility for one another's mistakes and shortcomings.

Some people deny that genuine community of action is possible. If it required individual persons to subordinate themselves to a good proper to someone else—the false ideal of altruism—then genuine community would be impossible. However, persons *can* love one another unselfishly if they are united in pursuit of values in which each person sees a fair promise of his own fulfillment, but which all together see as important enough to demand and to deserve frequent sacrifices of individual satisfactions.

Many people fear community. They are afraid that their own individuality might be more and more absorbed in another or in the others. However, true community takes nothing from individuality. The closer persons come together in dedicated love, the more they differentiate and fulfill themselves as individuals. Each can give as much as possible only by realizing his highest individual potentialities. Absorption follows, not from community, but from the abuse of a relationship which should be community and has become exploitation.

The community of persons in objective culture is so obvious that little explanation of it is needed. Men have a common language; no one can have a private language. Language exists only in the use of things to communicate. Yet each person uses the common language in a personal and special way. Each person can make a contribution to the common linguistic stock by creatively expressing himself in language.

Men share a common technology. No single person can understand the complex machinery well enough to make it work. All together men can do so.

One could cite many other examples of community in objective culture. One of the best is a fine orchestra. No one person can play a great symphony. The whole orchestra must work together to make beautiful music.

A good family exemplifies all aspects of a true human community. The members share the same flesh and blood. Husband and wife are one flesh; the babies are nourished from their mother's body. The members of the family think and learn together. They gain knowledge by conversation in which they share their experiences and insights. All fulfill themselves by serving and caring for one another. All share the same home and use the same property. Each contributes according to his ability; each receives according to his need.

Communities are mysterious. Social theories vainly try to reduce human community to one of the four orders. They cannot succeed, for persons complete one another in community in all of the four orders. Moreover, the mysteriousness of community is rooted in the mysteriousness of the person. As the unity of the person is immediately present to us, yet beyond rational discursive explanation, so in the unity of community there is an ultimate common ground: we are fellow creatures who together make up the creator's self-expression in a way impossible for any of us alone. The human family was regarded as an image of the creator by believers who said: "In the name of the Father. . . ."

24: Meaning, Revelation, and Christian Mysteries

"The creator speaks to man"

Is it meaningful to say that the creator has communicated to mankind some otherwise inaccessible truths about himself? In other words, does it make sense to say that God has spoken to man? If the concept of the creator's communicating is coherent, how could the *content* be meaningful? For example, how could it make sense to say that God is three persons, one of whom has become man?

The meaningfulness of many Christian doctrines presents no difficulty, at least no difficulty peculiar to Christian doctrine. Christians believed that God creates, that Jesus was crucified, and that it is wrong for any person to refuse to give another a cup of cold water when there is no special reason to justify the refusal.

The meaning of "an uncaused entity creates" was explained in chapter seventeen. "Jesus was crucified" is a straightforward statement of fact; it might pose a problem of verification, but its meaning is clear enough. (Here the truth of Christian doctrine is not under consideration; the problem of verification will be ignored.) "No one may refuse another a cup of cold water without special reason to justify the refusal" is a moral precept. Some philosophers, including many empiricists, think such precepts lack cognitive meaning—that is, that they cannot be true or false. But the problem concerns moral precepts in general; it is no different with respect to precepts peculiar to Christian teaching. I have dealt with the matter elsewhere and shall not deal with it here.[1]

The *meaning* of the Christian doctrine of the resurrection of the body—as

357

distinct from the philosophical thesis of the survival of the disembodied self—does not seem to me to pose any difficulties. It is generally agreed that one can coherently describe a state of affairs which would have to be called "resurrection of the dead."[2] Of course, whether a coherent description, based mainly on imagination, is at all likely to refer to anything is another matter.

The problem of meaningfulness to be considered in this chapter, therefore, is how those Christian doctrines which purport to express otherwise inaccessible revealed truths might be meaningful. Examples of such doctrines are the Trinity, the Incarnation, and the bodily presence of Christ in the Eucharist. These doctrines, and others similar to them, often are referred to as "mysteries of Christian faith." Christians did not claim to be able to explain the meaning or to prove the truth of such mysteries. They did think it possible to answer any specific objections attempting to show these doctrines meaningless.[3] Each of the Christian mysteries involves special problems of meaningfulness. I do not attempt to deal with all such problems here. However, I will try to show, against a few specific reasons to the contrary, how the three important Christian mysteries mentioned above could be meaningful.

Before taking up these three mysteries, however, I first consider the more basic problem whether the very concept of revelation is coherent. I think this question can be answered adequately in the Old Testament context. Moreover, what will be said about the purportedly revealed *content* in the Old Testament context will be relevant to the discussion of the content of the Christian mysteries. Therefore, I begin from the purported revelation of the creator, Yahweh, to Moses (Ex. 3).

Thomas Aquinas holds that God exists of himself, that God is his very obtaining.[4] He thinks this truth was taught to mankind when God, revealing himself to Moses, was asked by Moses to state the divine name, and answered this request:

> "I am who am." Then he added, "This is what you shall tell the Israelites: I AM sent me to you."
> God spoke further to Moses, "Thus shall you say to the Israelites: The LORD, the God of your fathers, the God of Abraham, the God of Isaac, the God of Jacob, has sent me to you." (Ex. 3:14-15)

Contemporary biblical scholars think that this passage should not be read as a philosophical doctrine.[5]

What, then, did the name mean? There are several suggestions. One is that in semitic thought knowing the name of an entity gave one a certain power of control over that entity. It might be that "I am who am" was meant to be an expression of a refusal to reveal, to imply that an adequate definition of God is impossible, and that God "does not make himself man's slave" as he would if he communicated a name which conveyed some power over himself.[6] A second possibility is that the name was regarded as revealing God's unlimited existence as against the unreality of the gods of other peoples; this notion has in support of it the fact that "Yahweh" probably is related to the archaic form of the verb "to be."[7] A third possibility, considered by some most plausible, is that the name means "he causes to be"; perhaps it is a shortened form of a fuller expression meaning either "he who brings into being whatever comes into being" or "the divinity who brings the hosts into being."[8]

If the first hypothesis is correct, the purportedly revealed name was meant to indicate that God is wholly transcendent; the "name" is a simple reaffirmation of his absolute otherness. If the second hypothesis is correct, the purportedly revealed name was meant to indicate that God truly exists. If the third theory is correct, the purportedly revealed name was meant to indicate that the transcendent principle is the creator of other entities.

These interpretations could all be correct; if so, then the allegedly revealed name indicated that God is not reducible to anything given in experience, but that he really exists and is a cause of all other entities. In other words, the name sums up the conclusion of the argument to an uncaused cause. Even if it is held by some scholars that "Yahweh" is merely a name, which perhaps was not correctly understood even by the Israelites, their conclusion—that this name applied to a personal being whose attributes could be shared by no other being—indicates transcendence and independence.[9]

The reference in the passage in Exodus to the "God of Abraham, the God of Isaac, and the God of Jacob" refers to an established religious context, assumed in the story of the revelation to Moses. However, this story itself is rather full; it can serve as a paradigm of revelation as understood in the Old Testament.

Moses observes a burning bush which is not consumed (Ex. 3:2-3); later at the theophany at Mount Sinai there are peals of thunder, lightening flashes, a dense cloud, and a trumpet blast (Ex. 19:16). In both cases he hears a voice which he is told is (Ex. 3:6) or recognizes as (Ex. 19:21-25) the voice "of God." In both cases the words which are heard are ordinary, recognizable words, but no normal cause of such sounds is experienced. Moses does not show himself credulous; rather the opposite is the case (Ex. 3:11-4:17). But the words refer to future events, and the events *prove* that the words are trustworthy, especially when the Israelites escape from the Egyptians (Ex. 14:15-31).

The events themselves recounted in Exodus were purportedly experienced. But they are recounted as unusual events. One need have no concept of a law of nature in order to regard a bush which burns but is not burned up as something out of the ordinary. The words which enter into the discourse are not special; the manner in which they are put together, to express a purported communication from God, is what is unusual. The events are taken to be caused by God to show his concern, his favor, and to carry out his purposes. The hearing itself is unusual, especially because of the relationship it establishes; the "person" who is heard by Moses and through him by the Israelites identifies himself by means of ordinary words as God.

The words which Moses hears and the events which occur mutually sustain each other. If the words alone were heard, Moses might well assume that he is having an hallucination; if the events alone occurred, he might think that these are simply natural happenings which he cannot explain. But the words predict and promise the events, and the events verify and fulfill the promise of the words. The unusualness of both—the fact that no visible speaker utters the words and that no usual explanation would account for the events— requires that the words-events unity be accepted at its claimed value, as a message and intervention of God.[10]

This story, if true, recounts a miracle as defined in chapter twenty-two. Words and deeds together indicate a cause outside human experience. If one thinks that the words were not heard *or* that no events occurred which could not be explained by natural causes, then one excludes, at least in this case, the reality of the alleged divine revelation. In other words, if one supposes that Moses did not hear a voice from a burning bush and did not later hear a voice on the mountain; or if one supposes that the various plagues, the parting of the sea, the manna in the desert, and so on *all* are susceptible of naturalistic explanations, then one must take the story as an expression of something which, even if it has religious significance, does not reveal more than one could learn about the creator by considering any state of affairs whatsoever.

If one assumes the story to be substantially true—which I do for the sake of this inquiry—then one can notice that the various sorts of statements in the story form a pattern. Some statements express in ordinary words with their usual meanings unusual things heard and unusual events happening. Some statements express in a negative way what God as speaker and agent is not; he is not merely a natural principle, nor an illusion, nor a human speaker, nor an entity which can be represented by any image. The speaker and the agent who does the saving deeds identifies himself as God. The characterization of Yahweh thus becomes a combination of two sets of relational predicates. He is the creator of heaven and earth and all things; he is the one who chose this people, who redeemed it from slavery in Egypt, who sustained and protected the people's lives, who guided and directed them toward a land of their own, who made covenant with them and was faithful to this covenant, who defended them in battle against their enemies.

The revelation to Moses—assuming it occurred—is an example of how words take on new meanings from their use in a peculiar context. To hear words which express a divine revelation would be diverse from hearing anything else. But the context which unites "hearing" and "God" is built up in such a way that the expressions are understandable. The manner in which both "hearing" and "God" are modified by their relationship in this peculiar context does not render either expression meaningless.

While one can say that God creates everything and that he is the cause of all caused causes, one cannot say that God utters all utterances or does all deeds. But the particular utterances and deeds which are attributed to God in Exodus can be appropriated to him to the extent that they do not seem to be utterances of anyone else or events explicable by created causes.

Once this peculiar order of divine words and deeds is initiated, many human acts and other events which fit into this order also can be appropriated to God. Thus, when Moses acts under God's direction, the words and deeds of Moses express the will of God. The fact that a great many entities which seem perfectly ordinary are thus integrated into this order—which may be called the "order of salvation"—provides an occasion for nonbelievers to explain away *all* of the order of salvation in terms of one or more of the other four orders. Such reductionism happens with regard to the four orders themselves, and for the same reason—namely, that the entities of each order also enter somehow into the others.

Of course, if acts and events which fit into the order of salvation also have their usual principles, there will be a tendency to suppose that these acts and events can be fully explained by their usual principles. The fact that they are enmeshed in the order of salvation makes them in a special way God's words or deeds; this fact need not exclude, nor even necessarily modify, the way in which they are human words and deeds, natural events, mere accidents, or whatever.

From the point of view of faith whatever pertains to the order of salvation is peculiar, whether or not it lacks its usual conditions, simply because it all occurs within the context of a special relationship. This special relationship is for the believer very much like his relationship to a human friend, father, ruler, or helper. But the relationship is odd in that it is to one who is not a human person, to one who identifies himself with the creator.

In all interpersonal relationships persons who accept another must proceed by faith. A rationality norm may indicate that one is reasonable to suppose that the experience one has is of the creator revealing himself, but both the acceptance of this judgment and a commitment to act on its truth are matters of free choice. Moreover, like any interpersonal relationship, this one cannot unfold unless one trusts the other party, accepts his statement of intent as sincere and his promises as authentic commitments. To the extent that the content of what is revealed provides information about the creator, his intent, and his promises, one who believes he is receiving a revelation and who trusts the one making it must believe this propositional content to be true, although one has no independent means of verifying it. Of course, to suppose the propositional content to be true does not mean that one claims to know exactly what this content is. Even in strictly human interpersonal relationships one often is mystified by the statement of a most intimate friend about himself. Yet one can believe that one's friend is expressing *some* truth—even though one is not sure precisely *what* truth—about himself.

The specific relationship one has to the creator who reveals himself in believing in him is distinct from the relationship one has to the creator in being caused by him. However, for the believer whatever the creator does can be seen as somehow integrated into the intent and promises of the friend, father, ruler, or helper in whom one believes. As in any intimate interpersonal relationship, one does not relate to the creator revealing himself only insofar as he reveals himself. One relates to the person himself, not merely to an abstract role or an isolated function of the person.

This analysis makes clear why many human statements, activities, and performances as well as many natural events which have proportionate causes were differently regarded by believers and nonbelievers. A believer, for example, read the Bible as the word of God, while not excluding human authorship and the normal literary history of such a text. The nonbeliever attends only to the latter conditions, does not read this book as part of the order of salvation, and hence sees no reason to attribute these writings to God any more than either believers or nonbelievers would attribute the authorship of ordinary books to God.

However, if *all* experiences can be sufficiently accounted for by their ordinary, immanent principles together with ordinary, universal, creative causality, then there is no reason to admit an order of salvation in addition to the usual four orders. Fulfilled prophecies and miraculous events are essential because only in them could one find a special relationship, one not shared by all creatures, which would require the creator who reveals himself as its term. Miracles need not be the most important entities in the order of salvation, but they are epistemically vital inasmuch as they make that order an irreducible subject matter for faith. If miracles are impossible, so is divine revelation.

The identification in Hebrew thought of the creator who can be known by reason with a person who reveals himself in an existential relationship explains why the Hebrews emphasized Yahweh's transcendence, yet freely used anthropomorphic expressions in speaking of him.

The Hebrews believed that Yahweh is holy, superhuman in a unique way, unlike any of his creatures, wholly other than creation. Yahweh was believed to be living. He gives and sustains life. But no image was to be made of Yahweh. Nothing in the universe was believed to resemble Yahweh, and so nothing was to be worshipped as his representation (Ex. 20:4, Dt. 5:8). The thoughts of Yahweh, it was believed, are not the thoughts of man, nor his ways like man's ways (Is. 55:8-9). Job's questions are not answered; in the end he is described as admitting his presumption: "I have dealt with great things that I do not understand; things too wonderful for me, which I cannot know" (Jb. 42:3).[11]

St. Paul carries on this aspect of the Old Testament tradition when he sums up early Christian belief in the transcendence of God:

> How deep are the riches and the wisdom and the knowledge of God! How inscrutable his judgments, how unsearchable his ways! For "who has known the mind of the Lord? Or who has been his counselor? Who has given him anything so as to deserve return?" For from him and through him and for him all things are. To him be glory forever. (Rom. 11:33-36)

For Paul transcendence is proper to the creator, and the relationship of creature to creator is neither displaced nor rendered less mysterious within the perspective of faith. Rather, the relationship of creature to creator is a condition without which the mysterious phenomena connected with Jesus Christ could not be regarded as anything other than a set of inexplicable experiences.

At the same time the Old Testament freely characterized Yahweh in anthropomorphic language. He is spoken of as having human organs such as eyes and hands, as performing human acts such as talking and walking, and as feeling human emotions such as anger and compassion. However, his fidelity is claimed to be extraordinary, more than human (Nm. 23:19).[12]

In the New Testament anthropomorphic expressions are used more cautiously but not eliminated. The transcendent principle who is wholly unoriginated is called "Father"; he is purported to hear prayer, to make promises and to keep them faithfully, and to hate sin but be quick to forgive sinners who repent.

Such anthropomorphic predicables are indispensable to Jewish and to Christian faith, for the relationship which Jews and Christians believed was established by revelation and faith between God and the believer is similar from the believer's side to a relationship between one human person and another within the existential order.

In applying relational predicables to the creator revealing himself believers greatly extended the use of the model of the human person, which already is suggested by the mode of the creator's causality, as I explained in chapter seventeen (pages 269-270). Creative causality suggests that the uncaused cause acts freely, by knowledge, and playfully. Revelation adds that he speaks, for one hears him; that he is faithful, for his promises are fulfilled; that he redeems, for one finds oneself rescued. The believer's relationship to the creator revealing himself has a practical significance; the believer is prepared to act in certain ways and to expect certain outcomes. However, the practical significance of what is believed does not mean that religious faith is nothing but an attitude toward the world of experience. One's belief in another in any interpersonal relationship always has a practical significance, but one does not *reduce* one's friends to the difference they make to oneself, to their involvement in one's own actions and sufferings.[13]

From the believer's point of view the vast extension of talk about God on the basis of revelation was a partial satisfaction of the desire to know the cause of the obtaining of the world of experience. From the nonbeliever's point of view the statements proper to faith inevitably seem a hopeless hodgepodge. But the believer supposed that each religious truth builds up the model of God as a person to whom man is related. The believer supposed that the explicit content of revelation—a precise set of words—controls the speculative extension of the model, while the lived relationship of the believing community with the God in whom it believes gives the relational predicables of religious discourse an irreducible descriptive content.

Relational predicables in expressions of faith still must meet conditions of predication concerning God clarified in chapters fifteen to seventeen. The way of negation limits the meaning of relational predicables such as "Father."

From the nonbeliever's point of view talk of God as a "Father" is meaningless. After all, one's father is one's male parent. With the descriptive content wholly removed by the way of negation nothing is left of the original metaphor. The believer accepted the negations; he knew that God is not a Father in any earthly sense. None of the descriptive language one uses to speak of human fatherhood can be applied *in the same sense* to the creator. The believer worked from the existential aspects of the relation of children to their father. Yet even this relationship was not applied to God *in the same sense.* The sense of "father" said of God was altered by the context of other expressions used in the formulation of the revealed message and in the lived relationship which believers supposed can develop from it.

Moreover, relational predicables known by reason to characterize the creator must be accepted as limits of any special relational predicables used by believers to express their faith. In the order of salvation acts and effects which are attributed to God cannot be thought of as rendering him dependent. God must remain wholly uncaused. This is one reason why believers maintained that everything which pertains to the order of salvation is a matter of God's wholly free gift. If one were to suppose that the acts of persons who receive revelation and who respond to it with faith in any way caused or required God to reveal himself, to grant something to mankind, or to keep his promises, then one would suppose that God is caused.

In short, the language of faith presupposed, built upon, and was conditioned by the language in which God can be spoken of by man even without faith. Yet the statements of believers were not wholly reducible to statements which could be made without faith. Believers thought that there is an order of salvation which includes the order of creation—that is, the order of entities within experience to the creator. There can be no order of salvation unless at least some of the entities included in it are miraculous. Only in this manner could the order of salvation be distinguished from the four ordinary orders. In other words, the miraculous is required to establish the order of salvation as irreducible, somewhat as *arguments* for their proper principles—for example, for free choice in the case of the existential order—are required for each of the four orders.

The preceding argument is not an attempt to show that there *has been* any divine revelation. Any attempt to argue this issue must deal with historical and literary critical questions which are beyond philosophical competence. The preceding argument is intended to show only one thing: the concept of divine revelation is coherent. In other words, Christian doctrines ought not to be rejected on the ground that divine revelation as such is logically impossible. Of course, the nonabsurdity of the *concept* of divine revelation does not imply that everything which is regarded by anyone as a divine revelation is coherent.

Christians, of course, not only believed that there could be a divine revelation; they believed that there is one. They also believed that it includes certain truths about God otherwise inaccessible to human inquiry. Leading examples of such purported truths are the so-called mysteries of Christian faith, including the Incarnation, the Trinity, and the bodily presence of Christ in the Eucharist. In what follows I propose to do two things: first, to state what Christians believed in each of these matters; second, to show against some arguments to the contrary that what Christians believed is not logically incoherent. Any argument for coherence can be extended indefinitely. I propose only an initial sketch.

The reader must bear in mind throughout that reference to documents displaying Christian faith is not made as an assertion of the *truth* of what was believed, but as evidence of the fact that this *content* was believed.

The Incarnation

Christians believed that a certain man, Jesus of Nazareth, began acting and speaking in a manner which was altogether unique, that he performed many miracles, that he was accused of claiming divinity for himself and did not deny it, that he was crucified for blasphemy, and that he rose from the dead.

Christians believed that Jesus's first followers accepted his words and deeds, sealed by his resurrection from the dead, as evidence of his divinity. Thus, they believed that John was a disciple of Jesus, and that John wrote the

Gospel attributed to him, introducing the story of Jesus with a statement of his divinity and his humanity:

> In the beginning was the Word; the Word was with God and the Word was God. He was with God in the beginning. Through him all things came to be, not one thing had its being but through him. . . . He was in the world that had its being through him, and the world did not know him. He came to his own domain and his own people did not accept him. . . . [He] was born not out of human stock or urge of the flesh or will of man but of God himself. The Word was made flesh, he lived among us, and we saw his glory, the glory that is his as the only Son of the Father, full of grace and truth. (Jn. 1:1-3, 10-11, 13-14)

John represents Jesus as revealing to his followers at the Last Supper that he and the Father are mutually in one another and are one (Jn. 15:17).

Christians also accepted Paul's summary of the Incarnation, passion, death, resurrection, and glorification of Jesus Christ as expressing equality between Jesus *as divine* and the Father, inferiority of Jesus *as man* to the Father (Phil. 2:6-11).

The very complexity of this notion naturally gave rise to many opinions regarding the makeup of Jesus Christ. Some believed him truly God but only apparently or incompletely human. Some believed him genuinely human, but only specially related to God or somehow partially God, not truly and fully God. To hold Jesus either fully human or fully divine seemed to many to require the denial of the other, since the creator-creature distinction seemed to them to be violated by the Christian belief that this man, Jesus, also is the Word through whom all things are created.

Several centuries were required for questions about Jesus Christ to be resolved to the satisfaction of the main body of Christian believers. The resolutions were hammered out in a series of general church councils held during the fourth and fifth centuries, when Christianity had spread widely and persecution of Christians had ceased. The clearest summary of Christian faith which emerged from this process is the profession of the Council of Chalcedon (451):

> We declare that he [Jesus Christ] is perfect both in his divinity and in his humanity, truly God and truly man composed of body and rational soul; that he is consubstantial with the Father in his divinity, consubstantial with us in his humanity, like us in every respect except for sin (see Heb. 4:15). We declare that in his divinity he was begotten of the Father before time, and in his humanity he was begotten in this last age of Mary the Virgin, the Mother of God, for us and for our salvation. We declare that the one selfsame Christ, only-begotten Son and Lord, must be acknowledged in two natures without any commingling or change or division or

separation; that the distinction between the natures is in no way removed by their union but rather that the specific character of each nature is preserved and they are united in one person and one hypostasis. We declare that he is not split or divided into two persons, but that there is one selfsame only-begotten Son, God the Word, the Lord Jesus Christ.[14]

This summary includes what is necessary to discuss the logical coherence of the Christian doctrine of the Incarnation.

First, if the doctrine of the Incarnation is taken to mean that Jesus is not truly man, then the doctrine is incompatible with its own datum: Jesus was a certain man from Nazareth.

Second, if the Incarnation is taken to mean that Jesus is not truly divine, the position contained in the introduction to St. John's Gospel is contradicted.

Third, if any attempt is made to suggest that "man" and "God" are partly true of Jesus, partly not, the attempt runs into the absurdity of supposing that what Jesus is—that is, his being such-and-such, man and/or God—could be divided. (Nothing is partly or somewhat the kind of entity it is in itself. Such concepts are all-or-none predicables.) Chalcedon excludes all these suppositions by affirming that Jesus Christ is perfect both in divinity and in humanity, truly God and truly man.

Fourth, if it is supposed that the Incarnation means that God is changed into man or that man is changed into God, the distinction between what is uncaused and what is caused is denied. Chalcedon excludes this supposition by affirming Jesus's distinct origin according to his divinity and according to his humanity. "Consubstantial" means that the same predicable, expressing what something primarily is in itself, can be said in precisely the same sense of two subjects. Thus, Chalcedon affirms that Jesus Christ and the Father are God in precisely the same sense; and that Jesus Christ and we are human in precisely the same sense. As God, he is "begotten" of the Father—a relationship which must be considered in the context of the doctrine of the Trinity. As man, he is born of the Virgin Mary.

Fifth, if it is supposed that what characterizes Jesus Christ as man affects or alters his divinity or vice versa, then predicables properly applicable to a creature—this particular man—would have to be applied to the creator, and vice versa. One would have to say that God the creator was created, that a certain man was uncaused, and so on. Chalcedon excludes such absurdities by affirming that Jesus Christ is both human and divine without any commingling or change in either nature.

Sixth, if it is supposed that the exclusion of commingling or change in Jesus Christ's divinity and humanity implies that he is two entities, existing separately, this division contradicts the datum of the problem: he is one person. Chalcedon excludes this incoherence by affirming that Jesus Christ is one person, not split or divided into separate entities, that his divinity and humanity are not separated from each other.

According to this doctrine "the Word was made flesh" does not indicate an intrinsic change in God. This predication is relational and the dependence is one-sided. This man, conceived of the Virgin Mary, is the same person as a divine person, the Word; therefore the Word was made flesh. The first statement expresses the being of Jesus as man, and says that this being is related to God not only as dependent upon the creator but as personally one with the creator. The second statement expresses the converse relation, but relational predications about God do not indicate mutual dependence, not even in this case.

If one were to assume that the unity of the divine and human in the single person of Christ were *unity* in the same sense as anything else is a unity, then absurdity could not be avoided. If the unity is the same as that of anything within one of the four orders, then the divine is reduced to one of these orders. If the unity is the same as that which can be said of God apart from the consideration of the Incarnation, then the human is reduced to the divine. This unity must be regarded as unique if contradictions are to be avoided. The precise point of the declaration of Chalcedon is to distinguish the unity of the person of Christ from any other unity, and to preserve the complexity of his makeup precisely by insisting upon the uniqueness of his unity.

No Christian would claim to understand or to explain this doctrine. The main point of theological arguments about it is to try to show that the concept of Incarnation is not logically incoherent. Therefore, the following points must not be taken as an attempt at explanation, but as indications of the coherence of the doctrine.

"Identical with itself" has various meanings. The self-identity of anything depends upon the sort of entity concerned. God could be called self-identical by an affirmative predication of the type discussed in chapter sixteen. But "self-identical" said of God could not mean exactly the same as the same expression in any other case, for said of God, this predicable, like all other affirmative and relational predicables, is conditioned by the whole way of negation. Identity of the person of the Word with the person who is Jesus of Nazareth therefore cannot be excluded as impossible from God's side, since we do not comprehend "self-identity" said of God any more than we comprehend "person" said of him.

From the human side the difficulty might seem more serious, for we do, after all, know what it is to be human. However, the difficulty is not overwhelming. We know that the human as such is created, but the doctrine of the Incarnation does not exclude that Jesus's human nature as such is created. As to the human person, I argued in the preceding chapter that the unity of the human person in any case is inevitably perplexing. The perplexity arises because a human self joins several distinct and irreducible orders of entity into one undivided reality. The ordinary human person is not several things, but one entity having several aspects which must be neither confused nor divided.

The unity of the divine/human makeup of Jesus Christ—as conceived in the Christian doctrine of the Incarnation—seems nearer to the unity of a human person than to any other unity we know of. The theological problems about his makeup are analogous to the philosophical problems, reviewed in the previous chapter, about the makeup of any human person. In one's own experience of one's self one's unity as a human person is immediately given, yet it is not reducible to a system, since the four orders of reality which are embraced in the complex unity of a human self do not form a single rational system. Thus it follows that while man's self-experience provides no reason to extrapolate the concept of human person to include identification with God, the concept of *person* one applies to one's self cannot exclude such extrapolation. Thus, from the human side, too, the doctrine of the Incarnation cannot be incoherent, for the concept of *person* as applicable to the human is necessarily open-textured enough to allow extension beyond intelligibilities which would be the basis for any argument demonstrating incoherence.

My point is not that Jesus Christ is merely a human person. To say that would be to deny the traditional Christian doctrine of the Incarnation, and while I am not asserting this doctrine here, I am not denying it either. What I am saying is that Chalcedon's declaration that Jesus Christ is both God and man, but a single person, the person of the Word, is incoherent neither with what one can intelligibly say of God nor with what one can intelligibly say of a person *who is* human.

A Christian who wished to speculate theologically by making use of the doctrine on the human person outlined in the preceding chapter would note that the ultimate principle of the unity of the human person is one's selfhood, a principle which is not restricted to one of the orders, but which underlies the unity of the person embracing the complex reality of all four orders. One's selfhood is not identical with, although it includes, the bodily *in itself,* the knowing subject, the self-determining agent, and the executive *ego.*

A Christian could say that Christ is truly man inasmuch as he like any man includes all the complexity of a human person, including everything which a human person has in all four orders and the unity he has in virtue of the mutual inclusion of those orders in one another, but that Jesus is not a human person just to the extent that the ultimate principle of unity—the selfhood of the created person—is absent in his case, replaced by the selfhood of the Word of God, through whom all things were created.

The Trinity

The doctrine of the Trinity derives from the same New Testament materials from which Christians developed the doctrine of the Incarnation. The Christian doctrine of the Trinity was never stated more clearly and completely than in the Decree for the Jacobites of the Council of Florence (1438-1445 in 1442):

> There is one true God, all-powerful, unchangeable, and eternal, Father, Son, and Holy Spirit, one in essence, but three in persons. The Father is not begotten; the Son is begotten of the Father; the Holy Spirit proceeds from the Father and the Son. The Father is not the Son or the Holy Spirit; the Son is not the Father or the Holy Spirit; the Holy Spirit is not the Father or the Son. Rather, the Father is only the Father; the Son is only the Son; and the Holy Spirit is only the Holy Spirit. The Father alone has, of his own substance, begotten the Son; the Son alone has been begotten of the Father alone; the Holy Spirit alone proceeds both from the Father and equally from the Son. These three persons are one God, not three gods; for the three persons have one substance, one essence, one nature, one divinity, one immensity, one eternity. And everything is one where there is no distinction by relative opposition.
>
> "Because of this unity, the Father is entirely in the Son and entirely in the Holy Spirit; the Son is entirely in the Father and entirely in the Holy Spirit; the Holy Spirit is entirely in the Father and entirely in the Son. None of the persons precedes any of the others in eternity, nor does any have greater immensity or greater power. From eternity, without beginning, the Son is from the Father; and from eternity and without beginning, the Holy Spirit has proceeded from the Father and the Son." [note omitted] All that the Father is, and all that he has, he does not have from another, but of himself; he is the principle that has no principle. All that the Son is, and all that he has, he has from the Father; he is a principle from a principle. All that the Holy Spirit is and all that he has, he has from the Father and equally from the Son. Yet the Father and the Son are not two principles of the Holy Spirit, but one principle, just as the Father and the Son and the Holy Spirit are not three principles of creation, but one principle.[15]

This formulation undoubtedly goes beyond the explicit content of the New Testament; it might be regarded by some Christians as excessively theological. However, it represents an orthodox expression of Christian faith; it is still regarded as normative by Roman Catholics.

Florence's decree clearly excludes any differentiation between Father, Son, and Spirit which would conflict with what must be said of the creator as such. The limitations set by human knowledge of the creator are not contradicted. Thus, Florence does not say that God is divided into several beings, or that there is more than one creative principle. It does not say that he is numerically one or numerically many *in the sense in which* those expressions can be predicated of any entities within experience.

The point of departure for the doctrine of the Trinity was the identification of Jesus as God, along with the distinction of him from another, identified as Father. "Son" and "Father" obviously cannot apply to the same. Also, in the New Testament Father and Son are distinguished from a third—the Spirit—who is "sent" by both, yet to whom is attributed unity with both and all the common divine predicables.

From this point of departure the doctrine of the Trinity unfolded. The difficulty in the doctrine is that it seems to violate the axiom that realities identical with something one and the same must be identical with one another. The Christian sought to avoid outright contradiction by saying that there is only one *God,* but that Father, Son, and Spirit are distinct *persons.*

This language, however, can conceal the difficulty and even lead to understandings of the doctrine unacceptable to Christians. If one supposes that divinity is analogous to humanity, and that just as there are many men having the same nature, although they are distinct persons, so there are many distinct divine persons, the doctrine of the Trinity might seem simple. However, in this case one denies what Christians believed, for this interpretation would mean that there are three divine entities, similar in nature but diverse in being. If one supposes that personality attributed to Father, Son, and Spirit is analogous to the various psychological personalities some human individuals display—the three faces of Eve—one again seems to have an easy solution to the problem of the Trinity. But, again, one denies what Christians believed, for this interpretation would mean that there are three roles played by God, perhaps corresponding to three distinct ways in which creatures are related to him, but no real distinction in God between Father, Son, and Spirit.

The latter approach might seem especially attractive on the theory of predication concerning God developed in earlier chapters of this work. However, the manner in which the doctrine of the Trinity is expressed in the New Testament does not admit such a solution. The distinction between the Son as God, on the one hand, and, on the other, the Father and Holy Spirit, is not established by different relations which believers have or should have toward the three persons, but rather by the *content* of revelation: many sayings attributed to Jesus himself, early Christian statements such as those found in the introduction to the Gospel of St. John, and the formula for baptism (Mt. 28:19). The way in which such statements are built up presents no great difficulty if one begins from the doctrine of the Incarnation. One need only add that there are two others, not identical with Jesus Christ nor with each other, who are God in the same sense he is.

Putting the matter this way, however, only sharpens the paradox. The resolution—not an explanation of the mystery, which Christians believed impossible, but a removal of the paradox—depends in the first place upon a rejection both of the supposition that God is one being in the same sense in which any entity within experience is one, and also of the supposition that divine persons are distinct in the same manner as human persons are distinct. Once these suppositions are rejected, the contradiction dissolves. Christians deny multiple divine entities in a set of perfectly ordinary senses, and they deny a unitary divine person in a straightforward sense. What is left to be affirmed is not clear, but for that very reason it cannot be clearly contradictory.

The resolution in the second place depends upon making a distinction between various sorts of distinction. The divine persons are said to be distinct relative to one another; they are one God apart from their mutual opposition. The Council of Florence makes use of this conception. Theologians developed it by suggesting that the divine persons precisely consist in opposed relations, relations not of anything other than themselves, but identical with the nonrelational divine reality itself.[16]

According to this view God as creator can be called "one" in the senses indicated in chapters sixteen and seventeen; thus "God" functions as a proper name. However, in the context of New Testament revelation "God" as a predicable is not a name—proper or common—except insofar as it is used in the same sense as "Father."

This approach can be clarified by referring back to what was said in the preceding chapter about reflexivity. In human knowledge and choice there is perfect reflexivity with respect to part of the content of knowing and choosing—namely, with respect to that which is knowing and choosing itself. To the extent that propositional knowledge is reflexive, the same is a knowing and a known.

God's knowledge and love do not depend upon anything other than himself; if they did, he would not be uncaused. Hence, in him knowledge and love were thought of as perfectly reflexive not only in some instance but with respect to their totality. Such knowledge and love need not lack content, because God is his own power to create as well as his own acts of knowing and loving. Yet, one can suppose, the distinctions between God knowing and God known, between God loving and God loved, hold. God knowing and God known, God loving and God loved, *is and are not* the same: divine unity with distinct persons.

Another conception which mitigates the paradox of the Trinity is that of community as experienced or approached even among human persons. There, as explained in the preceding chapter, greater unity and more perfect individuality can go together, though they seem opposed. Similarly, unity and distinction in the Trinity can be regarded as a community in which a higher form of unity is combined with more perfect distinctness.

The Eucharist

The last of the Christian doctrines to be commented upon here is that of the bodily presence of Christ in the Eucharist. This doctrine presents a different problem from the Incarnation and the Trinity. The doctrine of the Eucharist is drawn from some explicit New Testament texts (Mt. 26:26-29; Mk. 14:22-25; Lk. 22:19-20; 1 Cor. 11:23-25; Jn. 6:51-58). Christians believed that Jesus meant that bread and wine blessed as he commanded no longer was what it still appeared to be, but became his own body and blood. This doctrine was not taken to mean that Christ's body was divided, cramped in a small space, and subjected to chewing and digestion. It was taken to mean, however, that bodily contact with Jesus was accomplished by receiving the Eucharist, and that the multiplicity of Christians by sharing in the Eucharist were formed into one body of Christ, somewhat as mankind naturally forms one community by sharing the same human flesh and blood.

The difficulty with the doctrine is obvious. It seems to be falsified by experienced facts. Christians agreed less completely upon the details of this doctrine than they did upon the details of the doctrines of the Incarnation and the Trinity. I only propose some considerations which might point to a resolution of the paradox ("resolution" in the sense explained above).

One thing to notice is that normally one thinks of various entities according to their placement in one of the four orders. This way of looking at things causes a great many philosophical problems, not least the problem of the person discussed in the preceding chapter. If one supposes that what ultimately defines bread and wine, on the one hand, and the body and blood of Christ, on the other, is confined to the physical order, then the mystery of the Eucharist becomes an absurdity. For the consecrated bread and wine remain, from the point of view of natural science, just what they had been, and no Christian ever denied this fact.

A second point to notice is that when one considers subhuman entities, one can define them multiply; *what* one regards something as being, in many cases, depends upon the order in which one is considering it. For example, it would seem odd to take a great painting and to analyze it by saying that it really is only a piece of fabric bonded to certain complex, chemical substances in a certain spatial arrangement—"just so much paint smeared on a piece of canvas." Still, one can consider a painting in this way.

Human persons can be both regarded *as physical objects* and considered as subjects in the intentional order, in the existential order, and in the cultural order. Socrates serves as an example in innumerable logic books; an aborted child is treated as a mere blob; a functionary can be reduced to the status of a cog in the machine. In cases such as these something could be going wrong. If the manner in which the person is regarded as an object is not subordinated to selfhood of the person, something is wrong.

A third point to notice is that there are difficulties in determining just where a person's body begins and ends. Usually one supposes that the boundaries are obvious. However, in sexual reproduction part of the father's body is separated from him, perhaps by a considerable distance, at the precise time he comes to be a father—fertilization. One's senses extend one's body outward into the environment, to be affected by it; one's capacities for action also extend one's body to the point at which the effect is achieved. If this were not the case—I am taking for granted the outlook expressed in ordinary language—people would not see one another but only images on the retina.

A fourth point to notice is that communication normally means giving something of oneself. Perhaps the paradigmatic case is parenthood. A special aspect of parenthood is a mother breast-feeding her infants; they live from her very body by actually consuming not merely a substance which she "manufactures" but something of what she physically is. (A modern and artificial, but no less valid, example is giving a blood transfusion.) In verbal communication—the giving of a human word—one who receives the communication, even at a distance and perhaps by electronic means, in some real sense hears *the voice* of the person communicating with him.

These considerations together should not be taken as explaining what Christians meant by the doctrine of the Eucharist. Christians meant that the consecrated bread and wine brought about bodily unity with Christ in some way which cannot be explained. The key word, again, is "unity." The unity accomplished by the Eucharist must be of a unique sort, just as the unity of God and man in the Incarnation is of a unique sort, and the unity of the Trinity and of each divine person must be of a unique sort.

However, the considerations outlined suggest that one might think along the following lines. When one receives a telephone call from a friend, one hears *the voice* of one's friend, but one also hears sound waves electrically produced. One receives something of one's friend, but not his whole person; the medium remains as a vehicle. If one receives a blood transfusion, one receives part of another's very body, and there is no medium apart from the living substance itself which is received. But in this case the reality of the other is received only in part, and that part is alienated from the other person and turned into oneself.

If one supposes—which Christians believed—that the Eucharist communicated Christ himself, then the Eucharist must be regarded as combining various features which are separated in ordinary experience. The bodily presence is similar to biological cases of communication, cases such as sex, breast-feeding, and the blood transfusion. But there is no alienation from Christ of any part of himself; this aspect is rather like verbal communication. The classification of what appears to be bread and wine as *really* the body and blood of Christ is somewhat similar to what one does when one regards something in a particular order as *really* what it most significantly is—for example, one accepts a bunch of flowers as a token of friendship rather than as dying vegetation of a certain biological species.

If one combines these various aspects, a model for thinking about the Eucharist along the following lines emerges. Christ himself is communicated; the Word of divine conversation absorbs the medium into the message. But this communication occurs without physical division, unlike the biological examples. A medium is taken over, very much as a gift takes over the physical elements of what is given and transforms their meaning. However, since the medium communicates a person—and particularly since this person is one who ultimately cannot be subordinated to any created entity—what was antecedently the medium is displaced by the one who communicates. In other words, not only is the meaning of the bread and wine changed—though that certainly happens—but its appropriate ultimate definition is changed. However, this displacement does not mean that the bread and wine ceases to be physically—for the natural scientist—what they were. It simply means that the Eucharist is not defined by these physical characteristics; the use of this food and drink *demands* appraisal in other terms.

These sketches of ways in which I think one might go about trying to show that Christian doctrines need not be logically absurd are not altogether satisfactory. Each of these problems by itself would be suitable subject matter for a whole book. Still, these sketches will indicate the strategy I think is available to believers. Those who see contradictions in doctrines of faith must make some limiting assumptions regarding the meaning of the mysteries. My view is that such assumptions, if they lead to contradictions, must be denied. One need not thereby deny all positive meaning to the doctrines. Rather, one sets out to find a possible meaning which is really peculiar to the subject matter of the doctrine. If Christianity is true, perhaps such a quest for the true meaning of what is revealed is *all* that God expects of the intellects of those to whom he communicates.

25: Why Christian Doctrine,
If True, Is Important

Eliminating the negative

As I explained at the beginning of chapter twenty-two, a judgment whether Christian doctrine is true involves considerations beyond philosophical competence. However, there remains one question which can be considered philosophically. That question is, What difference would it make if Christian doctrine were true? The question must be answered from within the perspective of Christian faith itself. However, this fact does not mean that the question lies outside philosophy. If consideration of what Christians believed suggests that even if Christian doctrine were true, it would be irrelevant to human concerns, then a philosopher might reasonably suggest that inquiry be directed toward questions of greater existential significance. But if the content of Christian doctrine is such that it is important *if* true, a philosopher may reasonably commend to historians and to other scholars the inquiries which need to be conducted in their fields.

An analogy will clarify the point. If someone were to announce that the story of Snow White and the Seven Dwarfs is not necessarily absurd, that it might actually be true, one might reasonably react to this information with little enthusiasm. What difference would it make if this fairy story actually were a reasonably accurate chronicle?

Today many people feel that even if Christian doctrine were true, it would make little difference to anyone. What if Jesus Christ is God? What if God is a Trinity? What if Jesus is bodily present in the Eucharist? The world seems to go on pretty much as it always has. If Christian doctrine is true, it does not seem to make much difference. The first Christians had great expectations of an imminent revolutionary transformation of the world. Two thousand years later the world remains untransformed. If Jesus was raised from the dead, other people still die unjustly and nobody is raising them from the dead. To many people the Christian story seems an irrelevant tale from long ago.

Everyone recognizes that there is a great deal of evil in the world. There is poverty and pollution. There is ignorance and stupidity. There is disease and natural disaster. There is war, exploitation, and unjust institutions. There is meanness, cruelty, and addiction. There is duplicity. The innocent suffer while the wicked thrive.

There are many analyses and prescriptions for remedying evil. Some see the problem as one of lack of knowledge and control; they put their hope in research, science, and education. Some see the problem in terms of exploitation and unjust institutions; they put their hope in reform and revolution. Some see the problem in terms of sickness, including especially psychological illness; they put their hope in therapy. Some see the problem as inevitable, as something built into the human condition; they despair.

Christians believed that all the factors mentioned have a role in the unsatisfactoriness of the human condition. They believed that men should do what is humanly possible to overcome evil. But Christians also believed that all other forms of evil are symptomatic of the most fundamental evil. The most fundamental evil, according to Christians, was that the human race, created with a capacity to form an open community oriented toward friendship with God, failed to take advantage of the opportunity. This turning away on the part of mankind as a whole from an opportunity to somehow share in a special association with God was original sin. All other human evils, Christians believed, followed upon original sin, in the sense that human life and society would and could have been different and far better than it is if mankind had accepted its opportunity for intimate community with God.

Why should a failure at the beginning of human existence have affected the whole human race? Christians believed in the natural community of mankind. A favorable situation could and should have existed into which individuals, when born, would have entered naturally. Since it was not established, human persons are born as aliens rather than as citizens of a community oriented toward friendship with God.

Christians believed that the significance of the Incarnation is that by this means God grants each human person an individual opportunity to enter into a community of friendship with him. Jesus, because he is God, is not separated from divine friendship. He is capable of making other men friends of God by becoming friends with them himself.

The process of building up a human community of friendship with God was what Christians called "building the Kingdom of God," "building up the Body of Christ," and "building the church." The conception of "church" in

Christianity is that of gathering together of those who have accepted the offer of friendship extended by God to each human person through Jesus Christ.

The redemptive life, passion, death, and resurrection of Jesus was regarded by Christians as a mystery. A popular distortion of Christian doctrine was that God wished to take revenge for damage done him by sinful mankind, that he could not exact satisfying revenge on ordinary human beings, so he made his own Son suffer to restore his wounded dignity. A more accurate conception of what Christians believed is that God wished to make available to each individual human person the opportunity which had been available to the human race as a whole, that to do this he sent his own Son to be the leader of the new community, but that this project required as its first step the overcoming of existing alienation and evil.[1]

If the Christian idea of redemption was that of liberation of mankind from its self-imposed limits, one still wonders what the point of the passion and death of Jesus could have been. Why did God not simply restore the condition of mankind to what it had been before and allow each individual to make his own personal choice for or against divine friendship? A Christian could answer that such a procedure would have involved less human cooperation. Christians believed that Jesus is a man and that in this *man* mankind is saved. This conception agrees with the principle of divine inefficiency explained in chapter twenty-one.

Still, why should Jesus have had to suffer and die? Christians did not offer a single coherent response to this question. I think that they might have proposed a number of points.

Christians believed that Jesus's human love of the Father and of his own fellowmen was central to his community-forming project. One cannot love in any true, human sense without undertaking and doing something which is loving, for love is realized in a performance in which the whole person is engaged, not merely in a choice or disposition of one's freedom. From this point of view one might suppose that Jesus willingly suffered and died for the sake of the love which was necessary to do so.

Another factor to consider is that Jesus would not have been fully human had he not shared everything belonging to the human condition compatible with his divine personality. To commit sin was precluded. But the human condition, so far as it concerned him, was a condition of subjection to sin and its consequences. Full sharing in this condition required Jesus to become a victim of sin, a subject of suffering; he applied to himself the prophecy regarding the suffering servant: "And he was reckoned among the wicked" (Is. 53:12; Lk. 22:37). His Incarnation was complete, Christians believed, only when he was humanly forsaken by God.

Another factor is that Jesus's project was to overcome sin and evil. To overcome it he had to undergo it. St. Paul expressed this idea: "For our sakes

God made him who did not know sin to be sin, so that in him we might become the very holiness of God" (2 Cor. 5:21).

Finally, if the work of redemption was to be left, insofar as possible, to mankind itself, then Jesus, as the first of many brothers and sisters to be united in friendship with God, had to establish the pattern and mark out the way which was to be followed by others. Their liberation would have to depend upon their giving up of self-imposed limitations—a seeming sacrifice of identity and autonomy. Christians believed that Jesus provided a demonstration that one must lose his life in order to achieve it: "He died for all so that those who live might live no longer for themselves, but for him who for their sakes died and was raised up" (2 Cor. 5:15).

Even if such reflections of Christians could remove something of the scandal and foolishness of the cross, however, there remains the scandal of the existing condition of this world and the foolishness of any optimistic religious formula for altering the human condition in a radical and favorable way.

I think it beyond question that Christians often built up false hopes and such false hopes generated disappointment. The false hopes were for immediate and effortless salvation from all human ills. When this salvation was not forthcoming, otherworldliness sapped efforts to deal with human evils by human efforts. These matters have been considered in chapter twenty. Christians would have been more faithful to their own beliefs, I think, had they considered the redemption as a work in which they were called to share to the full extent of their capabilities. In this case the practical difference Christian faith could make would be to sustain hope despite all difficulties, frustrations, and setbacks. It could demand the maximum contribution from each individual, including creativity in dealing with human problems by all humanly available means. If true, Christian doctrine would provide the assurance that such creative efforts would not come to the melancholy end of mankind's extinction without a memory.

But to look at the significance of Christianity solely in terms of redemption, even if this redemption is seen as a liberation and overcoming of human evil, and as a task in which humanity itself is called to participate in every way possible, is still to regard Christian faith primarily from a negative point of view. The positive side of the picture, as Christians understood it, also must be sketched if one is to grasp the whole significance of what Christians believed.

If one were to ask Christians, "Why is your faith so important to you?" one would receive many answers, some rather negative, but others more positive.

Some Christians have said that their faith enables them to face evil without despair. Many believers who suffer serious losses, such as the death of a loved one, claim that their faith permits them to accept the reality of evil and yet to hope that good will prevail. Believers who take this attitude often contrast their outlook with that of nonbelievers, who seem either naively optimistic about the prospects of various human panaceas—education, technical development, psychoanalysis, revolutionary transformation of society, and the like— or cynically pessimistic about man's nature and condition.

Christians also believed that their faith enabled them to face existential evil—their personal sinfulness—without despair. One experiences one's self as divided, as subject to an alien power which one cannot succeed in mastering. With faith Christians experienced a sense of acceptance by God which they felt made it possible for them to accept themselves, although imperfect (cf. Rom. 7:15-8:11). Many Christians believed that without faith they would have been driven either to complete inauthenticity in an attempt to rationalize their own sinfulness or to complete self-hatred in an attempt to disown it.

Accenting the positive

Christians also believed that their faith gave them an identity; by faith they thought that they belonged to something great and lasting: "In Christ the fullness of deity resides in bodily form. Yours is a share of this fullness . . . " (Col. 2:9). The concept of the Church, the Kingdom of God, the Body of Christ, is basic to all Christian thought. A believer felt his place in reality secured; it was to make his personal contribution to the work of the redemption by which all creation would be perfected and united in Christ.

Dogmatism in the bad sense and fanaticism have not been absent from christendom. However, many Christians prized the sense of liberty which their secure identity brought with it. When role-playing is no longer felt to be necessary, one can play roles playfully. Moral earnestness and rational lucidity were not condemned by such Christians, yet they often prized equally levity, fantasy, and fleshliness. One who becomes a child by abiding faith in divine providence is relieved of the unbearable burden of upholding all value and all meaning; relieved of this burden, one can feel at ease even at the brink of hell and the margin of absurdity.

Christians believed that the universality of the reality in which their identity was secured embraced everything true, everything good, everything becoming (cf. Phil. 4:8). Only evil was to be excluded from the Body of Christ, but evil itself was to be excluded, not by destroying the good which suffered from it, but by loving that good, overcoming its evil by love, redeeming it, and restoring it to honor. Thus Christians believed that their faith permitted them to be tolerant without compromise, to be liberal without relativism, and to be creative of the new without infidelity to the old.

Christians valued security; they thought that their faith had freed them from radical anxiety. But this liberty was not to be used as an excuse for laxity. Rather, it was to make possible feats of trust which would be heroic. The martyr could die for his faith, secure in the belief that he died with Christ and would rise again with him. Encouraged by faith, Christians felt that they could venture out upon the thin ice of interpersonal relationships constituted by the commitments of weak and sinful persons. A couple in love, for example, could commit themselves, for better or for worse until death, in the indissoluble compact of Christian marriage.

Apart from such moral values many Christians felt that their faith was important to them because they found in it other personal values. One of these was the esthetic delight of the Christian way of life, made concrete in forms of worship, in the material culture of religious places and objects, in the language of faith and prayer, and in the customs of Christian life. This esthetic delight merged with the satisfaction which many Christians experienced in acts of public and private devotion—a deep sense of peace and joy in private prayer and meditation, a sense of rapture and exaltation in communal celebration of magnificent liturgical rites.

Certain Christians emphasized the transcendence of their faith to reason; they said that they believed because of the absurdity of faith. But many other Christians found intellectual satisfaction in their faith. The source of contingent being, which is indicated by reason, is only a theoretical entity, a possible explanatory principle which can be speculated about on the model of human agency, until one finds a more direct access to the inner reality of the uncaused cause. Christians believed that faith supplied further information about that which all men by nature desire to know. Things hidden from the wise were made known to mere children (cf. Mt. 11:25-27). Moreover, faith in what God has revealed of himself was not thought by Christians to be the end, but rather the beginning, of intellectual satisfaction:

> Now we see indistinctly, as in a mirror; then we shall see face to face. My knowledge is imperfect now; then I shall know even as I am known. (1 Cor. 13:12)

Thus, according to Thomas Aquinas, the goal to which faith was a means is the perfect knowledge of God.[2] And, in general, Christians believed that faith would lead to everlasting life with God, a life in which intellectual satisfaction at least would play an important role.

If "everlasting life" is taken to mean no more than endless existence, not much different from human life as it is, one might well wonder whether there is not more reason to fear than to hope that life might go on forever. Even if one adds golden harps and the like, one wonders whether endless life would not become boring. Perhaps eventually one would wish he could die but find he could not.

In chapter eighteen (pages 283-284) I sketched two worlds. In one a person might do as he pleased, but he would lack human companionship and opportunity for creative self-fulfillment. In the other each person would share a common life and therefore be limited by the desires and interests of others, while in a genuine community to which each would contribute according to his own abilities. Christians seldom considered what sort of human life they might expect after the promised resurrection of the body. They did picture a community free of misery and death, free of hatred and war, and free of ignorance and want. They might have added a positive vision of a human community sharing together in the forms of activity which are possible to human persons and valuable for their own sake.

So far as I can see, nothing which Christians believed prevented them from envisioning a life in which human persons would continue forever to engage in conversation, to know each other more and more intimately, to better understand the world in the light of acquaintance with its creator, to make beautiful things, and to enjoy them. Human abilities, Christians believed, will at least remain what they are. If the purpose of creation is to express the creator's reality, then everlasting life, if there is such a thing, would seem to imply continuous expansion of human achievements. If this conception is in accord with what Christians believed, then Christians also could propose that their efforts in human activities and in building up the human community here and now are beginnings of the everlasting life to which they look forward.[3]

Such a vision of mankind's future, if implied by Christian belief, shows that this belief, if true, is important.

Yet this vision of mankind's future falls short of what Christians did believe and hope for. Their belief was that God intended human persons to share his own intimate life. Christians regarded themselves as adopted children of God, as coheirs with Christ to what belongs to him as Son of the Father (Rom. 8:14-17). They believed that through Jesus and in him they were invited to become one with the Father and the Spirit as these three are one with each other (cf. Jn. 14:9-21; 17:20-24).

In other words, Christians believed that human persons are invited to become members of the divine family itself. They believed that human persons are asked to love one another as the divine persons love one another, with a mutual love which *is* the divine community. Christians believed that such love is not merely sentiment or merely human benevolence and altruism, but is entry into divine life. "Everlasting life" was understood by Christians not to express unending continuation of life much like the present life, even improved, but to express a life truly divine. The "beatific vision" for which Christians hoped was not passive gazing upon God, but knowing him even as one is known.[4]

Christian philosophers and theologians unduly narrowed the hope of their faith. Intellectuals are thrilled at the prospect of doing for all eternity what *they* enjoy. Most people have other tastes and other interests. The knowledge of God for which Christians hoped cannot be limited to a very restricted, highly refined experience of human intellectual knowledge.

The Christian doctrines of the Incarnation, of the Trinity, and of the bodily presence of Christ in the Eucharist—if these doctrines are true—have their importance only in the context of the hope of Christians to share fully in the life of God himself.

The Christian conception of the Trinity was that God's life is not that of a self-enclosed entity like Aristotle's unmoved mover. Christians believed that God is a community of persons and that the community of uncreated persons, the Trinity-creator, is not an exclusive circle closed to others. The doctrine of the Trinity meant to Christians that divinity is capable of being communicated. Christians believed that they were already "sharers of the divine nature" (2 Pt. 1:4), and that everlasting life meant the full development of this sharing.

The Christian conception of the Incarnation was that divinity and humanity can be united in a single person. Christians believed that Jesus is both God and man. Jesus they considered a divine person, but they regarded his makeup as a model of the way in which human persons were intended by God to be made into members of the divine family. Human persons would share in the divine nature while remaining human, without losing anything of their humanity, as the Word of God shared human nature while remaining divine, without losing anything of his divinity (cf. Jn. 1:13, 3:3-6; Eph. 1:3-14). Through and in Christ all things were to be restored to God. Creation was to become an embodiment of divine life (cf. Col. 1:15-28, 2:9-12).

The Christian conception of the bodily presence of Christ in the Eucharist was that this divine person who shares humanity is united with human persons who share divinity in a community *both* human *and* divine (cf. 1 Cor. 10:16-17). Christians believed that in receiving the Eucharist they receive the body and blood of Jesus, enter into his passion and death, overcome sin and evil with him, become one with his glorious resurrection (cf. Jn. 6:25-58; 1 Cor. 11:23-26). Christians believed that bodily unity with Jesus is important because a human being is bodily; they did not consider the bodiliness of human community to be an accident or something evil.

Christians often found their hope so difficult to believe that they reduced its grandeur. They thought of living *with* God, while remaining merely human. They thought of receiving grace from God, but living a life supernatural only in being beyond unaided human abilities.[5]

Christians in the beginning had high hopes, not merely great expectations. But as the Christian doctrines of the Trinity and the Incarnation were hammered out, the Christian doctrine of life everlasting was allowed to atrophy.[6] Partaking of divine life, being one with the persons of the Trinity as they are with each other, being adopted into the divine family, and knowing God even as one is known—concepts all found in the New Testament—became for many Christians little more than metaphors. Christian life became more a matter of avoiding sin than of living the life of God.

I think that if the first Christians had been able to make use of the later concepts in which Christian doctrines developed, they might have said something like the following, which I propose as a hypothesis to be investigated.

Divinity is communicable. The Father, the Son, and the Spirit are God, uncreated and creating. Human persons who are adopted into divine life also are God, created not creating.[7] A human person who participates in divine life does not receive *part* of it—God cannot be divided—but the divinity itself, the very same reality which the Father, the Son, and the Spirit are.[8] The human person to whom divinity is communicated has it as his own and has it whole. By his divinity a human person, being a creature, cannot create. However, whatever is not incompatible with one's also being a creature—the reality of divine life which would be enjoyed by the divine persons even if they did not create—is possible for the human person who becomes one with the Father, the Son, and the Spirit as they are one with each other.

As Jesus is both God and man, so human persons who are his brothers by adoption are truly and fully both man and God. Just as the two natures of the Word Incarnate neither mingle nor are separate entities, so the two natures of a human person who becomes God do not mingle and yet are not separate entities. The difference nevertheless remains according to Christian belief, for Jesus is God by nature, Christians God by adoption. The unity of the two natures in his case is in his person; his personal being is that of creator, not that of creature. In those who become God by adoption the unity of the two natures is in their acts of love and knowledge.[9] Thus, even now human persons can love the Father, Son, Spirit, and human persons who share in divine life with a love which is truly divine as well as truly human. "Life everlasting" means the fulfillment of this love, the perfection of this community, in a complete life which is beyond human imagining:

> See what love the Father has bestowed on us
> In letting us be called children of God!
> Yet that is what we are.
> The reason the world does not recognize us
> is that it never recognized the Son.
> Dearly beloved, we are God's children now;
> what we shall later be has not yet come to light.

We know that when it comes to light we shall be like him,
for we shall see him as he is. (1 Jn. 3:1-2)

* * *

In the first chapter of this book I set out as a philosopher but made my personal profession of faith. It seems to me appropriate that I end as I began, speaking as a believer.

When the Word of God became man, he was a light in the darkness of the world. Yet to worldly eyes his life in the midst of the blazing glory of the Roman empire was insignificant. Faith rejoiced that the darkness of the world's light did not overcome the brightness of the divine light.

The Roman empire collapsed; its glory was eclipsed in the cultural barbarism which later humanists called "the dark ages." But in those centuries the light of faith spread throughout Europe. Renaissance humanism led to the Enlightenment; worldly brilliance reached an altogether new intensity. The age of faith was past; the beliefs of Christians were admitted only as myths, to be demythologized again and again.

Today the bright vision of the Enlightenment is gone. Worldly humanism stumbles uncertainly in a night of problems too large for merely human wisdom. A believer may hope, must hope, that the darkness of today's world portends a new dawn of the life which is the light of man.

In our time there was a man sent from God whose name was John—Pope John XXIII. Unlike the brilliant intellectuals of the world, John made no claim to possess the light the world so desperately needs. He was a humble servant of the light; he called for an *aggiornamento* of the Church of Christ, so that the Incarnate Word himself might once more send forth his Holy Spirit to enlighten human minds and to enkindle love in human hearts.

A philosopher must revere human reason and must never concede anything to obscurantism. I do not believe a Christian philosopher detracts from the honor due to human wisdom when he admits how dim it is in comparison with divine wisdom. Therefore, I hope nothing other for this book than that it be some contribution to the preparation John undertook to make.

"The One who gives this testimony says, 'Yes, I am coming soon!' Amen! Come, Lord Jesus!" (Rev. 22:20).

Notes

1: INTRODUCTION

1. Antony Flew, "The Presumption of Atheism," *Canadian Journal of Philosophy*, 2 (1972), pp. 29-46. Flew makes the common mistake of treating Thomas Aquinas's "Five Ways" as if they were proofs (p. 43). A way (*via*) is a method, not a proof. As scholars on Aquinas have pointed out, Thomas's "Five Ways" presuppose much of Aristotle's philosophy and are completed by other passages in Thomas's own works. The only attempt he ever made to prove that God exists was in his early work, *De ente et essentia*. See Joseph Owens, C.Ss.R., *An Elementary Christian Metaphysics* (Milwaukee: 1963), pp. 341-351.

2. Donald Evans, "A Reply to Flew's 'The Presumption of Atheism,'" *Canadian Journal of Philosophy*, 2 (1972), pp. 47-50.

3. Antony Flew, "Reply to Evans," *Canadian Journal of Philosophy*, 2 (1972), pp. 51-53.

4. Malcolm L. Diamond, *Contemporary Philosophy and Religious Thought: An Introduction to the Philosophy of Religion* (New York: 1974), pp. 286-287, speculates that any cosmological argument which proceeds from the universe as a whole *might* be guilty of a fallacy of composition; he takes this as an adequate reason to prefer a sceptical to a theistic view of the outcome of all such arguments. (The argument I propose in part two does not proceed from the universe as a whole.)

5. *Ibid.*, pp. 60-67, admits there are extraordinary occurrences at Lourdes, but rules out *a priori* a nonnaturalistic explanation on the ground that the admission of such explanations would force scientists to sacrifice their autonomy. He gives no independent reason for supposing that scientists should have the sort of autonomy required by his argument. I answer this argument of Diamond's in the final section of chapter twenty-two.

6. For example, *De potentia dei*, q. 1, a. 2, c. James F. Ross, "Aquinas and Philosophical Methodology," *Metaphilosophy*, 1 (1970), pp. 300-317, makes

several criticisms of Thomas's metaphysical overconfidence with which I would agree. For Thomas's use of *ipsum esse* see John P. Doyle, *"Ipsum Esse as God-Surrogate: The Point of Convergence of Faith and Reason for St. Thomas Aquinas," Modern Schoolman,* 50 (1973), pp. 293-296.

7. Gerald F. Kreyche, "The Soul-Body Problem in St. Thomas," *New Scholasticism,* 46 (1972), pp. 466-484, argues that Thomas's treatment of the soul is incoherent because he fails to synthesize ideas derived from diverse and incompatible sources. In the first part of chapter twenty-three I propose an alternative conception of the human person.

2: A CHILD LEARNS TO TALK ABOUT GOD

1. Ludwig Wittgenstein, *Lectures and Conversations on Aesthetics, Psychology and Religious Belief,* ed. Cyril Barrett (Oxford: 1966), p. 59. These lectures are based on students' notes but are generally accepted as representative of Wittgenstein's own views.

2. For example, a child told to be silent in church because "this is God's house" wonders whether the person conducting the service is God. If he asks, he will be told that this is not God, that God is invisible but present. A child's idea of *God* can be built up from such a starting point, but reduction of the concept to its origins does not indicate whether "God" refers to anything transcendent to the immanent domain of religious actions, feelings, and so on.

3. Wittgenstein, *loc. cit.*

3: THE NECESSITY FOR REASONING TOWARD GOD

1. Thomas Aquinas, *Summa contra gentiles,* 1, ch. 11.

2. See Sylvain Bromberger, "Why-Questions," in Baruch A. Brody, ed., *Readings in the Philosophy of Science* (Englewood Cliffs, N.J.: 1970), pp. 66-87.

3. Norman Kemp Smith, "Is Divine Existence Credible?" in D. Z. Phillips, ed., *Religion and Understanding* (New York: 1967), p. 120.

4. Illtyd Trethowan, "Professor N. H. G. Robinson and Natural Theology," *Religious Studies,* 9 (1973), pp. 463-468.

5. John Hick, *Faith and Knowledge,* 2nd ed. (Ithaca, New York: 1966), p. 115.

6. A classic but somewhat bizarre collection of religious phenomena is William James, *The Varieties of Religious Experience* (New York: 1929).

7. See R. M. Bucke, *Cosmic Consciousness: A Study of the Evolution of the Human Mind* (New York: 1969), pp. 70-74; Keith E. Yandell, *Basic Issues in the Philosophy of Religion* (Boston: 1971), pp. 124-132.

8. Ronald W. Hepburn, *Christianity and Paradox* (London: 1958), pp. 24-59.

9. E.g., C. B. Martin, *Religious Belief* (Ithaca, New York: 1959), pp. 64-94.

10. Paul Helm, *The Varieties of Belief* (London and New York: 1973), pp. 140-164.

11. George Mavrodes, *Belief in God: A Study in the Epistemology of Religion* (New York: 1970), pp. 70-73, suggests that simple inferences have a role in some people's "experience" of God.

12. James, *op. cit.,* p. 438.

13. William James, *The Will to Believe and Other Essays in Popular Philosophy* (New York and London: 1897), pp. 1-31.

14. Ludwig Wittgenstein, *Lectures and Conversations on Aesthetics, Psychology and Religious Belief,* ed. Cyril Barrett (Oxford: 1966), p. 59.

15. The position is summarized and its fidelity to Wittgenstein rejected by Patrick Sherry, "Is Religion a Form of Life?" *American Philosophical Quarterly,* 9 (1972), pp. 159-167.

16. Kai Nielsen, "Challenge of Wittgenstein," *Studies in Religion/Sciences Religieuses,* 3 (1973), pp. 29-46, argues that Wittgenstein himself was a Wittgensteinian-fideist. James Kellenberger, "The Language-Game View of Religion and Religious Certainty," *Canadian Journal of Philosophy,* 2 (1972), pp. 255-275, builds up the case by using Wittgenstein's *On Certainty.*

17. In addition to Nielsen and Kellenberger, another critic of the position is Michael Durrant, "Is the Justification of Religious Belief a Possible Enterprise?" *Religious Studies,* 9 (1973), pp. 449-455.

18. D. Z. Phillips, *Death and Immortality* (London: 1970), p. 55.

19. *Ibid.,* p. 60. W. Donald Hudson, *A Philosophical Approach to Religion* (London: 1974), pp. 94-99, criticizes Phillips along similar lines.

20. This reformulation is suggested by the position formulated by Hudson, *op. cit.,* pp. 101-105, as his own, but I do not attribute the position I formulate to him.

21. This argument is pressed by Kai Nielsen, *Scepticism* (London: 1973), p. 32 and *passim.*

22. Søren Kierkegaard, *Concluding Unscientific Postscript,* trans. D. F. Swenson and Walter Lowrie (Princeton: 1941), p. 182.

23. Karl Barth, *Credo* (New York: 1962), pp. 11-12.

24. *Ibid.* In chapter five, note 27 and accompanying text, I suggest how the requirements of the faith-position which Kierkegaard and Barth are trying to protect might be satisfied without their extreme antirationalism.

25. Terence Penelhum, *Problems of Religious Knowledge* (London: 1971), p. 47; see also pp. 34-35 and 149-155.

26. This position is basic in Thomas Aquinas; see *Summa theologiae,* 1, q. 1, a. 1.

27. For his rejection of natural theology see Rudolf Bultmann, *Faith and Understanding,* trans. Louise Pettibone Smith (New York and Evanston: 1969), pp. 53-65 and 313-331. A brief account of Bultmann's demythologizing is given by Van A. Harvey, *The Historian and the Believer: The Morality of Historical Knowledge and Christian Belief* (New York: 1969), pp. 139-146. Jesus's sole revelation according to Bultmann is that he is the revealer; the content of this revelation is simply its reproof to all human self-assertions and norms. Harvey asks (p. 144) whether this does not render Jesus dispensable. A helpful critique of Bultmann is found in Hugo Meynell, *Sense, Nonsense, and Christianity* (London and New York: 1964), pp. 250-270.

28. Langdon Gilkey, *Naming the Whirlwind: The Renewal of God-Language* (Indianapolis and New York: 1969), pp. 73-106; see especially note

30 on p. 101, in which Gilkey reports the observation that the third generation of neoorthodox theologians find divine transcendence problematic; the paradox is explained by the neoorthodox rejection of objectivity and the younger generation's refusal to accept the category of the noumenal.

29. D. Scheltens, "Reflections on Natural Theology," *International Philosophical Quarterly*, 11 (1971), p. 78.

30. The fullest single study is Jonathan Barnes, *The Ontological Argument* (London: 1972); works cited by him (pp. 92-98) lead to a large literature.

31. Hudson, *op. cit.*, pp. 39-40.

4: PROVISIONAL STATEMENT OF THE ARGUMENT

1. Thomas Aquinas, *De ente et essentia*, ch. 4.

2. Peter Achinstein, *Law and Explanation: An Essay in the Philosophy of Science* (Oxford: 1971), pp. 137-138.

3. One finds this sort of criticism in marxists, who attack positions as ideological if they reach the wrong conclusion regardless of the arguments proposed for them; in Dewey, who was always ready to dismiss difficult counterpositions; in positivists, confident in their own dogmas, dismissing metaphysics and theology wholesale. One notes the same tendency in public debate of issues having philosophical aspects. If the philosophical community is to be of any service to society, it must be opposed equally to fallacies regardless of the position they support.

4. J. J. C. Smart, "The Existence of God," in Antony Flew and Alasdair MacIntyre, eds., *New Essays in Philosophical Theology* (London: 1955), p. 46.

5. *Ibid.* The difficulties Smart mentions here will be dealt with in chapter seven.

6. Ludwig Wittgenstein, "A Lecture on Ethics," *Philosophical Review*, 74 (1965), pp. 7-12; cf. *Tractatus Logico-Philosophicus*, trans. D. F. Pears and B. F. McGuinness (London and New York: 1961), 5.552, 6.432, 6.4321, 6.44, 6.522.

7. Martin Heidegger, *An Introduction to Metaphysics*, trans. Ralph Manheim (New Haven: 1959), pp. 1-8. Manheim renders "die Seinden" by "essents"; I substitute "existing entities."

8. G. W. Leibniz, *Monadology and Other Philosophical Essays*, trans. Paul Schrecker and Anne Martin Schrecker (Indianapolis and New York: 1965), pp. 84-85; see James Kellenberger, *Religious Discovery, Faith, and Knowledge* (Englewood Cliffs, N.J.: 1972), p. 59. Leibniz himself sometimes uses the "something rather than nothing formula"; e.g., "The Principles of Nature and Grace," in T. V. Smith and Marjorie Grene, eds., *From Descartes to Kant* (Chicago: 1940), p. 364.

9. This point is clearly developed by D. M. Armstrong, *Belief, Truth and Knowledge* (Cambridge: 1973), p. 49, who points out that the problem arises from the self-reference of the proposition and so remains regardless of the theory of propositions proposed.

10. See Etienne Gilson, Thomas Langan, and Armand Maurer, C.S.B., *Recent Philosophy: Hegel to the Present* (New York: 1962), pp. 145-150.

11. Smart, *loc. cit.*

12. For the following treatment of the proposition I depend on Richard L. Cartwright, "Propositions," in Ronald J. Butler, ed., *Analytical Philosophy*, 1st ser. (Oxford: 1962), pp. 81-103. Cartwright replied to criticisms in "Propositions Again," *Noûs*, 2 (1968), pp. 229-246. Armstrong, *op. cit.*, pp. 38-49, makes a number of the same points, but I do not think he deals adequately with other relevant questions about propositions.

13. Peter Geach, *Reference and Generality* (Ithaca, New York: 1962), pp. 22-46, and *Logic Matters* (Berkeley and Los Angeles: 1972), pp. 44-61 and 289-301, discusses the inner structure of propositions and makes the distinction between names and predicables. A predicable differs from a predicate in that the former is part of the latter; I prefer to think of the proposition as a systematic unity of any number of names and predicables rather than of any number of names and one predicate. I do not use "concept" in Geach's sense. In general Geach wishes to stay closer to language than I think possible.

14. The theory I am sketching is aristotelian in a broad sense. I worked out Aquinas's theory of the proposition and treated a number of these points more fully in *Basic Oppositions in Logical Theory* (unpublished Ph.D. dissertation, University of Chicago, 1959), pp. 175-196.

15. Roger Wertheimer, "Conditions," *Journal of Philosophy*, 65 (1968), pp. 355-364, points out that many current uses of "conditions" in philosophy depart from the meanings the word has in ordinary language. I use the word in the sense he clarifies. I also use the expression, somewhat clumsy and redundant, "prerequisite conditions." This expression leads me to use *prerequisites* and *requirements*. If these concepts seem to be begging questions against empiricist and kantian theories of causality, these problems will be taken care of in part three.

16. *Dc must meet the criterion*—in ordinary religious language this means that God's causing anything is not a necessary state of affairs; God creates freely. Not the uncaused cause—God the creator—but the uncaused entity—God—is the necessary being.

17. I am saying that even in the case of God, for him to be what he is is not the same as for him to obtain. This does not mean that God is divided; the real distinction as explained above does not mean that there are two nameable entities or that *x*'s obtaining is a state of affairs. God has what it takes to be known with knowledge like ours; we can know that he is without knowing what he is. If the distinction is given up at this point, either one has no knowledge of God at all or some minimal, positive essential knowledge. Comparison of the position I am developing with that of Thomas Aquinas is not as easy as might appear on the surface, since he works with *esse; obtains* is not precisely the same as *exists*.

18. The following objection might occur to a reader. If *Dc* is contingent because it is the cause of a contingent state of affairs, why is *D* itself not also contingent, since *D* is required for *Dc* to obtain. This question will be treated in chapter seventeen.

5: DEVELOPMENT OF THE ARGUMENT

1. Frederick Copleston and Bertrand Russell, "A Debate on the Existence of God," in John Hick, ed., *The Existence of God* (New York and London: 1964), p. 175.

2. Barry Miller, "The Contingency Argument," *The Monist,* 54 (1970), pp. 368-371, develops this point with unusual clarity.

3. Paul Edwards, "The Cosmological Argument," in Donald R. Burrill, ed., *The Cosmological Arguments: A Spectrum of Opinion* (Garden City, N.Y.: 1967), pp. 114-122.

4. G. W. Leibniz, *Leibniz Selections,* ed. Philip P. Wiener (New York: 1951), p. 539; the version quoted is from the *Monadology,* sec. 32.

5. Richard Taylor, *Metaphysics,* 2nd ed. (Englewood Cliffs, N.J.: 1974), pp. 103-105.

6. See Etienne Gilson and Thomas Langan, *Modern Philosophy: Descartes to Kant* (New York: 1963), pp. 145-171. Leibniz is talking about names rather than about predicables, but the distinction collapses if either is disposed of. The ultimate implications of Leibniz's position are worked out by Hegel.

7. Adrian Webster, "The Cosmic Background Radiation," *Scientific American,* 231 (August, 1974), p. 31.

8. James F. Ross, *Philosophical Theology* (Indianapolis and New York: 1969), pp. 279-304, made me aware of the problem.

9. Joseph M. Boyle, Jr., Germain Grisez, and Olaf Tollefsen, *Free Choice: A Self-Referential Argument,* forthcoming, discusses the "rule of intelligibility" in chapter six and answers the objection against free choice grounded in it in chapter ten.

10. The phrasing is taken from Edwards, *op. cit.,* p. 118, but the same point is made by many authors.

11. Roger C. Rosenkrantz, "On Explanation," *Synthese,* 20 (1969), pp. 337-340.

12. Many philosophers of science advocate a single model, but they do not all advocate the same model. One author who provides a more generous view of possibilities of explanation even within science is Ernest Nagel, *The Structure of Science: Problems in the Logic of Scientific Explanation* (New York: 1961), pp. 15-28; Nagel also provides more information about alternatives to his own positions than do most authors writing on this subject.

13. The objection mentioned here is dealt with in chapter seven. Reduction to a single model of explanation is primarily a strategy of positivists. Although discredited or seriously called into question in philosophy of science, the idea that all explanation must be of one sort is freely invoked in philosophy of religion.

14. P. AE. Hutchings, "God and Existence," *Sophia,* 2 (1963), pp. 5-8, makes a useful distinction between "taking for granted" and "accepting as given." Ernest Nagel, *op. cit.,* pp. 181-202, explains how Newton's laws function as principles in classical mechanics; Stephen Toulmin, *The Philosophy of Science* (New York: 1960), pp. 20-25 and 83-86, explains that the rectilinear propagation of light is indefeasible and more like an axiom than an ordinary law in optics; these and other examples are discussed in an illuminating article by John F. Miller, III, "The Logic of Scientific and Religious Principles," *Sophia,* 12 (1973), pp. 11-23.

15. Thomas S. Kuhn, *The Structure of Scientific Revolutions* (Chicago and London: 1962), pp. 110-134, expands on this point.

16. Max Black, *Margins of Precision: Essays in Logic and Language* (Ithaca and London: 1970), pp. 21-22.

17. *Ibid.,* pp. 86-88.

18. Henry E. Kyburg, Jr., *Probability and Inductive Logic* (Toronto and London: 1970), p. 78.

19. Michael Slote, *Reason and Scepticism* (London and New York: 1970), pp. 99-100.

20. I will say more about rationality norms in the third section of chapter nine. The necessary normativity of rationality norms is discussed in sections D and E of chapter eight of the work cited in note 9 above. Rationality norms cannot be logically necessary truths or they could not regulate *choices* in thinking; they must be cognitive or they would not ground assertions and exclude counterpositions; they cannot depend upon subjective purposes or they could not be used to settle disagreements among people having different purposes; they cannot be laws of nature or their violation would not be a matter of choice and would be a mere psychological abnormality.

21. "The First Principle of Practical Reason: A Commentary on the *Summa theologiae,* 1-2, Question 94, Article 2," *Natural Law Forum,* 10 (1965), pp. 168-201; coauthored with Russell Shaw, *Beyond the New Morality: The Responsibilities of Freedom* (Notre Dame and London: 1974), pp. 64-148.

22. Michael Durrant, *The Logical Status of 'God' and the Function of Theological Sentences* (London: 1973). R. Attfield, "The Individuality of God," *Sophia,* 10 (1971), pp. 20-27, criticizes an earlier version of a number of the arguments Durrant offers, expecially pointing out that "God" can function now in one way and again in another.

23. *Midrash Rabbah,* trans. H. Freedman and Maurice Simon (London: 1939), vol. 1, p. 313 (ch. xxxix, 1; commenting on Genesis 12:1). See Abraham Joshua Heschel, *God in Search of Man* (New York: 1955), pp. 113 and 367.

24. Aristotle, *Metaphysica* xii, 1074b1-14.

25. *Ibid.,* 1072b25-29.

26. *Ethica Nichomachea* x, 1177b31-1178a2.

27. Plato not only proposes arguments which lead to the Good, although he does not define it, in the *Republic* (cf. A. E. Taylor, *Plato: The Man and His Work* [New York: 1956], pp. 231-232, 285-289, 441-442, and 489-493), he also argues throughout his works for such a principle, which is the contradictory of *homo mensura*. Of course, "god" is not used by Plato to identify this principle, but it is perhaps significant how often this identification has been made.

28. In chapter three, notes 22-24 and accompanying text, I cited and discussed the position of Kierkegaard and Barth on the absolute priority of faith. I think the present consideration would meet the demands of the faith-position they wished to protect, but without the unnecessary antirationalsim in which they engage.

6: THE EMPIRICIST ALTERNATIVE

1. A Hume bibliography and general introduction to his thought may be found in D. G. C. MacNabb, "Hume," *The Encyclopedia of Philosophy,* vol. 4, pp. 74-90.

2. This reformulation is given by A. G. N. Flew, "Hume," in D. J. O'Connor, ed., *A Critical History of Western Philosophy* (New York, Toronto, London: 1964), p. 257.

3. *Ibid.*, p. 262.

7: CRITICISM OF EMPIRICISM

1. A. G. N. Flew, "Hume," in D. J. O'Connor, ed., *A Critical History of Western Philosophy* (New York, Toronto, and London: 1964), p. 257.

2. A. J. Ayer, *Language, Truth and Logic,* 2nd ed. (London and New York: 1952), pp. 35-38 and 114-120.

3. Keith E. Yandell, *Basic Issues in the Philosophy of Religion* (Boston: 1971), pp. 3-42, reviews developments in verificationism.

4. Regarding self-referential arguments see Joseph M. Boyle, Jr., "Self-Referential Inconsistency, Inevitable Falsity, and Metaphysical Argumentation," *Metaphilosophy,* 3 (1972), pp. 26-44.

5. The argument presented here is adapted with slight modifications from one stated in Joseph M. Boyle, Jr., Germain Grisez, and Olaf Tollefsen, *Free Choice: A Self-Referential Argument,* forthcoming, chapter seven.

6. Antony Flew, "Theology and Falsification," in Antony Flew and Alasdair MacIntyre, eds., *New Essays in Philosophical Theology* (London: 1955), pp. 96-99.

7. This point is made by a severe critic of cosmological argumentation, Ronald W. Hepburn, *Christianity and Paradox* (London: 1958), p. 12.

8. In Ayer, *op. cit.*, pp. 15-16, which is the second edition of the work, Ayer admits that the verification criterion is a definition; he rejects the idea that it might be a mere empirical hypothesis. He says it is not wholly arbitrary—which means it has some sort of necessity, but Ayer does not say what sort. He still thinks metaphysics can be excluded; however, its arguments must be analyzed in detail. He does not say how this analysis is to be done, but one can assume he intends to use the verification criterion in some form. In a radio debate with F. C. Copleston, S.J. ("Logical Positivism: A Debate," in A. Pap and Paul Edwards, eds., *A Modern Introduction to Philosophy* [New York: 1965], p. 755), Ayer says that the verification criterion "can be derived from an analysis of understanding." But he does not say whether he means by analysis of the word "understanding" or by empirical psychology; obviously neither will do.

9. Jerome A. Miller, *The Irrefutability of Metaphysical Truths* (unpublished Ph.D. dissertation, Georgetown University, 1973), examines a large number of empiricist authors and finds the unity of their antimetaphysics in their exclusion of extrapropositional necessary truths. Miller's work first made clear to me the importance of generalizing from Ayer to take in the whole movement with the stripped-down version of empiricism.

10. Ludwig Wittgenstein, *Tractatus Logico-Philosophicus,* trans. D. F. Pears and B. F. McGuinness (London and New York: 1961), 6.54, 7.

11. Max Black, *A Companion to Wittgenstein's Tractatus* (Ithaca, New York: 1964), p. 379.

12. *Tractatus,* 6.44, 6.45, 6.522.

13. Antony Flew, *God and Philosophy* (London: 1966), pp. 88-89; Terence Penelhum, *Religion and Rationality: An Introduction to the Philosophy of Religion* (New York: 1971), p. 36.

14. A. Michotte, *The Perception of Causality* (London: 1963), p. 265.

15. Jerrold L. Aronson, "Explanations without Laws," *Journal of Philosophy*, 66 (1969), pp. 541-557.

16. See B. A. Brody, "Toward an Aristotelian Theory of Scientific Explanation," *Philosophy of Science*, 39 (1972), pp. 20-31.

17. In Section VII, Part 1, note 3.

18. Richard Taylor, "Causation," *Encyclopedia of Philosophy*, vol. 2, p. 63.

19. Miller, *op. cit.*, pp. 282-283, rightly points out that for Aristotle, knowing that something is, is not equivalent to knowing its essence, but is equivalent to knowing that it has an essence. Carried to its conclusion, this means that knowing the essence of something fully would include knowing that it is. Cf. *Posterior analytics* ii, 89b22-94a18. Hegel carries out this line of thought to its ultimate implications.

20. *Dialogues concerning Natural Religion*, Section IX.

21. For a discussion and critique see Barry Miller, "Making Sense of 'Necessary Existence,' " *American Philosophical Quarterly*, 11 (1974), pp. 47-54.

22. Penelhum, *op. cit.*, pp. 40-41.

8: THE ALTERNATIVE OF A CRITIQUE OF KNOWLEDGE

1. Immanuel Kant, *Prolegomena to Any Future Metaphysics*, trans. Lewis White Beck (New York: 1951), pp. 108-109.

2. Kant's development can be followed in his early works: *Inaugural Dissertation and Early Writings on Space*, trans. J. Handyside (Chicago: 1929), pp. 52-66.

3. *Prolegomena*, p. 105.

4. Immanuel Kant, *Critique of Pure Reason*, trans. Norman Kemp Smith (London, New York, and Toronto: 1965), B xix-xxxvii. This and subsequent references to the *Critique* are to the pages of the German editions; the page numbers are carried in the margins of Smith's translation.

5. *Prolegomena*, p. 105.

6. *Ibid.*, pp. 88-89.

7. *Critique*, A 426-532; B 454-560.

8. Norman Kemp Smith, *A Commentary to Kant's 'Critique of Pure Reason'*, 2nd ed. (New York: 1962), pp. 485-492; P. F. Strawson, *The Bounds of Sense* (London: 1966), pp. 175-206.

9. Strawson, *op. cit.*, pp. 200-205. The fact that scientific cosmology is doing what Kant forbade is not insignificant. To what extent can Kant's false assumptions be removed?

10. *Critique*, A 538-558; B 566-586; this section is discussed in detail in Joseph M. Boyle, Jr., Germain Grisez, and Olaf Tollefsen, *Free Choice: A Self-Referential Argument*, forthcoming, chapter five.

11. A 452-455; B 480-483.

12. A 453, 455; B 481, 483.

13. A 559-561; B 587-589.
14. A 584; B 612.
15. A 584-590; B 612-618.
16. A 592-602; B 620-630.
17. A 600; B 628.
18. A 601; B 629.
19. A 603-608; B 631-636.
20. A 609-610; B 637-638.
21. A 614-620; B 642-648.
22. A 639; B 667.

9: CRITICISM OF CRITIQUE AS METAPHYSICS

1. Immanuel Kant, *Critique of Pure Reason,* trans. Norman Kemp Smith (London, New York, and Toronto: 1965), A 612; B 640.
2. A 203; B 248-249.
3. Robert Paul Wolff, *Kant's Theory of Mental Activity* (Cambridge, Mass.: 1963), pp. 281-282, suggests that Kant's difficulties with causal sequence might be solved by reducing causality to the functional conception which Kant treats as interaction; however, Wolff's treatment of this conception (pp. 286-287) indicates that this route of escape also is blocked. The suggestion is of course a version of the empiricist proposal to replace causality with correlation.
4. A 546-547; B 574-575.
5. Wolff, *op. cit.,* pp. 164-174, summarizes the problem and seems to think Kant can escape from it, but I find nothing later in Wolff's book which vindicates this hope. Norman Kemp Smith, *A Commentary on Kant's 'Critique of Pure Reason',* 2nd ed. (New York: 1962), pp. 611-638, shows that in his last work Kant was wrestling with this problem, evading it, and moving toward a more complete idealism. H. J. Paton, *Kant's Metaphysic of Experience,* vol. 1 (London and New York: 1936), p. 422, makes clear that Kant does hold that the unknown thing in itself literally causes its appearances. Paton is the most sympathetic of Kant's commentators.
6. A 592-593; B 620-621.
7. A 601; B 629.
8. A 695-696; B 723-724.
9. Immanuel Kant, *Prolegomena to Any Future Metaphysics,* trans. Lewis White Beck (New York: 1951), pp. 105-106. Paul Tillich, "The Meaning and Justification of Religious Symbols," in Sidney Hook, ed., *Religious Experience and Truth* (New York: 1961), pp. 3-11, takes a position strongly influenced by Kant; several others in the same volume criticize this position.
10. *Prolegomena,* p. 106.
11. A 669-702; B 697-730.
12. A 508-509; B 536-537.
13. A 642-668; B 670-696.
14. A 474; B 502.
15. A 642-648; B 670-676.
16. A 651; B 679.

17. A 647; B 675.

18. A 680; B 708.

19. A 682-688; B 710-716.

20. A 644-645; B 672-673.

21. A 689-694; B 717-722.

22. P. F. Strawson, *The Bounds of Sense* (London: 1966), p. 267.

23. *Ibid.*, p. 266, illustrates a logical deduction: "e.g., from any assertion to the effect that a certain individual has a certain property there follows an assertion of the existence of something having that property." Such a statement can be read as syntactical. However, to begin to distinguish sense from reference by saying that two expressions having different senses can nevertheless be used to refer to the same *thing* is to use "thing" to refer to extrapropositional entities, but without any accompanying empirical concept. Strawson himself elsewhere makes statements such as: "Since anything whatever can be identifyingly referred to, being a possible object of identifying reference does not distinguish any class or type of items or entities from any other" (*Individuals: An Essay in Descriptive Metaphysics* [London: 1959], p. 137). Carnap, of course, attempted to absorb semantics into syntax; Carnap's attempt did not succeed; see Jerome A. Miller, *The Irrefutability of Metaphysical Truths* (unpublished Ph.D. dissertation, Georgetown University, 1973), pp. 203-208.

10: THE ABSOLUTE IDEALIST ALTERNATIVE

1. *The Logic of Hegel*, trans. William Wallace, 2nd ed. (Oxford: 1892), sec. 44, p. 92.

2. *Ibid.*, sec. 124, pp. 231-232.

3. *Ibid.*, sec. 45, pp. 93-94; sec. 48, pp. 97-101; sec. 119, pp. 219-223.

4. G. W. F. Hegel, *The Phenomenology of Mind*, trans. J. B. Baillie (New York and Evanston: 1967), p. 80.

5. *Ibid.*, p. 765.

6. *Ibid.*, pp. 75-86.

7. *Ibid.*, pp. 756-783. On Hegel's transposition of Christian faith into philosophy see Emil L. Fackenheim, *The Religious Dimension of Hegel's Thought* (Bloomington and London: 1967), pp. 160-219; James Collins, *The Emergence of Philosophy of Religion* (New Haven and London: 1967), pp. 330-342.

8. Hegel, *Phenomenology*, pp. 105-107 and 115-116.

9. G. W. F. Hegel, *Lectures on the Proofs of the Existence of God*, in *Lectures on the Philosophy of Religion*, trans. E. B. Speirs and J. Burdon Sanderson, vol. 3 (London: 1962), p. 188; see Collins, *op. cit.*, pp. 293-310.

10. *Logic*, sec. 50, p. 103.

11. *Ibid.*, p. 104.

12. *Ibid.*, p. 106.

13. *Lectures on the Proofs*, p. 195.

14. *Ibid.*, pp. 228-230.

15. *Ibid.*, p. 232.

16. *Ibid.*, pp. 224-236.

17. *Ibid.,* p. 260.
18. *Ibid.,* pp. 261-274.
19. *Ibid.,* pp. 281-292.
20. *Ibid.,* p. 303; cf. *Hegel's Philosophy of Mind,* trans. William Wallace (Oxford: 1894), sec. 564, p. 176.
21. *Lectures on the Proofs,* pp. 313-327.
22. *Ibid.,* pp. 353-367; *Logic,* sec. 51, pp. 107-109.

11: CRITICISM OF ABSOLUTE IDEALISM

1. *The Logic of Hegel,* trans. William Wallace, 2nd ed. (Oxford: 1892), sec. 119, pp. 219-223.
2. G. R. G. Mure, *An Introduction to Hegel* (Oxford: 1940), pp. 139-141.
3. Aristotle, *Metaphysica* iv, 1005b35-1007a19.
4. *Logic,* sec. 24, pp. 49-52.
5. *Ibid.,* sec. 91-95 and 119-121, pp. 171-179 and 219-229. See also W. T. Stace, *The Philosophy of Hegel* (New York, Toronto, and London: 1955), pp. 297-313.
6. G. W. F. Hegel, *The Phenomenology of Mind,* trans. J. B. Baillie (New York and Evanston: 1967), pp. 80 ff.
7. *Ibid.,* pp. 149-160.
8. *Ibid.; Hegel's Philosophy of Nature,* trans. A. V. Miller (Oxford: 1970), sec. 250, pp. 24-27.
9. *Ibid.*
10. G. R. G. Mure, *A Study of Hegel's Logic* (Oxford: 1950), pp. 294-323.
11. G. W. F. Hegel, *Lectures on the Philosophy of Religion,* trans. E. B. Speirs and J. Burdon Sanderson, vol. 1 (London: 1962), pp. 63-64.
12. This argument against Hegel was worked out by Joseph M. Boyle, Jr., Germain Grisez, and Olaf Tollefsen, *Free Choice: A Self-Referential Argument,* forthcoming, chapter five.
13. James Collins, *God in Modern Philosophy* (Chicago: 1959), p. 213, maintains that Hegel holds the two sides together by sheer resolve.
14. Emil L. Fackenheim, *The Religious Dimension of Hegel's Thought* (Bloomington and London: 1967), pp. 116-159, makes a persuasive case for this thesis.

12: RELATIVISM AS A METAPHYSICAL ALTERNATIVE

1. Karl Löwith, *From Hegel to Nietzsche: The Revolution in Nineteenth-Century Thought* (New York, Chicago, and San Francisco: 1964), pp. 53-135.
2. James Collins, *God in Modern Philosophy* (Chicago: 1959), pp. 238-257.
3. *Hegel's Philosophy of Right,* trans. T. M. Knox (Oxford: 1942), pp. 12-13.

4. I do not know whether Wittgenstein himself indulged in metaphysics. Max Black, *Margins of Precision* (Ithaca and London: 1970), p. 268, says at the end of a chapter which sympathetically expounds Wittgenstein's philosophy of language: "Wittgenstein will not accept the language games of his philosophical predecessors as a form of life that is simply 'given'—he has his own language game, and a better one. But then the *critical* function of philosophical activity needs to be brought into the open—and not concealed behind a curtain of allegedly descriptive neutrality."

13: CRITICISM OF METAPHYSICAL RELATIVISM

1. The topic of fatalism is treated by Joseph M. Boyle, Jr., Germain Grisez, and Olaf Tollefsen, *Free Choice: A Self-Referential Argument*, forthcoming, chapter four.

2. W. Donald Hudson, *A Philosophical Approach to Religion* (London: 1974), p. 104. I refer to Hudson only for the passage quoted. The dialectic which follows is not a point-by-point critique of his view, which I find hard to understand.

3. I am not *trying* to interpret and criticize the *Philosophical Investigations;* therefore what follows ought not to be taken as a misinterpretation of Wittgenstein. I am trying to argue—partly, I think, in agreement with him—against a version of metaphysical relativism widely taken to represent his views. Patrick J. Bearsley, S.M., "Aquinas and Wittgenstein on the Grounds of Certainty," *Modern Schoolman*, 51 (May, 1974), pp. 316-334, interprets Wittgenstein as holding a conception of criteria nearer to that which I am defending than to that which underlies the demand I reject as unreasonable.

14: LIMITS OF REDUCTIONISM

1. Thomas Aquinas, *Expositio in libros ethicorum Aristotelis*, lib. 1, lect. 1.

2. See Germain Grisez and Russell Shaw, *Beyond the New Morality: The Responsibilities of Freedom* (Notre Dame and London: 1974), pp. 76-149.

3. Joseph M. Boyle, Jr., Germain Grisez, and Olaf Tollefsen, *Free Choice: A Self-Referential Argument*, forthcoming.

16: WHAT CAN BE AFFIRMED OF THE UNCAUSED ENTITY

1. Alastair McKinnon, " 'Existence' in 'the Existence of God'," *American Philosophical Quarterly*, 9 (1972), p. 351: "I cannot say 'God exists' precisely because I cannot think of him as not existing."

2. Mary Hesse, "The Explanatory Function of Metaphor," in Yehoshua Bar-Hillel, ed., *Logic, Methodology, and Philosophy of Science* (Amsterdam: 1965), p. 259.

3. Ian Ramsey, *Religious Language* (New York: 1963).

4. Cynthia B. Cohen, "The Logic of Religious Language," *Religious Studies,* 9 (1973), pp. 143-155.

17: RELATIONAL PREDICATIONS ABOUT THE UNCAUSED ENTITY

1. Joseph M. Boyle, Jr., Germain Grisez, and Olaf Tollefsen, *Free Choice: A Self-Referential Argument,* forthcoming.

2. Max Black, *Models and Metaphors: Studies in Language and Philosophy* (Ithaca, New York: 1962), pp. 219-243. Among other helpful points Black distinguishes between a model and a metaphor, while defending the usefulness of both as means of knowing. See also Mary Hesse, *Science and the Human Imagination* (London: 1954), pp. 134-146; *Models and Analogies in Science* (Notre Dame: 1966).

18: HUMAN FREEDOM IS COMPATIBLE WITH CREATURELINESS

1. See Germain Grisez and Russell Shaw, *Beyond the New Morality: The Responsibilities of Freedom* (Notre Dame and London: 1974), pp. 76-136.

2. See, for example, Psalm 19:9-11.

3. "Your decrees are forever just; they give me discernment that I may live" (Ps. 119:144); cf. Jn. 14:15-17; Rm. 7:7-12; Gal. 3:24; 1 Tim. 1:5; Heb. 8:10.

4. Rev. 21:1-7; cf. Is. 65:17-25.

5. Jn. 1:12; Rm. 8:14-17; 2 Cor. 6:18; Gal. 4:1-7; 2 Pet. 1:3-11.

19: EVIL IS REAL BUT IS NOT CREATED

1. Roger Trigg, *Pain and Emotion* (Oxford: 1970), p. 60. See also G. H. von Wright, *The Varieties of Goodness* (London: 1963), p. 57: "Pain is evil, I would say, only to the extent that it is disliked or shunned or unwanted."

2. Trigg, *op. cit.,* p. 166, describes the case of a young woman who did not enjoy a normal sense of pain: "As a result she suffered considerable physical damage regularly, and it merely went unnoticed or was regarded with indifference."

3. F. J. J. Buytendijk, *Pain,* trans. Eda O'Shiel (London: 1961), pp. 141-163, offers a suggestive analysis of pain from a phenomenological point of view. He sees its value as existential more than physical; man becomes aware of himself as a person, extends life into what is new, and manifests love by suffering pain. See also John Hick, *Evil and the God of Love* (New York: 1966), pp. 328-372.

4. Edward H. Madden and Peter H. Hare, *Evil and the Concept of God* (Springfield, Ill.: 1968), pp. 4-5.

5. *Ibid.,* pp. 32-34.

6. I have treated the problems of value theory more fully in: "The First

Principle of Practical Reason: A Commentary on the *Summa theologiae*, 1-2, Question 94, Article 2," *Natural Law Forum*, 10 (1965), pp. 168-201; "The Value of a Life: A Sketch," *Philosophy in Context*, 2 (1973), pp. 7-15; with Russell Shaw, *Beyond the New Morality: The Responsibilities of Freedom* (Notre Dame and London: 1974), pp. 55-96.

7. However, some theists have appealed to emotivism to solve the problem of evil; see Charles F. Kielkopf, "Emotivism as the Solution to the Problem of Evil," *Sophia*, 9 (1970), pp. 34-38.

8. Terence Penelhum, *Religion and Rationality: An Introduction to the Philosophy of Religion* (New York: 1971), pp. 227-228, invokes a subjectivist theory of value against the explanation of evil as privation; he invokes the opinion of "most philosophers"—meaning, of course, most who agree with him—as authority.

9. Mt. 13:19; 2 Cor. 4:4; Jn. 8:44; 1 Pet. 5:8.

10. This very clearly is the assumption of Alvin Plantinga in his various works on the free-will defense; see, e.g., "Which Worlds Could God Have Created?" *Journal of Philosophy*, 70 (1973), pp. 539-552.

11. The point is shown by Dewey J. Hoitenga, Jr., "Logic and the Problem of Evil," *American Philosophical Quarterly*, 4 (1967), pp. 114-126. It must be noticed that traditional Christian doctrine held that in heaven the blessed will be confirmed in goodness without loss of their freedom of choice. Thus it is not clear why God could not have created rational creatures preserved by grace from all sin—as Roman Catholics believe he did in the case of the Blessed Virgin Mary. Christians believed that the sin of Adam was a "happy fault" insofar as God brought out of it the greater good of the redemption.

12. See Nelson Pike, "Hume on Evil," *Philosophical Review*, 72 (1963), pp. 180-197; Keith E. Yandell, *Basic Issues in the Philosophy of Religion* (Boston: 1971), pp. 43-52.

13. Madden and Hare, *op. cit.*, p. 68.

14. Penelhum, *op. cit.*, p. 233.

15. Thomas Aquinas, *Summa theologiae*, 1, q. 25, a. 3. Thomas tries to argue that since God is *ipsum esse*, his power extends to whatever can be. I think this argument assumes that one can treat a metaconcept as if it were a first-level predicable.

16. These arguments are developed more fully by Peter Geach, "Omnipotence," *Philosophy*, 48 (1973), pp. 7-20.

17. Thomas Aquinas, *De potentia dei*, q. 5, a. 4.

18. I am taking for granted the even more basic point of Jewish and Christian faith that God has no obligations to anyone, since there is no one prior to creation to whom he might have obligations; those who make a point of evil often evidence a sort of resentment, as if they might have existed to enjoy the best of all possible worlds if they had not actually been created by God in this one. This point is developed by Robert Merrihew Adams, "Must God Create the Best?" *Philosphical Review*, 81 (1972), pp. 317-332. See also John King-Farlow and William Niels Christensen, *Faith and the Life of Reason* (Dordrecht, Holland: 1972), pp. 131-135.

19. David Hume, *Dialogues Concerning Natural Religion*, X (New York and London: 1966), pp. 61-70, treats the problem of evil in the context of a

refutation of an argument from design. Obviously if one appeals to order in the world to argue that God exists—which I do not—then one must admit that disorder in the world argues that God does not exist.

20: RELIGION NEED NOT CONFLICT WITH HUMANISTIC VALUES

1. Germain Grisez and Russell Shaw, *Beyond the New Morality: The Responsibilities of Freedom* (Notre Dame and London: 1974), pp. ix-137 and 190-200.

2. *Summa contra gentiles*, 3, chs. 121-122; *Summa theologiae*, 1-2, q. 19, aa. 9-10. Contrast this position with that of William of Ockham; see James Kevin McDonnell, *Religion and Ethics in the Philosophy of William of Ockham* (unpublished Ph.D. dissertation, Georgetown University, 1971), pp. 74-115.

3. The doctrine of the fall is not peculiarly Christian; the chief difference between Jewish and Christian doctrine is the remedy—viz, Torah or Christ. See William D. Davies, *Paul and Rabbinic Judaism*, 2nd ed. (London: 1958), pp. 31 ff.

4. Ludwig Feuerbach, *The Essence of Christianity*, trans. George Eliot (New York, Evanston and London: 1957), p. 226.

5. *Ibid.*, p. 26.

6. *Summa theologiae*, 1, q. 1, a. 8, ad 2; q. 2, a. 2, ad 1; q. 62, a. 5, c.; on divine law and natural law: 1-2, q. 90, a. 2, ad 1.

7. A critical examination of this point with references to relevant texts and various interpretations is in my article "Man, the Natural End of," *New Catholic Encyclopedia*, vol. 9, pp. 132-138.

8. *Summa theologiae*, 1-2, q. 94, a. 2; see my essay: "The First Principle of Practical Reason: A Commentary on the *Summa theologiae*, 1-2, Question 94, Article 2," *Natural Law Forum*, 10 (1965), pp. 168-201.

9. Vatican Council II, *The Church in the Modern World*, section 22.

10. Feuerbach, *op. cit.*, p. 260.

11. Feuerbach identifies what he takes to be Luther's position with the Christian position. The Council of Trent had a different idea; see Denzinger-Schönmetzer, *Enchiridion symbolorum definitionum et declarationum de rebus fidei et morum*, 34th ed, secs. 1520-1583.

12. Konrad Lorenz, *On Aggression*, trans. Marjorie Kerr Wilson (New York: 1966), pp. 236-274, describes the phenomena in question, although he does not take a religious perspective on them.

13. The days of the Messiah and of the world to come were distinguished from each other; see, e.g., Berakoth 34a, *The Babylonian Talmud: Seder Zera'im*, trans. I. Epstein (London: 1948), p. 215.

14. Vatican Council II, *Decree on the Apostolate of the Laity*, section 5.

15. Vatican Council II, *The Church in the Modern World*, section 39.

16. Vatican Council II, *Decree on the Apostolate of the Laity*, section 7. By citing a council of the Roman Catholic Church, I do not mean to suggest that this is not a view shared by most Christians, but rather that a fairly conservative Christian body has officially embraced the position.

21: DEVELOPING CREATURES AND A PERFECT CREATOR

1. Aristotle, *Metaphysica* xii, 1071b3-1072b29, argues to the reality of a primary principle of motion which he calls "God." Thomas Aquinas, *Summa contra gentiles*, 1, ch. 13, and elsewhere, maintains Aristotle's argument with some modifications. I think Thomas was inconsistent with his own best thought in this regard and that the use of the argument to an unmoved mover leads to an inadequate way of negation, one biased in favor of stability. At the same time Thomas is clear on the fact that creation is no change (*ibid.*, 2, ch. 17); he also maintains (ch. 30) that there is absolute necessity in created things. The last point was lost sight of by many later scholastic philosophers who emphasized the contingency of creatures as if this were on an immanent cause.

2. Raymond J. Nogar, O.P., *The Wisdom of Evolution* (Garden City, N.Y.: 1963), develops more fully many of the points I make in the following few pages.

3. Philip J. Donnelly, S.J., "Saint Thomas and the Purpose of Creation," *Theological Studies*, 2 (1941), shows (pp. 53-67) that Thomas Aquinas and Suarez exclude "extrinsic glory to be acquired" as the ultimate purpose of creation; note Donnelly's summary on p. 83.

4. See James F. Ross, *Philosophical Theology* (Indianapolis and New York: 1969), pp. 280-290.

5. *Summa contra gentiles*, 2, ch. 44.

6. Philip J. Donnelly, S.J., "The Doctrine of the Vatican Council and the End of Creation," *Theological Studies*, 4 (1943), pp. 21-29, shows that the "glory of God" of which Vatican Council I speaks can be identified with the goodness of creation itself.

7. *Summa contra gentiles*, 3, ch. 70.

8. *Ibid.*, ch. 69.

9. Thomas Aquinas, *ibid.*, ch. 21, cites with approval a statement of Pseudo-Dionysius: "Of all things, it is more divine to become a co-worker with God." He also uses with accommodated sense a statement of St. Paul (1 Cor. 3:9): "We are fellow workers with God."

10. *Summa contra gentiles*, 3, ch. 69. This sort of thinking has been endorsed by Vatican Council II, *The Church in the Modern World*, section 34: " . . . far from thinking that works produced by man's own talent and energy are in opposition to God's power, and that the rational creature exists as a kind of rival to the creator, Christians are convinced that the triumphs of the human race are a sign of God's greatness and are the flowering of his own mysterious design."

22: MIRACLES AS SIGNALS FROM THE CREATOR

1. This question is pressed by Alastair McKinnon, "Miracle and Paradox," *American Philosophical Quarterly*, 4 (1967), p. 313.

2. David Hume, *An Enquiry concerning Human Understanding*, ed. Charles W. Hendel (Indianapolis and New York: 1955), p. 122.

3. *Ibid.*, p. 123.

4. *Ibid.*, pp. 122-123.

5. *Ibid.*, pp. 124-130.

6. *Ibid.*, p. 136. Hume's statement here is, of course, a factual claim. One wonders how he knows it to be true. However, since it is an allegation which does not involve testimony for a miracle used to support religion, one can trust the testimony. Hume, of course, was unacquainted with modern advertizing. Richard Swinburne, *The Concept of Miracle* (London and Basingstoke: 1970), accepts Hume's terrain for the argument and answers these points in more detail than I shall.

7. Hume, *op. cit.*, p. 139.

8. Antony Flew, *Hume's Philosophy of Belief* (London: 1966), pp. 207-208.

9. McKinnon, *op. cit.*, pp. 308-310.

10. Patrick H. Nowell-Smith, "Miracles," in Antony Flew and Alasdair MacIntyre, eds., *New Essays in Philosophical Theology* (London: 1955), pp. 252-253.

11. Joseph M. Boyle, Jr., Germain Grisez, and Olaf Tollefsen, *Free Choice: A Self-Referential Argument,* forthcoming.

12. Hume, *op. cit.*, p. 119.

13. In this paragraph I have summarized what I take to be the kernel of truth in William James's concept of the *will to believe*. The trouble with James is that he does not limit the grounds.

14. Generally Hume stresses the revisability inherent in all empirical claims which go beyond immediate perception. Michael Scriven, "Explanations, Predictions, and Laws," in Baruch A. Brody, ed., *Readings in the Philosophy of Science* (Englewood Cliffs, N.J.: 1970), p. 100, states a view far removed from that of Hume: "The examples of physical laws with which we are all familiar are distinguished by one feature of particular interest for the traditional analyses—they are virtually all known to be in error. Nor is the error trifling, nor is an amended law available which corrects for all the error. The important feature of laws cannot be their literal truth, since this rarely exists. It is not their closeness to the truth which replaces this, since far better approximations are readily constructed. Their virtue lies in a compound out of the qualities of generality, formal simplicity, approximation to the truth, and theoretical tractability."

15. Hume, *op. cit.*, p. 122. Terence Penelhum, *Religion and Rationality: An Introduction to the Philosophy of Religion* (New York: 1971), pp. 272-273, proposes a similar criticism of Hume.

16. Werner Heisenberg, *The Physicist's Conception of Nature* (London: 1958), pp. 180-181.

17. Robert Young, "Miracles and Epistemology," *Religious Studies,* 8 (1972), pp. 115-126, develops a view close to that which I propose here, but Young supposes (p. 122) that if one identifies the unknown cause with God, one must be assuming that God is not the cause of all states of affairs generally. See also C. S. Lewis, *Miracles* (London: 1964), pp. 59-66. John King-Farlow and William Niels Christensen, *Faith and the Life of Reason* (Dordrecht, Holland: 1972), pp. 45-77, propose a view of miracles in many ways close to mine, but do not clarify sufficiently the signal aspect of

miracles, which is central in my view; they do provide useful historical information on the background of the definition of *miracle* as "violation of a law of nature"; they also comment on Tillich's extreme position.

18. O. Costa de Beauregard, "Irreversibility Problems," in Yehoshua Bar-Hillel, ed., *Logic, Methodology, and Philosophy of Science* (Amsterdam: 1965), pp. 313-346; notice note 19, p. 319, in which the opinion is cited that reversal of the ripples would be a "miracle."

19. Malcolm L. Diamond, *Contemporary Philosophy and Religious Thought: An Introduction to the Philosophy of Religion* (New York: 1974), pp. 64-67.

20. Alexis Carrel, *Man: The Unknown* (New York and London: 1935), p. 149; note also the footnote on p. 148: "Miraculous cures seldom occur. Despite their small number, they prove the existence of organic and mental processes that we do not know. They show that certain mystic states, such as that of prayer, have definite effects. They are stubborn, irreducible facts, which must be taken into account." Carrel goes on to add some facts about Lourdes. This objective approach contrasts with the dogmatism of Diamond and others. In effect, they hold that if miracles do occur, it is scientific to pretend that they do not.

21. Alexis Carrel, *Prayer* (New York: 1948), pp. 44-45.

22. Charles A. Lindbergh, "Preface," in Alexis Carrel, *The Voyage to Lourdes,* trans. Virgilia Peterson (New York: 1950), p. vii.

23. Diamond, *op. cit.,* p. 63.

24. The reference is to the allegations with respect to the shrine at Lourdes, France. See Louis Monden, S.J., *Signs and Wonders: A Study of the Miraculous Element in Religion* (New York, Paris, Tournai, and Rome: 1966), pp. 194-250, for an introduction, with references to works on both sides. On the compatibility of the definition of "miracle" I have given with Catholic teaching on the subject see John A. Hardon, S.J., "The Concept of Miracle from St. Augustine to Modern Apologetics," *Theological Studies,* 15 (1954), pp. 229-257; Liam S. Bréartúin, O.C.D., "The Theology of Miracles," *Ephemerides Carmeliticae,* 20 (1969), pp. 1-51 and 351-402. Hardon shows (p. 243) that "violation of the laws of nature" is not essential; Bréartúin shows the importance of the signal aspect of miracle in the theory of Thomas Aquinas. For the question of the supposed universality of miracles see Robert D. Smith, *Comparative Miracles* (St. Louis and London: 1965), pp. 106-163.

23: THE HUMAN PERSON AND THE HUMAN COMMUNITY

1. Thomas Aquinas, *Summa contra gentiles,* 2, chs. 56-78, argues cogently against many forms of dualism.

2. See P. F. Strawson, "Persons," in G. N. A. Vesey, ed., *Body and Mind* (London: 1964), pp. 403-424; Gabriel Marcel, *The Mystery of Being,* vol. 1, *Reflection and Mystery* (Chicago: 1960), pp. 127-153.

3. The argument is developed in Joseph M. Boyle, Jr., Germain Grisez, and Olaf Tollefsen, *Free Choice: A Self-Referential Argument,* forthcoming.

4. This position is argued cogently by Richard Taylor, *Action and Purpose* (Englewood Cliffs, N.J.: 1966).

5. J. R. Lucas, *The Freedom of the Will* (Oxford: 1970), pp. 114-172, develops a somewhat similar argument; his argument does not prove freedom of the will, but does seem to refute physicalism. H. D. Lewis, *The Elusive Mind* (London and New York: 1969), pp. 68-226, provides extensive critiques of various versions of the identity thesis.

6. Aristotle, *De anima* iii, 429a10-430a25, proposes his views on thinking mind in such ambiguous terms that his meaning has been debated ever since. Thomas Aquinas, *Summa contra gentiles,* 2, ch. 68, holds that the soul of a person is both an immaterial substance and the substantial form of the human body. He also thinks Aristotle held the same view (ch. 78). I do not see how the soul could be a substance if it were a substantial form. Thomas reaches his conclusion by elimination; his arguments against the alternatives he attacks are cogent. But I do not find his own solution satisfying.

7. Richard Taylor, *Metaphysics* (Englewood Cliffs, N.J.: 1963), pp. 24-29, argues the case well so far as the body/sentient mind is concerned; he does not take into account in this argument aspects of the human person irreducible to sensory awareness.

8. P. F. Strawson, *Individuals: An Essay in Descriptive Metaphysics* (London: 1959), pp. 87-116.

9. Hegel, however, erred in trying to treat bodiliness dialectically. The natural world cannot be mere nonthought. To treat it as such is to confuse its way of being with man's way of knowing it to be.

10. This theory of propositional knowledge is derived from Thomas Aquinas; see my *Basic Oppositions in Logical Theory* (unpublished Ph.D. dissertation, University of Chicago, 1959), pp. 175-197.

11. See Germain Grisez and Russell Shaw, *Beyond the New Morality: The Responsibilities of Freedom* (Notre Dame and London: 1974), pp. 1-41.

12. Many controversies, such as the is/ought controversy, arise from this problem. One cannot reason from a natural "is" to an existential "ought"; this was Hume's point and he was right about it, though he himself proceeded to try to reduce morality to natural factors. The argument of the following eight or nine paragraphs was worked out by Joseph M. Boyle, Jr., Germain Grisez, and Olaf Tollefsen in preparation for *Free Choice: A Self-Referential Argument,* forthcoming, although the argument will not appear in the published book.

13. Thomas Aquinas regarded the soul, insofar as it is a substantial form, as part of the body; he denied that the soul is the self: " . . . anima mea non est ego"; from this he concluded that the person is not saved unless the body rises from the dead: *Super 1 Corinthos lectura,* 15, lect. 2. See Peter Geach, *God and the Soul* (New York: 1969), pp. 17-29, who argues that without resurrection of the body hope of life after death is illusory.

14. Terence Penelhum, *Survival and Disembodied Existence* (New York: 1970), presents many of the arguments to which I refer, and he refers to other relevant authors in his bibliography, pp. 109-111. There is a more compact version in the same author's *Religion and Rationality: An Introduction to the Philosophy of Religion* (New York: 1971), pp. 345-355. H. D. Lewis, *op. cit.,* esp. pp. 227-248 and 324-325, criticizes many of these same arguments. See also John Hick, *Philosophy of Religion,* 2nd ed. (Englewood Cliffs, N.J.: 1973), pp. 97-117.

15. H. M. McElwain, "Resurrection of the Dead," *New Catholic Encyclo-*

pedia, vol. 12, pp. 419-427; Lucien Cerfaux, *The Christian in the Theology of St. Paul* (New York: 1967), pp. 176-202.

16. This point is argued effectively by Richard Purtill, "Disembodied Survival," *Sophia,* 12 (1973), pp. 1-10.

17. Purtill, *loc. cit.,* rejects the demand for a logically sufficient condition. I would maintain that this demand cannot be met even now; bodily continuity is *not* such a criterion; see C. B. Martin, *Religious Belief* (Ithaca, New York: 1959), pp. 97-102; also see John Hick, "Mr. Clarke's Resurrection Also," *Sophia,* 11 (1972), pp. 1-3, for a neat rejection of a demand for a logically sufficient condition of identity.

24: MEANING, REVELATION, AND CHRISTIAN MYSTERIES

1. For a position which denies cognitive meaning to ethical statements see A. J. Ayer, *Language, Truth and Logic,* 2nd ed. (London and New York: 1961), pp. 108-109; C. L. Stevenson, *Ethics and Language* (New Haven: 1944). I have treated this question in "The First Principle of Practical Reason: A Commentary on the *Summa theologiae,* 1-2, Question 94, Article 2," *Natural Law Forum,* 10 (1965), pp. 168-201.

2. See Terence Penelhum, *Religion and Rationality: An Introduction to the Philosophy of Religion* (New York: 1971), p. 353; see P. F. Strawson, *Individuals: An Essay in Descriptive Metaphysics* (London: 1959), p. 116; Peter Geach, *God and the Soul* (New York: 1969), pp. 1-29.

3. See, e.g., Thomas Aquinas, *Summa contra gentiles,* 4, ch. 1.

4. *Ibid.,* 1, ch. 22.

5. John L. McKenzie, S.J., *Jerome Biblical Commentary,* 77:12; Robert W. Gleason, S.J., *Yahweh. The God of the Old Testament* (Englewood Cliffs, N.J.: 1964), pp. 113-123.

6. *Jerusalem Bible,* Exodus 3:14, note h.

7. McKenzie and *Jerusalem Bible, loc. cit.*

8. William Foxwell Albright, *From the Stone Age to Christianity,* 2nd ed. (Garden City, N.Y.: 1957), pp. 257-266.

9. McKenzie, *op. cit.,* 77:13. Cf. Raymond Abba, "The Divine Name Yahweh," *Journal of Biblical Literature,* 80 (1961), pp. 320-328.

10. A point stressed by Vatican Council II, *Dogmatic Constitution on Divine Revelation,* section 2; cf. Dt. 18:21-22, where the combination of words and events marks the true oracle from God.

11. Cf. McKenzie, *op. cit.,* 77:8, 20, 106.

12. *Ibid.,* 77:21.

13. See an article along these lines by D. M. Mackay, "Language, Meaning, and God," *Philosophy,* 47 (1972), pp. 1-17.

14. This translation is taken from *The Church Teaches: Documents of the Church in English Translation,* trans. J. F. Clarkson, S.J., J. H. Edwards, S.J., W. J. Kelly, S.J., and J. J. Welch, S.J. (St. Louis and London: 1955), p. 172.

15. *Ibid.,* pp. 135-136.

16. See Thomas Aquinas, *Summa theologiae,* 1, qq. 39-42.

25: WHY CHRISTIAN DOCTRINE, IF TRUE, IS IMPORTANT

1. E. L. Peterman, "Redemption (Theology of)," *New Catholic Encyclopedia,* vol. 12, pp. 144-158.
2. Thomas Aquinas, *Summa theologiae,* 1, q. 12, a. 1; 1-2, q. 3, a. 8.
3. Vatican Council II, *The Church in the Modern World,* section 39.
4. This paragraph is based on the First Epistle of St. John.
5. See P. de Letter, S.J., "Sanctifying Grace and Our Union with the Holy Trinity," *Theological Studies,* 13 (1952), pp. 38-41, for some inadequate explanations proposed by Catholic theologians; most Christians probably tended to be even less realistic about the meaning of union with God.
6. The Greek church fathers spoke freely of the divinization of the Christian; they regarded the uncreated grace of the Spirit as prior to created grace. Some of them even argue that the Word and the Spirit are divine *a fortiori,* because these divine persons cause the divinization of human persons, which would be impossible were they not divine themselves. See Robert W. Gleason, S.J., *The Indwelling Spirit* (Staten Island, N.Y.: 1966), pp. 21-37.
7. See St. Augustine, *Expositions on the Psalms,* Ps. 49:2, in J. P. Migne, *Patrologia Latina,* vol. 36, c. 565; St. Athanasius, *Four Discourses against the Arians,* Or. 2:59, in J. P. Migne, *Patrologia Graeca,* vol. 26, c. 273.
8. The theologians who have accepted the theory of created actuation by uncreated act (see article of P. de Letter, S.J., cited in note 5 above, for references) approach the position I am suggesting, although they seem to assume that the uncreated act is the divinity of the Persons of the Holy Trinity; my suggestion is that the uncreated act is a divinity communicated to the created person as his own, not by procession, but by gift, in some way especially by the Spirit who is sent. See also Karl Rahner, S.J., "Scholastic Concept of Uncreated Grace," *Theological Investigations,* vol. 1, *God, Church, Mary, and Grace,* trans. Cornelius Ernst, O.P. (Baltimore: 1961), pp. 334-346.
9. Thomas Aquinas's theory of the beatific vision demands not only that in it one know God but that one know by means of the divine nature itself; see Rahner, *op. cit.,* pp. 326-333, for relevant texts and discussion. If the act of knowing is to be one's own, then it seems to me that the principle by which one acts also must be one's own. Many theologians beginning with Thomas himself have talked of "formal" or "quasi-formal" causality here; I think this is a mistake, since no relation involving creature and creator should be modeled on immanent modes of causality. What I am suggesting is that the analogy of the Christian to Christ be taken rather more seriously than it has been. I do not suggest that all Christians are *hypostatically* united to the divine nature; the human person remains human but is *dynamically*—in the power to act, not in the person—united with a divine nature which is freely communicated by the Trinity and which one who receives it has as one's own. There is no mixing, however, because God-the-Trinity-creator and God-the-adopted-creature remain distinct by opposition of relationships. This subject obviously requires an extended study, which I hope to undertake at a later date.

Index

Abba, R., 406
Abraham, 86, 323
Absolute Spirit, 60, 61, 65, 83, 170,
231, 238, 244, 281, 283, 284,
314, 319; exposition and critique
of theory of, 181-187, 191-204;
God's existence and, 187-190;
humanistic values and, 302, 305,
307, 310, 313; post-hegelian relativism and, 205, 206, 207, 208,
210, 211, 213, 221, 222, 223,
224
Abstraction, post-hegelian relativism
and, 217-221
Achinstein, P., 37, 389
Action, human: community and,
354-355; creator's causality
modeled upon, 270-271; post-
hegelian relativism and, 61, 209-
213, 217
Adams, R. M., 400
Adoption of sons, 383-385
Affirmation, predication of uncaused
entity by, 248-255
Agency, causality and, 126-127
Albright, W. F., 406
Analogy: between human choice and
divine causality, 268-272; Kant
on, 165-167; predication by,

248-255; schema of causality and,
262
Analytic philosophy, 211, 213, 224
Anselm, St., 32-34, 46, 173
Antinomies, Kant's, 143-147, 168
Arguments for the existence of God:
author's expounded, 36-58;
author's summarized, 82-83, 261;
Christian faith and, 29-31; cosmological argument, 4, 36-40, 63, 65,
68, 70-71, 86, 98-100, 125, 150,
163-164, 188-190; design argument and evil, 301; moral argument and Plato, 90; need for,
19-34; ontological argument,
32-34, 45-46, 64, 149-150, 174,
190; presumption in, 9; reference
of talk about God and, 6; Thomas
Aquinas's, 8, 84; utility of, 28
Aristotle, 12, 79, 88-89, 128, 129,
130, 177, 184, 193, 224, 317,
383, 392, 394, 397, 402, 405; on
God, 265; on human person, 344,
346, 347-349
Armstrong, D. M., 389, 390
Aronson, J. L., 394
Assertion: not obtaining, 177; not
proposition, 40-41
Athanasius, St., 407

408